GHOSTS
OF GREAT BRITAIN
AND IRELAND

GHOSTS
OF GREAT BRITAIN
AND IRELAND

A Compendium of 2,000 Hauntings

Jonathan Sutherland

breedon **books**
PUBLISHING

First published in Great Britain in 2001 by
The Breedon Books Publishing Company Limited
Breedon House, 3 The Parker Centre, Derby, DE21 4SZ.

ISBN 1 85983 219 9

Printed and bound by Butler & Tanner, Frome, Somerset
Cover printing by GreenShires Ltd, Leicester

Contents

Dedication

For Diane

Acknowledgements

I am indebted to my loyal band of ghost-hunters and researchers, who have provided me with much needed information as well as the impetus to collate this mammoth collection of British hauntings. Specifically I would like to thank Vera and John Sutherland, Betty-Jayne and Michael Scaddings, L. J. and Anne and Liz and Ken Prentice. This book would not have been feasible without the tireless dedication and skills of my partner Diane Canwell. I would also like to express my gratitude to various museums, tourist information centres and libraries around the country, especially the Halesworth and District Museum.

If you have any information about other British hauntings I would be pleased to consider including it in a future edition.

Jon Sutherland

Introduction

The term 'ghost', as we will see, transcends the stereotypical image of an apparition in a white bed sheet, clanking chains in a mouldy cemetery. Through these 2,000 entries, which only begin to catalogue the vast number of hauntings throughout Great Britain, we will discover that nearly every site in the country has the capacity to retain an imprint of something that happened there in the past. There is a vast range of different manifest-ations, from the simple 'feeling' of a presence to a full-blown and interactive apparition that has the capacity to respond to its own environment. There are benign ghosts, vengeful ghosts and ghosts that replay an episode, often their last act, without any reference to those changes that have occurred to the landscape.

Amid the kings, queens, nobles and historical luminaries are spirits of ordinary folk, perhaps caught up in extraordinary circumstances. There are victims, murderers, suicides, witches and those who are said to have made pacts with the devil. Many ghosts seem to have a mission, the circumstances of which are often forgotten. Some act as a warning, others seek to reveal the hidden. All have a reason for finding themselves in the continual loop of activity that we call a haunting.

The word 'ghost' derives from the Saxon 'gaste', or more commonly 'guest', and is simply a description of something that may appear, whether visible or not, to living people. Numerous experts have tried to explain these spirits or manifestations, and it seems from my own studies that these explanations tend to fall into five categories. First, ghosts may be a manifestation or reincarnation of ourselves, as we were in a previous life, which explains why we can see them. They are a half-conscious memory of something that we were. Second, they could be a manifestation born out of an intense, emotional situation, perhaps a conflict, which has in some way imprinted itself on a particular location. More recently this has been known as 'stone tape' theory. The imprint is left for those who have the psychic ability to read it. Third, they could be some form of disembodied spirit that has somehow separated itself from the mortal remains of someone who has died. To accept this theory we also have to realise that whatever has been left behind retains some rudimentary intelligence. The fourth category has more to do with our own memory and consciousness. These ghosts could be in our subconscious, then somehow projected externally so that we can view them. The fifth and final category may infringe too many religious taboos for many to consider it a viable explanation. Ghosts could be the next phase of life after death – dead people transform into a new existence, and from time to time those in our existence find themselves in a position to see them. One of the common difficulties in accepting any one category of explanations is the huge variety in which ghosts choose to manifest themselves. They are not all full-body apparitions; some are partial body or less. Inanimate objects appear, such as ghostly trains, ships, cars and buses. There are also horses, dogs, cats and bears that make themselves known to us in ghostly form.

There seem to be several common types of manifestation. There are many ghosts that simply appear and haunt a specific area and do not interact with people or their surroundings in any way. Numerous ghosts exist to provide warnings or messages, and there are often doubles created, as reflections of people who are about to die. Finally, there are those whose existence seems to be bent on bringing misery to the living. These poltergeist-type manifestations, often invisible, actively seek to destroy what is around them, or, at the very least, to make it impossible for the living to exist side-by-side with them.

I approached my research into ghosts with a healthy degree of scepticism, despite having had personal experience of a haunting in the past. It was interesting to discover that the type of manifestation I experienced was extremely common, and followed many of the patterns reported by witnesses over hundreds of years. What is striking in many of the haunting cases I have investigated is that descriptions have been given of the ghost in a completely isolated and objective manner. Witnesses have been able to describe a ghost, perhaps down to clothing details, without the prior knowledge that someone else, or perhaps several hundred other people, have described the manifestation in exactly the same way. Whether this is some form of serial hallucination or simply the product of an over-active imagination, triggered off by

something pertinent to the area of the haunting, may never be known. It is interesting that an individual intimately involved in the Borley Rectory hauntings, who claimed that they had faked a number of the manifestations, or at least created some of the mechanics that brought them about, could not explain some of the activities. He used the interesting word 'paranormal' to describe these inexplicable manifestations, which is a term that implies a mixture of the psychic, the subconscious and the suggested.

I remain sceptical, although there are certainly many stories that I have researched that I cannot explain. I have been approached by a number of people willing to recount their own haunting experiences. Many of these stories had remained untold for decades and were only revealed when they discovered that I was researching this book. In fact virtually everybody that I had a conversation with in relation to the book had a tale to tell.

I hope that this book will be a useful resource for those who wish to visit scenes of hauntings, or perhaps experience a manifestation of their own.

Jon Sutherland

A

Abbots Bromley to Ayot St Lawrence

Abbots Bromley, Staffordshire: Ye Olde Coach and Horses

It is said that a phantom coach and horses haunt the public house. Several witnesses claim to have seen the apparition. It is not known what has prompted this manifestation to make itself visible to the living. Abbots Bromley is an old village, between Stafford and Burton-on-Trent, which is famous for the annual Horn Dance that takes place in September. Henry Francis Cary (1772–1844) a clergyman, librarian, poet and translator, was vicar for four years after his ordination in 1796.

Abbotsford House, nr Melrose, Galashiels

The former home of Sir Walter Scott is said to be haunted by the ghost of George Bullock, Scott's steward, who died while in charge of alterations being made to the house. Bullock's ghost disturbed Scott with violent noises at around 2am, just as Bullock died. At the time that he heard the noises, Scott did not know of Bullock's death.

Abbotskerswell, nr Newton Abbot, Devon

John and Carol Durston lived in the ground floor flat of 200-year-old Aller House. After a few days they began to hear footsteps and shuffling noises in the middle of the night. The noises seemed to emanate from the corridor outside their flat, and sounded like someone walking up and down. Every time they checked to see what it was they could find nothing. After a few weeks, their living room, despite having a roaring log fire, felt stone cold. Ornaments were moved in their bedroom, especially a china donkey on the mantelpiece. A few days later the ghostly shape of a fat man materialised in their front room, even at times sitting between them on the sofa. The night-time poltergeist activity became more violent, and culminated in the couple seeking the help of the Revd Gordon Langford, the local vicar. Following investigations, they discovered that the ghost was one Victor Judd, who had committed suicide in the area of their flat in 1925. Other tenants corroborated the Durston's story, and the Bishop of Exeter sent Revd Sir Patrick Ferguson-Davie to perform an exorcism. Unfortunately it had little effect on the ghost, apart from moving it into the next door flat, which was owned by a Mr and Mrs Culley.

Abbots Langley, nr St Albans, Hertfordshire: The Vicarage

The ghost of an ill-treated servant girl, Mary-Anne Treble, haunts the vicarage. She worked as a maidservant and suffered greatly at the hands of the vicar's wife. She is also said to haunt the church on All Saints Day. An exorcism by a bishop has somewhat calmed her spirit, but she still makes quite a noise. Apparently, the fireplace in the room in which she died a horrible death will not stay mended, no matter how often it is repaired.

Abbot's Way, nr Buckfastleigh, Devon

As the Abbot's Way enters the moor at Cross Furzes, it is haunted by Squire Cabell (Capel), who died in 1677, and his great black hounds. His tomb is in the nearby church and it has a stone slab over it to keep him inside. Over the stone slab is a porch, which was built specifically to keep the stone slab in place. It is said that if you circle the tomb 13 times and then insert your finger into the keyhole, the spirit of the squire will rise and bite it off. In July his spirit can be seen rising from the tomb and setting off with his hounds toward his former home, Brooke Manor. In life he had a reputation for chasing the young women of the locality. When he died, his hounds howled at the approach of the devil, arriving to collect his soul.

Aberbeeg, nr Abertillery, Gwent

In 1911 Hosea Pope, a local policeman, was killed while trying to arrest and handcuff a local vagrant by the name of James Wise. The ghostly figure of the dead policeman can still be seen on the Cwm Road (A4046).

Aberdeen, Aberdeenshire: Amatola Hotel, Great Western Road

A portrait of the great-great-grandmother of the present owner hangs in the hotel. She lived and worked there in the 19th century and her apparition has been seen on many occasions, mostly on the landing in the older part of the hotel. Witnesses say that she appears just as she is portrayed in the painting.

Aberdeen, Aberdeenshire: Ardoe House Hotel, Blairs

The daughter of a 19th-century owner of the hotel was attacked and raped, and fell pregnant as a result of the assault. It is believed that she was so affected by the attack that she suffered from severe depression. In her despair she murdered the child and committed suicide. Her ghost still haunts the building.

Aberdeen, Aberdeenshire: His Majesty's Theatre

The ghost of a stagehand called Jake haunts the theatre. The unfortunate man was killed in an accident involving a stage hoist. It is said that the ghost is considerably more active than the stagehand ever was.

Aberdovey, off Towyn, Conwy

Aberdovey once lay on a rich and fertile plain, dotted with prosperous towns. One stormy night, the raging seas breached the wall and all but a few inhabitants were lost in the depths. Many say that the long-lost ghostly bells of Aberdovey can still be heard, ringing out from their watery grave.

Abergeldie Castle, nr Balmoral, Grampian

The Gordon clan originally built the castle in the 16th century, but it has other prestigious connections. Prince Albert rented the castle as a base for his summer adventures in Scotland, and both the future Edward VII and Queen Alexandra spent time there. It was Edward VIII, in his memoirs, who referred to the ghost of Kittie Rankie. It is said that she was burned as a witch on the hill overlooking the castle. She had been imprisoned in the dungeons before her execution, which may explain why some speak of a strange atmosphere there, while others claim to hear a bell pealing, which warns of disaster for the Gordon clan.

Abergele, Clywd

It is said that Prince Madoc sailed from Abergele to America in the 12th century. His magic vessel, *The Gwennan Gorn,* is often seen off the coast. It is said that the ship had stag horn instead of iron for nails, so that a lodestone could be used for navigation. In the late 18th century, visitors to America encountered a tribe of Indians, called the Mandan, who understood Welsh and knew of Welsh habits and legends. This may mean that Madoc actually got to America and that his settlers survived there for some years. A possible explanation for the ghost ship may be that it is simply the reflection of a real ship further out to sea, which in effect creates a mirage.

Aberglaslyn Pass, Gwynedd

A huge, but harmless, ghostly mastiff is likely to challenge you in the pass in the dead of night. If you should encounter a white lady, however, it is altogether more dangerous. Often those who see her become the victims of accidents or die suddenly.

Aberlemno, nr Forfar, Angus

The area around Aberlemno, including Careston and Finavon, is said to be haunted by Jock Barefut. He cut a stick from the Spanish chestnut tree in the grounds of Careston Castle. For his pains, the laird, nicknamed 'the Tiger', hanged him from the same tree. It promptly withered and died. The ghost of Jock Barefut is a testimony to the hanging and he is often seen in the area.

Aberystwyth, Dyfed

A headless dog haunts the road that runs south out of the town. The area called Pen Parcau was once populated by giants, and the dog was owned by a young giant. One day, the young giant's father was in trouble. In his haste to help his father, the young giant rode off so fast on his horse that his dog, still on a lead, could not keep up. As the giant galloped, the dog's head was pulled off.

Abington, Northamptonshire: Black Lion Inn

This public house has severe problems with poltergeists, which enjoy moving beer barrels, rattling doors, interfering with the lighting and causing mysterious mists. The building also boasts other strange manifestations, including that of a man accompanied by a large dog. On one occasion the apparitions were challenged and told to leave the building; they promptly complied. Researchers have observed flickering lights in the cellar, shadows and the sounds of a crying baby. Perhaps the most obvious explanation for all of this is that in 1892 Andrew McRae, a former licensee, was sentenced to death for killing his mistress and their baby on the premises.

Abthorpe, nr Silverstone, Northamptonshire

Jane Leeson, a 17th-century philanthropist who built the local school, can be heard with her rustling silk dress on quiet nights in the ruins of the old manor. She shares this location with the spirit of a Franciscan friar, who has also been seen on a number of occasions.

Acle, nr Great Yarmouth, Norfolk

The ghost of a man haunts the bridge. He is said to have avenged the murder of his sister by killing the perpetrator, her husband Josiah Burge, by slitting his throat. A year later the brother had his own throat cut by a ghostly skeleton. On 7 April each year the ghost appears and fresh blood is found on the bridge.

Aconbury, nr Hereford, Herefordshire

Sir Roger de Clifford is said to haunt the church. His dark figure can be seen stalking through the building and the churchyard. There was an attempt to exorcise his ghost, and it was thought that his spirit had been trapped in a bottle and buried beneath his tomb, which is in the wall of the church. However, it seems that the exorcism was unsuccessful. Local legend says that if the ghost touches you, you will die within the year.

Addenbrookes Hospital, Cambridgeshire

It is said that the ghost of a former nurse or doctor appears when morphine is being administered to a patient. Whether this is related to an unfortunate incident in the past, or whether the ghost appears to ensure that all is well, is unclear.

Addlestone, Surrey: St Paul's Church

In 1953, as Constable Battams patrolled his beat, he passed the churchyard at around 2am. He heard a rustling in the trees and then footsteps moving slowly toward him. Flashing his torch, he attempted to discover the source of the noise, but saw nothing. Instead the sound got louder and closer. He walked into School Lane and heard the footsteps slow and then stop. After discussions with the local vicar it was suggested that he had encountered the grey lady who haunts Sayes Court and the Addlestone crossroads. This apparition has been seen by others: an office cleaner in the 1970s experienced exactly the same encounter. The grey lady is apparently the restless spirit of a woman who went mad after her romance with a local man ended, in the early 1900s.

Airdit Farm, nr Cupar, Fife

The ghost of a witch haunts this farm. When she was finally hunted down and presumably killed, her ghost returned in the shape of one of her familiars. As a result, she has often been seen by witnesses in the form of a ghostly hare.

Airlie Castle, nr Kirriemuir, Tayside

The ghostly sound of a drummer, often accompanied by bagpipes, can be heard prior to the death of the head of the Airlie family. This has even occurred when the chief has died abroad. In 1881 Lady Dalkeith and Lady Skelmersdale both heard the drummer. When Lord Airlie was lying on his deathbed in America, the drummer was heard one hour before he passed away.

Alcester, Warwickshire: The Angel Inn

Although this former public house has been converted into two private homes, it is still the favoured site of the ghost of the murderer Captain Richard Hill. The public house was operating in the 17th century, and had an upstairs banqueting hall. Hill was last seen alive there in 1693. It is said that he was lynched and his body hidden by the local townsfolk. In the past his spirit took the form of a phosphorescent shape accompanied by footsteps which resounded around the building. It is not widely believed that the manifestation is particularly active at the moment. In the nearby church of St Nicholas, the ghost of Sir Fulke Greville has often been seen walking around the building. Greville is buried there and his tomb features an effigy to help identify the ghost.

Alderley Edge, nr Macclesfield, Cheshire

The village is said to be haunted by a naked man with long hair, who has a habit of peeping through windows. If approached or spoken to, he immediately disappears. Speculation regarding the nature of this manifestation has identified two possible explanations. It could be a similar kind of spirit to those seen in Cumbria, known as boggarts, supernatural creatures that can take a number of different forms, or the psychic imprint of a real individual. 'Peeping Tom'-type ghosts are very unusual, and it is not known how long this manifestation has been plaguing the area. According to a folk tale, a farmer from Mobberley once had his horse purchased by a wizard for the use of a king and his knights who were slumbering beneath the Edge. The story was told by Parson Shrigley (d.1776), who maintained that the events had occurred about eighty years before his time. There may be a connection between this story and the ghost.

Aldington Corner, nr Ashford, Kent: The Walnut Tree Inn

George Ransley and his two sons, notorious smugglers known as the Hawkhurst gang, operated from the inn 150 years ago.

Smuggled goods arrived via Romney Marsh and the gang used a lantern, hung from the window of the inn, to show that all was well. One night a quarrel over money led to a murder, and the body was disposed of in the well. Many people have reported hearing the sounds of quarrelling, cursing and fighting, followed by a heavy thump, footsteps and the sound of something being dragged toward the well. George Ransley was never tried for murder, but he was eventually deported for his smuggling activities.

Alfrick, Worcestershire

This is said to be one of the most haunted villages in Worcestershire. Not only does it boast animal ghosts, notably a black dog and a crow, but it also echoes with the sound of the village's agricultural past. A phantom wagon and horses has been seen and the sound of a hammer striking an anvil, which may be linked to a cooper, has been heard. Near the church the spirits of a couple with their dog have been seen taking a stroll to the old forge, just as they did when they were alive.

Allanton, Borders: Alanbank (sometimes spelled Allanbank)

In the 17th century the Stuart family owned and lived at Alanbank, but the ghost that haunts the house never visited Scotland. The house was pulled down in the 19th century, but the apparition has been seen at the site nonetheless, particularly at dusk. In the 1670s, Robert Stuart was in Paris and had an affair with a French girl, 15-year-old Jeanne de la Salle. After a while, his father called him home and Robert resolved to abandon his lover without telling her. As he climbed into the coach, Jeanne realised that she was to be left behind and pleaded with him to stay. She screamed that if he ever married another woman, she would come between them. Suddenly, she lost her grip on the coach and fell to her death under the speeding wheels.

After the tragic accident, Robert continued his journey to Scotland and arrived at Alanbank at dusk. To his horror, he saw the apparition of a woman in a white dress gazing down at him from the archway of the gatehouse. It was Jeanne, her head bloodied. Robert fainted. From then on 'Pearlin' Jean', as she became known, haunted Alanbank with screams, rustling silk, poltergeist activity, footsteps and full-body manifestations. By 1687, Robert had become a baronet and was married. He told his new wife about the spirit and they called in seven ministers of the Church of Scotland to exorcise it. The exorcism failed, but when Robert had a painting commissioned of Jeanne it seemed to appease the ghost. Whenever the portrait was put away, the hauntings began again, even after the deaths of Sir Robert and Lady Stuart.

Allington, Wiltshire

A curate fell from his horse while mounting it and broke his neck, probably after a good deal of drink. His friends panicked and threw his body into the well. To this day, horses take fright at the spot. When the hostess who had entertained the curate was on her deathbed she tried to explain what had happened, but she could not relate the tale in full before she died.

Alnwick Castle, Northumberland

The 12th-century monk William de Newburgh, writing in Yorkshire, told a tale of a vampire lord that lived in the castle. After the death of the vampire his nocturnal habits did not cease. He flew around the town attempting to suck blood from the inhabitants. His actions brought about an outbreak of the plague. Following this, his coffin was dug up and his body found to be very swollen. The diggers chopped through the body with a spade and fresh blood flowed. The body was then burned to put an end to the problem.

Altarnun, Cornwall: The King's Head

On occasions, the King's Head, a traditional 16th-century coaching inn, is haunted by former landlady Peggy Bray. The village, lying on the north-east edge of Bodmin Moor, has a 15th-century church known as the Cathedral of the Moor. The church is dedicated to St David's mother, St Non, and gives the village its name, which literally means 'Altar of St Non'.

Althorp House, nr Northampton, Northamptonshire

The home of the Spencer family is haunted by the spirit of a much-loved and long-serving household employee, who continues to make his rounds in the house after dark. It is said that he visits each of the bedrooms, particularly if there are guests in the house, to ensure that they have not left a candle or a lamp burning.

Alton, Hampshire: Crown Hotel

During the 1960s building work revealed the bones of a dog hidden behind a wall near a chimney breast. This gave credence to witnesses' statements that they had heard a dog scratching and whimpering. Many years ago, one of the landlords owned the dog and was extremely unkind to it, eventually beating it to death against the hearth. It is presumed that he chose to bury the dog near to the place of its death. Although the dog's bones have been found, the phantom scratching and whimpering continues.

Alton, Hampshire: St Lawrence's Church

During the Civil War royalists were besieged here. After a series of bloody skirmishes, which left sixty or more royalists dead, Roundhead soldiers entered the church. The royalist colonel made his last stand in the pulpit, despatching seven enemy soldiers before he fell. Several witnesses have heard savage fighting taking place in the church, although it is rare to actually see anything.

Alveley, Shropshire: Astley Bank

In 1945 a member of the Air Training Corps used to make the regular journey to and from parade from his parent's farm, down Astley Bank, to Alveley Old School. At around 11.30 one particular evening he swore that he could hear someone ahead of him. He heard the footsteps, and as he was walking in the middle of the road, decided to step to one side. Whatever was heading in the opposite direction walked straight through him. The apparition was wearing a black cloak, a large, brimmed hat and high boots with buckles. The witness remembers the cold shudder he felt as the apparition passed through his body.

Alveley, Shropshire: Coton Hall

A boy who lived at the hall was bought a white horse for his Christmas present. The impetuous youth could not wait for Christmas Day, and jumped on the horse and rode it through the park. As he galloped, the horse headed for some trees. The boy caught his head on a branch, fell and broke his neck. His ghost appears at midnight on Christmas Eve. Witnesses have either seen or heard him, particularly at the bottom of the park where the lane starts. The gate there inexplicably opens and closes, although no one is near it.

Alveley, Shropshire: Hall Close Farm

This old, possibly Tudor, farmhouse has three storeys. There is an upstairs room with a window that cannot be accessed from inside the house; it has no floorboards, as it was never completed. A man hanged himself from the rafters. In the 1980s the Jones family's daughters saw an old man and an old woman in one of the downstairs bedrooms. The old man wore a cap and had grey hair and the old woman was carrying a handbag. They asked the children whether they had seen Dolly. Several months passed and the children saw a photograph in the family album and recognised the old man and woman as being their mother's parents. One of the children also saw a stout man with white hair, wearing a suit and thick, round glasses, writing at the desk in a bedroom. The other daughter claims to have woken up in the middle of the night and seen a man standing over her, with his hands outstretched as if he were about to strangle her. Their brother saw the apparition of a woman who said to him 'Come with me, my husband is being hanged!' In the older section of the house, near the ghost room or on the landing, a woman sometimes dressed in white and sometimes in black has also been seen.

Alwinton, nr Rothbury, Northumberland

This strange and lonely place is said to be haunted by the figure of a cowled monk. Witnesses have said that the apparition appears to have no hands, feet or face, and it has often been seen hovering above the ground. An investigation in 1967 by the Newcastle Institute of Psychic Research failed to uncover the nature or purpose of this phantom.

Amberley, West Sussex

Two ghosts still actively haunt the Old Rectory: an old man and a little girl. During alterations in 1904 two skeletons were discovered under the floor of the dining-room cupboard. Forensic tests revealed that one of the skeletons was of a little girl, and the other was of an adult woman.

Amersham, Buckinghamshire: The Chequers Inn

A white-hooded figure haunts this public house, manifesting itself visually as well as opening doors and leaving cold spots. It may be that this is the ghost of a man called Auden who, in the 16th century, was responsible for imprisoning dissenters prior to their execution. Among those connected with Auden are William Tylsworth, who was burned at the stake in 1506, and the Amersham Martyrs, who met their fate in 1521. The present building did not exist in the 16th century, but it is likely that Auden haunts the site of a prison that stood here in the past.

Amersham Common, Buckinghamshire: Bendrose House

This was the former home of Dirk Bogarde. During his ownership of the house and later, at least seven people have had the unpleasant experience of feeling electric shocks. The episodes last a minimum of four minutes, and tend to occur between 4 and 5am. The experience was apparently most common in one particular room, although nobody has been able to suggest why.

Ampthill, Bedfordshire: Great Park

The ghost that haunts this 300-acre estate has been described as a knight in full armour with a plumed helmet, riding a white horse. However, in 1965 an ex-policeman, while strolling in the park with his family, encountered the vague shape of a man on a horse, who appeared where the castle used to be and disappeared near a small brook. The castle used to be the home of Catherine of Aragon. The site is now marked with an 18th-century cross, but nobody seems to know who the apparition is or why he haunts the area.

Amwell, Hertfordshire: The Elephant and Castle

Many years ago, the then landlord murdered his wife and then committed suicide in one of the bedrooms. Since then the apparition of a blonde woman, wearing a black dress and pearls around her neck, has been seen on the landing. Witnesses report that she holds out her hands as if pleading for help.

Amwellbury House, nr Ware, Hertfordshire

The phantoms of chanting monks can be seen moving past the house. The property occupies a site that formerly belonged to the Abbey of Westminster. Presumably these are the spirits of previous inhabitants of the building.

Andover, Hampshire: White Hart Hotel, Bridge Street

The manifestation of a tall woman in a dark green cloak can be seen gliding along an upstairs corridor. It is also said that Charles I stayed in a room on the ground floor and that the shadowy apparitions of a man and a woman haunt the room. Whether they are linked to Charles I is unknown.

Angmering, nr Worthing, West Sussex: The Pound

This site is near the former Ecclesden Manor, which was a monastic building. During the dissolution of the monasteries in the 16th century, some of the monks resisted eviction. One such monk may now be seen, often seated on a bank, reading a prayer book. Witnesses have stated that he is at least 8 or 9ft tall. His manifestation has been seen on a fairly regular basis for 500 years.

Annesley Hall, nr Nottingham, Nottinghamshire

The most notable ghost at Annesley Hall is a white lady, said to be a servant who died giving birth to the squire's child. Sadly, her relatives stole the money that she had put aside to ensure that the child had a decent upbringing. The ghost of another woman can be seen rising out of a well and sitting on a tree trunk to comb her hair, and a monk in black robes can be seen near the ruined church.

Apethorpe Hall, Northamptonshire

Lady Mildmay died in 1620. She was a much-celebrated philanthropist, who often distributed money to the children of the local area. Her ghost carries on this tradition, by dropping phantom coins as she makes her way around the mansion.

Appleby-in-Westmorland, Cumbria: Hanging Shaw

This bleak site on the moors to the north of Appleby was used for the hanging and gibbeting of criminals. It is so heavily haunted that a recent proposal to move the horse fair to the site was vigorously opposed by both locals and gypsies.

Appletreewick, nr Skipton, North Yorkshire: Trollers Ghyll

Trollers Ghyll is a stretch of moorland accessed from Bolton Abbey, and is a rather treacherous place to walk, as the ground is often slippery underfoot. The area is haunted by a phantom hound, known as the Barguest. It has yellow fur, saucer-like eyes and is said to be as large as a bear. Several different witnesses have encountered the Barguest, which is thought to have Norse origins.

Arborfield, nr Reading, Berkshire: St Bartholomew's Church

At midnight on New Year's Eve, the ghost of a young woman in full bridal dress can be seen standing by a yew tree beside the church. She was due to be married to a gardener from the nearby hall, but just before the ceremony she was murdered by a jealous butler.

Ardblair Castle, nr Blairgowrie, Perthshire

The silent ghostly figure of a green lady can be seen walking around the precincts of the castle. She is said to be Lady Jane Drummond, who committed suicide by drowning herself after her father forbade her to marry.

Ardchattan Priory, nr Connel Bridge, Strathclyde

The forlorn figure of a nun from Kilmaronaig Convent, which is on the opposite side of Loch Etive, haunts the priory. She was secretly smuggled into the priory by the monks and hidden in a hole beneath the floor of the oratory. The prior discovered her presence and had her buried alive, presumably in the same hole in which she had been hiding.

Ardvreck Castle, nr Inchnadamph, Highlands

In 1650 Neil McLeod of Assynt, then Lord of Ardvreck, betrayed the Marquess of Montrose, a royalist. Montrose was captured at Ardvreck Castle and taken to Edinburgh for eventual execution. Montrose's supporters, bent on revenge, burned down the castle and slaughtered the inhabitants. The figure of a giant man is seen near the shore of Loch Assynt, but whether he is linked in any way to the demise of Montrose, or his presumed stature, is unknown.

Arundel Castle, Arundel, West Sussex

This was the ancestral home of the Duke of Norfolk for over 700 years. The original castle was built during the time of Edward the Confessor. A ghostly man has been seen in the library, as has the spirit of a girl who jumped from one of the towers. The ghost of a kitchen boy has been seen and is described as wearing a light grey tunic with loose sleeves. He had long hair and was in his mid-twenties. The witness described the manifestation as being rather like an old photograph, with blurred edges. The spirit faded and disappeared as the witness watched.

Ascot, Berkshire

A phantom horseman has been seen on numerous occasions near a roundabout in the centre of the town. His purpose and intended destination are open to speculation.

Ashby St Ledgers, Northamptonshire

The ghost of Guy Fawkes is said to haunt the Manor House here. He has been seen on several occasions by a number of witnesses. Fawkes stayed here for some six weeks before his attempt, with a band of fellow conspirators, to blow up Parliament in 1605. He was captured before he could execute what became known as the Gunpowder Plot, and was subsequently put to death.

Ashdown Forest, West Sussex: Priest's House

The Priest's House, now owned by the National Trust, is said to be haunted by one of its previous inhabitants. The exact nature and purpose of the spirit is not known, but it has been seen by a number of witnesses over the years. Recent witnesses have described the spirit as a blue lady, who is often seen on the landing. Other witnesses have suggested that she wears a long, blue robe rather like a dressing gown. Local explanations relate the ghost to a murder where the victim was cut up and put into a settle, but there does not seem to be any evidence to substantiate this. Witnesses have also reported a sense of calmness as the ghost soundlessly glides past them, accompanied by a feeling of coldness.

Ashdown House, nr Forest Row, East Sussex

Lord Heathfield haunts this building. Every 6 July, his footsteps are heard on the stairs. However, the only connection that he has with the house is that his daughter married the man who built it.

Ashford-in-the-Water, Derbyshire

A ghostly procession of 12 men, carrying an empty coffin, can often be seen making its way down Shady Lane and into Longstone. It is said that this is a portent of death.

Ash Grange, Ash Magna, Shropshire

A ghostly monk has been seen near the entrance to the grange. He has been described as very solid, dressed in a long, black coat with a hood, and suspended about a foot off the ground, with no visible legs. The apparition seems to have the ability to glide across the road. Other witnesses have described feeling a cold rush of air, hearing rattling chains and seeing a strange light when the apparition appears. Although there is a farm nearby called Abbey Farm, it does not appear that there was ever an abbey here. The nearest abbey is Combermere, seven miles away. Another house nearby is haunted by the sound of bumping noises and the feeling that a figure is present in one of the bedrooms.

Ashintully Castle, nr Blairgowrie, Tayside

Spalding of Ashintully had a tinker hanged for trespassing on his land. Before he died the tinker laid a curse on the family, which has come true (the family has now died out), and his spirit haunts the avenue of trees where he was hanged. Another Spalding

killed 'Crooked Davie', who was a servant and hunchback. He joins the tinker in haunting this particular area. A one-time owner of the castle, Green Jean, appears in the private burial ground among the pine trees wearing a green dress. She was murdered by her wicked uncle. There is said to be an underground passage that leads from Ashintully to Whitefield Castle.

Ashleigh Barton, nr Plymouth, Devon

For many years a ghost that warns the inhabitants of an impending death in the family has haunted the upper floors of the house.

Ashmore, Cranborne Chase, Dorset

An ancient pagan camp that covered several acres is said to resound with shrieks, cries, groans and the clang of iron. It is said that the raiders who inhabited the camp preyed upon the local villagers, carrying off animals, loot and women. One night, after such a raid, as the warriors slept, the captured women broke free, signalled to their husbands and threw open the gates. All the sleeping raiders were slaughtered.

Ashover, Derbyshire: All Saints Church

The ghost of a headless woman haunts the churchyard. It is believed that she is the apparition of the wife of John Towndrew. He murdered her with a hammer in 1841, and cut off her head. He then committed suicide.

Ashton under Hill, Worcestershire

A white lady can be seen running up the main street of the village, screaming and wailing. The ghost of a robber monk, Benedict, who is notorious in this area, has also been seen and heard by several people.

Ashton-under-Lyne, Greater Manchester: The Tameside Theatre

It is said that Ernie, a violinist, haunts the building. He has often been heard, still playing his tunes long after his death. Presumably he once made his living at the theatre. Other witnesses have suggested that there are spirits at work in the theatre which are far more evil and aggressive than Ernie.

Ashwell, Hertfordshire: St Mary's Church

The apparition of a headless man in black is reputed to haunt the churchyard. Research has not uncovered who he may be or whether his mortal remains are buried in the consecrated ground.

Askerton Castle, nr Brampton, Cumbria

A phantom white lady is said to haunt the area surrounding the castle. One witness in the past claimed that the ghost actually spoke to him. She stepped out in front of his horse, grabbed the bridle and told him that she would only let him go if he promised that he would do something for her, but never tell another living soul. She threatened him with death if he ever divulged the secret. The man gave his promise and kept her confidence to the grave.

Askrigg, North Yorkshire: Nappa Hall

This 15th-century fortified manor was the place chosen to give Mary Queen of Scots a break from her imprisonment in Bolton Castle. She stayed at the manor house in 1568, and since then several people have claimed to have seen her ghost walking around the building.

Aspatria, Cumbria: Gill House

During World War Two, the Women's Land Army used Gill House as a hostel. Not only did they hear strange noises and smell something horrible, they also saw a phantom figure walking through closed doors. One of the girls even claimed to have felt that she was being strangled in her sleep. The haunting reached such a pitch that the worst infected room was closed. It is said that after the Women's Land Army left the building the intensity of the haunting subsided.

Aspley Guise, nr Woburn, Bedfordshire

The ghost of Dick Turpin, the famous highwayman, and his horse can be seen trotting along Weathercock Lane or Woodcott Lane, heading toward the old manor house. They ride up to a hedge, where the cloaked man dismounts and passes through the hedge and into the grounds of the old manor. In the past Turpin, intent on robbing the manor, discovered two corpses in a cupboard. The owner of the house had murdered his daughter and her lover after discovering them together one night. It is said that the pair were chased into a large cupboard in the kitchen, whereupon the father slammed the door shut and moved furniture in front of the cupboard to prevent them from escaping. They died of starvation or suffocation. Armed with the knowledge of the location of the bodies, Turpin was able to blackmail the father into allowing him to use the house as a hideout. His ghost re-enacts his discovery of the bodies and subsequent use of the building.

Astley, Warwickshire

Lady Jane Grey and her father Henry Grey, Duke of Suffolk, are said to haunt the castle, which was once their home but now lies in ruins. Lady Jane is seen as a fully formed apparition, but her father appears as a headless ghost. A further manifestation, this time a hooded monk nicknamed 'Willie', is often seen in the churchyard. There does not seem to be any particular reason for him to haunt this place.

Astley Abbots, nr Bridgnorth, Shropshire

A manifestation, which has been seen by several witnesses over a number of years around Severn Hall and The Boldings, is described as a woman around 5ft tall, wearing drab clothing, with a long skirt and a shawl around her head. She floats across the road and always just looks ahead of her. She may be the ghost of Hannah Phillips, who was due to be married at the church. One or two days before the wedding, she went to prepare for the ceremony. Unfortunately, she lived on the other side of the river and had to cross the ford in order to get to the church. She slipped and was presumed drowned; her body was never found. Several other witnesses have seen what may be the spirit of her fiancé, wearing a suit with a waistcoat and bowler hat. He even has a watch chain hanging from his pocket. Their intended home, of which there appears to be no record, has also been seen in ghostly form by a couple visiting the area. It appeared to be a roofless, ruined farmhouse, near The Boldings.

Aston, South Yorkshire: High Trees

The spirit of a one-time rector haunts this former rectory. It is said that he caught his wife embracing their butler. He murdered her, leaving an indelible bloodstain on the bedroom floor.

Aston, West Midlands: Victoria Road

In September 1971 two friends, Mrs Bagley and Mrs Heath, were walking to work. As they reached the site of the former police station, the apparition of a woman in a green frilly dress, standing in the middle of the road, confronted them. As they approached, she disappeared. Several months later a Mrs McFarland saw a woman in a yellow-green dress by the curbside. Again the apparition disappeared as she approached. It may be that this is the spirit of a former usherette at the Aston Cross Cinema. She died while crossing the road several years ago.

Aston Rogers, Shropshire: Pond House Farm

This building dates from the 16th century and is the stalking place of a female manifestation. Witnesses have felt someone breathing into their faces while they are in bed, and heard the sound of paper rustling. One witness saw a girl of around eight standing by her bed, wearing a blue frock with a white pinafore and white cap. As the woman reached out to touch the blonde girl, the apparition faded. This may be the spirit of a young girl who was burned to death in the house many years ago.

Atcham, Shropshire: The Mytton and Mermaid Hotel

John Mytton was an eccentric local squire who died penniless in London, and he is thought to haunt the Mytton and Mermaid Hotel. His funeral procession stopped at the hotel overnight en route to the family tomb. He was an odd character, who kept 2,000 dogs, 60 cats and a bear. He had a habit of risking his life every day and drank six bottles of port each night. He even set fire to himself in order to cure himself of hiccups. He came into a fortune at the age of 20, and devoted himself to ensuring that every penny of it was spent. Given the fact that he lived in the 18th century, spending £500,000 in 17 years was quite a feat. Unfortunately, nobody has been able to describe his apparition in detail.

Athelhampton Manor, nr Dorchester, Dorset

This mediaeval house not only has human ghosts, but it is also associated with some animal manifestations. A grey lady passes through the walls of the East Wing, as well as appearing in the Yellow and State Bedrooms. She was once confronted by a housemaid and told to leave, an order which she obeyed. Two Civil War duellists replay their fight in the house during some evenings, and a ghostly cooper can be seen mending barrels in the cellar. In 1957 Robert Cooke MP distinctly heard his cat, despite the fact that it had died over a week before. The house once belonged to the Martyn family, and during the 16th century they owned an ape (which can be seen in their coat of arms). Since the death of the last Martyn in 1595, the ghost of the ape has been heard scratching the panelling of the Great Chamber. It is said that the ape was sealed into a secret staircase behind the panelling.

Atherstone, Warwickshire

The area is haunted by the ghost of a farmer, who was killed by the low, over-hanging bough of a tree. He had made a bet on the time it would take him to get from Atherstone to Alderminster on horseback at night, but collided with the bough and was killed. It is said that if you see him once you will see him three times.

Attercliffe, South Yorkshire

A phantom army was first seen passing the river here in 1661. William Broome, then the vicar of Attercliffe, watched the procession of white-clad riders on white horses for one hour, recording the event in his diary.

Avebury Manor, nr Marlborough, Wiltshire

This fine Elizabethan house is said to be haunted by a ghost wearing a white hood, possibly a monk. A member of staff once asked the owner of the house whether the gentleman monk in the library was staying for lunch. The owner knew nothing of the visitor, and when they returned to the library the apparition had disappeared. Other manifestations have occurred at the house. A witness staying at the manor described a man in the garden as being dressed like a Cavalier, and at the Iron Gate, adjoining Truslow Manor, the figure of a lady in white lace with a white hood, perhaps a nun, was seen by a government official. Other individuals also experienced this manifestation throughout the 1970s.

Avebury Ring, Wiltshire

During World War One, the Wiltshire author Edith Olivier was driving through Avebury and saw lights around the circle of stones. She thought it was a fair that had been erected there and could hear the music and see the stalls. This was at dusk, and as she approached the stones, the whole apparition disappeared, leaving her among the sarsens. She was later told that fairs were held there 50 years before. Miss J.M. Dunn saw small human figures among the stones on a clear moonlit night. It is believed that these were the ghosts of stone age inhabitants of the area.

Avenbury Church, nr Bromyard, Herefordshire

Although the church is now in ruins, it is haunted by the melodies of ghostly organ music. It is said that the organist was murdered by his brother, and despite an exorcism the sound of organ music still pervades the ruins. A bell, which is now in St Andrew-by-the-Wardrobe in London, is said to be enchanted to the extent that it still tolls if an Avenbury vicar dies.

Aveton Gifford, Devon: South Efford House

The eccentric ghost of a naval officer hangs out of the window, cursing courting couples. It seems that the ghost continues a tradition that the man had begun in life. Within the house is found the ghost of a manservant who hanged himself from the staircase. A ferryman haunts the nearby river. The well-meaning owner of the land between the ferryman's cottage and the river considered the steps too dangerous for the old man to traverse, so he had them blocked. As a result the old man lost his livelihood and died of a broken heart.

Axbridge, nr Cheddar, Somerset: King John's Hunting Lodge

In 1978 an Elizabethan lady, dressed in white, was seen sitting in the mayoral chair. The chair dates from the Stuart period (1603–1714) and came from the Guildhall. The apparition's appearance is noted in the museum diary for August 1978. There is also a tale of a ghostly tabby cat that has been seen on the first floor or at the top of the stairs on several occasions. Several people have seen the feline and others have caught glimpses of its tail.

Aylmerton, nr Cromer, Norfolk

A white lady haunts the Shrieking Pits, intent on finding the body of her child. Although the pits were originally mediaeval iron workings, they now derive their name from the wailings of the ghost. Her husband murdered her and her child in a fit of rage.

Aylsham, Blickling Hall, Norfolk

The present building stands on the site of the birthplace of Anne Boleyn. She was executed on 19 May 1536. To celebrate this anniversary a phantom coach, drawn by headless horses and driven by a headless coachman, brings her headless body (she has her head on her lap) back to the hall. When it reaches the hall the coach and horses disappear. It is said that Anne Boleyn's father, Sir Thomas, is fated to drive over 40 bridges in the county each year, followed by a pack of screaming demons.

Ayot St Lawrence, Hertfordshire: Brocket Arms

The manifestation of a man dressed in brown, with a cowl, has been seen by a number of witnesses in the Brocket Arms, which was built in 1378. On one particular occasion in 1969 the witness stated that the spirit's head was facing downwards, but as she approached him he disappeared. The same ghost has been seen in the dining room, where guests have also heard muttered voices and footsteps. It is widely believed that this is the ghost of a pilgrim, who stayed in the building when it was a hostelry in the 14th century. He committed suicide by hanging himself in the room that is now the bar.

B

Backways Cove to Bygrave House

Backways Cove, Trebarwith Strand, Cornwall

There is some dispute about the reason for the haunting in this inlet in North Cornwall, where apparitions have been seen on the shoreline. Either they are drowned sailors whose bodies were cast ashore here, or they may relate to a sad story involving an inheritance dispute. When their father died, the elder of two brothers was left the entire estate while the younger was given nothing. The younger man was so jealous that he crept onto the farm in the dead of the night and set fire to it. However, unbeknown to him, his older brother had died the day before and left everything to him. It may be the ghost of the younger brother that haunts the area.

Badbury Rings, Dorset

This Iron Age fort has been a significant site for centuries, and is still a favoured place of modern druids. Witnesses have been watched and stalked by a strange-looking figure. It is described as being hairy and dwarfish, generally sticking to the edge of the site. The manifestation seems to have a particular interest in courting couples. Since the apparition's face is distorted by wounds, it may be that it is a warrior who was killed near the rings. Alternatively, it could be the ghost of a guardian said to protect a golden coffin buried under the old fort.

Badby, Northamptonshire

A white lady is said to haunt Badby Woods. She is seen picking her way through the trees, mounted on a horse, constantly repeating her last journey in life. Her husband murdered her as she rode home after visiting her lover.

Baddesley Clinton, nr Warwick, Warwickshire

You will have to wait until 2007 to have the chance of seeing the manic ghost of Nicholas Brome, as he only makes his appearance every 10 years. Despite the fact that he murdered the local priest, his mortal remains are buried under the doorway to the church. Brome was said to have had a very violent temper, so much so that when the local priest touched his wife in a way that he did not approve of, he killed the man in a rage. He made partial penance by supporting the church financially until his death, hence the fact that he was allowed to be buried on church ground.

Badger, nr Beckbury, Shropshire

This was once the site of a beautiful Georgian mansion, home of the poet and lawyer Hawkins Brown. Sadly the building has now been demolished A grey lady was said to walk along the blood-red painted corridor on the top floor. A witness writing in the 1970s recalled seeing a woman in a sheer, grey dress, with golden hair. On another occasion she stood by his bed and smiled at him. At a Christmas party, one minute before midnight, the assembled revellers all witnessed her as she walked across the dance floor and stood in front of the man who had seen her on several occasions. As he stretched his hand out to touch her, she disappeared. After the demolition of the house, the man walked across the park and saw the grey lady and smelt her perfume for the last time. When the land was ploughed an old jewel box was found, containing, among other valuable items, an engagement ring. It is felt locally that the grey lady probably died young of a broken heart.

Baginton, Warwickshire: The Old Mill Hotel, Mill Lane

Not only does the restaurant area still feature the mill pond and the mill wheel, but it is also haunted by the apparition of a grey lady. She has not been seen very often, but her voice has been heard on many occasions.

Balcombe, nr Horsham, West Sussex

During World War One a tragic accident occurred in the railway tunnel. A train in the gloomy tunnel killed four British soldiers. Their spirits have been seen and heard on several occasions by a variety of witnesses.

Balcomie Castle, nr St Andrews, Fife

At some point in the 16th or 17th century, the tower house was garrisoned by troops under a colonel. A boy working there had a habit of whistling while he worked. This so aggravated the colonel that he had him locked up in the dungeon. Straight after the incident, the colonel left to visit Fife. When he returned four days later, the boy was dead. Other versions say the starved boy was either a piper or fifer. Whatever he was, whistling can still be heard here.

Baldoon Castle, nr Bladnoch, Dumfries and Galloway

Sinister 17th-century events are the background for the hauntings at this castle, and also the inspiration for Sir Walter Scott's tale *The Bride of Lammermoor* and Donizetti's opera *Lucia di Lammermoor*. Janet Dalrymple, daughter of statesman Sir James Dalrymple, had fallen in love with the penniless Lord Rutherford. Her father had other plans for her and arranged a marriage with Rutherford's nephew, David Dunbar, then heir to Baldoon. Despite Janet's protestations, made with the active support of her mother, the wedding went ahead on 24 August 1669. The marriage was a short one. That night, after the couple had retired to their bedchamber, hideous screams were heard by the guests. Forcing the door open, they found Dunbar dead from numerous stab wounds and Janet crouching in the corner of the room. They could get no sense from her; clearly something had happened that had unhinged her troubled mind. One version says that she died within a month of the murdered bridegroom, while another, more sadly, tells that she survived for another 17 years, utterly insane. It is her bloodstained spirit that is seen in the castle to this day.

Ballechin House, nr Pitlochry, Tayside

The Society for Psychical Research was allowed access to this haunted home when the Marquess of Bute rented it on their behalf. Between February and May 1897, Adah Freer, the leader of the research group, catalogued a number of strange phenomena. The investigators witnessed a nun, accompanied by another spirit that was not identified, a shuffling man, a limping man, a priest, two old women, one of whom did not have legs, and a black dog. Most of the explanations offered for these manifestations derive from the oddly cursed Steuart family. The dog is apparently the spirit of Major Steuart, who has returned as the ghost of his favourite black spaniel. In 1873, the year before Steuart died, his 27-year-old housekeeper died in suspicious circumstances. Steuart's sister, Isabella, died in 1880, after a life as a nun. After Steuart himself died, the house was left to a John Steuart, a Catholic, who allowed a priest to live in the house.

Ballygally, Co. Antrim: Ballygally Castle Hotel

Set on the head of Ballycastle Bay, the building was constructed in 1625. A former owner, Lady Isobel Shaw, haunts it. She is said to make her presence felt by knocking on guests' doors and then disappearing.

Balnagown Castle, nr Ballchraggan, Highlands

The ghost of Black Andrew Munro, a convicted 16th-century rapist, haunts this 13th-century building, the former home of the Earls of Ross. The then Chief of the Clan Ross threw Munro out of one of the tower windows with a rope around his neck, as punishment for his crimes. It is also said that a considerable treasure lies buried somewhere in the castle.

Bamburgh Castle, nr Alnwick, Northumberland

The castle once belonged to the Forster family, later becoming the property of Lord

Crewe. The castle is said to be haunted by two apparitions. The first is a knight, about which we know nothing. The second is known as Green Jane. She continually re-enacts her own death, falling off the crag just outside the castle's clock tower. Her manifestation holds a bundle in its arms, perhaps a child, and many witnesses have sworn that they have heard screams and mocking laughter. Perhaps Green Jane was abandoned by her husband, or ignored by a lover to whom she had borne a child.

Banwell Abbey, nr Axbridge, Somerset

It is said that ghostly monks haunt the abbey, along with other apparitions related to its long religious history. However, in one of the nearby houses, there are witnesses who state that they have heard something that may be a more recent haunting than the monks. Footsteps are heard descending the staircase, often accompanied by the rustle of silk and the sound of a woman or girl sobbing. This must be related to a previous inhabitant of the house, perhaps with no religious connections, despite the proximity of the abbey.

Barbreck, nr Oban, Argyll

The ghostly figure of a young girl with a pale face has been seen several times beside Loch Craignish and the river valley of the Barbreck, particularly between Ford and Ardfern. This 'hooden maiden', as she is called, wears a tartan skirt, but the hood itself hides most of her features. If she is approached, she rapidly disappears.

Barcaldine House, Strathclyde

Deep in the territory of the Campbell clan, it is not surprising that the ghost of a Campbell is said to have been seen here on regular occasions. It is not clear who he may be or why he has chosen to haunt this particular castle. The only information that research has uncovered is that the spirit is seemingly bent on revenge. A blue lady is also present in the house, who, it is said, is attracted to music. She appears when anyone has a car radio on or is singing in the immediate vicinity.

Barnack, Cambridgeshire: Kingsley House

'Old Button Cap', who is said to walk through the house in flopping slippers, haunts this 14th-century former rectory. He may have been a former rector, who was often seen wearing his dressing gown and a bed cap with a button on top of it. Just before he died, it was said that he had conned a widow and her child out of an inheritance. His ghost is believed to be hunting for the incriminating papers that linked him to the scandal. He likes to stroke small children on their heads, and the author Charles Kingsley, as a child, recounted that the apparition turned the pages of a book he was reading.

Barnwell, Northamptonshire: The Old Abbey House

A link with St Radegund's Convent is the probable explanation for the appearance of the grey or white lady seen here. She is almost certainly a nun who used to use an underground passage to meet her Augustinian monk lover. Other manifestations that haunt the house include poltergeist activities featuring the ripping of bed linen while people are asleep. Squire Jacob Butler, known as the 'Giant Squire' because he was 6ft 4in tall, died there in 1765 and has been seen several times in the house. At the time of his death he was the oldest barrister in England. He appears as a sad ghost searching for his favourite dog, which died soon before him. A ghostly squirrel that reputedly haunts the grounds of the house is also accompanied by a phantom hare. The squirrel can be seen running along the wall of the garden and onto the grass, but whenever someone approaches it, it simply vanishes. The hare is seen in the garden too, especially when there is snow on the ground. Like the squirrel, it vanishes without a trace.

Barrasford, nr Hexham, Northumberland: Barrasford Arms Hotel

Once a well-known coaching inn, the Barrasford Arms Hotel was burned down toward the end of the 19th century. The fire has left at least one indelible mark as far as supernatural activities are concerned. A man died in the flames when the building was destroyed, and his apparition is seen running across the road with its clothes on fire.

Barrock Fell, nr Carlisle, Cumbria

Infamous highwayman John Whitfield was not executed by traditional means. Instead of being hanged and then having his corpse put in a gibbet, it was decided to put him straight into the gibbet and let him starve to death. In 1768, as Whitfield gradually starved to death in the metal cage, a coach driver happened to pass the spot. No one will ever know whether the motive was revenge because Whitfield had robbed him in the past, or whether the man took pity on the dying highwayman. In any case, the coachman shot him dead. On this part of the A6 you can still hear Whitfield's cries of agony.

Barton Ferry, nr Attenborough, Nottinghamshire

Several witnesses, mainly fishermen, have seen a troop of mounted Roundhead dragoons leading their horses across the river toward St Mary's Church. The witnesses say that they look tired and ill-kempt, so they may have been stragglers or deserters from a battle.

Basildon New Town, Essex: Church of the Holy Cross

The ghost of a man dressed in a reddish-brown robe haunts the church. The apparition is thought to be one of two rectors who were expelled and possibly murdered at the time of the Reformation. Footsteps and voices have been heard coming from the inside of the church when it is empty at night.

Basingstoke, Hampshire: Kingsclere Road

Dark, muttering figures have been seen in the shadows of the fir trees at a spot known as Catern's Grave. One witness reported a very frightening episode when he encountered a figure resembling a monk. He described the apparition as having a grey, lined face. The manifestation seemed to draw him toward itself, and even attempted to enter his body to possess it. After a mental or spiritual struggle, the witness escaped. Another witness told of being beaten away from the site by a group of muttering figures.

Bath, Somerset: Beehive, Lansdowne Road

The ghost of a serving maid has been seen on several occasions since the 1970s. She is described as having a happy expression and wears a mob cap, a bluish-grey gown that reaches to the floor, and black, shiny shoes. She has been seen both in the hallway and in an upstairs bedroom. Locals now refer to her as Bunty. The manifestation only lasts for a few seconds and then fades away.

Bath, Somerset: Garrick's Head Hotel, Shore Close

Beau Nash ran the Garrick's Head as a gaming house over 200 years ago. There were many duels and arguments in and around the building. A heavily-built man in Regency dress, with a long, brown wig, is often encountered. He has squeaky footsteps that leave no mark or print. The ghosts of a murdered man and his unfaithful wife have been seen since the woman's suicide, immediately after her husband had murdered her lover. The ghosts are particularly active when a new landlord takes over the hotel. Presences have been felt in the cellar, noises heard on the stairs and in the attic and house items have disappeared or been inexplicably moved.

Bath, Somerset: Gay Street

Dr Samuel Johnson often visited a house on Gay Street owned by Mrs Thale. They experienced ghostly voices coming from the drawing room, but whenever they investigated, the talking ceased and they found nothing in the room. In 1977 disturbances at a very haunted property in the road were attributed to a homosexual male ghost, with his white hair tied back with ribbon, seen by several men. Women with the men could not see the apparition. Military police were called to the property and were unable to explain the nature of the disturbances. One man who saw the ghost was so affected that he was taken to hospital and treated for shock.

Bath, Somerset: Grosvenor Hotel

William Wordsworth (1770–1850) once owned this building. It is now haunted by the ethereal form of a lady, who is accompanied by an obvious drop in temperature. She is said to walk along the corridor on the first floor. However, her appearance is indistinct and has a grey look about it. Several employees of the hotel have seen her from time to time and describe her as a 'misty' figure, but all report an icy cold feeling during her presence.

Bath, Somerset: Linley House, Pierre Pont Place

Staff and visitors to the building have often heard the sound of heavy footsteps going up the stairs into an empty room. In the 1960s the rooms above were flats. At least two residents reported hearing something walking up the stairs and stopping outside the flat. On a number of occasions the occupants opened the door to find nobody there.

Bath, Somerset: Pulteney Street

One of the houses in this road was formerly the home of Admiral Howe (1726–1799), First Lord of the Admiralty. His ghostly figure has been seen on several occasions, walking along the passage and entering rooms while they are occupied. The apparition behaves as if he is just checking the rooms, and ignores anyone he may encounter. On other occasions the ghost is heard to come in, remove his boots and outer clothing, walk up to the bedroom and disappear into a cupboard.

Bath, Somerset: Saville Row, Bennett Street

In 1905 Cynthia Montefiore approached the end of Saville Row and saw a man in a large, black hat coming toward her. He crossed the road, and as he neared her, she felt a strange sensation. As he momentarily passed out of sight, she turned and saw that he had disappeared. She was perplexed, as there was nowhere for him to have gone. In 1974 Eileen Parish witnessed the same phenomenon near the Assembly Rooms. She described the man in the same way and added that he wore black trousers and gaiters. The strangely dressed man has been seen on a number of other occasions in and around Saville Row.

Bath, Somerset: Theatre Royal

A grey lady is sometimes seen sitting in a box

BATH–BATTLE

above the audience. She is apparently the ghost of a woman who committed suicide by throwing herself into the stalls. Strangely, she has been seen passing from the adjoining Garrick's Head into the theatre through the walls. She also haunts the corridors to the lower circle and has been seen by many actors and actresses, including Dame Anna Neagle.

Bath, Somerset: Victoria Park, Gravel Walk

At one end of Gravel Walk schoolmaster Paul Buckley and a group from his class encountered a tall man with white hair. One particular boy, who had been standing near the steps, was extremely nervous and refused to discuss the matter. As part of the Bath Ghost Walk Tour, parties of would-be ghost hunters often visit this location. On one occasion one of the members of the tour asked the guide how they had managed to fake the disappearance of the white-haired man. On investigation the tourist described the same man that was seen by the school party. He apparently stood in the middle of the walk and then suddenly vanished. Most of these incidents appear to occur at around 8.45pm. Another witness from America further described the man as having his white hair tied behind his head with a ribbon.

Bath, Somerset: York Villa

This house was once owned by Frederick, Duke of York (1763–1827). However, the ghost dates from the period of George III, whose second son kept his mistress here with their two children. The prince decided to abandon his mistress, but she followed him back to London, leaving her children at the house. The servants had not been paid for some time and gradually left, abandoning the two children to starve to death. One of the prince's older servants returned to the house and discovered the bodies of the

children. He has haunted the building ever since. He is described as wearing a long cloak and dark trousers. There is also a tale of a woman in grey haunting the top floor of the property.

Battle, East Sussex: Battle Abbey

In the 1970s a Norman knight was clearly seen standing in the corner nearest the Chapter House. Later in the decade another visitor saw an old man in a brown leather jerkin and an apron. Monks have been seen near the abbey itself, and particularly in the churchyard of St Mary's Church. One figure was described as wearing a dark habit with a cowl, and glided toward the gateway of the abbey. In the Great Hall the sound of rustling silk has been heard. This sound and that of footsteps has been closely associated with the apparition of a lady in red. A woman in a long, red gown, probably Elizabethan, was seen by a group of visitors. She appeared in the corner of the room and faded after a few seconds. The ghost of a woman in a grey dress has also been seen walking along the corridor from the Great Hall to the Abbot's House. She is said to have a distinct limp.

Battle, East Sussex: Pyke House

The figure of a young girl has been seen running along the upstairs corridor near the flat occupied by the warden. She has been described as wearing a long, white dress or nightgown, and has the ability to glide through a bedroom and disappear near a window. The apparent explanation dates back to the time when the building was a pair of worker's cottages in the 19th century. The daughter of the owner, devastated after a failed love affair, committed suicide in the lake behind the house. Some witnesses claimed to have seen her indistinct image hurrying through the back garden. It is also said that the building contains a hidden and locked cupboard near the loft entrance.

Perhaps the contents may reveal the truth behind the manifestation.

Bawtry, South Yorkshire: The Crown, High Street

This 17th-century post house has three ghosts: a monk that haunts the stables where he died from a heart attack, a crinolined lady, who died in a fire many years ago and is said to walk the corridors of the old wing of the building, and the restless spirit of a serving girl, murdered by her jealous lover.

Bayham Abbey, nr Tunbridge Wells, Kent

These wonderful ruins are said to be haunted by the spirits of monks who once lived there. Several witnesses have said that they have seen a procession of monks in white robes pacing around the site. Others claim to have heard monkish plainchant and the tolling of bells.

Beaminster, Dorset: Bridge House

A blue lady haunts this area, and she was photographed just before the building was demolished. A local historian took some 20 photographs which, when they were developed, revealed the indistinct figure of a woman dressed in a long blue dress and high-heeled shoes. It also appears that there was a murder in the house many years ago, which left an indelible blood stain.

Beaminster, Dorset: St Mary's Church

In 1728, the body of John Daniel was found in a field close to his home. As he was said to have suffered from fits all his life, he was buried without an inquest being called. Six years later, on 27 June, while the church was being used as a schoolroom, several of the children claimed to have heard clanking metal. As they investigated the area, they heard singing. Some of the boys entered the church and saw a coffin lying on a bench. They then saw John Daniel, sitting with his pen in his hand, a book next to him. Four of the boys knew John, and his half-brother recognised his clothes. They threw a stone at the apparition and it disappeared. The local magistrate, Colonel Brodrepp, interrogated the boys, who accurately described the coffin and the fact that John's ghost had a bandage around it. He had injured his hand just before his death. Following the investigation, the body was exhumed and it was found that John had been strangled. In 1998 a local farmer encountered two figures disappearing into the ruined graveyard of the Daniel family. One appeared to be a young boy in dark clothing and the other a woman dressed in white. Psychic investigators reported a distinct drop in the temperature in the area following investigations soon after the event.

Bearsted, Kent

On the lane from the village to the Pilgrim's Way, you may encounter the manifestation of man who seems to be from the 17th or 18th century. He is described as being mounted on a horse, which may account for witnesses stating that he is wearing silver spurs. He is also said to be wearing a wide-brimmed hat.

Bearwood, West Midlands: Warley Park, Abbey Road

Built by the Quaker Hubert Galton, a Birmingham gunmaker, Warley Park was originally called Warley Hall. It was bought by the Birmingham Corporation in 1905 and the building was demolished in 1968. A grey lady is seen walking around the area at dusk, along a path leading from the car park to the woods. She vanishes part way along the path, and is thought to be the murdered heiress of the

Galton family, although another story runs that she may have committed suicide following a disastrous love affair. The apparition of a Chinese man, thought to have been a servant at the hall, has also been seen near the path. Some believe that he was in some way implicated in the death of the heiress.

Beauchief Abbey, nr Sheffield, Yorkshire

It would be surprising if this ancient religious site was not haunted by a shade of its past. Not only does the abbey claim to be visited by the ghost of a former monk, who has been seen by several witnesses over the years, but it also has a white lady. Although it is unclear who she is, several people have seen her. There are other less well-documented ghosts and apparitions at the site.

Beaulieu Abbey, Beaulieu, nr Southampton, Hampshire

Built in 1204, this abbey has a magnificent gatehouse now known as Palace House. It was converted into a private home in the 1500s. The estate boasts a number of chanting monks, notably seen by, among others, the sister of the owner, Lord Montague. Elizabeth Varley reported hearing the monks at dusk, which may coincide with the time that their services were held in the past. Other witnesses have reported hearing a Gregorian chant, which may not be the same as the type of songs sung by the monks. In the Palace House itself, two or three monks have been seen on a number of occasions. They are described as wearing white robes, with stripes of black cloth hanging down across the shoulders, which is an accurate description of a Cistercian monk. The black cloth, known as a scapulary, was worn as a sign of affiliation to the order. More recently, a witness saw two monks, with their heads bowed, walk along a path before passing through a hedge containing a metal fence.

Bebington, nr Birkenhead, Merseyside

Poulton Hall was once a nunnery, and Poulton Road is said to be haunted by the spirit of a nun, who has been mistaken for a hitch hiker on several occasions. One witness, late at night, stopped to give what he thought was a young girl a lift. She was wearing a long, dark coat and had long hair. As the driver pulled in and leant across to open the passenger window to enquire if she needed a lift, the figure slowly disappeared. Several other people claim to have seen the figure on this particular road, especially at night. The churchyard in Bebington is also said to be haunted by strangely floating monks, who appear around two feet off the ground. They wear grey robes and it is presumed that they are walking on the level that the ground was in Norman times. It has since been lowered, but the apparitions seem oddly oblivious to the changes.

Beccles, Suffolk: Roos Hall

On Christmas Eve you may well encounter a phantom coach drawn by four horses and driven by a headless coachman. In the park there is an oak tree from which a gibbet once hung. The tortured spirits of those who hanged there haunt the spot. One is described as wearing a mottled old brown jacket and tattered trousers. Many witnesses have reported that he appears from nowhere and glides toward the oak. As he reaches the oak he vanishes. Whether these stories are genuine or designed to scare off poachers will never be known.

Beckbury, Shropshire: Lower Hall

The ghost of Squire Stubbs is said to haunt his ancestral home, where in life he was able to indulge his passion for fox hunting. Apparently he used to hunt six days a week. On many occasions the sound of muffled

31

hoof beats making progress across cobbled stones has been heard, despite the fact that the local roads are all now tarmac. In the 1950s a witness heard the neigh of a horse and the sound of it hoofing the ground. It is widely believed that the spirit of the squire is unable to leave his familiar surroundings and abandon the joy of the hunt.

Beddgelert, nr Portmadoc, Gwynedd: The Goat Hotel

During the latter half of the 18th century, the inn was owned and run by David Pritchard. It seems that, for various reasons, his spirit cannot be separated from the inn. His presence and manifestation is most acutely felt and seen in room 29. One hundred years after his death, he returned to the inn and told the staff there of a secret that he had taken to his grave. Following his instructions, they lifted a hearthstone and found his hidden hoard of coins.

Bedford, Bedfordshire: The Magistrate's Court, Mill Street

Strange footsteps and knocking on doors are often heard in this former magistrate's clerk's office. In nearby Newnham Avenue the Methodist chapel is haunted by the figure of a man in black trousers and a tweed jacket. He exits the building through a wall, leaving a trail of mist behind him.

Bedford, Bedfordshire: Union Street

In 1670 Black Tom, a notorious highwayman, was hanged from the gallows that were once sited here. His spirit now lurks in the car park that has replaced the gallows. Drivers have described him as being a vague shape of a man, who seems to keep to the corners of the car park. Another witness described Black Tom's head as 'lolling about' – perhaps this indicates how he met his end.

Bedford, Bedfordshire: Willington Manor

This was the former home of Sir John Gostwick, Henry VIII's Master of the Hounds. Little remains of the house that he knew, as it has been burned down twice since he lived there. Witnesses have reported hearing footsteps and bells chiming at 3am on a number of occasions. At the beginning of the 20th century, a skeleton was found bricked up behind a wall, although it is not known whether this has any link to the haunting.

Bedlay Castle, nr Glasgow, Strathclyde

This 12th-century castle was once the palace of the Bishop of Glasgow. In the 14th century, the then inhabitant, Bishop Cameron, met a sticky end. Whether he was pushed or whether he fell we will never know, but he was found drowned in the fishpond. A manifestation matching the description of a cleric has been seen in the grounds.

Bedruthan, Cornwall: Bedruthan Steps

It is said that this is the site of an ancient castle, as well as a long disused tin and iron mine. Within the rock of the cliff that stands high above the crashing sea, many have heard the sounds of miners at work. Some claim to have heard their picks against the rock below, while others have spoken of muffled shuffling in unseen and forgotten galleries.

Beeleigh Abbey, nr Maldon, Essex

Connections with Lady Jane Grey give rise to the 450-year haunting of this site. Sir John Gates, a supporter of Lady Jane, awaited his execution here in 1553. He learned of his fate on 11 August, and on the anniversary of this date you can hear his wailing throughout the abbey site. Some witnesses state that they have seen Sir John, headless, walking around the abbey. He was beheaded in the Tower of London on 22 August 1553.

Beelsby, Lincolnshire
The ghost of Molly Briars, a local milkmaid, haunts the hillside where she was murdered many years ago. The stone on which she sat while milking the cows is still there, and locals believe that if it is moved then terrible ill-luck will affect the village.

Beer, Devon: Bovey House
Originally a mediaeval manor house, Bovey House was extensively enlarged in 1592 by its Elizabethan owner. The building's real claim to fame came in 1651, when it was the hiding place of Charles II after his defeat at Worcester. It is said that the house sometimes smells of lavender water, perhaps a supernatural reminder of the short stay of the king. Smugglers may be responsible for the tales of the other haunting in the house, that of a headless ghost. After all, they had good reason to dissuade people from venturing near the house while they were engaged in their nocturnal activities.

Belfast, Northern Ireland: Friar's Bush
This is one of the oldest graveyards in the city and was the resting place of many of the victims of a terrible cholera outbreak in the 1880s. It is also said to be the site of a 4th-century monastic building. There is a tunnel that runs near to it, linking two blocks of Queen's University. On several occasions, witnesses have reported a strange atmosphere in the tunnel, and one even suggested that a ghostly hand held his while he walked along the unlit passageway.

Belfast, Northern Ireland: York Road Railway Station
Poltergeist activity, in the form of a ring from a fire extinguisher being thrown across the platform, has been reported. Other witnesses have seen a strange figure in one of the sheds, which may be the same apparition that has been seen sitting in the locked canteen in the dead of night. Other staff on night duty have heard footsteps crunching across gravel.

Belmesthorpe, Rutland: Moody Inn
This public house was built on the site of a monastery, which once had a 30ft well. In recent years, several witnesses have reported the sighting of the manifestation of a hunchback, which seems to have some connection to the well that is now bricked up in the yard. Licensees and their families have also witnessed the ghost, particularly in the evenings, just before the public house closes.

Ben Macdhui, nr Braemar, Grampian
Not only is Ben Macdhui the second highest mountain in Great Britain, but it also has a manifestation fit to rival America's Bigfoot and the Himalayan Yeti. Whether this is, strictly speaking, a ghostly manifestation or folklore is not known for certain, but the 20ft-tall creature has reportedly been seen by a number of people. It seems to have a very malignant purpose. Known as either Am Fear Laith Mhor, or the Big Grey Man, the creature has a large head and short brown hair all over its body. It is most often seen near the Larig Ghru Pass, and its presence seems to entice unwary climbers to fall over Lurcher's Crag.

Benthall Edge, nr Ironbridge, Shropshire
In the 19th century a man was taking wages to limestone workers when robbers attacked him. After they had taken the money, they bound and gagged him and threw him in a pit. To give themselves time to get away, they rolled a large stone over the pit. Despite his

screams, no one heard him. Ultimately a search was organised and it was found that the stone had slipped into the pit and crushed him. His screams still echo around the Benthall Edge. In a nearby pool, the ghost of a murder victim appears in a distressed and bedraggled state. It is said that the young girl's blood seeped into the pool, causing the water to change from muddy brown to red.

Bentley, Hampshire: Jenkyn Place

This 17th-century house is said to have no fewer than three different hauntings. Some are obviously connected with events that happened in and around the house at times in the past, but others are less under-standable. The spirit of Mrs Waggs, a former housekeeper, has been seen on several occasions, presumably finding it difficult to leave a place in which she was once happy. An unknown white lady can also be seen walking around the house. Finally, witnesses near the house have seen a coach and four on a number of occasions.

Beoley, nr Redditch, Worcestershire: Moat House

Murderer Captain Richard Hill, who mysteriously vanished from the Angel Inn in London in 1693, fled here after killing an actor. The apparent reason for the murder was that they were both courting the same woman and Hill wanted to do away with his rival. Hill took refuge in Moon's Moat (now probably Moat House) in Beoley. However, it is not his spirit that is seen in the house but that of a woman, possibly another of his murder victims. The apparition appears on 20 January each year (St Agnes's Eve). Rumour has it that it is the ghost of a daughter of the house.

Berry Pomeroy Castle, nr Totnes, Devon

This castle is said to be the most haunted in

Great Britain, and is named after the Norman family that built the castle. The Duke of Somerset, brother of Jane Seymour, third wife of Henry VIII, built a mansion within the castle walls at the beginning of the 16th century. A white lady appears in the dungeons and on the ramparts – perhaps she is Lady Margaret Pomeroy, who was imprisoned in St Margaret's Tower by her sister Lady Eleanor. They had both fallen in love with the same man. Margaret starved to death in the tower. Witnesses who have seen her report feelings of malevolence, fear and depression. Sir Walter Farquhar, an 18th-century physician who made a home visit to the wife of the castle's steward, saw a young blue lady wringing her hands in distress. He watched her go up a stair and vanish into one of the rooms. It is said that she portends disaster at the castle and is seen when a death is imminent. She was a baron's daughter who was raped by her father and became pregnant – she killed the baby at birth and both the child and the mother can be heard and seen. The castle is now open to the public and volunteers there have seen shadows in the gentlemen's toilet. In the teashop a ghost touches the shoulder of unsuspecting visitors.

Besford Court, nr Pershore, Worcestershire

This house is said to be haunted by either a nun or a grey lady. Witnesses differ in their descriptions of the manifestation, but it does seem that the figure is likely to be seen in one of the upstairs bedrooms. While there does not appear to be any particular reason why either a nun or a grey lady is related to the building, it is just as likely that there are two hauntings as one.

Best Beech, Sussex

The phantom of a man with a sack slung over his back has been seen on several occasions near Beggar's Bush. He is most likely to be seen when the fruit is ripening and it is nearly dusk. Perhaps this is the apparition of a man who did a good deal of scrumping in his life.

Bettiscombe House, nr Lyme Regis, Dorset

The manor house is home to a particularly haunted and significant skull. If it is ever removed from the house, then all sorts of problems will occur. It is said to have dripped blood just before the commencement of hostilities in World War One. The skull, probably taken from a prehistoric burial site, cannot be traced to its original owner. At Bettiscombe Manor, particularly on the south side of the house, you may encounter a phantom funeral procession passing by.

Bexley, Kent: Hall Place

The Black Prince has been seen at Hall Place at twilight, wearing black armour and accompanied by the sound of mediaeval music. Many people have seen the apparition and it is now often related to some family disaster. During World War Two a set-back for the British often followed the ghost's appearance. The wife of Sir Thomas Hall, Lady Constance, also haunts the house. She threw herself from the tower after her husband had been killed in an accident in the 13th century. A third ghost can be seen in one of the attic bedrooms and is said to be the manifestation of a long-dead servant girl.

Bicester, Oxfordshire: Weston Manor Hotel

This 11th-century country mansion had substantial additions made to it in both the 14th and 16th century. 'Mad Maude' is said to haunt one of the bedrooms and a phantom coach has been seen driving through the courtyard of the hotel.

Bickley, Greater London: The Chequers Inn

Staff and guests at the inn have reported the sighting of a man in green velvet, wearing a hat with a plume, sat at a table with a quill pen. Women in 18th-century dress have been seen in the passage in the upper quarters, and although they are silent, they are prone to slamming doors. Beds have been shaken in the night and it is said that both Charles Dickens and Samuel Pepys encountered ghostly characters here. Most of the hauntings seem to emanate from the older rooms, but investigations have never revealed anything to explain the visions and sounds.

Biddenden, nr Ashford, Kent

At the beginning of the 19th century, a local squire found a baby girl on the doorstep of his London home. Nobody could find her family, and the girl was put into an orphanage. Subsequently, they adopted her and named her Susannah Lost. They only had one child of their own and the girl gradually fell in love with her adopted brother. On her 18th birthday, a ball was held at Ibornden Park in celebration. Her adopted brother refused to dance with her, so she left the party at midnight and apparently drowned herself in the pond in the park. Investigations have discovered that this probably happened in around 1837. Her ghostly spirit has been seen on many occasions on the anniversary of her suicide, around the lake now known as Lady Pond.

Biggin Hill, Greater London

Unsurprisingly, a ghostly Spitfire haunts this vital World War Two RAF airbase. RAF officers, residents and visitors have all heard, but not necessarily seen, a Spitfire coming into land. The key date of 19 January seems to be the most important for hearing these sounds. The Spitfire comes in, makes a low victory roll and then lands. Some have even heard men's voices, glasses clinking and other associated sounds.

Bildeston, Suffolk: The Crown Inn

The ghost of a man who wears a long over-coat and an old-fashioned hat haunts this 15th-century building. It is widely believed that this character was a former customer of the place. Throughout its recent history, the inn has also been a site of tremendous poltergeist activity, including hammering on the front door and mysterious footsteps.

Billinge, Merseyside: Stork Hotel

Heavy footsteps have been heard emanating from the room above the bar, particularly at closing time. Guests that have stayed in the hotel have reported that the noise is loud enough to keep them awake. The building was originally constructed in 1640 as a gaol and was used extensively during the Civil War. Royalist officers and soldiers were imprisoned in what was the crypt and is now part of the cellars. It is thought that the sounds either relate to Cromwellian soldiers or to the death of a royalist soldier during his imprisonment.

Billingham Manor, Isle of Wight

The fact that a ghost and the smell of madonna lilies haunt this building can be traced back to a duel that occurred here in the past. Miss Leigh, married to an Englishman, had taken a French lover. There was a duel between the two men. Unfortunately, we do not know the outcome, but one certainly died in the fight, for it is he that haunts the house. As for the scent of lilies, we can only presume that this was Miss Leigh's favoured flower. The house, it is also said, has another ghost, that of a phantom monk. The English novelist J.B. Priestley (1894–1984) once lived at Billingham Manor.

Bindon Hill, nr Lulworth, Dorset

It is said that on some nights you may see the forms of Roman soldiers marching in this area. They apparently come from Flower's Barrow, march over the hill and then disappear. There are a great many soldiers in the manifestation, but no indication that there was a major battle here to explain their presence.

Bircham Newton, nr Fakenham, Norfolk

This former airfield, now disused, is haunted by a number of World War Two ghosts. Particularly interesting is the sports car full of laughing aircrew, which speeds across the base only to crash into one of the hangers. Three of the crew of an Avro Anson, keen on squash in life, haunt the squash court. Their bomber crashed nearby, killing them all. The ghosts of two other airmen have been seen engaging in a fencing match.

Birmingham, West Midlands: Alexandria Theatre

It is said that the presence of a former director, Leon Salberg, can be felt at the back of the stalls. Also, the spiritual imprint of a wardrobe master who died in his office can be heard in the form of soft footsteps. Witnesses have reported hearing the sound of a man walking over concrete and then wood along a passageway that leads to the room where the wardrobe master was found dead. Despite the fact that the whole passageway is now carpeted, and that the wardrobe master wore carpet slippers, the sound definitely differs as the apparition walks from the concrete to the wood part of the passage.

Birmingham, West Midlands: Aston Hall

Sir Thomas Holte built Aston Hall between 1618 and 1635. He previously lived at

Duddeston Manor, where he is said to have killed his cook in a fit of rage, splitting the man's head in half with a meat cleaver. He was accused of the killing, but took out a libel case and won. He was married twice; his first wife produced 15 children, one of whom was Sir Edward Holte who was was killed at the siege of Oxford (1643). His second wife, Anne, daughter of Sir Edward Littleton of Pillaton, bore him no children. By this time, Sir Thomas was having an incestuous relationship with one of his own daughters. The girl was eventually locked up in one of the upper rooms, where she remained for 18 years before she became insane and finally died. It is believed that she is the white lady that haunts the hall and is often seen in the Long Gallery.

Birmingham, West Midlands: BBC Broadcasting Centre, Pebble Mill Studios

This centre, when opened in 1971 by Princess Anne, was said to be the most expensive, largest and most modern television centre in Europe. In 1977, when the play *Ritual of Stifling Air* was being produced by Michael Rolfe, strange and mysterious noises, as well as an unpleasant atmosphere, were experienced by the staff and crew. This may relate to the fact that one of the builders involved in the construction of the centre had fallen off the scaffolding and been killed. The man had been seen on several occasions by staff and security men.

Birmingham, West Midlands: Birmingham General Hospital, Steelhouse Lane

Members of staff have often seen a kindly old man with a clay pipe in his mouth vanish as he reaches a recently-built wall. Staff seem to believe that the apparition is that of a patient. The manifestation seems to be a friendly ghost, who does not seem overly concerned at being seen by people.

Birmingham, West Midlands: Bristol Road, Rednal

In 1966, a nurse working at the Bromsgrove General Hospital was waiting for a number 144 bus to take her to work. As she waited at the bus stop she saw a friend, John Bevan, walking toward her. She had not seen him for three years. She greeted him and asked him why he was in the area, but he ignored her. The nurse described him as looking very ill. As she boarded the bus she looked through the window and the man had disappeared. Later in the day she met another friend who knew John Bevan and related the tale. Her friend questioned her and she accurately described his clothing and appearance. She was then told that John Bevan had died in the hospital two days earlier and was lying in the hospital mortuary.

Birmingham, West Midlands: Cross Roads, Erdington

A stone bench near Tyburn House is said to be haunted by a strange figure dressed in a long, grey garment. Numerous witnesses, including a nurse from Goodhope Hospital, have seen him. The apparition appears for around 20 seconds before fading away. One explanation links the haunting to a murder that occurred in 1745, when a drunken colonel of the Duke of Cumberland's regiment left his sword in an inn and grabbed hold of a young man, demanding to know where he could find his weapon. The boy was not only frightened, but had a speech impediment and could not provide the officer with the information. The colonel ordered that the boy be decapitated. His body was thrown into Pype Hayes Park, and his head thrown into a tree at New Shipston. The skull was found when the tree was felled in the 19th century. Another possible explanation for the haunting suggests that the apparition could be the ghost of Mary Ashford, who was murdered after a dance at the Tyburn Inn on Whit Monday in 1817. A local farmer, by the name of Thornton, was tried but acquitted. Locals believed him to be guilty and he emigrated to America. More perplexing is the fact that in 1974 another murder occurred on Whit Monday, and again the accused man was named Thornton. He, too, was acquitted of the murder.

Birmingham, West Midlands: Dudley Road Hospital, Dudley Road

A middle-aged man, in a long white coat, has been seen walking near the petrol station near the hospital. Numerous nurses have seen the apparition appear and disappear, as have several other witnesses. The police no longer bother to investigate reports. One possible explanation relates to the fact that the petrol and service station is built on the site of a former mortuary. A staff nurse had an affair with one of the doctors and died under mysterious circumstances. The doctor visited the mortuary to see the corpse on numerous occasions after her death. The assumption is that the doctor still visits the site where his beloved lay even though he himself is dead. A phantom staff nurse has also been seen in the Neuro-surgical wing, described as being blonde and in her twenties, wearing a grey uniform. She apparently visits those who are very ill and several witnesses have said that patients that do see her often rapidly improve in health.

Birmingham, West Midlands: St Nicholas Church, Cardworth

Despite the fact that many witnesses have described the apparition of a tall figure of a woman dressed in a long, green gown in the graveyard, it is more likely that it is not a woman at all. A mass grave was dug in the church grounds for the burial of soldiers following a battle during the Civil War, so the apparition may be a royalist officer or, if it is a woman, a relative of one of these officers. There is also a rumour that a hoard of treasure is buried in one of the graves, so the spirit may have been sent to ward off any grave robbers.

Birmingham, West Midlands: Smallheath Police Station

Hilda, the former cleaner at the police station, haunts the building. She has been positively identified by a number of police officers. Interestingly, none of the police officers are particularly keen on investigating doors slamming and other strange noises emanating from the top floor.

Birmingham, West Midlands: Snow Hill

Near to the Roman Catholic cathedral of St Chad's is a house that is said to be very haunted. In the early part of the 20th century, tenants heard screams and groans on the ground floor. They also saw a tall, stout man, accompanied by a large dog, standing by the fireplace in the sitting room. Particularly striking about the apparition was the fact the man's face was featureless. On another occasion, witnesses saw a misty cloud over the fireplace in the shape of a man and a dog. In 1829, a supposed body snatcher and probable murderer lived in the house. His occupation was selling bodies to medical students for their studies and research. Locals at the time claim to have seen numerous people enter the house, but never leave. It is believed that the groans and screams emanate from the victims of the corpse provider.

Birmingham, West Midlands: Warstone Lane Cemetery

It is said that the ghost of a white lady haunts the cemetery and the surrounding streets.

She is described as wearing a crinoline dress, which should aid the dating of the manifestation. Otherwise, the only other significant feature is that witnesses report the distinct smell of pear drops.

Birmingham, West Midlands: The White Swan, Harborne Road

Dating back to around 1714, the pub is haunted by the ghost of John Wentworth. In 1830, following the death of his girlfriend, who had been crushed to death under a wagon that overturned after speeding down a hill out of control, he hanged himself in the pub.

Bisham Abbey, Bisham, Berkshire

This former 13th-century haunt of the Templars was also the home of Lady Elizabeth Hoby, who had six children. Her youngest child, William, was not a very intelligent boy, and was extremely messy. His mother, incensed by his failures, beat him to death. Her ghost can be seen in the corridors, attempting to wash the blood of her son from her hands. In many cases she is seen 'in negative', with a black face and a white dress. In 1840 workmen renovating Bisham Abbey discovered some old, smudged schoolbooks that had a connection with the Hoby family. It may be this discovery that has led to the legend that explains the apparition.

Bishop's Stortford, Hertfordshire: George Inn

This former coaching inn boasts the manifestation of a grey lady. The woman was stabbed by a burglar when she stepped out of room 27 onto the balcony, and she fell back into the room and died. Nowadays the door to the balcony is sealed, but on numerous occasions witnesses have seen swirling grey mist around the bed. Guests allocated this room have asked to be moved to another. Another witness has seen the apparition of a woman in a grey gown

bending over her bed with her arms raised. The spirit disappeared when the guest screamed.

Bishop's Stortford, Hertfordshire: Windmill House

The ghost of a volunteer army officer has been seen walking around the grounds of Windmill House. Apparently he was the victim of an accidental shooting, which killed him. It is not known whether this event happened here or whether the officer had a particular connection to Windmill House during his life.

Blackburn, Lancashire: Samlesbury Hall

A white lady, said to be the daughter of a previous owner of the hall, haunts this mediaeval building. She is seen with her lover, a knight, who was killed by her brother. Two apparitions have been seen floating a foot or so above the ground. They appear roughly at the site of the murder. It is presumed that the level of the ground was higher in the past.

Blackpool, Lancashire: The Promenade

On stormy nights witnesses claim to hear the sound of a phantom tram rolling along the Promenade, but no one, to date, has actually seen the tram in question. The spirit of a pointsman has been seen at night, walking along the tracks with a lantern in his hand. The particular place to spot this apparition is said to be Bispham. The tram noises may be explained away as the sounds of electrically-charged air being created by the storm.

Blakesley Hall, Northamptonshire

Those facing religious persecution probably used this 15th-century yeoman farmhouse as a refuge. It may be that the building was once a private chapel, as there is a tunnel leading from the house to the nearby church. In recent years, during the redecoration of a bedroom, the owners discovered religious motifs in wall paintings. Several witnesses have seen the ghost of a woman dressed in a blue gown. It is said that she is the ghost of a mother looking for her child. During a party at the hall, a woman was engaged in a conversation with a strange-looking man, who simply disappeared while she was talking to him. She further reported that she became ill and almost fainted. When she described the character to the owner of the house, he showed her an old family painting that matched the description. The man in the portrait had died 150 years earlier.

Blanchland, nr Hexham, Northumberland: Lord Crewe Arms

The female ghost that haunts this former manor house was once a fully formed apparition, but has, over the years, been reduced to 'just a feeling' witnesses have that there is a presence. It is thought that the ghost is that of Dorothy Forster. Her presence is felt in one of the bedrooms, which is accessed by passing through a huge doorway at the top of a stone staircase. The door itself was actually the original inn sign. A female guest who stayed in the haunted bedroom reported feeling something inexplicable at the bottom of her bed.

Blanchminster Castle, Binhamy Farm, nr Stratton, Cornwall

When Sir Ralph de Blanc-Minster returned from the crusades, he discovered that his wife had remarried, thinking him dead. He became something of a recluse. As he was a great benefactor of Stratton, his body was buried in the church when he died. His tortured spirit, however, still haunts the moat of this castle. The castle is also known as Binhamy Castle, derived from the French

bon ami meaning 'beloved friend'. An alternative story says that Sir Ralph was actually killed in the Holy Land in 1270, and returns to haunt the castle in the form of a white hare. The Revd Hawker, writing in the 19th century, featured Sir Ralph in an epic poem. Hawker is also credited with inventing the Harvest Festival.

Bleaklow Hill, nr Glossop, Derbyshire

Walkers and ramblers on the Pennine Way have often reported seeing phantom Roman soldiers. Even the rescue teams that operate in this area claim to have seen either a small group of Roman legionaries or a whole legion marching around the hills. It is said that the manifestations are most likely to reveal themselves on the first full moon in the spring. Strange lights have also been reported in the area, notably the pinprick lights known as the Longendale Lights and the blue beam lights near the Torside Reservoir. It is probably more sensible to discount the supernatural and pass this sighting on to UFO enthusiasts!

Blenkinsopp Castle, nr Haltwhistle, Northumberland

Although partially burned down, this castle is still haunted by the spirit of a white lady. The story runs that she was married to a man who decreed that wealth was more important than any woman and promptly vanished. It is also said that the phantom woman only appears to children and that her purpose is to reveal to them the treasure that she had hidden from her avaricious spouse.

Bletchingly, Surrey: St Mary The Virgin, Church Street

This church has a memorial to Robert Clayton, where it is said that the temperature drops noticeably at a range of about 8ft. Witnesses have also seen the ghost of a woman in a 17th-century gown. Others have referred to the clothing as possibly being of the William and Mary period (1688–1714). Local residents confirm that the spirit of a woman haunts the church, but research has not indicated who she may be or what her purpose is.

Blithfield Hall, nr Rugeley, Staffordshire

This impressive Elizabethan manor has five ghosts, the most notable being that of the grey lady of Blithfield. It may be that this apparition no longer haunts the hall, but certainly her wailing used to be heard near the well in the garden. An unseen spirit that creates a sound akin to the rustling of skirts is often heard shortly after 11pm. in the lower gallery. At 3 o'clock in the afternoon a cleaner saw a man dressed in dark clothing staring intently at the floor. She described him as rubbing an unusual-looking ring on the finger of his left hand. The apparition faded as the cleaner walked toward him. Near some azalea bushes in the eastern part of the garden, the manifestation of a woman wearing a long frock, covered by a grey mackintosh with wearing a flat, straw bonnet has been seen on a number of occasions.

Bluebell Hill, nr Maidstone, Kent

In 1965, four girls were driving toward a pub when their car lost control on a sharp bend on Bluebell Hill. Three of the girls were killed and the survivor was badly injured. One of the girls, Judith Lingham, is now the celebrated phantom hitch hiker of Bluebell Hill. She appears on the roadside and accepts a lift, often saying either that she wants to go to Rochester, or that she has just been involved in a car accident. Whatever the reason, she disappears after getting into the car. Nine years after the tragic accident, a motorist rushed into Rochester Police Station

saying that he had hit a girl on Bluebell Hill. He had wrapped her in a tartan rug and left her there while he went for help. When the motorist returned to the scene with the police, the rug was lying on the ground, with the girl missing and no mark on his car. What is particularly strange is that the motorist actually picked up the ghost and wrapped it up. There are very few descriptions of ghosts having substance and weight.

Blyford, nr Halesworth, Suffolk: The Queen's Head

This small thatched public house, overlooking what was the Blythe Estuary, has strong smuggling connections. A tunnel was discovered in the cellar leading to the church across the road. It is said that smugglers deposited their contraband in the crypt of the church and moved it, unseen, into the public house at night. What is particularly interesting about this story is that the sounds of the hauntings only began once the tunnel was opened. Numerous witnesses, including tenants, have reported hearing the sounds of gunfire, footsteps, explosions and seeing the flashing of lights. To all intents and purposes one would assume that this is an echo of battles that took place between customs officers and smugglers. The haunting may have taken a more sinister turn in recent years. An inexplicable fire gutted the public house, which has since been restored.

Blythburgh, Suffolk: Toby's Walk

Blythburgh boasts one of the most magnificent parish churches in England, often referred to as the Cathedral of the Marshes. It has strong connections with the apparition of Hugh Bigod manifested as a large black dog, or the Black Shuck. Indeed, score marks appear on the church door that have often been attributed to this manifestation or that of the devil. Toby's Walk, however, has an altogether sadder story attached to it. In

1754 Toby Gill (Black Toby), a black dragoon in the British Army, raped and murdered a girl from Westleton on the heath now known as Toby's Walk. He was tried and executed and left to hang on a gibbet beside what is now the A12. Numerous witnesses have reported seeing either Black Toby, who was a drummer but does not sound his drums in death, or a horse-drawn hearse arriving to collect his body, complete with a headless driver.

Blythburgh, Suffolk: Westwood Lodge

A lady in a long, silver dress haunts this place. In 1972 three policemen tried to capture the ghost. Their traps were sprung and they recorded strange noises on a tape recorder. The men also felt a sudden chill. They did not, however, see anything. Several locals, including a gamekeeper's son, will still not go anywhere near the lodge at night.

Blythburgh, Suffolk: The White Hart

A little old man haunts this public house, situated on a bend on the A12. He has been variously described, but most witnesses agree that he looks like a monk. This could mean that this is one of the many locations linked with pilgrims en route to Walsingham. However, after a truck crashed into the public house, killing the driver, and a later burglary and a fire, the ghost has not been seen as often as it was in the past.

Bodmin, Cornwall: Bodmin Gaol

Although the building is around 200 years old, it is the period when it was used for public hangings that seems to be the source of many of the odd events. Witnesses claim to have seen vague figures and felt a sense of depression within the walls. Others have heard heavy footsteps and the sounds of clinking keys.

Bodmin, Cornwall: Lanhydrock House

The National Trust acquired this old house in 1953. Despite having suffered a ruinous fire in 1881, it still boasts the ghost of a grey lady. She may be Isabella, second wife of the second baron, John Robartes, who died in 1685. Isabella, if it is she, tends to be seen sitting in a beech wood chair in the drawing room, or walking along the gallery in the north wing. Another spirit has been seen and felt in her ladyship's room, which may be a later Lady Robartes, who in 1881, at the age of 68, was saved from the house fire. She never recovered from the shock of the loss of her home and died soon afterwards, followed by her husband in 1882. It is also said that the smell of cigar smoke permeates the smoking room on the ground floor of the house.

Bolton, Greater Manchester: Smithhills Hall

In the 14th century, this building was owned by the Knights Hospitallers, and is one of the oldest in the country. The Corporation of Bolton purchased it in 1938. In 1977 a witness saw the apparition of a priest who moved through the green room. It is believed that the apparition is of George Marsh, a local preacher in the 16th century. There is also rumour of a 'bloody foot print', which appears on the stone-flagged floor in the hall.

Bolton Abbey, nr Skipton, North Yorkshire

This 12th-century ruined abbey is located close to the River Wharfe and is in a very picturesque setting. In 1864 the nave of the priory was rebuilt, and is now used as the local parish church. In 1975 Reverend Griffiths witnessed the apparition of an Augustinian monk wearing a brown hassock. The manifestation walked through the wall of the rectory toward the ruined abbey. A number of visitors to the ruins have also reported seeing the figure of a monk near the rectory. He is a black-robed monk and he carries the smell of incense with him. He is often seen in the daytime and tends to appear most frequently in July.

Bolventor, Bodmin Moor, Cornwall: Jamaica Inn

Some years ago a stranger to the area was having a drink of ale when he was called outside. He disappeared into the darkness, only to be found murdered the following morning. His ghost has been seen on several occasions, perhaps finishing off the beer that he did not get a chance to enjoy. He is seen wearing a tricorne hat and a long, high-waisted overcoat. The manifestation has also been seen outside the inn, sitting on the wall, and in one of the upstairs bedrooms. Witnesses of the bedroom sighting describe the room as being very cold when he passes. One of Daphne du Maurier's novels was called *Jamaica Inn* and featured the inn.

Bonnyrigg, nr Edinburgh, Midlothian: Dalhousie Castle Hotel

This castle's history spans more than 800 years, and is haunted by a grey lady. She is believed to be the mistress of Ramsay, one of the former holders of the castle. She was imprisoned in one of the towers and bricked up by Ramsay's wife. The ghost is also responsible for strange noises and gusts of wind.

Borley Rectory, nr Clacton-on-sea, Essex

Amazing stories of truly horrific hauntings surround this place. It was built in 1863 and destroyed in a fire in 1939. Most of the remaining superstructure was demolished in 1944. Hundreds of independent guests and visitors to the rectory, including clerics, former rectors and doctors attest to having seen a range of manifestations at various times. The rectory was probably built on the site of an old monastery, and it is said that a nun from a nearby nunnery was about to elope with one of the brothers. They were discovered and the monk was hanged and the nun bricked up alive. A ghostly nun does haunt the site, a solid apparition, gliding along the path known as the Nun's Walk. The manifestation's face is not visible. Loud pealing bells have awoken the household on a number of occasions and after the death of the Revd Harry Bull (d.1927), mothballs were said to have flown around the rooms. A phantom coach and horses has also been seen in the drive, immediately after which bells rang and footsteps were heard. During the 1930s the hauntings reached fever pitch, with messages discovered on pieces of paper and on the walls, household articles appearing and disappearing and flying around the house accompanied by ghostly figures. Later, there was an unexplained fire, with doors locking and unlocking themselves. In 1938, the house was sold after the last rector was forced to move out, but a fire gutted the building less than a year later. In 1939, excavations were carried out in the cellar following a theory put forward by Canon Phythian-Adams about a murdered female French Catholic of the 17th or 18th century. A female jawbone was found and this has since been linked with the manifestation of the nun. When the Ghost Club visited the site in 1948, they reported being showered by stones and bottles, and the 30 bells in the hall all rang without explanation. Witnesses report smelling incense, violets, decaying flesh and other aromas around the site to this day. Others claim to have heard dogs panting, furniture being moved, crockery smashing, laughing voices and unexplained thuds in the vicinity.

Boroughbridge, nr Ripon, North Yorkshire

A highwayman has been sighted haunting a pathway in the town that meets with the Great North Road leading to Scotch Corner. The apparition is believed to be that of Tom Hoggett, who is said to have drowned in the River Swale while attempting to escape from troops.

Borth, nr Aberystwyth, Dyfed

A seven-foot tall female apparition, known as Yr Hen Wrach, is said to haunt the marshlands called Cors Fochno, at the mouth of the River Dovey. She is to be particularly avoided on misty nights, as it is said that if she breathes on your face you will suffer a great illness.

Borthwick Castle, nr Edinburgh, Lothian

Mary Queen of Scots is believed to have been imprisoned in this castle. It is said that she escaped from the castle one day disguised as a young boy. The castle is haunted by a small figure, believed to be that of a young boy, or perhaps Mary Queen of Scots in disguise, which has been seen walking between the castle and the churchyard.

Boscastle, Forrabury, Cornwall

Forrabury was a hamlet that has now been claimed by the sea. The ghostly peal of Forrabury church bells can be heard tolling from under the waves. It is said that when the bells for the church were brought by ship from the foundry, the captain made a blasphemous curse, and as a result a storm brewed up and engulfed the ship. Not a single crewman survived. It is also said that ghostly ships have been seen in and around the area where the boat carrying the bells went down with all hands.

Boscastle, Cornwall: Penally House

Overlooking Boscastle harbour, this house was built in 1836 by William Slogatt, who was a local wine and spirits merchant. Locals believe that he was active in the smuggling trade, and that he used the house as a store for the illicit alcohol. There are numerous stories of underground tunnels and many report hearing footsteps and hoof beats on the private road leading to the house, which was cut out of the rock by Slogatt. Faces have also been seen in the bedroom windows at night. These may be phantoms looking out for their illicit cargo to arrive.

Boscastle, Cornwall: The Wellington Hotel

This 16th-century coaching inn is haunted by a frock-coated figure on the landing. He has a ruffled shirt, pony-tail and leather gaiters, and is often referred to as a coachman or stable-hand. A ghostly girl has also been seen on the landing at the top of the tower. She appears to be perfectly solid, but has been seen emerging from a wall and disappearing through a closed window. The spirit of an old lady caused great consternation in rooms 9 and 10 when she was seen sitting on a bed, despite the fact that the room was vacant. Apparently she then disappeared through a locked door.

Boscombe, Hampshire

Margaret Best, reporting events in the 1960s, had a strange and chilling tale to tell about the flat in which she lived. For several months, she sensed that something was in her bedroom; the manifestation tucked her up in bed and occasionally even moved small objects around the room. During the latter stages of the haunting, Margaret had the distinct impression that something was trying to strangle her in her sleep. She even noted marks on her throat. Suddenly, however, the hauntings ceased.

Bossiney, Cornwall

In one of the older buildings in the Bossiney area, several unexplained happenings and sightings have been reported. Large paintings with heavy frames have been turned to the wall. Witnesses have seen a little old man who sits cross-legged, staring out to the sea. This manifestation is reputed to be the ghost of a hunchback who once lived in the house. Animals are terrified of the building. The centre of activity appears to be one of the bedrooms.

Boston, Lincolnshire: St Botolph's Church

Because of the flat landscape surrounding this church it can be seen from several miles away, and has become known as The Stump. Witnesses have reported seeing a woman, with a child in her arms, leaping from the tower of the church. The history of this apparition is not known.

Botathan, nr Launceston, Cornwall

The ghost of Dorothy Dinglet prompted an attempted exorcism in a field called Higher Brown Quartils some years ago. The death of Dorothy seems to be connected with the two sons of the Bligh household. The elder brother left the area immediately after her death. On several occasions the form of Dorothy has been seen pointing into the distance. It is also said that Dorothy died in childbirth. The Bligh family approached the Reverend John Ruddle, curate of Launceston, about the haunting. He not only saw the apparition, but also performed a successful exorcism, although it is said that Dorothy's spirit can still be seen on misty mornings.

Bottesford, Leicestershire

This former World War Two air base boasts a ghostly bomber. The bomber can be heard flying over the now abandoned airfield.

Witnesses have also reported seeing eerie lights above the derelict control tower.

Bottlebush Down, nr Tarrant Gunville, Dorset

A Bronze Age horseman is said to haunt this area. To the side of the old Roman Road is a barrow, and it is said that this is where the ghostly horseman ends his ride. He has also been seen near Squirrel's Corner.

Boughton Malherbe, nr Ashford, Kent: The Old Rectory

The ghost of a hunchback monk in a grey habit has been seen in and around the house on numerous occasions. The building dates back to the Tudor period, although it may have been a monastery or manor house before then. The monk has been seen since the middle of the 17th century and is described as wearing coarse, rough cloth, like tweed, which is grey in colour. The apparition's favoured room is now known as the haunted room. The ghost of a lady with flowers, dressed in grey silk, has also been seen, either writing letters or reading the Bible.

Boverton Castle, nr Llantwit Major, South Glamorgan

A black lady, said to be Hadwisa (Isabella), daughter of the Earl of Gloucester and divorced wife of King John, haunts the castle. She is described as being a tall woman with long black hair. The castle was dismantled in the early 19th century, but this does not appear to have affected her haunting. She is described as a black lady because she habitually wore mourning clothes in recognition of the fact that her husband's love for her had died. She has been heard weeping, having spent the rest of her earthly years in exile in this castle, following her husband's marriage to Isabella of Ang-oulême. Locals call her 'Wissie'.

Bovingdon, Hertfordshire: Box Lane

Box Lane is haunted by a gleaming manifestation. Whether it is related in any way to the hauntings of the churchyard is unknown. It is said that the churchyard was desecrated by bloodshed and as a result the spirits of those buried there cannot rest.

Bovington Camp, nr Wareham, Dorset

A man known locally as Herman the German haunts the tank museum. It is thought that Herman may have died inside a Tiger tank when it was shelled during World War Two. His manifestation peers through the window of the museum and stares at a Tiger tank. The lowest panes of glass in the window are 8ft from the ground, but Herman can still be seen from the inside.

Bower Chalke, Applespill Bridge, Wiltshire

Applespill Bridge is said to be the site of a hidden store of gold. A nearby barrow was looted, and a gold coffin was found. The ghosts of seven men carrying the coffin have been sighted, as has a phantom shepherd who, it is said, got lost and died in a snowstorm. Witnesses have heard the shepherd's cries of 'I want to go home' on a number of occasions. Patty's Bottom is the site of a battle between the Romans and the Britons, and on moonlit nights the sound of trampling feet can be heard and headless horses can be seen.

Box, nr Bath, Wiltshire

Brunel designed the staggering mile and three-quarter long tunnel here, which lies 300ft underground. Constructed in 1841, it has been the centre of a haunting that track workers often refer to in dread. They claim to hear and feel an on-coming steam train, which disappears just as it seems that it will run them down.

Bracknell, Berkshire: A329

On a section of the road between Ascot and Bracknell, presumably as a result of a past accident, the ghost of a dreadfully mutilated policeman appears. His face is supposedly fearful to behold.

Bradford, West Yorkshire: Alhambra Theatre, Manchester Road

This theatre was the training ground for several well-known personalities, including the disc jockey David Hamilton. One evening, while sitting in his dressing room, David Hamilton saw the face of a man in his mirror. He instinctively swung around to see who was standing behind him, but no one was there. He looked back into the mirror and could still see the apparition, although it was beginning to fade away. The apparition smiled and then disappeared from view. A while later David Hamilton was looking through photographs of former actors when he recognised the face of the apparition. Other witnesses have also experienced similar sightings in that particular dressing room, and the ghost always smiles at them.

Bradford-on-Avon, Wiltshire: St Lawrence's Church

Whether the spirits that haunt this church are mediaeval worshippers or lepers is a contested point, but they have been seen by a variety of witnesses. The church dates from the 10th century, but spent many years as cottages, until it was re-consecrated after 1856.

Bradford Pool, nr Drewsteignton, Dartmoor, Devon

Near the three massive granite slabs of Spinster's Rock lies the oddly named Bradford Pool. A ghost, it is said, lures unsuspecting travellers to their deaths. Whether this was originally a cautionary tale to prevent young people from drowning is unknown.

Bradgate Park, nr Leicester, Leicestershire

Lady Jane Grey was queen for just nine days before she was beheaded, aged 16, in 1554. This was her former home, in what may have been happier days, and her spirit returns to the ruins on Christmas Eve. Four headless black horses pull a carriage with Lady Jane on board, which stops outside the house so that her headless body can carry her head inside.

Bradwell-Juxta-Mare, nr Southend, Essex

The chapel of St Peter ad Murum is said to be one of the oldest in Great Britain, having been built in 654 by St Cedd, on the site of an old Roman fort. After falling into disuse, then spending time as a beacon tower, cattle shed and smuggler's hide, it was reconsecrated in 1920. Many people have witnessed strange, shadowy figures inside the building and odd lights shining out of the building when nobody was there.

Braemar Castle, Grampian

Appearing only to newly-wed bridegrooms, the ghost that haunts this castle has a sad tale to tell. In Victorian times, a newly-wed bride awoke to find her husband gone. In desperation, she committed suicide. Her husband had left early that morning to go hunting. It is also said that the Black Colonel of Inverey, John Farquharson, haunts the building. He leaves a candle burning in recognition of the fact that he burned the castle down in 1689.

Brailes, nr Shipston on Stour, Warwickshire

Dressed in a cape with a tricorne hat on his head, the famous Quaker George Fox can be seen walking past the old Meeting House. Granny Austin, one of the Brailes witches, appears on New Year's Eve, with no legs. A headless ghost, of unknown origin, can be seen by the bridge on the Shipston Road. In addition to this the ghost of a nun whose child was taken away from her to avoid a scandal is often seen near the Roman Catholic church.

Braishfield, nr Romsey, Hampshire

An Edwardian lady searches the lanes and footpaths of the area for her money and jewels, which she buried before she died.

Bramber Castle, nr Worthing, West Sussex

The ghosts of William de Braose's family, starved to death at Windsor at the hands of King John, have been seen in the castle and in the nearby village. William and some of his children escaped, but his wife and at least one son died. The apparitions are seen begging for bread or just staring at the ruins of the castle, and are most likely to appear in December.

Bramhall Hall, nr Stockport, Greater Manchester

In 1630, a traveller dressed in red arrived at the hall on New Year's Eve. He was given a bed and the hospitality of the house. In the morning the owner, William Davenport, was found murdered in his bed and the stranger had disappeared. A ghostly red rider now appears in the courtyard every New Year's Eve.

Bramshill, nr Basingstoke, Hampshire: Bramshill House

The house stands on the site of an old manor house, built in 1327 by Sir John Foxley. That building was demolished in the early 17th century and replaced in 1612 by the present house, constructed for Lord Zouche, a prominent Roman Catholic. The Cope family lived in the house from 1690–1935. The bridal chest of Bramshill, or the mistletoe bough chest, found in the long gallery, has a sad tale attached to it. Many years ago, a young Italian bride died on her wedding day at the age of 18. Just after the wedding feast, she and the bridegroom played hide and seek, but she disappeared and was never found. Many years later her skeleton was discovered in the chest; she had chosen it as her hiding place, but when she climbed in the lock snapped shut and she suffocated. During the 17th century the chest was purchased and moved to Bramshill. During World War Two, King Michael and Queen Marie of Romania lived in the house and described the ghost of the Italian bride as beautiful, with auburn hair hanging down in ringlets and wearing her white ankle-length wedding gown. She is seen, in particular, in the library and the long gallery, and she leaves behind a smell of lily-of-the-valley. The Black Prince was murdered here and his body dumped in the lake. Several witnesses have seen the figure of a green man, and it is thought that this has some connection with the murder. Bramshill is now a police training college.

Bramshott, nr Farnham, Hampshire

Apart from the fact that Boris Karloff once owned a house here, sufficient to generate any number of ghostly stories, Bramshott claims to be the most haunted village in Hampshire. St Mary's churchyard, for example, has two manifestations; one is of a horrific apparition dressed in a white shroud, while the other is the ghost of a Victorian girl wearing a bonnet.

Branston Hall Hotel, Branston, Lincoln, Lincolnshire

Witnesses have heard ghostly music in the form of 1920s jazz in and around the building. On a spiral staircase, witnesses have also heard, but not seen, a woman crying.

Braunstone, nr Leicester, Leicestershire: Braunstone Hall

James Oldham, later Lord Mayor of Leicester, built Braunstone Hall in 1775. The hall is thought to be haunted by the ghost of one of the builders who worked on the house. During its construction two workers apparently fell to their deaths.

Braunton Barrows, nr Barnstable, Devon

The ghost of William de Tracy, one of the knights involved in the murder of Thomas Becket in 1170, is condemned to twist ropes out of sand. Just as he manages to succeed, a black dog appears and fires a ball of flames that burns through the strands of the freshly made rope.

Breamore House, nr Fordingbridge, Hampshire

The apparition of William Dodington's wife, whom he murdered in 1629, haunts the blue bedroom. Her appearance foretells the imminent death of the present owner of the house. William's father, another William, completed the house in around 1583. A portrait of his wife, Christian, still hangs in the house. Legend has it that if the painting is ever touched, then the perpetrator will die within the day. As a result, it hangs there, dusty and faded.

Breckles Hall, nr Thetford, Norfolk

George Mace, a former soldier who had fought in the Crimea, was the leader of a gang of poachers in the latter part of the 19th century. By day, he worked at a farm in Ovington. He arranged a meeting of the gang on the Breckles estate, intending for them to do their poaching and then return home to divide the spoils. All the gang members arrived as planned, but there was no sign of George. They waited, and soon heard the sound of carriage wheels coming up the drive to the hall. As they watched, the coach glowed, the door opened and the step was pushed down. Then the coach disappeared. The gang all knew that the appearance of the coach meant that someone had just died. In the morning, George's body was found on the drive, just where the coach had stopped and vanished. There was no sign of foul play or illness, and the corpse's face had a fixed smile upon it. The phantom coach has been seen on every occasion that someone has died in the immediate area.

Brecon, Powys: The Welsh Bookshop

The apparition of a woman dressed in 18th-century clothing haunts this shop, in The Struet. She has been seen to appear and then glide across the room and vanish into the wall. It is believed that during the 18th century the building was a surgeon's workplace, and the ghost is probably one of the patients that did not survive.

Brede Place, nr Hastings, East Sussex

Several ghosts, some of whom are unknown, haunt the house. Father John, the apparition of a friendly priest has been seen, as have a 16th-century servant girl called Martha, hanged for stealing from the house, a headless man that has been photographed and a lady in an Elizabethan-style ruff.

Brentford, Boston Manor House, Essex

The apparition of a woman, dressed in a flowing white gown, has often been seen gliding down the back lawn toward the lake, or near the back door of the house, along a paved area near a cypress tree. She is known locally as 'the lady of the lake' and may be the ghost of Lady Boston, who was murdered by her husband after he discovered that she was having an affair with Lord Fairfax. Another suggestion is that she was a woman who committed suicide in the 19th century after a disastrous love affair. Whichever is the case, the skeleton of a woman was discovered in the grounds of the house in recent years, and was given a Christian burial on the estate.

Brentwood, Essex: The Golden Fleece

Standing on the site of the 12th-century priory of St Peter's, this pub is frequently haunted by the figure of a monk or priest. The monk is often seen in the reflection of a mirror in one of the bedrooms, but if the witness looks behind, the room is empty. There is also poltergeist activity in the building, taking the form of kitchen items and glasses being moved around.

Brentwood, Essex: The Swan, High Street

Formerly The Argent and The Gun, the pub became The Swan in 1783. William Hunter, who was held there for two days before being burned to death, haunts the building. He was executed at The Butts, on Shenfield Common, on 26 March 1555, aged 19. William appears as a man wearing a hat, and is responsible for poltergeist activity, including plate smashing, furniture moving and bumps in the night. Doors lock and unlock, papers are moved, dogs will not go into certain parts of the building and a strange cold sensation, coupled with the feeling of a presence, has been experienced by several people on the stairs to the cellar.

Bretforton, nr Evesham, Worcestershire

A headless female phantom haunts the churchyard and the surrounding area. She carries her head under her arm. The village is also visited by the apparition of a spectral coach coming from Littleton, and the manifestation of a ghostly funeral cortege approaching from Weston Subedge.

Bridestowe, Devon: Royal Oak

The ghost of Wicked Lady Howard and her Coach of Bones can be seen and heard in these parts, particularly outside the Royal Oak public house. She is said to have murdered all four of her husbands and to have built the coach from their bones. She has a headless coachman and headless horses, as well as a skeletal dog.

Bridge, nr Canterbury, Kent

A country club, the building of which dates back to the 17th century, is said to be haunted by the figure of a serving maid. She has been seen carrying a linen basket that she places on the floor. Local gossip relates the apparition to a maidservant who had a child by the owner of the building. The child was murdered and hidden in the linen basket. This may account for other reports of a baby crying near the chimney on the ground floor. When the serving maid's ghost is seen, she walks toward the witness, and then disappears.

Bridgnorth, Shropshire: Abanazer's Cottage

This unassuming property was built in 1810, but has been owned by the current owner since the 1980s. During vital renovation work to make the house habitable, the witness stated that on two occasions a little old man met him on the stairs and walked right through him. It has become apparent that the ghost lives in the attic and moves around at night. He does not appear to cause any particular problems, but it is felt that the spirit of this old man is unwilling to leave the house that he loved.

Bridgnorth, Shropshire: The Bridgnorth Croft Hotel

Bells have been heard in the night, which may relate to the fire station that was once based in the stables at the rear. Guests staying in room 12 have complained that something has tugged at their feet in the middle of the night. In room two a strange apparition appears beside the bed and a black lady has been seen walking through the dining room.

Bridgnorth, Shropshire: Crown and Raven Hotel

At a séance in this pub, contact was made with the spirit of a 19-year-old chambermaid who killed the lover of the man to whom she was engaged. She was executed for murder. The events which culminated in the séance included loud noises at night, footsteps, dogs inexplicably not wishing to go to the upstairs flat, compressed air switching itself on and off and lights flickering. It is generally believed that the girl's name was Eva. There is also a rumour that the pub has a second apparition, a Cavalier.

Bridgnorth, Shropshire: Hospital Street

A former grocery shop is the home of a mischievous poltergeist that enjoys throwing tins of food around the shop. Foods such as oranges and eggs have materialised in the shop, often witnessed by customers. In the 18th century the building was a pub called The Buck's Head. Apparently many witnesses saw the spirit of a little boy who was killed outside under his father's dray horse. The couple that live in the house now have felt the presence of two little girls who haunt an upstairs room. Two old-fashioned night-dresses appeared draped on the stairs, food has been moved around and they have even felt fingers running through their hair. In more recent years a photograph was found among a collection of dolls that was kept in one of the upstairs rooms, and it is believed that this photograph depicts one of the girls who is haunting the house.

Bridgnorth, Shropshire: Magpie House Restaurant, Cartway

The building was constructed in the 16th century and is supposed to be haunted by a woman dressed in black. In the 1600s two children were drowned in the cellar of the building when they accidentally found themselves locked in a room that was rapidly filling with water. There are still marble busts of the children, erected by their parents, in the terraced garden. It is said that on stormy nights you can hear crying and banging on the cellar door. In recent years a dog that used to sleep in the cellar died one night for no apparent reason. On many other occasions strange noises have been heard, beds have been shaken and uncontrolled laughter and weeping has been heard.

Bridgwater, Somerset

A phantom black horse and a black dog have been seen along the lanes near this town. The figure of King Alfred has also been spotted, reliving his flight after the Danes overran his kingdom in the 9th century. On the road to Westonzoyland, the ghostly voices of Monmouth's rebel soldiers can be heard singing hymns as they retreat into Bridgwater from Bristol. On the road to Stogursey, the chance discovery of bones ended periodic hauntings by a red-coated soldier, who had been hanged at the crossroads by Colonel Kirk, after having deserted to join Monmouth. The ghostly footsteps of Judge Jeffreys can also be heard, just before he knocks on the 17th-century Marycourt building in St Mary's Street. He apparently stayed in the building on a number of occasions. The Bloody Assizes accounted for the deaths of over 200 people and about 800 transportations to America. Throughout the West Country many had rallied to Monmouth's flag, then paid the price as neighbour fought neighbour after Monmouth's failure on the battlefield.

Bridgwater, Somerset: Sydenham Manor

James Scott, Duke of Monmouth and Buccleuch, was born on 9 April 1649 and was the illegitimate son of Charles II. He adopted the name of his wife, Anne Scott, and was made a duke in 1663 and Captain General of the Armed Forces in 1678. It was claimed that Charles had actually married Monmouth's mother, Lucy Walter, and that he was therefore not illegitimate. Charles sent Monmouth abroad, but he returned in 1684 to plot the murder of Charles and James in the Rye House Plot. When Charles II died in February 1685 and his brother, the Duke of York, became James II, Monmouth landed in June on the beach near Lyme Regis to claim the crown that he thought to be rightfully his. The campaign was a disaster, culminating at Sedgemoor in July, and although Monmouth fled from the battlefield disguised as a shepherd, his badge of the Order of the Garter was found in his pocket and he was taken to London and executed seven days later on Tower Hill for treason. The Monmouth Room at Sydenham Manor houses a portrait of Monmouth himself. Next door to his bedroom, which he looked out of to view Sedgemoor, is a small room, once used by him for praying. His spirit haunts this closet and many people have commented on the strange atmosphere in the room.

Bridport, Dorset: The Art Gallery and Museum

This 16th-century mellow stone, mullion-windowed building has been an inn, bank, working man's club and Conservative club, and now houses the art gallery and museum. A manifestation widely believed to be a former female owner is seen wearing a pale yellow Edwardian afternoon gown, which once formed part of the museum's display. The temperature drops and witnesses report an uneasy feeling of being watched. At times the room in which the spirit manifests itself becomes unbearably hot. It is believed that the woman earnestly wishes to be with her dress, in which she had asked to be buried.

Bridport, Dorset: Broomhill Farmhouse

This 16th-century thatched farmhouse boasts the lingering spirit of a member of the Golding family, which owned the farm for several generations. The present owners and holidaymakers have seen a woman dressed in a cloak leaning over the gates near the farmhouse. Her apparition has also been seen inside the farmhouse itself.

Bridport, Dorset: The Bull Hotel

This hotel has been the venue for psychic fairs, during which many mediums agreed that there was a good deal of spiritual activity within and around the building. Many believe that the hotel is actually built on an ancient graveyard. The land directly behind the building is called Mortarhay, The Field of the Dead. During the Monmouth rebellion in 1685, Monmouth's army landed at Lyme Regis. A portion of the army force-marched to Bridport, precipitating a number of skirmishes in the town, most notably between Edward Coker and a Colonel Venner. Venner, despite being wounded, shot Coker dead. At the same time Wadham Strangways received a mortal wound through a window in the hotel (which is now blocked up) and he still haunts the room in which he died. Children's voices are often heard on the first floor and several witnesses have reported feeling distinctly uneasy in the function room, which was once a hayloft.

Bridport, Dorset: Chantry House, South Street

Believed to be the oldest building in the town, Chantry House is said to have tunnels which pass under the road to the nearby St Mary's Church. The building itself has an eerie atmosphere and is haunted by the manifestation of a priest. Unfortunately no one has been able to describe it in more detail.

Brightlingsea, nr Clacton, Essex: St Osyth's Priory

This site, which certainly pre-dates the 13th-century chapel and tower, was at one time used as a convalescent home. A phantom monk has been seen, dressed in a white robe and scapula, gliding toward the water. The apparition stands there for a few seconds and then vanishes. It has been speculated that the monk in white may be a novice, or that his habit may be mauve, which would indicate that the monk had some form of medical qualification. Another monkish apparition has also been seen. One witness, who was a patient in the 1970s, awoke just before 4am. The door to her small ward opened and a monk, dressed in a brown habit with a cowl over his head, walked into the room. His hands were tucked into his sleeves and a small crucifix hung from the girdle around his waist. The apparition stared at the witness for a few seconds, then turned to walk back through the door but disappeared. On closer inspection and following conversations with staff, it transpired that the monk had not walked through the existing door to the ward. The spirit had actually walked through a bricked up and plastered door. Later in the 1970s another witness apparently saw the ghost of a tall woman dressed in white.

Brighton, East Sussex: East Street

A tall, dark figure haunts a stationery shop; it

is believed that the site was once linked to a monastery by underground passageways. The apparition is described as wearing robes and a cowl. Witnesses also report that the ghost is faceless.

Brighton, East Sussex: The Lanes

The apparition of a pre-Reformation nun haunts this maze of small shops and cafés. She wears a grey habit and has been seen in a wide variety of places in this area. It is not known who she is or why she should choose to haunt this place.

Brighton, East Sussex: Preston Manor

The original house was built in 1250, although the present structure dates from 1738 and is essentially a Georgian house. In 1934 Mrs Magniac, the half-sister of the then owner, visited the curate of the manor in order to discuss the ghost that was haunting the house. Several people had seen a white lady standing on the stairway. On a number of occasions individuals had not recognised the manifestation as being a ghost but had assumed it was another guest in the house. On one particular occasion Mrs Magniac herself walked up to the strange figure and offered her hand; it promptly vanished. A Captain Sandeman also witnessed the apparition. In the mid-1970s a visitor to the house claimed to have seen the ghost of a dog run through two rooms and then disappear. The description of the animal matched that of Kylin, Lady Thomas-Stanford's pet.

Brimington, Derbyshire: Ringwood Hall Hotel

This former house, now a hotel, is said to have a hidden tunnel, which for some strange reason leads to the nearby church-yard. Witnesses have also reported seeing spirits playing a ghostly game of snooker in one of the rooms. Presumably they are previous residents of the house.

Brimpton, nr Newbury, Berkshire: Brimpton Lane

In the 18th century, this place was the site of a horrific coaching accident. A carriage carrying a group of people to a Hunt Ball fell into the river at Abel Bridge. In January each year, on the anniversary of the tragedy, screams and the noise of injured horses can be heard. Some witnesses claim to have actually seen the carriage itself.

Bristol, All Saints' Church

The church was once a monastery, closely linked with the Guild of Calendarers, who were keepers and maintainers of valuable documents. When Henry VIII dissolved the monasteries the prior hid the monastery's accumulated wealth, some of which was later found by Henry's men. As long ago as the 1840s the apparition of a black monk was reported, producing clearly audible footsteps at night. A servant sleeping in the building was disturbed by the monk opening her locked door and shaking her bed. On another occasion a monk gestured to two visitors, then turned and disappeared into a wall. It is widely believed that this monk remains on the site in order to protect the remainder of the treasure.

Bristol, Bristol Cathedral, Deanery Road

A perplexing monkish ghost has been witnessed by a number of individuals over the past few years. The fact that the apparition wears a grey habit does not sit easily with the fact that the Augustinians who founded the original priory church wore black. The library adjoining the cathedral is actually built on the foundations of the older priory. The same monk is often seen at about 4.30pm, which coincides with Benediction, an afternoon service.

Bristol, Duchess Lake, Stoke Park Hospital

The main building of the hospital is the former home of the Duchess of Beaufort. Witnesses have reported seeing the figure of a woman riding a horse through the trees surrounding Duchess Lake. Those witnesses who have waited for the apparition to return from the trees have not seen her reappear. In 1965, a group of young people saw the apparition and they were very sure that it was the duchess herself. One of the youngsters was quoted as saying 'She is known to have frequented the lakeside'.

Bristol, Leigh Woods, nr Clifton Gorge

The woods, which are close to the Clifton Suspension Bridge, are said to be haunted by the designer of the bridge, Isambard Kingdom Brunel. Unfortunately Brunel died before the bridge was completed. Strange sounds have been heard in the vicinity of the bridge and it is thought that the ghost of Brunel returns to supervise the unfinished work.

Bristol, Llandoger Trow, King Street

This inn, built in 1664, is named after a small village and boasts the ghost of a young man who was born and died there. The boy was physically disabled and limped quite badly. In the early days of the apparition, it was seen in the yard near a wall of what used to be the boy's bedroom. The bedroom is situated over the Old Bar. Witnesses have seen the ghost of the young man moving slowly up the stairway, but in more recent years only the sound of his dragging limb has been heard.

Bristol, Vassal Park, Fishponds

It is said that the Duchess of Beaufort, presumably a busy apparition, haunts Vassal Park. She also haunts Duchess Lake at Stoke Park Hospital. The spirit of a monk, dressed in a dark brown gown and hood, has also been seen floating over the path near a small bridge. Witnesses have said that the spirit reaches a wall a few feet from the bridge and then disappears. It may be that this spirit has ceased to haunt the area, as it has not been seen for more than 20 years.

Brixham, Devon: The Black House

The 14th-century Black House was built or used by monks. Doors get locked inexplicably. The owner has been locked out of both the bathroom and the house itself. The ghost is said to be that of Squire Hilliard, whose son, 400 years ago, fell in love with a country girl from Cheriston. The father forced the girl to marry someone else. His son, riding through the woods, saw her coming out of the church on the arm of another man. Young Hilliard hanged himself from a tree and his horse returned home rider-less. His father's ghost searches for his son, in order to ask forgiveness for the pain that he caused him.

Broadford, Isle of Skye: Broadford Hotel

This hotel boasts not only the ghost of a former employee, but also considerable poltergeist activity. The apparition of an old housekeeper is said to walk around the building searching for her favourite chair, which has long since gone. The poltergeist activity manifests itself as fog and mist in the rooms and inexplicably moved lamps and ladders. Some witnesses also claim to have seen a mysterious figure on the staircase.

Broadway, Worcestershire

The bells of the church were hidden in

Middle Hill beech wood during the Reform-ation. They are still heard pealing at night and were said to sound an alarm during World War Two, despite the fact that bell ringing was prohibited.

Brockley, Somerset: St Nicholas Church

Several people have seen a little brown lady, either cleaning or simply walking along the aisle. It is thought that she was a kindly individual who died in 1907. An investigation by the Society for Psychical Research reported hearing footsteps and whispers, but did not actually see the woman. It is thought that the spirit of this church supporter was drawn to the building out of sentiment.

Brockley Combe, nr Bristol

Many claim that this village, which boasts a 14th-century manor house, is one of the most haunted places in the West Country. A ghostly horseman can be seen at around midnight on moonlit nights. The 'bounding ghost', a tall, thin apparition, is seen ahead of travellers on the road. The 'phantom girl' is the ghost of a woman who died of a broken heart. The ghost of Dinah Swan (d.1833), who was found dead in her cottage, literally frightened to death, has also been seen, as has a phantom coach driven by a man in 19th-century clothes. A ghostly male has been seen dressed in black, with a large, white collar.

Brodick, Isle of Arran: Kilmichael Country House

Said to be one of the oldest buildings on the island, Kilmichael Country House was con-structed on land given to the original owners by Robert the Bruce. A mysterious grey lady haunts the hotel, but her identity is unknown. She tends to be seen in one or two of the guest bedrooms.

Brodick Castle, Isle of Arran

This site probably dates back to Viking times and certainly some of the present structures were built in the 14th century. However, it is from the Cromwellian period that the ghost of a white lady probably originates. During the time when troops were garrisoned in the castle, one of the serving girls became pregnant by a soldier. She killed herself in order to avoid the shame. Another theory revolves around three women who lived in the castle. They fell ill, and it was widely believed that they had caught the plague. Their bodies were apparently buried within the precincts of the castle; perhaps one of them has chosen to continue to haunt the building. There is also a tale of an apparition who haunts the library. He wears a wig, a green coat and breeches. There does not appear to be any historical episode at the castle to explain this manifestation.

Brooklands, nr Byfleet, Surrey

The spectre of Percy Lambert, a motor-racing ace, haunts the circuit. He was killed at the end of Railway Straight. Another theory sug-gests that the ghost, who wears goggles and a leather jacket, is the first driver to be killed at Brooklands, a man by the name of Herman.

Broughton, Northamptonshire: Church of St John the Baptist

The site next to the church used to be the village gaol. Prior to his hanging for horse stealing in 1825, the leader of a local gang of villains was held here. His ghost has chosen to haunt the church, despite the fact that his body is not buried there. He appears at Christmas time, usually at night. The apparition is described as being a large shadowy man who moans very loudly at times.

Broughton Astley, nr Leicester, Leicestershire

The sad apparition of a grey lady can be seen at dawn beside the river. She fell in love with a soldier during the English Civil War. He went away to fight and she waited for him to return. He never did, and she spent the rest of her life grieving.

Broughton Hall, nr Eccleshall, Staffordshire

During the English Civil War, the owners of the hall supported the king. When the Roundheads arrived to take the hall, the young heir poked his head out of a window and shouted 'I'm for the king'. The soldiers promptly shot him. His red-stocking clad apparition can still be seen walking in the long gallery.

Brownsea Castle, Brownsea Island, off Poole, Dorset

A large black figure, described as having broad shoulders and a hooded head, has been seen in the corridors and rooms of the servants quarters. Witnesses have also claimed that the apparition appears to be wearing a cloak. It is not known what or who the manifestation relates to, but other locals and former employees also attest to having seen the ghost.

Brownsover, nr Rugby, Warwickshire: Brownsover Hall Hotel

During the reign of Elizabeth I, a one-armed ancestor of the Boughton family used to drive around his estate on a coach drawn by six horses. After his death the manifestation of one-handed Boughton and his coach and horses continued to haunt the area. In 1755 the family enlisted the support of a team of clergymen in order to carry out an exorcism.

The rector of Harborough Magna, who apparently persuaded the ghost to enter a bottle that he then sealed and threw into the lake, carried it out. During the 1880s the bottle was discovered and given back to the family. Since then the sound of horses hooves has been heard in the area. Numerous witnesses before, during and after World War Two, reported hearing hoof beats and the sound of wheels on the drive. Dogs are apparently terrified to be in the vicinity.

Bruern Abbey, Oxfordshire

It is said that there is a four-mile underground passage to Tangley Hall from the abbey. Why this passageway should exist is perplexing, but it may have some connection with secret religious rites. Whatever the explanation, it is said that a ghostly monk traces the path of the tunnel by walking above it on solid ground.

Bryanston House, Bryanston, nr Blandford, Dorset

The ghost of old Aunt Charlotte is said to walk around the building at night, often entering bedrooms and staring at the terrified individual under the sheets. A pack of phantom hounds, known as the Portman Hunt and led by one headless dog, also haunts the area. Several older locals claim to have seen these apparitions on a number of occasions.

Buckfast Abbey, Devon

Pre-Reformation monks haunt the abbey. They have been seen at regular intervals, particularly while the building was unoccupied. Whether the recent habitation or renovation work has disturbed these monks is unknown. A small boy, out fishing in 1872, saw a procession of the monks. He described them as walking in single file and in perfect silence. They slowly disappeared before his eyes.

Buckfastleigh, Devon: Brook Manor

John Capel, who died in 1677, had a formidable reputation as a ravisher of young women. Legend has it that when he died, the Devil came to claim him. His tomb is enormous, and it is said that if you circle it 13 times and then poke your finger into the keyhole, then the ghost will rise and bite your finger off. Capel's spirit is seen, accompanied by spectral hounds, on the drive to his former home, Brook Manor.

Buckholm Tower, nr Galashiels, Borders

A former laird of Buckholm called Pringle, who lived there in the late 18th century, haunts these ruins. He was an unpleasant piece of work. His wife and son left him after suffering from his cruelty, and no woman for miles was safe from his advances. Pringle used his hunting dogs to track down Covenanters, and on one occasion helped to catch and imprison two locals, Geordie Elliott and his son William, believed to be sympathisers. The pair were murdered by Pringle, who may have been too drunk to realise what he was doing. Isobel Elliott, the wife and mother of the men and a former employee of Pringle, appeared at the door and confronted Pringle. He dragged her down to the dungeon. She screamed loudly as she saw, hanging from hooks attached to the old oak beam, the bodies of her men-folk. The old woman slowly struggled to her feet, her eyes burning with hatred. She faced the drunken laird and cursed him for what he had done. Shortly afterwards Pringle died a painful death, and at the point of death was racked with convulsions as if being attacked by his own hounds. Strange noises are heard in the dungeon to this day, and a bloodstain marks the spot of the murders. On the first anniversary of Pringle's death, his ghost was seen, being chased by spectral hounds. He was calling for help and when he reached the door, he hammered on it until one of the servants opened up. The servant could see no one there. Since that time, every June, the same sounds and heavy banging on the dungeon door are heard.

Buckingham, Buckinghamshire: Castle House, West Street

This 12th-century castle was built from stones taken from an earlier structure destroyed by Danish raiders. The Barton family were the first new owners, but it then passed, in the 15th century, to the Fowlers. Catherine of Aragon was imprisoned here while Henry VIII argued with Cardinal Wolsey and the Pope about divorcing her to marry Anne Boleyn. In 1965 Buckingham Town Council moved into the house and discovered that the building was also home to a 400-year-old ghost. The ghost is that of a Jesuit priest who was Catherine's confessor, who risked his life on a number of occasions to celebrate mass with her. In 1908, a priest's hole was discovered over the entrance to the great parlour. It contained the skeleton of a male, which was dated to the 16th century. It is believed that the skeleton is that of Catherine's priest, and is the source of the haunting. The apparition has been seen heading toward the priest hole, mainly during the late evening.

Buckland, nr Dover, Kent: Buckland Hospital

While recovering from a heart attack in the hospital, Bill Ridgeway, the deputy mayor of Dover, encountered the manifestation of a young boy on a trolley. Not only did he see the ghost, but he also had a conversation with it, on the subject of death. The ghost asked Ridgeway whether he thought he was going to die, and Ridgeway replied that he just wanted the will to live. At this the ghost disappeared. Ridgeway was not the only individual in the ward to have witnessed this apparition.

Buckland Abbey, Devon

Sir Francis Drake made extensions to this Cistercian abbey, allegedly with the help of the Devil (the extension work was said to have been completed in just three nights). The story runs that in payment for his help, the Devil condemned Drake to drive a black hearse, drawn by headless horses and followed by headless hounds, along the road from Plymouth to Tavistock after his death. Drake is also said to have left his drum to be used as an alarm if ever a new Armada came from Spain to invade Britain. He promised that, wherever he might end up after his death, he would come to his country's aid from beyond the grave and defeat the Spanish again. Drake's drum has never been used to signal the approach of a Spanish Armada, but it was said to have sounded itself during the Battle of Britain in World War Two.

Buckton, Northumberland

A cloaked figure haunts the country lane connecting Buckton with Detchant and Fenwick. The apparition has been seen walking in the spinney called Grizzy's Clump. It is the manifestation of the Scot, Grizelle Cochrane. In 1685, Grizelle's father, Sir John Cochrane of Ochiltree, was sentenced to death for supporting the cause of the Duke of Argyll against James Stuart. A royal courier was bringing the death warrant from London to Edinburgh. Grizelle dressed as a highwayman with a brace of pistols and held up the stage and took the warrant. Her actions delayed the execution, giving her father's supporters enough time to gain a pardon for him.

Buildwas Abbey, nr Ironbridge, Shropshire

The Black Abbot, John Burnell, once the abbot of Buildwas, haunts the grounds of this ruined abbey. Sir Thomas Tong and a band of renegade monks stormed the abbey in 1342 and fatally stabbed Burnell. It is said that Burnell's ghost joins another monk in part of the ruins sometimes. Following a recent fire on the nearby bridge, the sound of ghostly screams and the smell of burning has been reported.

Bungay, Suffolk: Bigod's Castle

The ruins of Bigod's Castle are haunted by the transformed spirit of Hugh Bigod, one-time pretender to the throne. He is seen in the form of a phantom hound known as the Black Shuck. In this form he has been seen as far afield as Blythburgh.

Bungay, Suffolk: St Mary's Church

During a service in the church on 4 August 1577, a flaming black dog hurtled through the congregation, immolating two of them. Another member of the congregation lived but was shrivelled by the event. The Black Shuck, or Hugh Bigod, was blamed. However, it is much more likely that a lightning strike hit the church, as there was a storm at the time. To commemorate the event the weathercock in the town centre boasts a black dog.

Burford, Oxfordshire

A terrifying black cloud, which drives animals frantic, can be encountered on the road leading to Witney. In the town the former priory is haunted not only by screams, singing and bells, but also by a host of apparitions, including that of an old-fashioned gamekeeper and a little brown monk.

Burgate, nr Fordingbridge, Hampshire: Tudor Rose Inn

This 14th-century public house echoes to the inexplicable sound of footsteps. The sound emanates from the stairway or, at least, very near to this part of the building. Staff have also reported seeing the vague outline of a woman gliding up the stairs. Despite a ghost research team's investigation in the 1970s, no light has been shed on this matter. The hauntings show no signs of ceasing. Recent landlords have reported the mysterious figure and the same strange noises near the staircase.

Burgh Castle, nr Great Yarmouth, Norfolk

This former Roman fort once faced the North Sea, although it now only overlooks marshland. The manifestation that haunts it may or may not have anything to do with the occupation of the Romans: no plausible explanation has been given for the vision seen by many witnesses. A figure, draped in a white flag, jumps from the battlements. The best day to observe the phenomenon is said to be 3 July.

Burgh Island, nr Salcombe, Devon

Tom Crocker, the infamous pirate, used the island as his base in the 14th century. He was hanged in 1395, and his ghost can be seen in the third week of August, the anniversary of his death.

Buriton Manor, nr Petersfield, Hampshire

A ghost haunts this house, the former rectory of Buriton. It is said that there is an underground passageway that links the manor to the church. Whether the apparition is of a former rector or a secret visitor to the rectory is unknown. A chambermaid hanged herself in the old tithe barn many years ago. Her spirit returns from time to time to relive the last few minutes of her earthly life. She is heard walking to the front door, along the path and into the barn, where she took her own life.

Burnley, Lancashire: St Peter's Church

Trash, or Old Striker, a phantom dog that is said to be very unlucky, haunts the church and surrounding area. It is described as being a large shaggy dog with big feet. Witnesses have said that when it approaches, it sounds as if the dog is walking through water. The degree of ill fortune it brings depends on how the witness sees the hound. If it is a clear apparition, then the person or a close family member will die soon. If the manifestation is less distinct, then the death will occur much later. Luckily, some witnesses have only heard his howls.

Burton Agnes Hall, nr Driffield, East Yorkshire

The manifestation of a young girl, known as 'Awd Nance', has often been seen around the house, particularly during the evenings. She is the ghost of Anne Griffith, daughter of the man who built the hall, who died after she was mugged while on her way to visit neighbours. On her deathbed she asked that her head should be kept somewhere in the house. Her family ignored her grisly request, and the hall suffered from immense poltergeist activity. Reluctantly, her body was exhumed and her head removed. The skull was kept in the house and the poltergeist activity ceased, although her ghost is still seen. If ever the skull is removed from the house, screams and poltergeist activity recur.

Burton Constable Hall, nr Hull, East Yorkshire

Nurse Dowdall, a nanny at the hall during the 19th century, haunts the building. She has been seen on a number of occasions, wearing a shawl over a long dress and a bonnet on her head. A number of other apparitions are present. A phantom Roman legion marches on the drive, a ghostly nun walks the long gallery and a spectral black Labrador has been seen on the stairs. The hall also has the apparition of a woman dressed in a brown checked shirt and matching shoes.

Burton Dassett, nr Banbury, Warwickshire

'Jenny Burn Tails' is the local name for a strange manifestation that may be a form of will-o'-the-wisp. On occasions, the intensity of the glowing object has been very intense. It is also interesting to note that the apparition always seems to move in the same direction.

Burtonwood, nr Warrington, Cheshire

This old airfield boasts the apparition of a headless pilot. During World War Two, the base was used for incoming American production aircraft. An unfortunate pilot attempted to bail out of his aircraft before it plummeted into the ground, but he somehow got decapitated by the canopy. One of the hangars is now a museum, within which is a bus. The bus was once the home of an old gamekeeper. His apparition has been seen wandering around too.

Burwash, East Sussex

Bateman's, the former home of Rudyard Kipling, is haunted, but the ghost of David Leary is far more fascinating and well documented. He appears as a ragged form, coughing, choking and moaning in Gladwish Woods. He was wrongly hanged for the murder of his friend Russell and vowed to haunt the people that had been involved in his conviction.

Bury St Edmunds, Suffolk: Moyses Hall

A dagger, a pair of pistols, a scalp and a book bound in skin are some of the gruesome relics in this museum. The artefacts relate to William Corder, who murdered Maria Martin at the Red Barn. When he was executed at Bury St Edmunds 7,000 people came to see his last moments. After Corder was hanged and his body dissected, a death mask was made and stored at Moyses Hall. The head itself is said to have brought such bad luck to the hall that it was eventually buried. Corder's tortured spirit can be seen in the vicinity.

Bury St Edmunds, Suffolk: The Nutshell, Cornhill

This is said to be one of the smallest public houses in the country. The ghost of a small boy, who was apparently murdered many years ago, haunts it. Numerous regulars, as well as a succession of landlords, have seen the apparition. One particular regular, who sometimes spends the night in a small bedroom on the third floor, also reports that the temperature is considerably lower in this room than in the remainder of the building. This may be the seat of the haunting.

Bury St Edmunds, Suffolk: St Edmundsbury Abbey

In 1446 a nun by the name of Maud Carew poisoned the Duke of Gloucester while he was imprisoned here. Her often-sighted spirit, which is now referred to as the grey lady, has been seen passing between the walls of houses built into the west side of the ruined church. Many other witnesses have also reported ghostly monks, clad in brown, gliding across the grounds near the gateway. The abbey gateway has been described as one of the most spiritually powerful places in England, and the former rector of Risby, the Revd Webling, claimed that he received messages from his two dead sons there, and that the ghostly monks had helped him write his book about the life of St Edmund. Apparently, the information they gave included the fact that the saint's body had been taken out of its sarcophagus and hidden somewhere near the high altar.

Bury St Edmunds, Suffolk: The Suffolk, Buttermarket

A priory stood near here, a casualty of Henry VIII's dissolution policy. There is, apparently, a tunnel that leads from the pub to the site of the old priory, and in this passageway, the ghost of a monk, has been seen.

Bury St Edmunds, Suffolk: Theatre Royal, Westgate Street

It is said that the ghost of the original builder of the theatre, William Wilkins, haunts the building. Several witnesses have reported seeing the misty shape of a man in a grey suit. Whether this is Wilkins or 'Stage Door Johnny', an apparition often seen by the stage door, one can only speculate. Johnny is apparently the manifestation of a man who died suddenly while having an affair with one of the actresses.

Buttsbury, nr Ingatestone, Essex

The road from Stock to Ingatestone near Buttsbury is said to be haunted by the ghost of a Cavalier. The particular area to note is known as White Tirells.

Buxted, East Sussex

Nan Tuck was accused of being a witch and suffered trial by water (ducking). She managed to escape but was found hanging from a tree in what is now called Tuck's Wood. Perhaps she committed suicide rather than face death at the hands of the villagers, or perhaps she was lynched. Her tormented spirit is still seen in Tuck's Wood and Nan Tuck's Lane.

Bygrave House, nr Baldock, Hertfordshire

There are three ghosts living in this building. One is the spirit of a peddler who was murdered here many years ago. The other two phantoms are those of a mother and child, whose bodies were buried under the drawing room floor.

C

Caerphilly Castle to Cwn

Caerphilly Castle, nr Cardiff, Mid Glamorgan

A Gwrach-y-rhibyn (Welsh hag), which has been described as a green lady with a large head and bulging eyes, haunts the castle. It is believed that the flag tower is the probable centre of the activity, but she has been seen in other parts of the structure. She shares the castle with as yet unidentified ghostly soldiers.

Cairngorms, Ben Macdhui, Grampian

A big grey man haunts Ben Macdhui, one of the six main peaks of the Cairngorms. He is described as being over 10ft tall, with long arms and a terrible, almost guttural voice. In 1891, Norman Collie, later a professor at the University of London, heard footsteps following him in the mist, but by the time he reached Rothiemurchus Forest, the footsteps had stopped. Mountaineer Dr A.M. Kellas was on the summit one June night, when he saw a figure climbing out of Lairig Ghru Pass. George Duncan saw the same figure in 1914, wearing a large black robe and waving its hands. In 1941 the Scottish naturalist, Wendy Wood, heard a booming voice close beside her. The strange figure has been seen on numerous occasions since.

Caistor, nr Grimsby, Lincolnshire

The apparition of a monk that has a tendency

to play the organ in the middle of the night haunts the church at Caistor. In January 1967, the vicar left a tape recorder running in the church and locked up for the night. When he listened to the tape in the morning, he could hear footsteps walking through the empty church, followed by the playing of the church organ. He also heard banging noises that had not been reported thus far.

Caldbeck, nr Carlisle, Cumbria

John Peel, Caldbeck's famous huntsman, who was immortalised in the song *D' ye ken John Peel, with his coat so grey'*, does not haunt the village, but a spectral black dog has been seen on numerous occasions. A ghost that has the habit of rattling chains haunts the rectory beside the church. The gardens of Bushay House are home to a strange display of floating lights.

Calgarth Hall, Lake Windermere, Cumbria

Built in the 16th century, Calgarth Hall was once owned by the Cook family, but the local magistrate, Miles Phillipson, wanted the property for himself. Shortly before Christmas, Phillipson invited the Cooks for dinner on Christmas Day. He planted a small silver bowl in one of their pockets during the meal, and the couple were arrested, despite their protestations of innocence. Phillipson tried them himself and sentenced them both to death. When he passed the sentence, Dorothy Cook laid a curse on Phillipson, saying that his family would come to ruin. She also swore that she and her husband would haunt Calgarth Hall as long as the Phillipsons owned it. The Phillipsons moved into the house just after the execution and all was fine until the first Christmas. Mrs Phillipson was walking upstairs when she saw the terrifying apparition of two skulls staring at her; her husband, hearing her screams, rushed to her and saw the horrible objects

himself. The skulls were thrown out of the window, but just after midnight horrible screams were heard and the skulls were back where they had first been seen. Phillipson threw the skulls into the pond, but by that evening, they were back again. Over the next few years Phillipson suffered setback after setback, and the screaming skulls accompanied each misfortune. By the time he died, all he had left was the hall, and the skulls still came back each Christmas to remind him of the curse. His son was sensible enough to sell the place.

Callow, nr Great Malvern, Worcestershire: Callow Farm

This farm was once an inn, where it is said that passing travellers were robbed and murdered. The footpads would take the bodies across the fields and hide them in a cottage out of sight of the road. The cottage was pulled down several years ago, but several witnesses have reported seeing not only phantoms of the footpads carrying a corpse across the field, but also the building appearing as a shadowy vision.

Callow End, Worcestershire: Prior's Court

Three ghosts haunt Prior's Court. One is of a lady who was murdered while sheltering from a storm. Another is a Cavalier whose skeleton was found up a chimney, and the third is a girl who wanders from the courtyard to the orchard. A ghostly shape, perhaps related to one of these, can be seen in one of the bedrooms. Human bones have also been found buried in the garden.

Calverley, nr Leeds, West Yorkshire

'Old Calverley, Old Calverley, I have thee by the ears, I'll cut thee into collops, unless thee appears' – this was the rhyme which the local boys used to sing, running around in a circle, with their caps thrown into the middle. They would throw a mixture of crumbs and pins on to the caps, and then whistle through the keyhole of the church to summon the ghost. In life Walter Calverley was a reckless man, and by 1604 he was being continually plagued by moneylenders. Having spent the fortune left by his father he was, by all accounts, a little mad. On 23 April 1604 he finally snapped, and murdered two of his children and stabbed his wife. Thinking her dead, he rode off to Norton to kill his other son. His wife, however, had survived the attack and alerted the authorities. Riders overtook Walter and arrested him. At his trial in York, he refused to plead. A guilty verdict would have meant that his remaining property would go to the crown. His penalty for not pleading was death by pressing (peine forte et dure). This grisly punishment involved the victim being covered with a large plank of wood, so that progressively heavy weights could be placed on top until the victim was crushed to death. Death would not occur for several days and was excruciatingly painful. After his death, Walter's body was buried at York, but it was later moved back to Calverley. His ghost has been seen on many occasions at the church and on horseback, re-enacting his last ride to kill his surviving son. As for the village boys and their rhyme, it worked once and they ran for home!

Camborne, Dead Man's Cove, Cornwall

The apparition of a man dressed in black has been seen by the shoreline. It is not known who he is. Despite the fact that several witnesses claim to have seen the manifestation, many believe that the phantom was a story originally invented by smugglers to keep people away from their activities.

Cambridge, Cambridgeshire: Christ's College

Christopher Round's ghost haunts the mul-

berry tree in the Fellow's Garden. He killed a fellow student at the college and his spirit can be seen, bent and stooped in remorse, slowly shuffling around the tree.

Cambridge, Cambridgeshire: Clare College

When Dr Robert Greene died in 1730, his directions were that his body should be dissected and all, barring the bones, buried in All Saint's Church. The bones were to be displayed in the library. Providing the college adhered to these instructions they were to receive Greene's house and a proportion of his shares. The college did not accept his bequest until 1742, by which time Greene was already buried in Tamworth. Eventually the bones were displayed in the library but moved in 1763, 1818 and 1890. By the end of the 19th century the bulk of the skeleton had disappeared; students had taken the bones as last-minute souvenirs. The authorities believe that Greene haunts the college as a result of their delay in accepting the bequest, and their non-compliance with his instructions.

Cambridge, Cambridgeshire: Corpus Christi College

One of the upper rooms in the old court is haunted. There is some dispute over the identity of the ghost. Some contend that it is the ghost of Dr Butts, who was Master of the college between 1626 and 1632. Others believe that it is more likely to be a suitor who courted the daughter of Dr Spencer, a Master during the 17th century. The suitor haunts the kitchen; it was here that he hid in order to avoid Dr Spencer. The unfortunate man suffocated in one of the cupboards.

Cambridge, Cambridgeshire: Emmanuel College

It was not until the late 1860s that the ghost of Emmanuel House began to trouble the occupants. On several occasions heavy foot-steps were heard near the drawing room, descending the staircase into the hall below. Over a decade later a witness saw a short figure, perhaps dressed in a bridal gown, in one of the bedrooms. The veiled lady, as she became known, was seen on a regular basis by a number of different people until 1893 when the building was demolished. It is not known whether the ghost has chosen to haunt the structure that replaced the earlier house.

Cambridge, Cambridgeshire: Girton College

Although the ghost seen in and around the college buildings is said to be a Roman centurion, it seems unlikely that this is the case, as parts of the college are built on an Anglo-Saxon cemetery. The college also has a grey lady, immortalised by the spiral staircase known as the Grey Lady Staircase. It is believed that she is the apparition of Miss Taylor, who was accepted by Girton but died before she could take up her place.

Cambridge, Cambridgeshire: Jesus College

Arthur Gray was Master of Jesus College from 1912–40. He wrote extensively regarding the ghosts of the college, describing the ghost of Charles Ballasis, extensive poltergeist activity and a number of former students and staff that he claimed haunted the college.

Cambridge, Cambridgeshire: Montague Road

During the 1920s, a young boy encountered the spirit of a woman lying in a hammock in the summerhouse. The family realised that it was almost certainly the apparition of the boy's aunt, who had died in the summer-house in her youth.

Cambridge, Cambridgeshire: Newnham College

Henry and Eleanor Sidgwick were late 19th-century ghost hunters. Over a period of years they made contact with a number of spirits, often conversing with them in Greek or Latin. They also developed some of the first ways of authenticating ghostly contact. It is believed by many that some of the ghosts that they disturbed remain active on the premises.

Cambridge, Cambridgeshire: Peterhouse

Frances Dawes committed suicide by hanging himself with the bell ropes in the college chapel. Dawes was a Senior Fellow, but had disputes with Dr James Yorke, Bishop of Ely and visitor to the college, particularly regarding the election of a new master. The apparition that is said to haunt the college may well be Dawes, or, perhaps, Frances Barnes, who became Master for Life in 1788 and died in 1838.

Cambridge, Cambridgeshire: St John's College

The phantom figure of an 18th-century undergraduate has been seen on one of the staircases at this college. The figure is thought to be that of Dr James Wood (1760–1839) who eventually became Master of the college. As a student he was so short of money that he used to sit on the stairs clad in straw to keep warm and used to study by the lighting on the staircase.

Cambridge, Cambridgeshire: Sherratt and Hughes, Trinity Street

Founded in 1581 and said to be the oldest bookshop in Great Britain, the premises are haunted by two ghosts. The manifestation of a man dressed in a Victorian evening suit has been seen, as well as a white lady. It is not known why these two apparitions have chosen to haunt this building.

Cambridge, Cambridgeshire: Sidney Sussex College

An apparition that is said to be a pale yellow head without ears haunts the south wing of Chapel Court. Others have reported seeing a large, pale blue eye. These hauntings may be related to the fact that Oliver Cromwell's head was buried in the ante-chapel of the college in 1960. After the Restoration in 1660, Cromwell's body was exhumed (he had been dead for two years) and hanged. His head was cut off and put on a pole at Westminster Hall, where it remained for 20 years until it was blown down in a storm. The head was embalmed, and after 1680 it changed hands many times until it was presented to the college by a Dr Wilkinson in 1960. There is a plaque commemorating the head's interment, but its actual resting place is unknown. The hauntings at the college date from the arrival of Cromwell's head.

Cambridge, Cambridgeshire: Trinity College

Christopher Wordsworth, the poet's brother, was Master at the college and received a complaint from a student given lodgings in a college room. The student stated that a spectral 19th-century child, with its hands turned outwards, had appeared in the room and groaned and screamed. The odd apparition of a man in hunting gear has also been seen in the New Court.

Cambridge, Cambridgeshire: Trumpington Street

In the 1890s one of the houses in the street was put up for sale. The maid showed a potential buyer around the house and after the tour she told the buyer that the house was haunted. She described the ghost as wearing a green dress and having a red feather in her hat. The buyer responded by saying that he had seen this woman in a portrait in the first room he had been shown. Both the maid and the owner were stunned by this as there was no such portrait in the house.

Camelford, Cornwall

The ghost of a knight has been seen near the square in the centre of the town. One of the buildings, apparently built during the Queen Anne period, still has traces of its old Tudor cellars and walls. The ghost is never seen as a whole figure, which leads experts to suggest that the manifestation is standing on what was the floor, but has now been significantly raised. Perhaps the knight is related to the fact that this is the supposed site of the Battle of Camlann (537), in which both Arthur and Mordred may have died.

Camfield Place, Essendon, Hertfordshire

Formerly the home of Beatrix Potter, who herself saw a dozen candles snuffed out by an unseen ghostly hand, this house has also been home to Barbara Cartland. She has apparently seen the ghost of one of her spaniels, Jimmy.

Cammeringham, nr Lincoln, Lincolnshire

A ghostly light, thought by some witnesses to be a woman in a chariot, has been seen here. It is known as the Cammeringham Light and it is thought by many to be the apparition of Boudicca (Boadicea) herself.

Canewdon, nr Southend-on-sea, Essex

The churchyard and surrounding lanes are favoured spots for the ghost of an old woman. She can be seen wearing a crinoline and bonnet. She may be the ghost of a woman executed for being a witch.

Canley, nr Coventry, West Midlands: The Phantom Coach Inn

A fatal coaching accident not only gives the pub its name, but is also the source of the apparitions and the poltergeist activity in the building itself. In the past, marshland surrounded the village and a coach strayed into the boggy ground, causing the death of all of those riding in it. The phantom coach has been seen on the road near the inn.

Cannard's Grave Inn, nr Shepton Mallet, Somerset

The public house stands at the junction of five roads and takes its name from Giles Cannard, a 17th-century innkeeper. He was strongly associated with local smugglers and highwaymen. Cannard was a forger and probable murderer, and dealt in stolen goods. When the authorities finally hunted him down, he hanged himself rather than face trial and execution. He was buried at the crossroads, where many an unfortunate traveller had fallen victim to his robber friends. Unwary travellers often see his ghost in winter.

Cannington, nr Bridgwater, Somerset: Blue Anchor Inn

Maude de Meriett was one of three vow-breaking nuns who lived in a convent that was pulled down to make way for a house in the 17th century. The nuns were beaten to death in the early 13th century, around the time of Magna Carta. Maude's sad-faced phantom has been seen in the public house, and crossing the nearby bridge. Whenever anyone approaches her, or attempts to talk to her, she simply disappears. Maude's heart is buried a few miles away at Combe Florey.

Canterbury, Kent: Canterbury Cathedral

The spirit of Simon of Sudbury, who was murdered in 1381, has often been seen and heard in the Sudbury Tower. Simon, then Archbishop of Canterbury and Lord Chancellor, was killed by Wat Tyler's men during the Peasant's Revolt. His severed head was displayed on London Bridge before being taken to St Gregory's Church in Sudbury, Suffolk. His manifestation, however, is not headless, and is described as being tall and dignified, with a grey beard and cloak and a fresh-looking complexion. The ghost of Nell Cook haunts the dark entry of the cathedral. She caught her master, a canon, with a young woman and poisoned them both. After her execution, her body was buried beneath the paving stones of the entrance. Her spirit rises each Friday night. It is also said that the ghost of Thomas Becket can be seen in the crypt. He is described as being of medium height, thin and wearing a cassock. Although the apparition is quite distinct, it is commonly referred to as 'Becket's shadow'.

Canvey Island, Essex

The ghost of a Viking haunts the north-eastern mudflats of the island. It may be an apparition of one of Halfdan's invaders, who were very active in the area in the 9th century. Edward, King Alfred's son, defeated Halfdan. The ghost of an old Dutchman with buckled shoes, rosettes on his knee and breeches has also been seen on the island, carrying a bundle over his shoulder.

Capesthorne Hall, nr Congleton, Cheshire

In 1861 the hall was gutted by fire, but the chapel and the wings survived. A grey lady haunts the east wing, particularly near to the staircase. The apparition is said to float rather than walk. Another mainfestation has been seen walking along one of the corridors, then descending the stairs toward the chapel. It disappears into a wall and is described as being a shadowy grey figure. The ghostly arm of a man has been seen at the window of one of the bedrooms, but when this was investigated there was nothing to be seen.

Cape Wrath, Highlands

A Polish ship was driven ashore at Cape Wrath over 300 years ago. Since then, the apparition of a tall bearded man, dressed in a long dark coat, knee-length boots and a tricorne hat has been seen near a ruined cottage beside the lighthouse. An old shepherd, who had decided to bed down in the cottage one night, was kept awake by heavy footsteps. He saw nothing, but never slept there again.

Capheaton, nr Morpeth, Northumberland

In 1783, 1821 and 1940, a ghostly piper warned of danger to the village. The first two occasions preceded serious fires and the third signalled the fact that German bombers were passing overhead.

Cappoquin, Melleray Grotto, Co. Waterford, Republic of Ireland

Whether it is a religious miracle or a true haunting, the statue of the Virgin Mary came to life on 16 August 1985, and gave messages to visitors. Following this event, several statues across the country followed suit, notably those in Ballinspittle and Asdee.

Caractacus Stone, nr Higher Combe, Somerset

The ghost of a carter who tried to uproot the stone in order to find the treasure buried beneath haunts this place. The stone crushed him to death and on foggy nights he can be seen and heard lamenting his folly at the attempt. The stone is probably named after Caractacus, chief of the Silures tribe, who was defeated and taken to Rome by the Romans in AD 46. A Latin inscription linked to the stone reads *Carataci Nepus,* which means 'clansman of Caractacus'.

Cardiff, South Glamorgan: Cardiff Castle

In the mid-1970s the custodian of the building, while clearing up after a civic reception, encountered a ghost that had been haunting the building for decades. The man came face-to-face with the figure of a male ghost in the doorway at one end of the hall. He walked toward the stranger and enquired as to whether he could help him. The manifestation faded away. The custodian's children and a guest staying with them claimed to have seen the figure of a man looking at them in a bedroom. After the event numerous poltergeist activities took place, including doors being locked, furniture being moved and a drastic effect on the sanity of the family dog. The possible explanation may involve the death of the 2nd Marquess of Bute. He died in what is now a small chapel behind the library. The apparition of a man in a long cloak has been seen in the area by a number of witnesses. He appears to always be in a hurry, and often scowls prior to vanishing. Several individuals have claimed that the manifestation bears a remarkable resemblance to a portrait of the 2nd Marquess, which hangs on a wall in the building.

Cardiff, South Glamorgan: National Museum of Wales

Dunbar Smith, who designed the building, moves chairs about in the night. His spirit is said to haunt the museum because his ashes were moved to make way for a gent's lavatory.

Carew Castle, nr Pembroke, Dyfed

The daughter of Nest, the last king of this area, haunts the castle. She takes the form of a white lady and has been seen for many years by a wide variety of witnesses.

Carleton Castle, nr Girvan, Strathclyde

Sited atop a rocky crag, this ruin is haunted by horrific screams. A one-time laird murdered seven of his eight wives at Gamesloup Crag. May Cullean, his eighth wife, had the better of the serial killer. He took her to the edge of the crag and told her to take off her clothes and jewellery before he threw her off. She told him that she was too shy and asked him to turn his back. When he did so she pushed him off.

Carlisle, Cumbria: Carlisle Castle

Carlisle Castle was built in the 11th century by William Rufus, in an attempt to protect his territory from the Scots. Mary Queen of Scots was imprisoned there in May 1568, and after the Battle of Culloden in 1746 Scottish rebels were held there. In 1835, during alterations to the building, the skeleton of a woman was found bricked up in the second floor of the keep. Her identity is unknown, but she was wearing silk tartan, her feet were on a silk tartan stool and she had valuable rings on her fingers. In 1842, a soldier on sentry duty was approached by a figure resembling the woman. He lunged at her with his bayonet and she disappeared. However, the shock caused him to collapse, and he died several hours later. He regained consciousness long enough to retell his story.

Carlisle, Cumbria: Citadel Restaurant

Originally a late 19th-century Temperance Hall, the building has two ghosts: a grey lady and a medieaval figure thought to be a monk. The site was once occupied by a structure somehow related to the abbey and the castle, and there are tunnels that run from these buildings to this site. It is believed that they were constructed as an escape route should the Scots attack. They were also used during the English Civil War. The same grey lady that haunts the Temperance Hall has also been seen at the castle.

Carlisle, Cumbria: Wardew House, Gisland

Wardew House was orginally built as a watchtower during the Border Wars with Scotland. A green lady that tends to manifest herself as a billowing green shape, accompanied by a disembodied wailing, haunts it.

Carreg Cennen Castle, nr Llandeilo, Dyfed

The sleeping spirits of Owen of the Red Hand and his 51 warriors rest here. It is said that they will rise after 1,000 years and purge Wales of her enemies and bring peace to the world.

Carrigaphoca Castle, nr Macroom, Munster, Republic of Ireland

Standing atop an enormous rock, nestled in the trees, is a fairytale castle that is home to an evil spirit or 'pooca'. It is said to prey on unwary travellers if it has the chance.

Carter Bar, nr Jedbergh, Northumberland

The Redeswire Raid of 1575 is taken to be the last real battle of the Border Wars, which took place to the east of Carter Bar at Leap Hill. A headless ghost haunts the treacherous moorland here, which is said to be Thomas Ellesden, who was decapitated by a Scottish claymore, a sword used by noblemen and highlanders.

Cartmel, nr Kendal, Cumbria

Many years ago, a charcoal burner was killed here when he was struck by lightning. His wife, or lover, was so grieved by his sudden departure that she could not bear to leave the small cottage that they had shared. Eventually depression and exposure took her life and she has been heard, more often than seen, plaintively calling her man's name.

Cassiobury, nr Watford, Hertfordshire

This was once the home of the Earls of Essex. Lord Capel's ghost appears on the anniversary of his execution, 9 March 1649. He had, rather foolishly, changed his allegiance from Parliament to that of the king, and paid a high price for the switch.

Castell Coch, nr Cardiff, South Glamorgan

Castell Coch was built in 1870 in 13th-century style by William Burgess for the Marquis of Bute. It is on the site of the fortress of Ifor Bach, a Welsh hero. Ifor, it is said, bewitched two men to become eagles to guard his treasure. During the English Civil War, a royalist was decapitated in a cannon accident and now guards Ifor's treasure, which he had discovered before his death. When Burgess obtained the castle in the 19th century, it had lain unloved for nearly 200 years, and he spent 20 years restoring it to its former glory. During the restoration work, the son of Dame Griffiths fell into a pit and drowned. She died of grief and also haunts the castle.

Castle Acre, Norfolk: Castle Acre Priory

Dating back to the latter half of the 11th century, this site boasts phantom monks and another less obvious apparition. The monks have been seen walking through the gateway and along the walkway to the priory, while the second manifestation, which is not a monk, has been seen in the solar of the priory's lodgings. This ghost may be connected to the time when the site was used as a farm.

Castle Ashby, Northamptonshire: The Falcon Hotel

During the English Civil War, Arthur, a blacksmith, was a loyal royalist. When Parliamentarian cavalry passed through the village and demanded that he re-shoe their horses, he refused. They hanged him from the walnut tree in his garden. His apparition has been seen on the anniversary of his death, 14 June.

Castle Donington, Leicestershire: Donington Manor Hotel

Built as a coaching inn in 1794, the fact that the buiding is haunted even appeared on the property details published when the hotel was sold in 1967. During renovations following the sale, various witnesses reported seeing an unpleasant-looking woman in one of the rooms. Since that time a number of other incidents have occurred that confirm that the hotel is still haunted.

Castle Green, Somerset: Castle Hotel

This hotel was once a part of the castle. It is now an impressive 50-room hotel. The Duke of Monmouth's army was garrisoned here, but it is the apparition of a female violinist that appears to cause the guests some consternation. She has been seen by several of the guests and many have heard her playing the violin. It is not immediately obvious who this woman may be.

Castle of Mey, nr Wick, Highlands

This 16th-century castle is the most northerly in Great Britain, standing around 6 miles from John O'Groats. It is also known as Barrowgill Castle. The ghost of Lady Fanny Sinclair, known as the green lady, haunts the castle. She committed suicide by throwing herself from one of the towers. She had fallen in love with a servant of the castle, a ploughboy, and had been forced to end the relationship by her father. She was so distraught that she took her own life.

Castle Rising, nr Kings Lynn, Norfolk

The Norman Earl of Sussex built this castle in 1150, apparently on a Roman site. Isabella, mother of Edward III, was imprisoned here after the murder of her husband. She died a mad woman, and her shrieks of maniacal laughter can be heard echoing around the castle. It is also said that her ghost can be seen wandering around the ruins of the castle church.

Castle Rushen, Castletown, Isle of Man

An enormous number of executions have been carried out within the precincts of the castle. One such execution seems to be the root cause of the haunting. Many years ago a woman was hanged for murdering her own son, despite the fact that the boy actually died of natural causes. The apparition of a woman in a long, grey dress, accompanied by a boy, has often been seen near the drawbridge. If the figures are approached they disappear. The woman has also been seen alone at the top of Eagle Tower, and staff suggest that she has appeared in the dungeons.

Castle Stuart, Petty Parish, nr Inverness, Highlands

Many years ago, the Earl of Moray offered £20 to anyone who would dare spend the night in the 17th-century castle tower. A local poacher, by the name of Big Angus, said to be afraid of neither man nor beast, took up the challenge, thinking it easy money. The next morning, the unfortunate man was found in the courtyard below, with a frozen look of horror on his face. The three-turreted haunted bedroom at the top of the east tower is still available for overnight stays.

Castleton, Derbyshire: The Castle Hotel

A ghostly bride, presumably a white lady, has been seen in the hotel at various times, as has the spirit of a man in a pin-striped suit, accompanied by an Old English Sheepdog. The bride is said to be the ghost of a woman left standing at the altar. It is also said that the unseen spirits of former employees haunt the kitchens. The manifestation of a grey lady, who is only partially visible because the rest of her ghostly form walks on the level of the floor in her times, also haunts the building.

Catcleugh Reservoir, nr Jedbergh, Northumberland

The manifestation of Percy Reed, the keeper of Redesdale, assists lost hikers and members of the public, steering them away from danger and putting them on the right path. Percy was murdered somewhere on the moors by two members of the Hall family, who had invited him to go hunting with them. His apparition has been seen in several places in the area, but particularly near to the reservoir.

Catton, nr Norwich, Norfolk: White Woman Lane

The spirit of a young woman has often been seen crossing this narrow road. It is said that she was the former owner of the nearby manor house, and engaged in an illicit affair with a coachman. He lived on the other side of the road, and it is believed that even in death she insists on honouring her commitment to meet him each night.

Cawdor Castle, nr Nairn, Highlands

When the daughter of one of the Earls of Cawdor fell in love with a man from an opposing clan, her father was outraged. The tension between them grew to such a point that he chased her into one of the highest towers of the castle and she hung desperately out of the window to escape his wrath. When he reached the windowsill, he chopped off her hands and she fell to her death. Her handless apparition has been seen by a great number of people.

Caxton Gibbet, nr Cambridge, Cambridgeshire

Of great historical interest, this site was the location of one of the first 17th-century tollgates, a much-used gibbet and a triple murder. At some point in the 18th century, three wealthy travellers retired to bed, quite drunk, to be awoken by the landlord's son going through their bags and pockets. He murdered all three of them and dumped them into the well. The killer was eventually tried, hanged and gibbeted outside his father's pub. The scene of the murders is constantly colder than the rest of the building. Witnesses report hearing footsteps walking from the room, along the balcony and then stopping at the foot of the stairs, where the well is sited. Villains seem to be attracted to the pub, for in 1753, another son of a landlord was hanged and gibbeted (for five months) for robbing the mail. Another man, in the 18th century, committed a murder in a nearby field and fled to America. He foolishly returned only seven years later, got drunk in the pub and told the assembled crowd about his crime. He was subsequently arrested, tried, hanged and gibbeted. He was still alive that night when a baker passed by and took pity on him. The baker cut the

murderer down, only to join him on the gibbet some days later.

Chalford, Gloucestershire: The Ragged Cot Inn

This stone-built 17th-century inn is haunted by a mother and her child. The first landlord of the public house murdered them both.

Chanctonbury Ring, nr Worthing, West Sussex

This prehistoric hill-fort is covered by beech trees and haunted by an old man with a grey beard, as well as the sound of galloping horses. It is said that if anyone can count the number of trees on the site and speak the number out loud, then Julius Caesar himself, at the head of a phantom Roman army, will appear.

Chapmanslade, nr Frome, Wiltshire: Black Dog Woods

Legend has it that a highwayman used a dog to pounce on unsuspecting coachmen as they descended the steep hill that passes through the woods to the east of the village. Unfortunately for the highwayman, the drivers quickly adapted to his scam and were able to shoot him dead when he appeared on the side of the road one night. It is not the highwayman that haunts this stretch of road and immediate area, but his hound, which takes the form of a large spectral dog with fiery red eyes.

Chard, Somerset: The Chough Hotel

Judge Jeffreys haunts a nearby building, which he used as a courthouse. During his short period here he had twelve men hanged from the large oak tree at the end of the town. However, it is in the hotel in which he lodged that several people have seen his ghostly form. He has been variously described as 'an old man sitting by a fire', or as 'a nasty old chap'. A female guest at the hotel heard whispering and laughing voices, and on her second visit to the hotel was told by the landlord that a man had stayed in a particular room and had heard the same sounds, but had left in haste with a red whip mark across his face. Alterations to the hotel revealed a small chamber beside the bedroom. Other guests have reported a ghostly figure in armour, phantom figures passing windows and a little old lady near the back door.

Chardstock, nr Axminster, Devon: St Andrews Church

A middle-aged woman in an old-fashioned long grey dress has often been seen walking from the vicarage path toward the church. Several witnesses have reported that as she reaches the gate she disappears. The most likely time to see this apparition is at about 5.30pm, or at dusk. There does not appear to be any obvious reason why the woman should haunt the path, although it is assumed that she is buried in the graveyard.

Charlecote Park, nr Stratford, Warwickshire

The apparition of a young girl is said to haunt the lake that stretches out beside this magnificent building. Witnesses have seen a young girl enter the water and then disappear. It is believed that she is the ghost of a suicide victim.

Charlton Marshall, Dorset

Shortly before World War Two, several boys boarding at the preparatory school located in the old manor house saw a grey lady wearing a grey cap travel down a corridor and vanish through a wall at the end. On some occasions staff and pupils were actually passed by the apparition in the same corridor. Unfortunately, the old manor house was pulled down several years ago and replaced by a housing estate.

Charmouth, Dorset: Charmouth Lodge

Many years ago a woman was murdered in the house and her body was thrown into a well. Her ghost now appears as a white lady. The second apparition is a little more difficult to link with the house, as it appears to be the ghost of a monk.

Chartham, nr Canterbury, Kent: Howfield Manor

The manor stands on the grounds of a former monastery and boasts the ghost of a monk. The monk apparently died shortly after a fire swept through the monastery. He ran into the building in order to save one of the brethren, but died as a result of the injuries that he sustained. Although some claim to have seen the monk himself, you are more likely to hear ghostly chanting.

Chatham, Kent: Dockyards

Nelson's ghost has been seen here, interestingly with his eye and arm intact. It may be significant that he does not appear in Great Yarmouth or in Portsmouth, both places that were important in his life.

Chatham, Kent: Invicta Bingo Hall, High Street

The ghostly figure of a man in green has been seen walking about the foyer and upstairs in the balcony. It was first supposed that this was related to the time when the building was used to house evacuees during World War Two. Local churches had arranged for the building to be used as a temporary home for families bombed out during the Blitz. Unfortunately it suffered a direct hit, killing four people, including three children. Since the 1940s a green ghost has been seen, and is often described as looking 'military'. During the 1970s a clairvoyant identified the individual as William Malan, who worked as a commissionaire in around 1940 and wore a green uniform at work. Children's voices have been heard at night, but witnesses have been unable to detect the source of the noise. This may relate directly to the unfortunate deaths during the war.

Chatham, Kent: Magpie Hall Road

For nearly 25 years, two adjoining houses in this street have been haunted by strange footsteps that tend to stop when lights are switched on. Witnesses complain that the activity seems to take place between midnight and 5am. The only plausible explanation seems to be that a man once cut his own throat in one of the houses, but this does not explain why the haunting has begun.

Chatham, Kent: St Mary's Barracks

During the middle watch the sound of limping footsteps can be heard, as can the tapping of a crutch or wooden leg. The source of the sound is likely to be the ghost of a former sailor, or someone related to the naval history of the area.

Chatham, Kent: 'Snob' boutique, High Street

This 19th-century building, once apartments, is haunted by the ghost of a Victorian woman that lived on the top floor. In the run up to Christmas 1969, a shop assistant saw the apparition of a woman standing by one of the dress racks. She described her as wearing old-fashioned clothes and standing there brushing her hair. However, the shop floor was empty. Other staff checked and found nothing. Later, while taking a lunch break on the fire escape, a woman's face was seen in one of the upstairs windows. Four witnesses in the 1970s also claim to have seen a glass of water disappear in front of their very eyes.

Cheadle, Greater Manchester: Malt Shovels Hotel, Oxford Road

The ghost of Tom Ward, a former landlord who died in 1971, has been encountered by a number of landlords since, as well as by regular customers. He is described as being short and grey haired. He seems particularly active near the beer pumps in the cellar. It has been suggested that he mouths a warning to those working on the pumps that may relate to an accident that happened in the past.

Checkley, nr Uttoxeter, Staffordshire

In 1895, Mrs Hutchinson, the vicar's wife, died. She now haunts her former home, the rectory, as well as the memorial school that she helped to set up. She was a terrifying individual, who had the habit of verbally abusing those who had failed to attend church to listen to her husband's sermons. Witnesses have seen her, sometimes with her little white dog, dressed in a frilly blouse, waistcoat, grey dress and mob cap.

Cheltenham, Gloucestershire

In a large house in Pittville Circus Road (formerly called Garden Reach), the apparition of a tall woman appeared between 1882 and 1889. She was seen by at least 10 people and heard by twice that number. The ghost, holding a handkerchief to her face, has also been seen in recent years in a nearby house. It is said that she could be the ghost of Imogen, second wife of Henry Swinhoe.

Cheltenham, Gloucestershire: Hallery House

A smoking ghost, who seems to revel in the fact that he is enjoying a relaxing cigarette in the non-smoking dining room, haunts this villa-style property. Although the apparition has not been seen directly, the owners believe it to be a woman. The ghost seems to prefer a particular chair and animals in the house are extremely frightened to enter the dining room.

Chenies Manor House, nr Amersham, Buckinghamshire

The building has had an interesting and chequered history, playing host to King Henry VIII, Anne Boleyn, Catherine Howard, Elizabeth I, Charles I and 200 Parliamentarian soldiers. Who it is that now haunts the house is unknown, but the apparition seems to have a limp. In the 1970s, alterations were made to the house that revealed a bricked-up room next to the Pink Room. This was one of the rooms in which the soldiers had slept. When the wall was demolished it was found that the hidden room was a prayer room and priest hole. There was an inscription on the wall inside that read '9th September'. Since then, it has been impossible to keep the windows and doors in the Pink Room shut on that date.

Chepstow, Monmouthshire: St Pierre Hotel Country Club

Said to date from the 14th century, this former stately home is haunted by the ghost of a grey lady. Popular belief is that she died in an accident on her wedding night.

Cheshunt, Hertfordshire

The Great House is said to be haunted by the spirit of a grey lady. There are also, reputedly, indelible bloodstains upstairs. Nearby, several ghosts haunt Old Palace House.

Chester, Cheshire: Barlows, Bridge Street

Many years ago one of the landlords was an extremely proud individual who devoted all his waking hours to making his inn the best in the city. After he died successive landlords heard groans and banging noises emanating from the cellar. It is believed that the manifestation of the old landlord is particularly active if something is happening in the pub that he would not have approved of.

Chester, Cheshire: The Bluebell Restaurant, Northgate Street

The apparition of a beautiful, blonde-haired woman, dressed in a 17th-century cream gown, has been seen in the front left window of the first floor. It is believed that she still looks into the street, hoping to glimpse her royalist lover.

Chester, Cheshire: city walls

From Morgan's Mount you may see the spectral figures of royalist soldiers and their wives retreating from the city. An icy blast of air precedes them. The headless ghost of a royalist can also be seen; he lost his head when a canon ball smashed through his room.

Chester, Cheshire: Dee Hills Park

A ghostly monk that seems to particularly enjoy scaring people in the middle of the night haunts No.14. He stands at people's bedsides, waiting for them to notice him. When they let out a scream and leave the room he vanishes.

Chester, Cheshire: Eastgate Street

In the middle of the 19th century, a woman who was deserted by her husband hanged herself on the premises. Since then, witnesses have heard wailing emanating from the first floor and the storeroom, lights have been switched on and off and doors have opened despite the fact that they were locked. The ghost has never been seen, but she is now known as Sarah and most witnesses seem to think that she is friendly.

Chester, Cheshire: Falcon Inn, Lower Bridge Street

The apparition of a girl, often accompanied by extreme poltergeist activity, haunts the pub. It is said that many years ago the landlord threw out one of his servants. She was forced to live on the streets for a short while until she died.

Chester, Cheshire: George and Dragon Hotel, Liverpool Road

Standing on the site of a Roman cemetery, the pub is haunted by the sound of marching feet. They seem to pass through the pub, following the old Roman road.

Chester, Cheshire: Grosvenor Park, Union Street

Billy Hobby was once the keeper of the spring that was situated in the park. It was believed that the water had magical properties, and as a result, Billy made an enormous amount of money, until two customers caught a chill and died. Billy's spring was closed down, but he still haunts the park by locking the gates.

Chester, Cheshire: Marlborough Arms, St John's Street

An oppressive presence, coupled with the terrifying sound of someone cutting their own throat, has been reported by a number of staff working in the cellar. In 1885 the landlord committed suicide down there.

Chester, Cheshire: Old King's Head

A sword was found under floorboards in bedroom four in the 1930s, during renovation work. It is believed that the find is related to the indistinct apparition of a man seen wandering around the building. Messages appear on a mirror in room four, items disappear in room six and kitchen equipment has been moved.

Chester, Cheshire: Pepper Gate

Ellen was the daughter of Alderman Rauff Aldersey, and she fell in love with Luke, a local armourer. Her father disapproved of their relationship and they were forced to elope. Luke took her away on his horse and they married in Wales. The alderman was beside himself with rage and believed that the gate guards should have been more vigilant. He ordered Pepper Gate to be locked. Later the three were reconciled, but the muffled hoof-beats of Luke's horse can still be heard clattering up the approach to Pepper Gate at night.

Chester, Cheshire: Pepper Street

Two ghostly monks haunt the premises now occupied by a furniture store. They are known by the locals as Charlie and Herbert. They are described as being black-cowled figures.

Chester, Cheshire: The Pied Bull, Northgate Street

Toward the end of the 19th century an ostler went out to check the horses in the middle of the night. Somehow the lantern he was carrying set the straw ablaze and he was burned to death. He now seems to haunt the cellar of the pub and has been seen to try to open up beer barrels.

Chester, Cheshire: Roman Amphitheatre

The apparition of a Roman legionary patrols the ampitheatre and the foundations of the tower. Witnesses have been able to clearly identify the uniform and it is believed that he was a soldier in the XI Legion. The popular story is that he fell in love with a local girl and used to leave his post in order to meet her. One night he was ambushed and killed by Celts.

Chester, Cheshire: The Rows

The odd apparition of an old-fashioned sailor has been seen here. Witnesses suggest that he appears to be searching for something.

Chester, Cheshire: St John's Church

In 1881 the Great Tower partially collapsed. Soon afterwards, a hooded figure, sometimes described as wearing a long cloak, was seen in the ruins. It is believed that it could be a ghostly monk, perhaps Anglo-Saxon. He is best seen near the bowling green.

Chester, Cheshire: St Mary's Hill

The last house was formerly the home of a cowman. He died in his sleep and the cows were left unattended for a number of hours. Consequently, many witnesses claim to have heard the sound of cattle complaining, particularly early in the morning. During World War Two an ARP Warden challenged a man on the premises, but the figure vanished as soon as the light was flashed on him.

Chester, Cheshire: Stanley Place, Watergate Street

A grey lady, said to be contemporary with James Stanley, 7th Earl of Derby, haunts the gallery and the Queen Anne room. He was executed in 1651 for his support of the future Charles II. Although he was executed in Bolton, he can be seen in many of the ground floor rooms. Interestingly, his apparition appears to be in negative form.

Chester, Cheshire: The Top Rank Club, Brook Street

During World War Two staff were startled to hear incendiary bombs falling on the roof of the building. When they checked the premises nothing was found, and the noise was coming from inside the roof. Since then, witnesses have reported hearing heavy boxes being dragged around in the same area, but can offer no explanation for it.

Chester, Cheshire: Vicar's Lane

The apparition of an old woman haunts the top floor of an old convent situated on this road. On many occasions witnesses have not necessarily seen the ghost but have certainly felt its presence.

Chesterfield, Derbyshire: The Pomegranate Theatre

Built in 1893 as an extension to the Civic Hall (constructed as a memorial to Chesterfield's George Stephenson), the Pomegranate Theatre is haunted by a grey man. Many believe that he haunts this building as well as his own former home, Tapton House.

Chesterfield, Derbyshire: The Royal Oak

There seems to be evidence that this building was used by the Knights Templar as a way house during the Middle Ages. The building did not become a public house until 1772. Manifestations include those of the Templars, some of which are believed to be foreign knights. There are also the spirits of an elderly man and woman, and a ghost that has not been described by witnesses.

Chettledown, nr Blandford, Dorset

As a result of a bloody encounter between poachers and gamekeepers, a man lost his hand. The hand was buried in Pimperne churchyard and the man, when he died, was buried in London. The ghostly hand is often seen searching for its body at Bloody Shard Gate.

Chicksands Priory, nr Shefford, Bedfordshire

Although the priory was built in 1150, it became an Air Force officer's mess just after World War Two. In 1954 an airman witnessed a woman with a ruddy face and untidy hair, wearing a dark dress with a white lace collar, sitting on the side of his bed. She was holding a notepad. The apparition rose, walked to the foot of the bed and disappeared. There are several possible explanations, but the most popular is that a nun, having been made pregnant by one of the canons at the priory, was walled up alive after the murder of her lover, and that her ghost is responsible for the haunting. Dr Richard Layton apparently recounted this story in 1534, in a letter to Oliver Cromwell himself. A woman in black was seen in the 1960s in St James's Room disappearing through a wall, and another apparition in white glided past a member of staff.

Chiddingstone Castle, Kent

The ghost of Anne, daughter of the Earl of Leicester of Penshurst, who married Henry Streatfield, haunts the property. In the 400 years up to 1936 the house remained in the Streatfield family. It is, therefore, extremely unlikely that the unfortunate Anne knows that this is no longer the family home.

Chideock, nr Bridport, Dorset

The graveyard here seems to be at the centre of a haunting involving a terrifying black dog. It has been seen by a number of witnesses and always tends to disappear near to the cemetery.

Childe's Tomb, nr Princetown, Dartmoor, Devon

During the reign of Edward III, Childe, a hunter from Plymstock, got caught in a blizzard. He killed his horse and disembowelled it so that he could shelter in the carcass, but died of exposure despite his efforts. He supposedly left a message 'The first that brings me to my grave, my lands at Plymstock he shall have'. The monks at Tavistock undertook to bury the body. Between the wars witnesses saw ghostly figures of monks with a bier at this spot.

Childswickham, Hereford and Worcester: Childswickham House, nr Broadway

A blue lady haunts this house, despite the fact that an attempted exorcism took place in 1870. The ghost is still seen at the windows of the buildings and it is also said that the exorcism failed on account of the fact that one of the twelve priests involved died within a year of the service.

Chilham, Kent: Chilham Castle Keep

Numerous staff and guests have seen the ghostly figure of a mediaeval woman during weekend banquets held in this building. The ghost appears as a fully-formed human, but has the ability to walk or melt into walls. Strange and mysterious sounds have been heard directly above the women's lavatory; they are said to resemble the sounds of heavy furniture being moved. This is despite the fact that there is only a roof and a water system above the lavatories. Others have reported a severe drop in temperature in the room below.

Chilham, Kent: White Horse Inn

Of 15th-century origin, this building had a short career in the 17th century as a vicarage, as it adjoins St Mary's Church. During this time, the Reverend Samson Hieron was the incumbent, but he was dismissed on account of his Non-conformist beliefs. He died in 1677 and was buried in the churchyard. A grey-haired, black-gowned and gaitered Samson Hieron has been seen warming himself beside the inglenook fire in what was once his home.

Chillingham Castle, nr Alnwick, Northumberland

This 12th-century structure has numerous ghosts that reflect its long and varied history. There is a 'radiant boy' in the Pink Room who can be heard crying and moaning at midnight. Witnesses have seen the manifestation wearing a blue suit, surrounded by a strange glow. At the end of the 19th century the skeleton of a child was found in the wall of the Pink Room, but the apparition still haunts the north-west tower. A grey lady, Lady Mary Grey, haunts the castle with her rustling silk dress and an icy chill. Her husband abandoned her for her sister. In the Topiary Garden a spectral funeral cortège has been seen.

Chilton, nr Ramsgate, Kent: Canterbury Road

The manifestation of an awkward monk appears to be one of the many reasons why drivers are often involved in car crashes in this area. Given the fact that this is a major crossroads and close to a railway line, it is not immediately obvious why a monk should haunt this spot. However, he appears in the middle of the road, and is described as wearing a habit, or what looks like a naval duffle coat. It is possible that he is not a monk at all, but an apparition related to World War Two.

Chilton Cantelo, nr Yeovil, Somerset: Higher Chilton Farm

This is the site of the skull of Theophilus Broome, who died in 1670. He requested that his head should be preserved in the house that he loved. He was a Republican, who moved to Somerset to avoid the same fate as Oliver Cromwell. Several owners of the farm in the succeeding years attempted to rid themselves of this gruesome object. When a grave was dug to bury the skull in the nearby churchyard, the spade broke and other attempts were deterred by strange noises. In 1977 two researchers removed the skull and were involved in a car accident en route to London. The skull remains in the house in a cabinet above the door.

Chingford, Essex: Chingford Mount Cemetery, Old Church Road

Although some believe that the footsteps and strange ghostly voices can be attributed to either Lord Nelson or Dick Turpin, their spirits are probably kept busy elsewhere. It is more likely that this haunting relates to a member of one of the royal hunting parties that roamed the area. The land was once part of Lady Hamilton's estate, hence the Nelson connection. The specifics of the haunting are that a man on a black horse is seen in the area of the Cemetery Lodge, riding slowly over the grass. He is accompanied by the sounds of footsteps and voices.

Chingle Hall, nr Preston, Lancashire

Built in 1260 by Adam de Singleton, Chingle Hall was an important centre for Catholics after the Reformation. The ghostly manifestation of a Franciscan monk has been seen both in the hall and walking over the bridge. Witnesses also state that they have heard footsteps and that doors open and close of their own accord. John Wall, who was executed in Worcester in 1679, was born here, but his head was kept in a convent in France until the French Revolution. It was then returned home. During the late 1960s, two witnesses were sleeping in what was believed to be a haunted room. They not only heard footsteps, but also experienced a strange light, which hovered in the room and then disappeared into a wall. The point of disappearance is said to be the resting place of Wall's skull. There is also said to be a body sealed up near a window in one of the rooms, which might have a connection with the Franciscan apparition. When a medium visited the hall, it was established that the body does have something to do with the hauntings, as there are secret documents sealed in with the remains. The medium went on to say that if the body was exhumed and the papers read, then the hauntings would cease. Other witnesses claim to have seen a second monk, black-caped and cowled, praying with the first monk in front of a wooden cross.

Cholderton, Wiltshire: Cholderton House

In 1896 a clergyman either fell, jumped or was pushed down the well. His spirit haunts the sacred druid grove of yew trees. His slippers were found neatly placed beside the well, giving the impression of a suicide. Strange noises, but no physical mani-festation, constitute the haunting.

Christchurch, Dorset: Priory Church

Within the Draper Chapel, named after John Draper, the last Prior of Christchurch, who died in 1552, the apparition of a monk has been seen. It is said to be Draper himself, who saved the church during the dissolution through his friendship with Thomas Cromwell. The church itself boasts strange tapping noises, which are either triggered or stopped by building work in the church. During the tapping periods one of the doors in the south of the priory opens without

reason. Also, there are strong smells of incense during these times.

Christchurch, Dorset: Three Arches Bend

The Rattenbury murder case in the 1930s received a great deal of publicity at the time. Alma Rattenbury and her young lover, George Stoner, were both tried for the murder of her elderly husband. Stoner was found guilty and sentenced to death. Four days later Alma went to Three Arches Bend and stabbed herself six times, puncturing her heart three times before she fell into the water. By all accounts Alma had been broken by the events, but her actions managed to save her lover, whose death sentence was commuted to life. In fact, he served only seven years. On still June evenings the apparition of a silent female ghost can be seen sitting by the water. It then stabs itself repeatedly and falls face down into the water. The key date is 4 June.

Christleton, nr Chester, Cheshire: Plough Lane

A gibbet once stood at the end of this lane and many individuals met their end here, two of whom still haunt the spot and are believed to be Irishmen.

Chudleigh Knighton, South Devon

A ghostly dwarf is said to lead those who will follow him to a cache of buried treasure. South of the village a new bridge crosses the Teign; the Dewar, or the Devil, haunts it.

Church Lawford, Warwickshire

A phantom vehicle in the form of a large truck with dim headlights may speed toward you on the old road between Rugby and Coventry. Whatever your reaction, the truck will continue its journey, passing through you or past you and then disappearing into the distance. Many motorists have suffered near-fatal crashes as they have attempted to leave the road or swerved into the path of oncoming traffic.

Church Stanton, Somerset

The swirling mist at Merlan Corner sometimes transforms into the shape of a headless rider. Witnesses have also stated that they have heard the sound of a trotting horse when this manifestation makes its appearance.

Cirencester, Gloucestershire: The Black Horse Inn

Said to be the town's oldest inn, the Black Horse was the site of an exorcism in 1933, during which the name James was written on one of the bedroom windows. The ghost that haunts this pub is described as being an obese old woman, wearing a fawn dress and sporting an angry expression.

Cirencester, Gloucestershire: The King's Head

After being attacked by supporters of James Stuart, Lord Lovelace died of his injuries in the pub. It is believed that it is his apparition, which has been described as looking like a royalist Cavalier, that haunts the building. In 1980 poltergeist activity became so intense that it literally shook some guests out of their beds.

Clachtoll, nr Lochinver, Highlands

A ghostly black dog with burning eyes and a human-like face, topped with deer-like antlers, has been seen around the area. It is said that if the animal gallops past you or barks at you more than once then you will die. Legend has it that as it disappears it cackles like a hyena.

Clacton-on-sea, Essex

Opposite the Martello tower is the site of an old ballroom, once part of a Butlins Holiday Camp. A soldier was involved in a fight in the ballroom and was killed. His ghost has been seen on many occasions.

Claife, nr Ambleside, Cumbria

In 1635 nearly 50 wedding guests died when their over-laden boat sank in Windermere. It may be this story or that of Thomas Lancaster, who poisoned his wife, six other family members and a servant in 1671 and was hanged at his birthplace, that explains the eerie voice and apparition seen here. A ferryman, before the car ferries were established, heard someone calling for passage across the lake. He rode across to collect the passenger, but returned terrified and died the next day. The spirit that caused this death is known as the Caller of Claife.

Claines, nr Worcester, Worcestershire: The Old Mug House

It is said that this pub is the only one in the country to stand on consecrated ground. It was probably built when the neighbouring church was rebuilt in the 15th century. Various landlords, past and present, have reported hearing strange footsteps going down the stairs, items going missing and even on one occasion a plate of biscuits having been eaten during the night. In the 1990s the landlord was sitting in the lounge eating a meal with friends and neighbours when they all heard a shelf full of glasses being swept onto the floor. This kind of activity continued for several months. Dogs are very uneasy in the kitchen and near the cellar of the pub, and on several occasions beer and cider taps have been turned off in the cellar. Despite having infrared security devices, the pub still has some kind of manifestation moving about in the middle of the night. Doors will slam and it is only then that the alarms are set off. A possible explanation concerns a strange, misty figure, seen in the cellar in the 1950s. Beyond this nobody knows who may be responsible for the haunting.

Claydon House, nr Whitchurch, Buckinghamshire

The house is haunted by the spirit of Sir Edmund Verney, the king's standard-bearer at the Battle of Edgehill in 1642. Cornered by Parliamentarians, he refused to give up the colours. They killed him and even had to hack off his hand to take the standard. It was recaptured, along with Sir Edmund's hand, which was recognised by the signet ring. The hand was sent for burial at Claydon; the rest of his body was never found. His phantom now seeks to reunite the body with the hand. He is often seen on the Red Stairs. There is also a grey lady in the Rose Room. This may be Florence Nightingale, whose sister Parthenope married Sir Harry Verney.

Clayton-le-Moors, nr Blackburn, Lancashire: Dunkenhalgh

A French governess, whose name was Lucette, haunts the ballroom and grounds on Christmas Eve. She was seduced and then abandoned by a member of the Petre family, who owned the house until 1940. She committed suicide by throwing herself off Boggart's Bridge.

Cleve Court, nr Alcol, Kent

The spirit of an unhappy woman is seen pacing around the room in which her cruel husband imprisoned her. She is said to appear in the form of a grey lady, with an old-fashioned dress. She is seen standing by the beds of sleeping children, and is observed by children in the house, adding fuel to the notion that she may have died childless.

Cliffsend, Kent

This is both the former site of a gibbet and a burial ground for criminals and suicides. A glowing light has been seen here which takes the form of a human figure.

Clifton Hampden, Oxfordshire

The ghost of Sarah Fletcher has haunted the Georgian house, Courtiers, for some years. She arrived just in time to stop her husband, Captain Fletcher RN, from bigamously marrying an heiress. He fled to sea and she hanged herself on 7 June 1769. She achieved this by tying a pocket-handkerchief around her neck, and that to a cord which was attached to the curtain rails around the bed. She has been seen in a black silk cloak, with a purple ribbon in her auburn hair.

Clouds Hill, nr Dorchester, Dorset

This is a little way from the former home of T.E. Lawrence, or Lawrence of Arabia. Since Lawrence died in a motorcycle accident, it would not be unreasonable to link the ghostly sound of a motorcycle engine with him. However, another motorcyclist did die near this spot a few years ago.

Cobham, nr Leatherhead, Surrey

Campanologists in St Andrew's Church claim to have seen the particularly unusual apparition of a blue donkey. The uncharitable would say that they had perhaps spent too long in the local public house, but other witnesses also claim to have seen this manifestation.

Coggeshall, Essex

This is said to be the most haunted town in Essex. The Cistercian abbey, built in around 1140, and the gatehouse have been sites of hauntings. A house in Church Street is also said to have restless spirits. The Guild House in Market End boasts mysterious lights in an attic window at night. A little old man has also been seen at the foot of a bed in this building.

Colchester, Essex: Colchester Castle

In May 1656 the Quaker martyr James Parnell died in the dungeon of the castle. He was made to climb a rope from the dungeon in order to get his food. On one fatal occasion he fell from the rope and died. His ghost is still seen here.

Colchester, Essex: The Red Lion Hotel

In 1633 Alice Mellor was murdered in one of the rooms. The bedroom was so badly haunted by her spirit that it had to be bricked up. It was, however, reopened in 1972.

Cold Ashton, Gloucestershire

Olive Snell, the portrait painter, got lost looking for her friend Lady Winifred Pennoyer's house. She stopped at a house with wrought-iron gates, surmounted with pineapples. She opened the gate and rang the front doorbell. A butler appeared and gave her instructions on how to get to the friend's house, in return for which she gave him half a crown. Recounting the story to Lady Winifred, her friend exclaimed that the house was empty. They went over the next day to check; the gate was locked, but they found the key in the garden shed and went up to the front door, only to find a half crown lying on the step.

Cold Norton, Essex

De Laches House has a bedroom that no animal will enter. Apparently, at 2am a small woman in a Victorian dress appears at the window. Her facial appearance is said to be very frightening.

Colebrook, nr Crediton, Devon

The hilly lanes around this area are said to be haunted by a particularly strange and aggressive manifestation. Witnesses claim to have seen the apparition of a red monkey near the village. The monkey has sometimes attacked people.

Coleford, Devon: The New Inn

An apparition known as Sebastian haunts this thatched, 13th-century former monks retreat. The ghost has been seen in many of the bedrooms and witnesses have also complained about icy breezes and doors with a mind of their own, which accompany his presence.

Colnbrook, nr Windsor, Berkshire: The Ostrich

Dating back to 1106, the building was originally used as a hostelry and hospice for pilgrims. During the 14th century it was run by the Jarmans, who were early examples of serial killers on an enormous scale. They had a bed built in one of the bedrooms over the kitchen, which could be collapsed through the floor by removing two bolts. The unfortunate sleeping guest would then tumble into a cauldron of boiling water. The body would then be dumped into the river and the valuables disposed of. One of their last victims was a rich clothier from Reading, by the name of Thomas Cole. After the body was disposed of, the Jarmans went to the stable to get rid of the horse. They had left the stable door open and the horse had wandered off. One of the inn's servants found it and brought it back, but something made Mr Jarman panic and run off. The servant went straight to the local JP and after the bed was discovered Mrs Jarman confessed to the murder. Soon afterward, Mr Jarman was picked up in Windsor Forest. Just before they were both executed they admitted to at least 60 other murders. It is the apparition of Thomas Cole that still haunts the inn.

Coltishall, Norfolk: The Red House

At one time, this Victorian building was used to house RAF personnel. During the 1970s, a family briefly moved into the house and experienced a number of strange episodes. They reported feeling very sudden drops in temperature, particularly in the kitchen and the scullery, despite the fact that the rest of the house was warm. They also sensed a presence, perhaps a woman or an old couple, benevolent and clearly happy that the house was being lived in once more. It is believed that the manifestations may be of previous occupants of the house.

Combe Bank, nr Sundridge, Kent

Lady Frederick Campbell, wife of Lord Ferrers, haunts the path. Ferrers was hanged at Tyburn in 1760 for the murder of his steward, who had given evidence against him in divorce hearings brought by his wife. Before he died, he cursed her to suffer a death more painful than his own. In 1807 she died in a fire at the house. The only part of her body that was found after the fire was her thumb. Her spirit is doomed to search for the rest of her physical body for evermore.

Combe Gibbet, nr Newbury, Berkshire

At nearly 1,000ft, this spot on the top of Inkpen Hill was the last resting place of many criminals. Several witnesses have reported seeing and hearing strange visions and noises in and around the area. A man and his lover, who drowned the man's wife but were overheard by his son, are seen along with a mother and father who drowned their children at Murderer's Pool, which is located nearby.

Combe Manor, nr Newbury, Berkshire

This is an ex-priory where Charles II brought Nell Gwyn. Period figures have been seen in the garden and the chanting of monks has been heard in the house. In the recent past a

small skeleton was discovered under the stairs.

Combermere Abbey, nr Whitchurch, Shropshire

The Cotton family acquired the site at the time of the dissolution of the monasteries. The abbey is haunted not only by a distraught little girl, thought to warn of an immediate death in the family, but also by ghostly monks.

Combe Sydenham, Somerset

The white figure of the ghost of Sir George Sydenham rides a headless grey horse. He was the father of a girl who was once engaged to marry Sir Frances Drake. There does not appear to be any particular reason why his apparition has been seen.

Comlongon Castle, Clarencefield, Dumfries and Galloway

In 1564, Marian Carruthers was either murdered or committed suicide shortly after having been forced into an arranged marriage. She disappeared soon after the wedding, but her body was not found until some months later. It is said that she was buried without a funeral, and as a result, her restless spirit still haunts the grounds of the castle.

Compton Abdale, Gloucestershire: Puesdown Inn, High Street

On several occasions, the manifestation of a man dressed in dark clothes, astride a horse, has been seen riding silently away from this 13th-century coaching inn. At regular intervals scuffling noises and footsteps have been heard in one of the rooms above the main doorway. It is said that both phenomena are highwayman-related. There is a tale of a highwayman who was shot while trying to rob someone on the nearby road, and then fled to the inn for sanctuary. The wound was a mortal one and he passed away in the night, leaving only his spirit to haunt the building.

Compton Castle, nr Torquay, Devon

The castle is said to be haunted by an apparition that creates an eerie and unpleasant atmosphere, although nothing has been seen. Unfortunately the identity and purpose of the ghost is not known.

Congleton, Cheshire: The Lion and Swan

First registered as an inn in around 1496, this pub is remarkable for its apparition of a naked lady. She has been seen on several occasions and witnesses report that she only wears clogs! The pub also boasts a magnificent carved fireplace.

Conington, nr Peterborough, Cambridgeshire

On 16 October 1948 Colonel Mellows drove his car straight into the path of the 4 o'clock London train on the East Coast main line. It was an unfortunate accident, which resulted in the death of the colonel, but came as no great surprise. Motorists wishing to pass this way had to open the gates to cross the railway line. From then on signalmen at the nearby Conington box could see the tragic accident being replayed over and over again.

Coniston, nr Ambleside, Cumbria

The ghost of an old miner can be seen clinging to the rock face of Simon's Nick. Other witnesses, mainly climbers, have heard strange voices while they have been climbing this rock. The area around Coniston had numerous lead and copper mines and it is presumed that one of the unfortunate victims of a mining accident still haunts this place.

Conwy, Gwynedd: Plas Mawr, High Street

A castle boasting 15ft-thick walls in the shape of a Welsh harp surrounds this mansion. The Lantern Room, in which it is said a 16th-century owner killed himself after finding the bodies of his wife and small children, is haunted by the sounds of a man frantically searching. The owner had left a doctor to care for his wife and children, but could not find him on his return. A misty shape is often seen at the bottom of the stairway, accompanied by a sharp drop in temperature. The possible explanation may be that the mother and children lay on these steps prior to their removal to the Lantern Room for treatment.

Corby Castle, nr Carlisle, Cumbria

An apparition that neatly straddles the supernatural and mythology has often been seen here. Known as the 'radiant boy', the manifestation appears to be a child, dressed in white, who seems to fluoresce a brilliant white. It is said that those who see the manifestation will achieve power and fortune but will meet a violent end. One such was Lord Castlereagh, who became an MP at 21, later becoming Secretary of State for War, Foreign Secretary and Leader of the House of Commons. He became insane and committed suicide in 1822. The most stunning account of the ghost relates to the rector of Greystoke, who observed the boy standing by his bedside for some minutes, before he disappeared into the side of a chimney.

Corfe, Dorset: Corfe Castle

This was one of the castles built by William the Conqueror, but it is said that it was the site of a former Saxon hunting lodge. Edward the Martyr was murdered here as part of a plot by his stepmother to clear the way for her own son, Ethelred the Unready. It is said that the strange lights and headless figure that can be seen on the road below the castle relate to this incident. Other theories hold that the manifestation is that of Lady Banks, who commanded royalists there during the Civil War. King John also used the castle as a prison, and 22 French noblemen starved to death in the dungeons.

Corfe Mullen, Dorset: Corfe Lodge

The apparition of a lavender lady has been seen on a number of occasions by a variety of staff, family members and guests. She is described as being a beautiful young woman, with long plaits on either side of her head. She tends to be seen in the bedrooms and stands over those asleep until they notice her, before fading away.

Corfe Mullen, Dorset: Lavender Farm

In addition to occasional sightings of the lavender lady of Corfe Lodge, farm workers have seen a phantom coach and a strange-looking figure that resembles John Bull wandering around the area. The farm is famous for its lavender, which is distilled and sold as perfume.

Corgarff Castle, nr Tomintoul, Grampian

Built in 1537 as a hunting lodge, Corgarff Castle was besieged in 1571 by Adam Gordon of Auchindoun. He burned it to the ground, killing Margaret Forbes and 26 other people. Witnesses report hearing the screams of the victims as they were burned to death, a clear indication that their spirits are still restless.

Corsham, Wiltshire

At under 3ft tall, a misshapen dwarf is said to haunt the churchyard. His clothes might suggest that he was a monk. Although the apparition has been seen on numerous occasions it is not known who it is or why it is there.

Corsock Hill, nr Dumfries, Dumfries and Galloway

A headless phantom piper is said to play his pipes furiously on the hill. It is believed that the apparition may be that of a man who tried to warn the area of an oncoming enemy.

Cortachy Castle, Forfar, Tayside

A ghostly drummer can be heard in and around the castle prior to the death of a member of the Ogilvy clan. The drummer had fallen in love with the countess, and the Earl tied him to his drum and threw him out of one of the windows of the castle. Another story tells that the drummer was from either Clan Campbell or Clan Lindsay, and was captured by the Earl of Airlie and thrown from the battlements. The drummer was heard prior to the death of Lady Airlie in the mid-19th century, and at various other times over the years.

Corwen, Denbighshire: Owain Glyndwr Hotel

Originally built as a monastery in 1329, but later converted into a coaching inn, the building is haunted not by a monk, but by the lover of a monk. A local woman was having an affair with one of the monks until the abbot found out and sent him away from the area, never to return. The woman was never told and continued to wait for him. She does so even now, from beyond the grave.

Cotehele, nr Calstock, Cornwall: Cotehele House

The house was built in 1353 and acquired by the National Trust in 1947. There are many stories attached to the house, including a powerful smell of perfume that is often described as being herbal, and the sound of plaintive music. A man was killed beneath the archway in the 17th century, his blood stained a stone that was subsequently moved to Cotehele Quay. The 5th Earl of Mount Edgcumbe and his nurse saw a woman in white pass through the bedroom. The ghost of a young girl with long hair, wearing a white dress, has been seen on one of the staircases.

Coughton Court, nr Alcester, Warwickshire

From the beginning of the 15th century this was the home of the Throckmorton family, well-known Catholics. The apparition that haunts the Tapestry Bedroom is believed to be one of the daughters of the family, who was married to one of the conspirators involved in the Gunpowder Plot. She is described as being a pink lady, and she walks through the bedroom into the dining room and then descends the staircase.

Coventry, West Midlands: Coventry Cathedral

Considering its ruin during World War Two, it is not surprising that the sounds of German aircraft have been heard over the remains of this ruined mediaeval cathedral. Several witnesses claim to have heard the piston-engine aircraft droning over, just as they did during the war.

Coventry, West Midlands: Rugby Road

The apparition of a ghostly lorry with dimmed sidelights haunts the road to Rugby. It approaches cars on the wrong side of the road, but disappears just as a crash seems imminent.

Coverham, nr Leyburn, North Yorkshire

Just after World War Two, peat diggers on the moor discovered the body of a woman. This may explain the manifestation of a black lady who has been seen walking from the church toward Middleham.

Crackenthorpe, nr Appleby, Cumbria

Elizabeth Sleddall was married to Lancelot Machell during the 17th century. She reverted to her maiden name after Lancelot's death, when she discovered that she had been disinherited in his will. When she died, she made numerous appearances in the form of a banshee to Machells on their deathbeds. In desperation they disinterred her body and buried it beneath a boulder in the riverbed. Her ghost still appears in the hall once a year, having made the walk from the river. Locals call the ghost Peg Sneddle and she is most likely to be seen in September. A phantom coach bearing a ghostly woman, drawn by four black horses and manned by a ghostly coachman and outriders, also blights the area. This may be Peg, but her ghost has been seen walking around the area as well.

Crafthole, Whitsand Bay, Cornwall: The Finnygook Inn

The Finnygook Inn was once known as the New Inn and was used by a well-known smuggler named Finny. Finny and some of his gang were killed in a skirmish when the authorities unexpectedly raided the inn. The ghost of Finny is said to revisit the old headquarters of his gang frequently, but it appears to be a happy experience for him. In 1950 the managers of the brewery decided to rename the premises after Finny, hence the new name of The Finnygook Inn.

Cranbrook, Bakers Cross, Kent

This is said to be the home of the English pirate Bluebeard, Sir John 'Bloody' Baker. His wife saw Sir John and his gang carrying a body out of the house. The corpse's stiffened hand got caught in the banister, Sir John hacked it off and it fell into the lap of the hidden wife. There was a ring on one of the fingers, and this was the evidence that brought Sir John to the gallows. His ghost is still to be seen here.

Cranbrook, Kent: The Pest House (The Pestilence House), Frythe Walk

Built in 1369, the building was first used as a hospital for plague victims. Rather ghoulishly, the bodies were simply buried in the cellar. This area was sealed when the building was converted into a private house ten years later. When a second wave of plague came in the 1660s, the building was again used as a hospital and the cellars became the preferred burial site once more. Among the many apparitions that haunt this place of death is a woman called Theresa Benenden, the unmarried daughter of the house. She had been receiving £8 as an annuity, but the payments stopped and she failed to have the decision reversed in court. She committed suicide in 1779, and chose the cellar as the place of her death. Many witnesses have seen her in the upper part of the house and on the staircase.

Cranmere Pool, nr Okehampton, Devon

The ghost of Benjamin Gayer, known locally as Bingie Gear, haunts this place. He was a former mayor of Okehampton. His spirit sometimes takes the form of a misshapen dwarf or a black colt. This is as a result of an exorcism by 24 clerics in the 17th century.

Craster, nr Alnwick, Northumberland: Craster Tower

Although the bulk of the building was not completed until 1730, the Pele Tower is 14th-century and there are still vestiges of the Anglo-Saxon settlement. A grey lady has been seen in the tower. Her apparition enters the front door, goes up the stairs into a bedroom and then into the drawing room. Witnesses also state that they have heard rustling silk and footsteps. Extensive poltergeist and aural hauntings have occurred on at least two occasions when members of the Craster family have died in the building. The sound is described as being very loud and rather like someone using a sledgehammer. On investigation, nothing was found and there was no obvious damage. In the 17th century, a Craster family member killed an opposing Fenwick over a land dispute, by running his throat through with a sword. Consequently, witnesses have seen the sword fight re-enacted in the kitchen garden, together with the sounds of a man gasping for breath. An invisible phantom coach is heard to stop outside the front door, then make its way around the back of the house toward the stables.

Crathes Castle, nr Ballater, Grampian

After 40 years construction, the castle was finally ready for occupation by the Burnet family in the early part of the 17th century. A green lady haunts the room now known as the Green Lady's Room. There is some dispute over the exact circumstances surrounding the haunting, but the story seems to revolve around a young Burnet, dating from around the time that the castle was completed, who fell pregnant after an affair with a local gillie. It is here that the two stories diverge. Either he was sacked and sent away and she died of a broken heart, or both the girl and the child 'conveniently' disappeared. The latter seems more appropriate given that in the middle of the 19th century the skeletons of a girl and young child were found buried under a hearthstone. Many people strongly believe that the family murdered them both to avoid a scandal. The Burnet family was certainly plagued by the ghost during the 18th century, but nowadays she is more likely to be heard than seen. Witnesses describe her as looking very sad and carrying a baby in her arms. Her appearance is also linked to an imminent death in the Burnet family.

Crawley, West Sussex: The George, High Street

Probably built in the early part of the 17th century, this pub was an important coaching inn for the area. In order to dissuade would-be highwaymen, the George had a dedicated night watchman. Mark Hurston's spirit, still restless and watchful, patrols the corridors of the hotel to this day.

Crazywell, nr Burrator, Dartmoor

Also known as Claiswell or Classenwell, this place is scrupulously avoided by locals at night, because of a mysterious voice. It comes from the middle of the pool and announces the name of the next person in the neighbourhood to die.

Creech Hill, nr Milton Clevedon, Somerset

A tall ghostly figure, said to have a terrifying and maniacal laugh, haunts this area at night. It is said that you may ward this spirit off if you have a lantern and a hazel staff tipped with iron.

Creslow Manor, nr Whitchurch, Buckinghamshire

In 1120, the land here was owned by the Knights Templar and later the Knights Hospitaller of St John of Jerusalem. After the dissolution of the monasteries it passed into the hands of the Crown and was eventually leased to Cornelius Holland in 1653. When the monarchy was restored in 1660, the manor was leased to Sir Thomas Clifford. His wife, Rosamund Clifford, haunts one of the bedrooms, with her light footsteps and rustling silk dress. In the 1850s, a former High Sheriff of Buckingham stayed the night in the Haunted Chamber. He was not concerned and refused a lantern or candle, although he did take a box of matches, two pistols and a cutlass. Morning came and the man did not appear for breakfast. There was no reply to knocks on the door, and a jug of water left for him outside the room was still on the floor. At first they thought that he had left early, but his horse was in the stable. Eventually he came into the room with a strange story to recount. Just after midnight, the soft tread of a woman's feet and the rustling of silk had awakened him, but when he investigated he found nothing. He went back to sleep and awoke again to louder sounds. Again he sprang out of bed and lunged toward the direction of the noises. There was nothing to be seen and the sounds simply faded away. Unable to sleep, he went for a long walk to consider what the explanation may have been. He had come to no certain conclusions.

Cresswell, nr Morpeth, Northumberland

During the Dark Ages some local fishermen killed a man that they believed to be a pirate on the beach. He was, in fact, the lover of a woman who lived in a tower overlooking the beach. The man was a Viking and had landed to visit the woman. As a result, she appears as a white lady on the shoreline, close to the tower from which she saw her lover being murdered. There are also spectral hounds in the area that do not appear to be hell-hounds, but more closely resemble hunting dogs.

Crewe, Cheshire: The Lyceum

The manifestation of a ballerina who committed suicide by hanging herself in one of the dressing rooms has been seen. An actor believed to be of the Victorian period sometimes accompanies her. They have both been seen standing at the back of the auditorium.

Crewkerne, Somerset
The main road to Chard is haunted by the sound of galloping horses and the sight of a phantom battle between smugglers and customs men. Several witnesses have also reported hearing the sound of a wounded customs man fighting for breath.

Crockern Tor, Dartmoor
Riding a skeleton horse, Old Crockern's ghost can still be seen in the area. He is said to be buried beneath a mound.

Croft, nr Leicester, Leicestershire
In December 1124, Ralph Basset executed 44 locals for evading tax. Six of them were brutally tortured by having their eyes and testicles cut out before they were hanged. On stormy nights in December you may still hear their screams. Some witnesses also report seeing white figures on the hill at night, although these are believed to be the apparitions of ghostly druids. The hill, for them, was a sacred place.

Croft Castle, nr Leominster, Herefordshire
The Oak Room of this 14th or 15th-century castle boasts the apparition of a large, leather-clad manifestation, widely believed to be the Welsh leader, Owen Glyndwr. Another male apparition is often seen, dressed in Elizabethan clothing, walking through the walls of the hall.

Croglin, nr Brampton, Cumbria: Low Hall
A vampire is said to stalk these parts and was once cornered in a vault in the churchyard after having attacked a young girl. It was shot and the body was burned. This

happened in the 17th century, but many believe that the vampire still roams the area in spectral form.

Cromer, Norfolk
The road from Runton to Overstrand is known as Shuck's Lane. If you are unlucky enough to encounter a dog that is the size of a small cow and has large, yellow eyes, do not look it in the eye or you will be dead within the year.

Crondall, nr Farnham, Hampshire: All Saint's Church
Strong Civil War connections seem to be responsible for the hauntings in and around the church. The manifestation of a Roundhead horseman in armour can be seen in the road leading down to the church. Within the church several witnesses have seen a soldier in thigh-length boots kneeling to pray before he vanishes. During the Civil War Roundheads used the church. On 27 January 1645, after a brief skirmish with royalists, the Roundheads captured their foes and executed them near the church. Also, just after Wellington's victory at Waterloo, a messenger carrying the news from Portsmouth to Aldershot, was attacked and murdered by footpads. The ghostly sounds of his gasping breath can be heard in Alma Lane. Strangely, Crondall also boasts a flock of ghostly sheep.

Cropthorne, nr Evesham, Worcestershire: Cropthorne Heath
In the middle of the 18th century a yeoman farmer called Dutton died and his funeral procession passed across the heath. The manifestation of Old Dutton's funeral can still be seen taking the same route.

Cropthorne, nr Evesham, Worcestershire: Holland House
The apparition of a Welsh soldier, who died

in 1651 at the Battle of Worcester, haunts this house. There is also a grey lady and the manifestation of Mrs Holland, an early occupant of the house, who can be seen in the library.

Croston, Lancashire: Royal Umpire Museum, Moor Road

The ghostly figure of a woman, now known as the Sascoe lady, has been seen since the removal of a stone cross from the garden of the museum. She was seen standing near a bus stop beside the museum, prompting a bus driver to stop, thinking that she was a passenger. The apparition walks down from Sascoe Farm until she reaches the bus stop. Witnesses have also reported hearing the sound of heavy breathing. When ghost researchers visited the museum in 1975, they were subjected to a shower of stones that may or may not have been supernaturally related.

Crowland, nr Spalding, Lincolnshire: The Abbey Hotel

Henry Girdlestone, a local farmer, bet his assembled cronies in the bar that he could walk a thousand miles in a thousand hours. He set off in 1844 and managed to cover 1025 miles in 1076 hours. His footsteps can still be heard in the attic where, no doubt, he slept for hours after his feat.

Crumbles, nr Eastbourne, Sussex

Irene Monro, who was murdered in 1920, and Emily Kaye, butchered in 1924, have both been seen haunting the place of their death.

Cuckfield, West Sussex: The King's Head

Geranium Jane haunts the pub. She was either the victim of an accident, or murdered. Either way, a pot of geraniums struck her on the head. Local gossip at the time claimed that she was pregnant and that somebody wanted her out of the way. It is interesting to follow this train of thought, as she only tends to appear if one of the male members of staff at the pub is being unfaithful to his partner.

Cullen House, nr Banff, Grampian

The 6th Earl of Findlater was something of a madman. He murdered his most faithful servant and then cut his own throat. Known as the Mad Earl, he still haunts the Church Room, where the murder and suicide took place.

Culloden, nr Inverness, Highlands

Culloden Moor saw the last pitched battle fought on British soil. On 16 April 1746, hopelessly outnumbered by the Duke of Cumberland, Bonnie Prince Charlie's Catholic highlanders were slaughtered. No quarter was asked or given and most of the dead rebels were buried under a huge cairn of stones on the battlefield. Many witnesses have seen and heard strange things that hark back to the one-hour pitched battle that settled the issue. A dark-haired highlander, said to be wearing the Stuart red tartan, has been seen resting by the stones. Others have seen the two phantom armies locked in combat, their tartans identifying them as the ghostly figures fight amid the din and smoke of combat.

Culmhead Blagdon, nr Taunton, Somerset: Holman Clavel Inn

The ghost that haunts this public house is known as Charlie. Legend has it that he was a defrocked monk, and he has been seen in the bar, one of the bedrooms and other places within the inn. The building is over 600 years old, and may well have been a rest house for pilgrims en route to Glastonbury. Charlie is said to enjoy playing skittles at night and pads around the building, sometimes generating sounds of falling stones or glass being broken. On investigation, nothing is ever found, nor is any sign of his nocturnal movements discovered.

Culzean Castle, nr Girvan, Strathclyde

In the 16th century, Gilbert Kennedy, 4th Earl of Cassillie, held the castle. He captured Alan Stuart, Commendator of Crossraguel Abbey, and had him taken to the Black Vault. After having him stripped he proceeded to roast him in front of a huge fire until he signed over the lands of the abbey to him. Kennedy was fined £2,000 by the Privy Council, a huge sum in those days, but kept the land. He was also forced to pay Alan Stuart a life pension. On Sunday mornings you may still hear the sound of a fire crackling, accompanied by the screams of a man being burned. In the 1970s, three servants saw the apparition of another character contemporary with all of this. It is believed that it was the ghost of a Kennedy piper, murdered in the castle.

Cumnor, nr Oxford, Oxfordshire: Cumnor Place

Despite the fact that the Elizabethan house here was replaced in 1810, it is still haunted by Amy Robsart, wife of Robert Dudley, Earl of Leicester. She died in mysterious circumstances in 1560. Dudley was probably having an affair with Elizabeth I. Amy's neck was broken when her body was found at the foot of the stairs. The fact that her ghost still haunts the house may give a clue about whether she was murdered or whether this was simply an accident. She also haunts the grounds, in particular, Lady Dudley's Pond, where attempts to calm her spirit by exorcism have failed in the past. The water in this pond is said never to freeze.

Cupar, St Andrew's, Fife: The Royal Hotel

This 19th-century building was constructed on the site of the graveyard of the nearby monastery. While the hotel is plagued with poltergeist activity, a more obvious manifestation in the form of a cowled monk has also been seen in the Function Room.

Curdworth, Warwickshire: St Nicholas and St Peter Ad Vincula

Dating back to the Norman period, this graveyard was used to bury a great many casualties of both sides during the English Civil War. It is also believed that there is gold buried with the bodies, but the would-be treasure hunter must first gain the approval of a headless ghost. There is also the apparition of a green lady, said to be tall and wearing a long green dress. She has been seen wandering in between the graves. A possible explanation is that she is contemporary with the English Civil War and that she is a woman who committed suicide after her husband's or lover's body was cast into one of the mass graves.

Curry Mallet Manor House, nr Taunton, Somerset

A male and a female, dressed in Elizabethan clothes, haunt this building. It is thought that the woman may have been a housekeeper. Clashing swords are heard in the Banqueting Hall and the rustle of silk upstairs. Footsteps are also heard in the Minstrel's Gallery.

Cutcombe, Somerset

A phantom hearse, drawn by four black headless horses, haunts the sharp bend at Sully, near Cutcombe. A number of accidents have been attributed to the sighting of this phantom coach.

Cwn, nr Rhyl, Clwyd: Blue Lion Inn

This building originally housed monks that had built the nearby church, but in the 17th century it became a farm. In 1646, a farmer and his two sons occupied the site and one evening the local beadle had to be called to break up a fight between them. A couple of days later, he was called back and told that one of the sons, John Henry, had left the farm and gone to find his fortune abroad. From then on the buildings were haunted by what is believed to be the ghost of John Henry. Footsteps have been heard above the bar and walking along a corridor and a 'rattling bang' has also been reported. Other witnesses have seen the apparition of man dressed in working clothes, tied at the knee with string and some sort of sacking over his shoulders. Sometimes the manifestation also wears a waistcoat. Toward the end of the 19th century, the church was enlarged and some of the graves had to be moved. When one of the coffins was exhumed, the diggers found another skeleton lying on top. It is now believed that the father and the other son killed John Henry, buried him and made up the emigration story.

D
Dallington Church to Durham

Dallington Church, Northamptonshire

A strange apparition of a congregation said to be made up of 'bubbles' haunts this 13th-century church. This was how the manifestation was described by two schoolgirls in 1907. It seems that this is some kind of time slip, and the transparent ghosts, kneeling in prayer in the pews, are a whole ghostly congregation from the past. It is quite rare for ghosts to be transparent; more often they appear as whole or partial figures that seem to have substance like a living thing. The church is also haunted by a grey lady, the

ghost of a former Lady Spencer, who appears dressed in a grey cloak.

Darley, nr Matlock, Derbyshire: Ghost Lane

Running alongside the churchyard, this road is haunted by the apparition of a peddler who was murdered in the 17th century. His sad manifestation has been seen on several occasions, making its way along the road that was the scene of his death.

Darlington, Co. Durham

The Reverend Harry Kendal, a congregational minister in late 19th-century Darlington, investigated the following strange statement by James Durham, who was a night watchman at the Darlington and Stockton Station. The statement was dated 9 December 1890:

'I was a night-watchman at the old Darlington and Stockton Railway Station, at the town of Darlington, a few yards from the first station that ever existed. I was there 15 years. I used to go on duty about 8pm and came off at 6am. I had been there a little while, perhaps two or three years, and at about midnight, or 12.30am, I was feeling rather cold standing here and there, so I said to myself, I will go away down and get something to eat. There was a porters' room, where a fire was kept on, and a coalhouse was connected to it. So I went down the steps, took off my overcoat and had just sat down on the bench opposite the fire, and turned up the gas, when a strange man came out of the coalhouse, followed by a black retriever dog. As soon as he entered, my eye was upon him and his eye upon me, and we intently watched each other as he moved on to the front of the fire. There he stood, looking at me, and a curious smile came over his countenance. He had a stand-up collar and a cut-away coat, with gilt buttons and a Scotch cap. All at once he struck at me and I

had the impression that he had hit me. I upped with my fist and struck back at him. My fist seemed to go through him and struck against the stone above the fireplace, and knocked the skin off my knuckles. The man seemed to be struck back into the fire, and uttered a strange unearthly squeak. Immediately, the dog gripped me by the calf of my leg, and seemed to cause me pain. The man recovered his position, called off the dog with a sort of a click of the tongue, and then went back into the coalhouse, followed by the dog. I lighted my dark lantern and looked into the coalhouse, but there was neither dog nor man, and no outlet for them except the one by which they had entered. I was satisfied that what I had seen was ghostly, and it accounted for the fact that when the man had first come into the place where I sat, I had not challenged him. I was certainly not under the influence of strong drink, for I was then, as I have been for 49 years, a teetotaller. My mind at that time was perfectly free from trouble. What increased the excitement was the fact that a man, a number of years before, who was employed in the office of the station, had committed suicide and was carried into this very cellar. I knew nothing of this circumstance, nor of the body of the man, but Mr Pease, and others who had known him, told me my description exactly corresponded to his appearance and the way he dressed, and also he had a black retriever just like the one that gripped me. I should add that no mark or effect remained on the spot where I seemed to be seized.'

The Reverend Kendall noted that Durham had attended his church for over 25 years and that he was a very strong man, both mentally and physically. He passed the information on to Professor Sidgwick, President of the Society for Psychical Research, and they were both convinced that Durham was not asleep at the time. Equally, he would have been awakened when the skin was taken off his knuckles. Finally, they discovered that a clerk called John Winter had committed suicide by blowing his brains out with a pistol. The description fitted Winter and he had a black retriever dog.

Darlington, Co. Durham: Civic TheatrE

Opened in 1907 as the Darlington Hippodrome, the building is haunted by its early benefactor, Rino Pepi. Many witnesses have seen him walking up and down the aisles. Witnesses have also seen the apparition of a ghostly stagehand, who committed suicide by hanging himself from one of the fly ropes.

Darlington, Co. Durham: Darlington and Simpson Rolling Mills

Five workmen died in the early 1920s when the overhead cable railway at the mill collapsed and crushed them. Later, several workers saw a transparent apparition in the finishing shop. They claimed that if it was approached then the manifestation would groan, wave its arms and then vanish. In July 1970, eight men walked out after the apparition had continually frightened them. One even threw a stone at the ghost. On another occasion, several men chose to follow the ghost and saw it pass through the wall into Longfield Road, and then sit on the wall where the dead men used to take their lunch breaks.

Darlington, Co. Durham: King's Head Hotel, Priestgate

Albert the butler appears in rooms 419 and 426, and the hotel now makes quite a feature of its resident ghost. If guests have dinner in their rooms, the hotel will give them free wine with the dinner, a nightcap and breakfast in bed. By all accounts, Albert is perfectly friendly.

Darlington, Co. Durham: Town Hall

The present building was constructed on the site of a 12th-century manor house. The site itself, although few claim to have seen the apparition in the past few years, is haunted by a one-armed manifestation. The ghost is said to be that of murder victim Lady Jarrett. She died of shock after a robber, bent on relieving her of her rings and bracelet, cut off her arm.

Dartington Hall, Dartington, Devon

A white lady, said to be the harbinger of death of members of the Champerknowe family, haunts the hall. A grey lady, the apparition of a woman who committed suicide by throwing herself off the church tower, has also been seen. The Lower Gate is haunted by a headless horseman, and the drawing room, even when locked, has a grand piano that plays by itself. A woman in a Norman-style dress, said to be the wife of Gaven Champerknowe, haunts the Countess's Room.

Dartmouth, Devon: Royal Castle Hotel, The Quay

Staff and guests have heard the sound of horses' hooves and the crunch of coach wheels on gravel in the early hours of the morning. This is not surprising, considering that the hotel now incorporates what used to be a coaching yard. Witnesses have also reported hearing footsteps in the hallway immediately after the sound of the horses and coach wheels.

Datchet, nr Windsor, Berkshire: The Royal Stag

The marks left by an apparition haunting this pub were photographed in 1979 and 1984. A boy, many years ago, was left outside the pub by his drunken father in the middle of a blizzard. The unfortunate child attempted to call his father and write messages on the window, but he died of hypothermia. His marks have since been seen on the window of the pub during the winter. The cellar has a tombstone that is said to return of its own accord if it is ever removed from the premises.

Datchworth, Hertfordshire: Bramfield Road

Both in this road and in Whitehorse Lane, you may encounter the indistinct shape of a horse pulling a struggling human form, coupled with the sounds of a man begging for mercy. Others have also heard the sounds of a horse's hooves clattering along. The haunting goes back many years to when Pieman Glibbon ran a pie stall at Hertfordshire markets and fairs. Naturally, he conversed with his customers, and showed great interest in their movements. Many of his customers, carrying cash from the sale of their livestock, were robbed by a highwayman on their way home. When the highwayman was caught, it turned out to be Glibbon. Some of the local farmers, so outraged that he had preyed on them like this, took the law into their own hands and beat him, then tied him to a horse which dragged him along the road, killing him.

Daventry, Northamptonshire: The Wheatsheaf Hotel, Sheep Street

Charles I used the hotel as his headquarters in June 1645, encountering an apparition of his old friend Thomas Wentworth, Earl of Strafford, who had been executed at the insistence of Parliament despite the king's best efforts, on 12 May 1640. When the manifestation appeared on the night of 13 May, it warned Charles that the impending clash with the Parliamentarians would end in disaster for the king's cause and that he should ride north with his army. The king told his commanders, but Prince Rupert in particular was convinced that they had the manpower to defeat Cromwell once and for all. At Naseby, Wentworth was proved right and after losing 3,000 men, the royalist army was routed. With hindsight, if the king had moved north, he would have been able to pick up more troops on the way, and could have met the Parliamentarians on more equal terms.

Dawley, Shropshire: Swan Hotel, Watling Street

A traveller was robbed and murdered in one of the bedrooms of the hotel in the middle of the 19th century. Not only have witnesses heard footsteps walking toward one of the bedrooms, then fading away when they reach the door, but they also claim to have seen something much more tangible. One of the recent staff claims to have seen a man in a long dark coat and trousers. She described the clothing as looking like untanned leather. This was a former coaching inn and the manifestation may be related to a murder that occurred on the premises.

Dean Castle, nr Kilmarnock, Strathclyde

When a terrified servant saw the head of the 4th Earl of Kilmarnock roll past her on the floor, it was only a premonition of the fate that would befall her master. Just a year later, as a supporter of the Jacobites, he was beheaded in the Tower of London.

Deddington, Cheshire

A former vicar, Maurice Frost, haunts the vicarage here. His apparition has been seen wandering around the grounds by a number of locals and his own cousin positively identified him.

Dedham, nr Colchester, Essex: The Sun Hotel

Elsa, a maidservant at the hotel, was the last victim of the witch burnings in Essex. She was burned alive at the stake within sight of the building. She has been seen on the staircase and upper floor. Witnesses relate that she sits, weeping, with her head in her hands.

Denbigh Castle, Clwyd

A white lady haunts the Goblin Tower. The tower was built by Henry de Lacy, Earl of Lincoln, in order to protect the castle's water supply. The apparition of his own 15-year-old son also haunts the tower; he died when he fell from the scaffolding during its construction. Several people have seen his face peering out of one of the windows.

Dent, nr Sedbergh, Cumbria

Either 14th-century Scots or much earlier Danes are said to haunt the fells to the south. The phantom army descends Whernside into Dentdale. Witnesses claim that they have seen many hundreds of figures in the mist.

Denton Hall, nr Newcastle upon Tyne, Northumberland

In the 17th century a jealous sister strangled a girl living at the house. As a result, she appears as a white lady, often called either 'Old Barbery' or 'Silky' due to the fact that witnesses often hear her rustling silk dress. She does seem to favour two of the rooms in the house, but has been seen in other places.

Derby, Derbyshire: Assembly Rooms

An assembly was built in 1714, but a larger structure was completed in 1763 in the Market Place. The new assembly, completed in 1977, stands on the site of this 18th-century building, which was gutted by fire in the 1960s. It incorporates the site of the Duke of Newcastle's house, where Charles I stayed in 1637. The apparition of a Victorian woman, who appears to float and has no legs, has also been seen. A ring of dancing children, accompanied by laughter, has been seen in the Darwin Suite.

Derby, Derbyshire: The Bell Hotel

The figure of a ghostly nanny or maidservant has been seen in one of the bedrooms. She is described as appearing to be from the 18th century, wearing a mob cap. The apparition stands there for a few seconds before fading away.

Derby, Derbyshire: Derby Cathedral

A ghost, believed to be Prince Charles Edward Stuart, has been seen dressed in Jacobite style, walking into the Cathedral. Bonnie Prince Charlie did visit Derby in 1745 and it is perhaps this event that is recalled in the haunting. Many other witnesses have seen this vague shape and claim to have heard his footsteps. The apparition may be the same one that has been seen in the vicinity of the Silk Mill pub.

Derby, Derbyshire: The George Inn

Built in around 1693, the pub was a favoured place of the Duke of Devonshire, who used it as his headquarters during the Jacobite Rebellion of 1745. The inn has many ghosts, but perhaps the oddest story revolves around the 'George skull'. A female human skull was found under the cellar floor, but no other human remains were found there. It was once the custom to bury a human skull, a pair of shoes or a dead cat to ward off evil spirits and witches. Perhaps this is the explanation for the skull. The ghost of a man in a blue coat with long hair has been seen on the landing; he disappears in the bar area. Kitchen items have been moved, buckets thrown at staff and beer taps have been fired at the cellarman. The cellar is also haunted by a strange disembodied groaning noise. It may have a link with the skull that was found here.

Derby, Derbyshire: Georgian House Hotel

The apparition of a male ghost, believed to be a naval officer, haunts this building in Ashbourne Road. It was originally built for a naval officer who served under Nelson in the 18th century. The manifestation has been described as wearing a blue suit, perhaps a uniform, and tends to be seen in the hallway and on the stairs.

Derby, Derbyshire: Guildhall Catacombs

During World War One Alice Wheeldon sheltered conscientious objectors and was imprisoned. After she was released, she lived as a virtual recluse and when she died was buried in an unmarked grave. It is believed that the sightings of a woman in the catacombs are the apparition of Alice. Her manifestation is accompanied by the sound of ghostly footsteps. Workmen have also seen a ragged young boy in the catacombs. When they search for the boy, there is no sign of him. The identity of this young apparition is unknown.

Derby, Derbyshire: Headless Cross, Friar Gate

The apparition of a white or grey lady has been seen to emerge from the stone itself. Some witnesses believe that this is the same ghost that has been seen on Friar Gate and in the Arboretum. Other witnesses have seen the forlorn manifestation of a small dog sitting beside the cross.

Derby, Derbyshire: The Jacobean House

Built in 1611, this was once the home of Mrs Gisbourne, not only the wife of the Mayor of Derby, but also the first woman to have her own coach. It is perhaps this connection that explains witnesses' accounts of seeing a phantom coach, driven by a headless coachman, emerging from the archway. Another apparition has been seen standing outside the Wardwick entrance to the building. A blue lady has been seen on the stairs, with a white shawl around her shoulders. She is described as being gentle and non-threatening. She does have a tendency to move things around and hide small items, but this may be the work of the other 11 ghosts that are said to inhabit the building.

Derby, Derbyshire: The Noah's Ark

In the 17th century Noah Bullock built a boat and moored it at Morledge on the River Derwent. He seemed to be a god-fearing man, as his sons were called Shem, Ham, Japhet and Benjamin, but looks can be deceptive. In 1676, he was discovered to be a counterfeiter. Standing before Sir Simon Degge, the Recorder of Derby, he promised to sink the boat and stop his operations. In this way he escaped the hangman's noose. The pub, named after his floating home and counterfeiting centre, is still haunted by his apparition to this day.

Derby, Derbyshire: St Helen's House

Built in 1767 for John Gisbourne of Yoxall Lodge, Staffordshire, St Helen's House stands on the site of an Augustinian monastery. The building seems to be quite heavily haunted. The apparition of a woman has been seen running down the stairs, as if she were being chased. A ghostly monk has also been seen, perhaps the culprit that scared a teacher there when the building was being used as a school. On several occasions, while working late, the teacher heard her name being spoken in a whisper. The building has numerous cold spots and on another occasion in 1992, a witness saw a grey figure float down from the ceiling and disappear into a wall.

Derby, Derbyshire: St Mary's Church, Bridge Gate

Augustus Pugin, who also drew the designs for the Houses of Parliament, built the church. Prior to 1840, Derby Catholics were restricted to practicing their faith in the chapel in Chapel Street. The massive railway building programme changed all that, as many Irish Catholics moved into the area. The enlarged Catholic community purchased the land on Bridge Gate and commissioned Pugin to design a new church for them. It is haunted by the apparition of a priest, who has been seen on numerous occasions. On one occasion, a newly ordained priest was descending the stairs with three other priests and commented that he had not expected that there would be five of them at the church. The three other priests told him that he was mistaken and there were only the four of them. The new priest explained that as they had been sitting upstairs another priest had joined them. He described the man as being quite old, with grey hair. In this instance, only the new priest had seen the apparition and it had not made itself known to the other three.

Derby, Derbyshire: St Werburgh's Churchyard

A grey lady, said to be the apparition of an old woman, haunts the churchyard and Seymour's Wine Bar and Restaurant. Just before she appears, witnesses report smelling the strong scent of lavender in the air.

Derby, Derbyshire: Shire Hall

In 1665, a deaf-mute woman was sentenced to be pressed to death at the Shire Hall; she was the last victim to suffer this fate. Her ghost can still be seen walking around the cells in the basement of the building. The Shire Hall was built in 1659 and witnessed many famous murder trials, including that of the Pentrich Martyrs. In 1817, they were the last people in Britain to be sentenced to be hung, drawn and quartered.

Derby, Derbyshire: The Silk Mill

Now the Industrial Museum, this building is haunted by one of the many children said to have died here during the time that it operated as a silk mill. Several witnesses have heard the pitiful sounds of a child crying at the foot of the stairs in the tower, where the boy bled to death. The lift here also has a habit of working on its own, perhaps related to the same incident.

Derby, Derbyshire: The Smithfield

Inexplicably, pipes running from the cellar of this pub continually seem to be switched around, and on other occasions beer will come out of the pumps even if the gas is off. One of the landlords saw an old man sitting in the chair in the bar area. The only suggested explanation is that this is the apparition of a man who was killed in the stables.

Derby, Derbyshire: Ye Olde Dolphin Inn

Dating from around 1530, the pub is haunted by the apparition of a blue lady. She has been seen in and around the building for years. At one time, doctors used the building to dissect the bodies of executed criminals. Given the inexact science of hanging before the changes in 1760, some of the 'dead' would wake up on the dissection table. On one such occasion, in the cellar of the building, a doctor plunged a scalpel into a 'corpse' and it woke up. Both men are believed to have died of shock. These events may explain the intense poltergeist activity in the cellar. The presence turns beer kegs off and then frightens staff who go down to deal with the problem.

Derby, Derbyshire: Ye Olde Spa Inne, Abbey Street

In 1773 Dr Chauncey opened a mineral spring here, but when he died the business folded. Eventually a cottage was built on the site, which later became a farm and then a pub in the 19th century. Dr Chauncey is still active on the site, in the form of strange voices and the sense of a presence in the cellar.

Derrygonnelly, nr Enniskillen, Northern Ireland

A strange knocking noise was reported in this house as early as 1877. In that year, the psychic researcher Sir William Barrett successfully communicated with the ghost by asking it to guess how many fingers he had extended inside his pocket. It is said that the manifestation was right each time.

Devereux Wooten Farm, nr Weobley, Herefordshire

Lady Berrington haunts the farm. It is believed that she had connections with this area and that for some inexplicable reason she still chooses to haunt this spot.

Devizes, Wiltshire

On 13 July 1643, the royalists, under Lord Wilmott, defeated the Parliamentarians under General Waller. Waller's cavalry was driven down a slope and into an area that has become known as Bloody Ditch. Eight hundred men died here. This was the culmination of the Battle of Roundway Hill. Witnesses have seen horribly injured phantom horses in the area.

Diamond Cottage, nr West Peckham, Kent

Jack Diamond, the highwayman, lived here. The house was burned down one Friday 13, but the shell still stands on a hill above the village. It is said that ghosts are visible there on any Friday 13.

Dilston Castle, nr Hexham, Northumberland

In 1716 James Radcliffe, the Earl of Derwentwater and a Jacobite, was executed in the Tower of London. At the moment of his death it was said that the gutters of the castle ran red with blood. His apparition can be seen galloping across the countryside at the head of his men, while the ghost of his wife stands in the ruins of the castle, wringing her hands.

Dingwall, Highlands: Tulloch Castle Hotel

The Davidson clan owned this 16th-century castle in the Victorian period, and it is from this time that the haunting seems to originate. The young daughter of the master of the house stumbled into her father's bedroom to find him in bed with a woman who was not her mother. She took fright and fell down the staircase and broke her neck. As a result, she now appears as a green lady.

Disley, Cheshire: Lyme Park, Buxton Road

A white lady became particularly active in this 16th-century manor house, following renovation work in the late 1970s. She is described as being a tall woman in an attractive white gown, and has been seen by staff and visitors in the Ghost Room that leads from the Long Gallery. Witnesses have only seen her for a few seconds. She has also been spotted beneath one of the trees at the front of the building. It is widely believed that she is Blanche, the mistress of Sir Piers Legh, who built the original hall in 1541.

Ditchingham, Norfolk: Lion's Grave

Situated along the old Bungay to Norwich road, this site boasts the ghostly apparition of a coach and four horses. Several motorists have narrowly avoided collisions with the manifestation, which apparently gets to within a few feet of oncoming vehicles before fading away.

Ditteridge, Wiltshire: Cheney Court

Once the home of Queen Henrietta, the house is haunted by an unknown apparition. It is believed that the haunting may relate to the period when she lived here.

Dixton, nr Monmouth, Gwent

In the meadows beside the river, walkers often encounter the apparition of a man walking with his ghostly white dog. Around the rectory the manifestation of a tramp has often been seen carrying a parcel. Many years ago he was drowned in the river.

Doddington Hall, nr Lincoln, Lincolnshire

Built by Thomas Taylor in the 16th century and extensively modernised in the 19th century, this hall is haunted by the apparition of a girl that has been seen to throw herself off the roof. Explanations revolve around an over-amorous squire with designs on the girl. At her wits end and, presumably with the squire close at hand, she chose death rather than the bed of the man. The events apparently occurred around the time of the alterations in the 19th century. Another ghostly figure haunts the building in the form of a brown lady, seen standing on the first floor landing in a long brown dress. She has only been seen for a few seconds before vanishing. A witness saw the strange apparition of a man proposing to a girl in the drawing room. Of particular note is the fact that the bottom few inches of the manifestation were missing. What the witness did not know at the time was that the floor had been lower in the past.

Dorchester, Dorset: The Antelope Hotel

The building was used as a court during Judge Jeffrey's Bloody Assizes after the Monmouth Rebellion of 1685. Witnesses have heard ghostly footsteps, the clink of metal against metal and have seen light streaming into their rooms at night. The ghostly activity seems to take place around 2.30am each morning.

Dorchester, Dorset: St Peter's Church

The ghost of a former rector, the Reverend Nathaniel Templeman (d.1813), has been seen on several occasions. The most notable sighting occurred on Christmas Day 1814. Two churchwardens were taking a break from decorating the church when Templeman sat down between them. The apparition looked at them, shook his head, displaying his disappointment, then got up. The ghost then floated down the aisle, sank through the floor and disappeared.

Dorchester-on-Thames, Oxfordshire: The George Hotel

Built in the 15th century, the building is haunted by a white lady. Witnesses claim that she appears to be a sad-looking girl, wearing a white gown. It is not known why she has chosen to haunt this pub.

Dornoch, Highlands

In 1772, Janet Horne was burned at the stake as a witch. Her place of death is marked by the Witches' Stone, now on the edge of a golf course. Her ghost can be seen on autumn nights, just as the moon is waning.

Dover Castle, Dover, Kent

The present castle dates from around 1180. During the reign of Henry II a massive £6,500 was spent on improving the castle. The site is also connected with a Roman lighthouse and an Anglo-Saxon fortified town. Both the Georgians and the Victorians made considerable changes to the structure. The keep boasts the ghost of a Cavalier dressed in 17th-century costume, with a black, wide-brimmed hat and plume, a purple coat and knee-length boots. A lady in a red flowing dress has also been seen by members of staff. The Mural Gallery is home to a figure in blue. In the king's bedroom staff have also seen the lower half of a man's body purposefully walking near the doorway. In the underground works a 17th-century pikeman has been seen in the guardroom, walking through a wall and coming out the other side. Another blue figure has been seen in passageways nearby. Visitors have also spoken of moans and screams that may or may not be related to the apparitions mentioned.

Downe Park, nr Orpington, Kent

There are several ghosts here, including a bedraggled and wet girl who was drowned in the old moat. She stands and sobs by guests' bedsides. A severed arm has also been seen, as has an old man in the barn. There are other manifestations as well as these that haunt the library, hall, pantry and stairs.

Dowsborough, Somerset

On autumn nights you may hear the sound of soldiers, at first happily drinking around their campfires and then engaged in deadly combat. This was the site of a Danish raiders' camp. Witnesses also say that they can hear a boy singing and it is believed that this was the sole survivor of a surprise attack by the English.

Dozmary Pool, Bodmin Moor, Cornwall

Not only is this said to be the resting place of King Arthur's sword Excalibur, but it is also the haunting place of the evil Tregeagle. His spirit was doomed to remain here until he managed to empty the pool with a limpet shell. In life he was an evil and rapacious lawyer.

Drem Airfield, East Lothian

In 1934, as Air Marshall Sir Victor Goddard flew over Scotland, he saw a line of yellow aircraft, surrounded by ground crew in blue overalls. This was a very strange apparition as the airfield was disused at the time and not reopened until 1938. Aircraft were not painted yellow in 1934, and neither were the ground crew issued with blue overalls.

Drewsteignton, Dartmoor

At Bloody Corner a thin trickle of blood is said to seep under the door of a cottage where, many years ago, a murder was committed.

Drightlington, nr Leeds, West Yorkshire: Lumb Hall

A strange, cloaked figure, believed to be related in some way to the English Civil War, haunts the hall. He is now known as Charlie and is described as being a fairly harmless cloaked apparition. On many occasions his shuffling feet have been heard near the front door.

Drumlanrig Castle, nr Thornhill, Dumfries and Galloway

This pink granite castle, dating from the 17th century, has an odd manifestation that was probably once a family pet. The Countess of Dalkeith and one of her sisters were heading for their bedrooms when they saw a huge, hairy figure moving toward them. Some years later the countess saw the large ape-like apparition again, sitting on a chair. The castle was used as a hospital in World War One, and several nurses slept in the building. One of

the matrons, who had been assigned the Yellow Monkey Room, fled from her post after having seen the apparition on a number of occasions. Whether the manifestation is that of an ape that may have been brought back to Scotland in the past, or whether the witnesses were mistaken, may never be known. The daughter of the Duchess of Gloucester claims to have seen a girl by her bedside at the castle, and it is also said that the ghost of Lady Anne Douglas is often seen walking around the castle, carrying her head in her hands.

Dublin, Republic of Ireland: Portobello Harbour, Rathmines Bridge

Many years ago, a lock keeper drowned himself here after being sacked for continual drunkenness. His apparition, taking the form of either a brilliant light emerging from the canal water or a wave that transforms into the shape of a man, has been blamed for two accidents here. In November 1857, a soldier from the nearby Portobello Barracks was walking with his girlfriend along the canal path when the manifestation emerged from the water. The soldier was blinded by the light and tripped, fell into the water and drowned. On the evening of 6 April 1861, Patrick Hardy, a horse-drawn bus driver, had just dropped a passenger off when his horse suddenly reared as it saw the apparition. Unable to control the beast, Hardy and his conductor, the bus, the horse and six passengers plunged into the water. Hardy and his work colleague were saved but the others perished.

Dublin, Republic of Ireland: St Patrick's Cathedral

Captain McNeill Boyd was lost in February 1861, attempting to save drowning sailors who had been pitched into the waters at Dun

Laoghaire. A memorial to the brave man can be seen at the cathedral, along with the ghost of Boyd's faithful black Newfoundland dog. The manifestation has also been seen at his master's grave in Glasnevin Cemetery. On the fateful night of 8 February, Boyd and his men were swept off the rocks and into the sea by a massive wave. When his body was finally recovered from the sea it was buried with great reverence. During the funeral, the dog walked beside the coffin and refused to leave the grave until it died of hunger.

Dublin, Republic of Ireland: St Stephens Green

In the 1840s, Colonel and Mrs Launey moved into the house, but after a short period, they began to experience strange apparitions. Mrs Launey saw a dark figure walking up the staircase, and to her horror she realised that it was headless. Within a few days, her husband and some of the servants had witnessed the apparition too, along with the sound of a spinet being played in the drawing room. Guy Lorrimer, Mrs Launey's brother, saw a dark figure emerge from under his bed, crawl on all fours toward a cupboard built into the walls and disappear with a loud chuckling laugh. On Christmas Eve, the family encountered a strange light in the drawing room and the body of a headless woman on the floor. A tall man, with a knife in his hand, stood over the corpse. Another woman, dressed in an 18th-century dress, stood close to him. Hanging off the tree was the woman's head, with the Christmas presents scattered all around the room. There was a scream and a laugh and the manifestations disappeared. The Launeys cancelled their lease and left the house on Christmas Day.

Dublin, Republic of Ireland: 118 Summerhill

This was the site of a house that was owned by a coach-building family in the 19th century. When the house was demolished in the 1960s, workmen claimed to have seen a strange apparition. The manifestation of a man, quite tall and dressed in overalls, was seen standing in the corner of a room. The hauntings became so frequent and had such a marked affect on the workmen that they refused to work in the house unless it was broad daylight.

Duddlestone, Somerset

Although the apparition's identity is unknown, many witnesses have reported seeing the ghost of a headless rider passing through the village. This may be the same ghost that has been seen in Corfe, but there he is described as being a white rider. In Duddlestone he appears in a flowing cloak astride a grey horse.

Dudley, West Midlands: Dudley Castle

Disappointingly, despite the fact that this castle was mentioned in the *Domesday Book*, its hauntings relate to the 17th or 18th century. Near the keep, walking arm in arm, an elderly couple have been seen on a number of occasions. The man is described as holding a crooked walking stick and wearing a tall hat. The couple have also been described by other witnesses as appearing to wear clothes of the 1930s.

Dudley, West Midlands: Dudley Zoo

Within the grounds of the zoological gardens, strange sounds, including the clash of steel and human murmurings, have been heard. While many attribute these noises to the animals, others firmly believe that they have supernatural connotations. In the late 1970s, an employee in one of the restaurants saw the shape of a white lady in a white gown. She was originally believed to have seen an albino peacock. Interestingly, the local police force considered it important enough to carry out an investigation of their own, but unfortunately they turned up nothing.

Dudley, West Midlands: The Jolly Collier

Tragic events followed the untimely death of a landlord's wife here many years ago. The landlord was left with a young daughter and a business that was all but broke due to poltergeist activity. No one would stay at the inn on account of the fact that objects were thrown around the rooms, crockery was smashed, bells rang at odd hours and there was the threat that you might even be thrown out of your bed. The situation, as far as the landlord was concerned, worsened to such a degree that he murdered his own daughter and then committed suicide. In addition to the poltergeist activity, the man and his daughter have also been seen. Witnesses have seen the ghost of a man in a brown suit, accompanied by a young blonde girl.

Dumfries, Dumfries and Galloway: Castle Street

Red Comyn was killed in Castle Street in 1306 on the site of the Minorite friary, by Robert the Bruce. The latter is seen, together with the apparition of Roger de Kirkpatrick, who provided the dagger that ended Comyn's life. Another manifestation shares the area: a headless horseman, the ghost of a young Mac-Milligan boy. He was courting a local girl and was chased off by her brothers. In the ensuing race to reach safety he failed to notice a low bough that struck his head clean off.

Dumfries, Dumfries and Galloway: County Hotel

Bonnie Prince Charlie, or more correctly Prince Charles Edward Stuart, haunts the room in which he stayed in 1745. Witnesses

sitting in Prince Charlie's Room, which is now a lounge area, have seen him in his Jacobite clothing, deep in thought.

Dumfries, Dumfries and Galloway: Dumfries and Galloway Royal Infirmary

Demolished two decades ago, the original Dumfries Hospital was owned by St Joseph's College. Many witnesses have reported a strange atmosphere and an odd feeling in a particular place in the grounds of the Royal Infirmary. The original hospital focussed on the mentally ill. Among the cures or remedies for the mentally disturbed, doctors prescribed chaining to the wall of cells. Clearly, many violent activities occurred in these 'treatment' rooms. In later years the rooms were sealed off or used for storage purposes, but the iron-barred doors and the manacles remained on the walls. Ultimately the hospital was closed down following a number of complaints about moans and shrieks. It became a boarding school and the building was used as a dormitory for parents. After that it became a block of flats. The reputation of the place led to the flats being levelled in 1963. Many people who visit the site have claimed to experience terror, or say that they have felt disorientated. Despite all this, not a single physical manifestation has ever been seen; it is more a sense of evil and pain that pervades the site. Dogs, for example, will not venture anywhere near the site of the old treatment rooms; it seems that a grim reminder of the past has left its indelible mark here.

Dunham Massey Hall, nr Altrincham, Greater Manchester

An Elizabethan manor house stood on this site before the hall replaced it in the 18th century. It is the architect of the newer building that haunts the site. He either fell or was pushed from the roof. It is a popular conception that his demise was immediately preceded by a dispute with the builders.

Dunnose Point, nr Ventor, Isle of Wight

The ship HMS *Eurydice* went down in poor weather on 24 March 1878, claiming the lives of 300 novice sailors. There were only two survivors. Several witnesses claim to have seen the phantom ship off the point.

Dunnottar Castle, nr Stonehaven, Aberdeenshire

Picts were active in this area long before the first castle was built here in the 12th century. William Keith made huge improvements in the 14th century. The castle was twice besieged by Montrose during the Civil War, and in the latter part of the 17th century was used as a prison for Covenanters. A green lady, perhaps an earth spirit, is said to haunt the castle, relating to the time when the Picts were converted to Christianity. Others have seen a tall, blonde-haired, leather-clad man near the guardroom, and the drawing room reverberates with strange voices. In later years both tourists and staff have reported sighting a young, scrawny, deer-hunting dog, which disappears if approached. In the brewery tourists have also seen a young girl in sackcloths who walks out of the doorway and disappears.

Dunphail, nr Forres, Grampian

The old Highland Railway Line used to run through this area until the tracks were removed several years ago. However, this does not seem to inhibit a phantom train from clattering along through the station, several feet above the ground.

Dunrobin Castle, nr Golspie, Highlands

This was the stronghold of the Dukes of Sutherland in the 18th and 19th century. Margaret, the daughter of the 14th Earl, haunts the original building, a mediaeval stone keep. She fell in love with Jamie Gunn, who was a young groom at the castle. The Earl was livid and banished Jamie and locked his daughter up in the old tower. Presently Jamie returned with a plan to release Margaret and elope with her. After smuggling rope into her room, Margaret was literally at the point of descent when the Earl's steward arrived with her father. Rather than face life without Jamie, she let go of the rope and fell to her death in the courtyard below. Her apparition is often seen sobbing in the room at the top of the old tower.

Dunsmore Heath, nr Rugby, Warwickshire

The terrifying apparition of a phantom lorry appears out of the darkness on one of the bends on the A45 as it crosses the heath. The apparition speeds straight toward oncoming vehicles and vanishes at the last minute.

Dunstaffnage Castle, nr Dunberg, Strathclyde

Situated on Loch Etive, the castle was built on the site of an Iron Age fort. 'The Scanniag' or 'Elle Maid' haunts it. She is either a white or green lady, and probably has some kind of connection with the Campbells who once controlled Dustaffnage. She has been seen to be happy in good times for them and very sorrowful if one is about to die. The apparition is not averse to causing problems in the castle; she stamps on the floor to wake people in the mornings and pulls bedclothes off sleeping guests.

Dunstanburgh Castle, nr Alnwick, Northumberland

Thomas, Earl of Lancaster, built the castle in 1316. He was not a great friend of Edward II, and as a result, lost his head at Pontefract Castle. The exact circumstances of his death perhaps explain why the apparition appears with a somewhat messy head and a face contorted with pain. It took the executioner 11 attempts to remove Thomas's head. A white lady, believed to be Margaret of Anjou, wife of Henry VI, also haunts the castle, together with the apparition of Sir Guy. The story runs that Margaret had been magically imprisoned in the cliff-top castle and Sir Guy had fallen desperately in love with her. Despite his best attempts, he could not release her from the magical bonds that held her there, and they now spend their ghostly existence together.

Dunster, nr Minehead, Somerset

William de Mohun held the castle here for Matilda against King Stephen. There have been numerous reports of the sounds of clinking coins, particularly on nights with a full moon. A phantom in 17th-century costume is seen walking around the castle during thunderstorms, which may have some connection with Colonel Wyndham, who held it for the king for 160 days. The ghostly figure of a Roundhead soldier has been reported in the Leather Room. In the nearby nunnery, guests were alarmed by the presence of a bare-headed apparition dressed in flowing robes. Others who are sure that the figure resembles that of a monk have also reported this.

Duntroon (Duntrune) Castle, nr Kilmartin, Argyll and Bute

Although most of the remaining structure of this castle is 17th-century, the site actually dates from the 13th century. In the 17th century, Ulster MacDonnell Coll Ciotach sent a piper to the castle. He planned to attack the Campbells. The piper was imprisoned, and as Coll Ciotach's men approached the piper signalled a warning that the Campbells were

prepared for them. The Campbells cut the piper's fingers off and then murdered him. As proof of these events, in 1910 a skeleton was found bricked up in the castle with its fingers missing. There are also reports of doors being knocked, objects being thrown around rooms, pictures falling off walls and ghostly footsteps patrolling the castle.

Dunvegan Castle, Sligachan, Isle of Skye

MacLeod of MacLeod had his stronghold here in the 13th century. It claims to be the oldest castle in Scotland that is still inhabited by the same family. The Fairy Bridge has evil connotations: horses will not cross it, and dogs are especially frightened at this point.

Dunwich, Suffolk: Dunwich Heath

This was once part of the land that belonged to the Barnes family, who lived in Sotterley Hall during Victoria's reign. Miles Barnes was particularly fond of horses and his apparition has been seen riding a phantom steed across the heath. You are most likely to see his ghost when there is a full moon, when you can watch it glide across the heath and disappear over the cliff.

Dunwich, Suffolk: Greyfriars

In the Middle Ages, Dunwich was a large and thriving seaport. In one spectacular storm over a million tonnes of sand and shingle sealed the harbour and heralded the decline of the town. Over the years, cliff and beach erosion has eaten into the ruins of the town and little now remains. Most of the town, several churches and major buildings that were once at the heart of Dunwich, lies under the North Sea. The ruins of Greyfriars are at the centre of the hauntings. Several Franciscan monks have been seen walking toward the ruins, chanting prayers. Greyfriars remains on the cliff-top, year by year finding itself closer to the raging seas below.

Duporth Holiday Camp, Cornwall

Built on the site of an old manor house, the holiday camp is haunted by the apparition of a ghostly nun called Flo. She was heard to be striking matches and opening a lock on the cabinet in the drawing room. Despite the fact that the original house is now gone, she still interferes with things, including a sewing machine, an electric kettle and a children's roundabout. One of the members of staff has an ongoing relationship with the apparition, and he always thanks Flo when she turns on the kettle for him. Flo has also been seen chatting to children near the old farmhouse, and she is described as an old lady in a black dress (perhaps a nun's habit).

Durham, Co. Durham

Near Neville's Cross, on the path to Cradlewell, you may encounter a pitiful apparition on St Thomas's Eve (20 December). Witnesses have seen the ghost of a woman carrying a child. She was the victim of a murder here many years ago.

E

Eardisley to Eynesbury

Eardisley, nr Hereford, Herefordshire

The Dogs of Hell haunt Parton Cross. They are believed to be the same beasts that rampage across the border in Wales and are known there as the *Cwn Annwn*.

East Bergholt, Suffolk

Friary Lane is said to be haunted. It was once a Benedictine convent. The temperature drops and a door slowly opens itself before 11pm. During World War Two a soldier stationed here felt cold hands on his face.

When he woke in the morning he discovered that his hair had turned white.

Eastbourne, East Sussex: Beachy Head

This is the most southerly point of the South Downs and the highest cliff on the south coast. It is a popular spot for suicides. There are some strange, perhaps supernatural, forces afoot on this cliff, which entice individuals to jump more than 500ft to their doom. It is said that many people have seen a horrifying monk in black beckoning them to the edge, despite the fact that there is no record of a monastery near this site. Whatever the reason, it does seem to affect animals as well as humans. A man walking a dog saw an apparition of a grey lady in the 1970s. The apparition had a terrifying effect on the dog, and on his return home the owner spoke with friends who had also seen the grey lady. She may be the ghost of a suicide in the past, but she has been seen at least three times a year over the past few years. From descriptions her clothing seems to be dated to the mid-19th century. Another ghost has been seen, dressed rather like a farmer's wife in an apron, carrying a bundle that is believed to be a child. The apparition is seen on the edge of the cliff, then takes a step over the edge and vanishes. It is widely believed that she is the widow of a farmer who was murdered during Victoria's reign. She is particularly seen in the evenings.

Eastbourne, East Sussex: Eastbourne College

This boys' school near Compton Park is haunted by the tortured spirit of a former student who hanged himself in one of the dormitories. It is said that he was suffering from concerns about his forthcoming examinations, and had family problems. Staff and students report that there is an icy spot in one of the corridors and others say that they feel distinctly uncomfortable at the same place. Other members of staff have reported seeing the strange, opaque figure of a young boy standing near a doorway to a bedroom in the evening.

Eastbourne, East Sussex: The Plantation

This is the site of an old manor house owned by Lord Willingdon, a former Viceroy of India. It lies in a small copse of trees to the north-west of Ratton. While decorators were renovating the building, they found a blood-stain on the floor of one of the bedrooms. This may be related to a time when Canadian soldiers were billeted here during World War Two. They reported hearing scraping sounds and strange noises coming from this room. Many also complained of a terrifying atmosphere in the whole of the building. Soon afterwards, the building inexplicably caught fire and was virtually razed to the ground. Following the fire, the building was completely demolished. Local stories relating to the haunting revolve around various sightings of a monk, or the figure of a man in a monk's habit. One particular witness saw a man walking across her garden, dressed in what appeared to be a dressing gown and sandals. The apparition disappeared through a wall at the bottom of the garden. The same witness believed that the figure was headless. It is difficult to understand why a monk is associated with this site, as there is no record of any religious history.

Eastbourne, East Sussex: Towner Art Gallery

The famous Lamb Inn and the Jesus House, with its well and underground chapel, help date the surrounding buildings to the mediaeval period. Various masonry marks in the stones in the cellars have intrigued archaeologists. The actual building was originally known as Manor House and was occupied at one stage by the Reverend Towner. After his death the building was left to the local council. Numerous individuals have claimed to hear strange noises that cannot be readily accounted for. As the building changed use over the years, several previously sealed rooms were discovered. Other witnesses have stated that they can smell horses in the building, but it is well over 100 years since horses were kept in the original stable part of the building on the ground floor. Other witnesses have reported hearing people murmuring but they cannot distinguish particular words. Most of these occurrences seem to take place after the building has closed to the public.

Eastbury, nr Tarrant Gunville, Dorset

A headless coachman, driving a coach and four with headless horses, stops to pick up the ghost of the scoundrel William Doggett. He wears knee breeches tied with yellow silk ribbon. The coach moves off and rattles across the cattle grid at the beginning of the drive, then drives under the yew trees and up to the house. Doggett had defrauded his master, Lord Temple, and on the eve of discovery, he committed suicide.

East Chinnock, nr Crewkerne, Somerset: The Old Rectory

This 16th-century building became a rectory in the late 18th century, with an extra wing being added for one of the rectors, who had seven daughters. One of the daughters fell in love with a man that her parents disapproved of, and the young couple decided to elope. The man found a ladder, climbed up to the girl's room and brought her safely down to a waiting coach. On several occasions the sound of footsteps and a ladder being placed against an upstairs windowsill has been heard, despite the fact that it is not now known how the pair met their fate.

East Cowes, Isle of Wight

During World War Two an unfortunate pilot was somehow decapitated in an accident. Witnesses have seen a headless parachutist slowly drifting toward the ground.

East Harptree, Somerset: Coley House

The ghost of a Roundhead soldier has been seen on numerous occasions and has also been documented in the national press. Apparently the figure is clear enough for eyewitnesses to describe its uniform and habits. One old man who lived there would regularly talk to the ghost after the manifestation had walked up the staircase and opened the latch on the door on the stairs. When the old man died the ghost apparently disappeared with him, never to be seen or heard of again.

Easthope, nr Bridgnorth, Shropshire

John de Easthope, a local squire, murdered William Garmston in 1333. Shortly after the killing he committed suicide. It is the murder victim that is seen at dusk in the churchyard. He has been described as being quite a short apparition. He has the unnerving habit of visiting newcomers to the village, and scares the living daylights out of them on their first night by appearing at the foot of their beds.

East Kirkby, nr Horncastle, Lincolnshire

During World War Two the airfield here was used as an American bomber base. The apparition of a pilot who died when his B17 crashed nearby has been seen walking toward the control tower, with his failed parachute in tatters behind him.

East Lavant, nr Chichester, West Sussex: The Royal Oak

The pub used to be called Fanny Glover's. One of the former landlords, Wilfred Miles, purchased a grandfather clock, and after cleaning it and getting it to work, he proudly installed it in the pub. The same night, his two sons, who slept in one of the upstairs bedrooms, fled into their parents' room, complaining that something had come into their room in the middle of the night. Wilfred himself saw the apparition of a man dressed in old-fashioned clothing. He became convinced that while the clock was running the manifestation would continue to haunt the building. He stopped the clock and the hauntings ceased. Whenever the clock is started, the back bedroom is best avoided.

East Meon, Hampshire: Buriton Manor

Several ghosts, including that of an old nanny in 18th-century uniform, haunt this building. Children often see her. The manifestation of a phantom maid runs across the courtyard in silence and vanishes when she reaches the brick wall. The brick wall used to have a gateway through which one could reach the local church. The ghost of a friar in a brown gown with a white cord around his waist has been seen on a number of occasions, particularly in the stable yard near the beech-lined avenue which is now known as Monk's Walk. So significant are the hauntings that in 1957 a Colonel Bonham-Carter successfully applied to the local council to reduce the rateable value of the manor because of the ghosts. The president of the tribunal said that 'if the haunting was genuine, then a reduction should be allowed'.

East Retford, Nottinghamshire: Town Hall

In the mid-1970s, several members of staff at the Town Hall reported seeing a ghost, wearing either a wig or a flowery hat, bending over one of the desks in the Committee Room. One witness, on spotting the apparition, turned on the light and it promptly vanished. Later, in 1975, the Town Clerk was in the same room when he felt the room go icy cold. He looked at his watch and realised that it was the same time that many other members of staff had reported encountering the ghost. The most obvious conclusion is that this is the ghost of a former judge who, presumably, used the Committee Room as one of his chambers. Why he should choose to haunt the Town Hall is unknown.

East Riddlesden, nr Keighley, West Yorkshire

A black dog, said to be the size of a donkey, haunts the area and carries a curse. If you look it in the eye, you will die. A black bear howls through the windows of houses containing someone close to death, and a large, black cat also stalks the area.

East Riddlesden, nr Keighley, West Yorkshire: East Riddlesden Hall

A white lady haunts the area near the duck ponds. She was knocked from her horse by a low-hanging branch and died. The apparition of a Scottish merchant, who was murdered for his money by a servant at the hall, has also been seen, together with a blue lady whose purpose and identity are unknown. Finally, the friendly ghost of a grey lady, cruelly starved to death by her wicked husband, makes an appearance on New Year's Eve.

East Scrafton, nr Leyburn, North Yorkshire

The Pennine Light is a flickering light that is said to haunt the B-road passing through this small village. There does not appear to be any particular explanation for the manifestation and has caused problems for motorists. It is locally believed that the light could be in some way connected with the nearby ruined St Simon's Chapel, which stands by the riverside.

East Stoke, nr Nottingham, Nottinghamshire

Lambert Simnel was born in 1475 and was said to be an imposter who first claimed to be Richard, Duke of York, the younger son of Edward IV, and then Edward, Earl of Warwick, nephew of Edward IV. He was crowned Edward VI in Dublin, which prompted Henry VII to show the real Earl of Warwick to assembled crowds in London. One of his supporters, the Earl of Lincoln, led an ill-armed force to its doom at the hands of the armies of Henry VII. In June 1487 seven thousand of Lincoln's men died. The road to Fiskerton Ferry has become known as the Red Gutter, as this was where most of the slaughter occurred. Many witnesses claim to have seen the apparitions of naked men around the area. They are believed to be the ghosts of the many Irishmen that fought and died for Simnel, the pretender to the throne.

Eastwell Park, nr Ashford, Kent

This spot is very close to the Pilgrim's Way. On Midsummer's Eve you may see a spectral rider approach the house and head toward the lake, into which he vanishes.

Eastwell Park, nr Ashford, Kent: Eastwell Manor Hotel

A white lady has been seen entering the bar. She seems to float across the floor and then disappears. In one of the function rooms a housekeeper saw the terrifying apparition of a man hanging from the ceiling with a noose around his neck. Other members of staff have heard loud noises that seem to emanate from the floor or the walls.

East Wellow, nr Southampton, Hampshire

Colonel William Morton was one of the men who signed the death warrant of Charles I. He lived in the village, and his ghost has been seen walking from the site of his old manor house toward the parish church and graveyard. It is also said that there is a spectral coach with four horses that travels from Embley Park to the church, although it is not known whether this is connected with Morton in any way. Also in St Margaret's churchyard is the grave of Florence Nightingale. Her ghost has been seen both inside the church, where she attended many services, and at her own graveside.

Ebbw Vale, Gwent

The apparition of a young woman carrying a baby in her arms haunts both the millstream and the churchyard. She is described as being white and rather indistinct. She walks along the path beside the stream, with her eyes fixed to the front, and disappears as she reaches the bridge. In the churchyard she walks straight through locked gates and then disappears part-way up the path. It is said that she was a black-haired Welsh girl, who was romantically involved with the son of a wealthy farmer during the reign of Queen Victoria. His father opposed the relationship, but the young man was determined, at least, to have his way with the girl. She would not consider anything until they were married, so he tricked her into believing that a ceremony officiated by one of his friends was a genuine union. She remained at home with her father and William spent as much time with her as he could. To all intents and purposes she was a wife to him. After a short while, William tired of the girl and saw her less and less. She pleaded with him to make their marriage more public, but he refused and explained that his father would disinherit him if he found out. Eventually he told her that their 'marriage' was over, but she was pregnant. When her father threatened to throw her out of the house, she told him about the secret wedding with William. Her father immediately went round to see the young man's father, who adamantly refused to allow the marriage, as he had already arranged for his son to marry another woman. Just before William's real wedding, the girl, now with a babe in arms, went to see him to try one last time to convince him to marry her properly. We do not know what happened, but the girl and her child were never seen alive again. Their bodies were found in the millstream soon afterwards. To this day, it is not known whether she committed suicide or was murdered by William or his father. William's life was short itself. He drowned on his honeymoon, but not before he had made his new wife pregnant. That baby was never to know its father either.

Edgehill, Warwickshire

The first major battle of the English Civil War took place on 23 October 1642. Although the outcome was inconclusive, there were over a thousand casualties. On Christmas Eve 1642 local farmers witnessed a ghostly re-enactment of the battle going on around them. More locals and sightseers turned up the following night and also experienced the phenomenon. Charles I sent some of his officers to witness the events and they actually recognised some of their comrades who had fallen on the battlefield. Although the phenomenon seems to have decreased in frequency in the intervening years, some witnesses have seen Prince Rupert on his white horse and, more chillingly, Sir Robert Verney holding the royal banner, despite having lost one of his hands in the battle.

Edgeworth, Turton Bottoms, Lancashire

The Ashworth Museum is housed in an enlarged 12th-century house, known as Turton Tower. Turton Bottoms is close to Edgworth and is linked to it by a Roman road. In November 1978 a witness from Tonge

Moor was travelling by bus to visit friends when he saw a couple waiting under a street lamp at the bus stop. The girl was about 19 years old and wearing a fawn raincoat. The man was older, with dark hair, and was wearing an anorak. As he got off at his stop, the witness noted that the couple had disappeared. He looked around, but there was no sign of them. On his return journey he had a conversation with the same bus driver, who also recalled seeing the young couple. Several other bus drivers have reported seeing the vanishing passengers, but no one seems to be able to link them to any particular incident. In nearby Chapelton Road, a misty figure has also been seen, but whether there is any link to the couple is unknown.

Edinburgh, Lothian: Charlotte Square

Four ghosts haunt this part of the city, including a phantom coach, a monk, the apparition of a Georgian woman and a sad, ill-kempt beggar.

Edinburgh, Lothian: Edinburgh Castle

Probably dating from the mid-17th century, a phantom drummer beats out long-forgotten marches from the castle walls.

Edinburgh, Lothian: Holyroodhouse

Mary Queen of Scots and her secretary, David Rizzio, both haunt this building. Rizzio was murdered here in 1566 and witnesses have accurately described him and his Tudor costume.

Edinburgh, Lothian: West Bow

Major Weir was burned at the stake on 11 April 1670, and his sister was hanged the following day in Grassmarket. By all accounts Weir had lived a blameless life. He was Commander of the City Guard, a lay-preacher in the Presbyterian Church and protector of his older sister Grizel. In 1669, following a string of accusations about him that amounted to the fact that he had a pact with the Devil, Weir confessed all and added that he had an incestuous relationship with his sister. Although their house was demolished in 1878, Weir's ghost can still be seen heading down the High Street toward West Bow, in a sheet of flames, riding a headless black horse. Grizel has also been seen, her face contorted and her skin blackened by the flames from the pits of Hell.

Egremont, nr Whitehaven, Cumbria

Many years ago a farmer, very familiar with the inns of the area, set out toward his home on his horse, roaring drunk. Neither the horse nor the rider was ever seen again, except as ghosts that appear on Christmas Eve.

Egryn, nr Harlech, Gwynedd

Mary Jones, an evangelist, claimed to have incredible talents, which some say that she did indeed display. She was believed to be able to speak to Jesus, and while doing so her body was said to be bathed in a strange light. It is believed that these occurrences, which took place in 1905, have their roots in paranormal activity that was present in the village many years earlier.

Eilean Donan Castle, nr Kyle of Lochalsh, Highlands

The apparition of a Spanish mercenary soldier who was killed during a siege here in 1719 haunts this amazing Highland castle. Also of note is the fact that Farquhar MacRae, following a dream-like vision, extensively restored the castle. His vision was later confirmed by other documentation to be an accurate interpretation of the original structure of the castle.

Elland, Yorkshire: The Fleece

The Fleece, in Elland's Westgate, is haunted by the ghost of Leathery Colt, a peddler who was brutally murdered in an upstairs room at the inn. When his body was dragged downstairs after the killing, a trail of blood was left on the wooden stairs that no amount of scrubbing could remove. Leathery Colt always stabled his horses and carriage in an adjoining barn while staying at the Fleece, and it was not long after his murder that his ghost was seen driving his carriage out of the barn late at night, furiously driving along Dog Lane to Old Earth, accompanied by a violent rush of wind.

Ellesborough, Buckinghamshire: Church of St Peter and St Paul

Several times a tall phantom in mediaeval clothing has been seen to glide into the church and move over to one of the memorial tablets, where it vanishes. In the late 1940s, the figure was seen by the church organist while he was practising. In the 1950s the same phantom was seen by a lady arranging flowers, and in 1970 a visitor witnessed the apparition. This visitor was interested enough to walk over to where the apparition had vanished and found that the only tablet there was the Hawtrey memorial plaque.

Ellingham, nr Alnwick, Northumberland

For many years this village has experienced the recurring apparition of a man chasing a horse down the main street. It is not known who the man is or when the original event occurred.

Elm, nr Wisbech, Cambridgeshire: Elm Vicarage

Built in the 18th century, the vicarage is haunted by the apparition of a ghostly monk called Brother Ignatius and the sound of a bell. Brother Ignatius is described as a man in his thirties, with dark curly hair and a thin face. He wears a brown habit and tends to be seen around dusk. The monk lived in the 12th century and was a watchman for the area when floods threatened. For some reason, he failed to raise the alarm and several monks were drowned. He now rings the bell whenever there is danger or when a villager is about to die. The vicarage is also haunted by a much more malevolent spirit in the form of an apparition with a large head and a red face. It attacked a vicar's wife, but the ghost of Brother Ignatius drove the manifestation away. The malign spirit is said to be the ghost of a man who was murdered at the scene of the attack over 100 years ago.

Elsdon, nr Rothbury, Northumberland

William Winter was a nasty piece of work. No sooner had he returned from being transported abroad than he was involved in a murder. With the aid of two gypsies, he robbed and murdered an old woman who lived in a remote cottage close to the village. In 1791 he finally paid for his crimes and was hanged and gibbeted in Newcastle. The site where the gibbet once stood is now known as Winter's Gibbet, or Steng Cross, and usually his ghost is seen some distance from the spot where he died. This may mean that his body is buried in the woodland.

Elterwater, nr Ambleside, Cumbria

A gunpowder factory used to occupy a site beside the water here and in 1916 four men were killed in an explosion. Since the late 1970s a number of witnesses have seen the apparition of a man walking around the area. From their descriptions he appears to be John Foxcroft, one of the four who lost their lives.

Emborough Chilcompton, Somerset: Court Hotel

This was the former courthouse, in which Judge Jeffreys presided over numerous cases. Members of staff and several guests have seen him, wearing clothes contemporary with his period. His manifestation has been seen to walk through the front door, which is now sealed, to stand underneath an oak tree in the garden. After a few minutes, the manifestation disappears. Other witnesses have reported hearing the front door opening and closing.

Epworth, Lincolnshire: Epworth Rectory

John Wesley, the preacher and co-founder of Methodism, was born at Epworth in 1703, the son of Revd Samuel Wesley. In December 1716 and January 1717, a series of hauntings took place in the rectory. On the night of 2 December 1716, strange knocking sounds were heard. Servants then heard someone appearing to stumble over boots. Knocking was also heard the following morning. That night Holly Wesley was sitting in the dining room when the door opened, she heard the rustle of silk and was aware of a presence in the room. The poltergeist activity increased, carrying on all day and night. When Samuel Wesley decided to omit the king from his prayers, 'Old Jeffrey' as the poltergeist had now become known, stopped the knockings. On one occasion, one of the girls, Hetty, actually saw the apparition of a man walking down the stairs in his nightshirt.

Erdington, nr Sutton Coldfield, West Midlands: Castle Vale

Many years ago monks built a shrine to Our Lady The Blessed Virgin on this former marshland. Several people have seen the apparition of a monk in the area. Some describe him as wearing something like a duffle coat, but this may be a monastic robe. The ghost of what may be a Polish RAF pilot who died when his plane crashed has also been seen. A grey man has been seen near the old airfield, and a young Victorian girl also stalks the vicinity.

Erdington, nr Sutton Coldfield, West Midlands: Erdington Hall

The ghosts of several members of the de Erdingtons, who were formerly Norman warlords, are said to revisit their ancestral home. They may be Peter, who died in the crusades, Sir Thomas, who was killed in the War of the Roses or even Giles or Richard, who both died in strange circumstances.

Erdington, nr Sutton Coldfield, West Midlands: Gravelly Hill

A young brown lady is said to visit one of the houses along this road. She is thought to date from the Edwardian period, and may have been a suicide victim who jumped from the middle window of the house.

Erdington, nr Sutton Coldfield, West Midlands: Pype Hayes Hall

Built in the 1630s by the Bagot family, and later occupied by Hervey, who married Dorothy Arden, Pype Hayes Hall is haunted by Lady Bagot. This was the title Dorothy acquired after her marriage, but she fell in love with the butler. Their affair was discovered and they agreed to commit suicide together. She has been seen in an old-fashioned yellow dress, staring out of the window. She is most likely to be seen on Friday 13.

Erdington, nr Sutton Coldfield, West Midlands: The Roebuck Inn

Back in 1791 the landlord, John Gorton, heard noises in the street outside. As he opened the window someone shot him with a pistol. During the 1940s another landlord died when the ship he was serving in was sunk while protecting convoys to Russia. Yet another landlord, during the 1950s, disappeared while out for a walk and his head was found on the railway line. Consequently the pub seems to be haunted by one or all of these former landlords. Extreme poltergeist activity has been reported, noises have been heard, dogs will not enter parts of the building and the burglar alarm is set off for no apparent reason. On one occasion a barmaid saw a man in a white shirt sitting in a room near the restaurant.

Erdington, nr Sutton Coldfield, West Midlands: Shepherd's Green House

This Victorian building has a haunted room believed to contain the ghost of the Earl of Leicester. From descriptions it appears that the manifestation is of 18th-century origin. The ghost has spoken to a variety of different people and is described as having tied-back light brown hair, and wearing a velvet jacket and trousers that narrow at the ankle. Other witnesses have reported seeing a young female apparition with long, black hair. A face seen peering through a window in the attic was described as looking like a nun. When this apparition appears, witnesses report hearing a woman's voice and smelling honeysuckle.

Erdington, nr Sutton Coldfield, West Midlands: Station Road

A strange apparition seems bent on monopolising the telephone box. She has often spent a considerable amount of time making other potential users wait. After a while she simply vanishes. She is described as being in her thirties and wearing clothes that appear to be contemporary with World War Two.

Erdington, nr Sutton Coldfield, West Midlands: Woodend Road

The ghostly figure of a young girl has been seen at the top of the stairs in one of the 1930s houses on this road. She is described as wearing Edwardian clothes, having long blonde hair and blue eyes, and being aged about 16. She appears for only a few seconds before disappearing.

Ethie Castle, nr Arbroath, Tayside

David and Ethie Beaton moved into the castle in 1524. He was the Abbott of Arbroath, and they had seven children. David Beaton was murdered at St Andrews on 29 May 1546. His ghost has been seen on many occasions, particularly on the narrow staircase that leads to a secret door in his old bedroom. On other occasions, witnesses have heard footsteps and the sounds of something being dragged across the floor. When a new governess was given a room in the older part of the house, she was kept awake by the sounds of a child playing with a toy with wheels. Sometimes she would hear the child sobbing gently, but could never discover where the sounds were coming from. Bent on discovering the reasons for the noises, the family found that the room above her bedroom was bricked up and panelled over. When this was demolished they found the skeleton of a small child beside the rotted remains of a wooden cart. As soon as the bones had been buried, the hauntings stopped. The castle also houses the apparition of a woman who is sometimes seen in the garden. Her appearance, however, is not welcomed, as it heralds the death of a family member.

Eton, Berkshire: Brewhouse Yard, Eton College

The college is haunted by Jane Shaw, who was instrumental in saving the college from being destroyed by her lover, Edward IV. In recognition of her devotion she was allowed to live in Lupton's Tower until she died in 1526. Several witnesses have seen a light emanating from the tower and others have reported spotting a woman in a long, mediaeval gown. One particular witness believed that he was being followed, only to turn around and see a strange flashing light. Another apparition, also in mediaeval clothing, has been seen in the Provost's Lodge, accompanied by the sound of footsteps.

Eton, Berkshire: Three Tuns Inn, High Street

It seems that poltergeist activity, as well as a more straightforward manifestation, has been experienced in this public house. Pints of beer have been tipped over customers, doors have been opened and landlords have felt someone push them. A cleaner has seen the apparition of a man in modern clothing in the central bar, but when she looked at the ghost intently it faded away. These spirits seem to have haunted the public house for a number of years, outliving many of the licensees.

Ettington Park, nr Stratford-upon-Avon, Warwickshire

A grey lady, believed to be the apparition of a servant girl who fell down the stairs in the Elizabethan period, has been seen. The ghosts of two children are often seen playing in the park. They were drowned in the river and their gravestones can be seen in the ruined church nearby.

Everingham, nr Market Weighton, East Yorkshire

Two female ghosts haunt this area. The first is of a suicide victim that worked in the nearby hall. She was a cook and drowned herself in a pond. The second ghost, complete with bicycle, is often seen near to the entrance of the hall. She was killed in a road accident.

Evershot, Dorset: The Acorn Inn, Fore Street

This 16th-century inn is said to be haunted by the ghost of a highwayman. It is believed that he used the pub as a base at some point during his short career.

Exeter, Devon: Cowick Barton Inn

This former farm became a public house in 1963, but is haunted by more ancient inhabitants of the area. Before the farmhouse the monastery of St Thomas stood on the site, and as a result the ghostly figure of a monk has appeared in the bedrooms of the pub. Interestingly, the apparition has also been seen walking across the fields toward the river in broad daylight, by residents and visitors.

Exeter, Devon: Exeter Cathedral

At around 7pm, particularly in July, you may be able to see the figure of a ghostly nun that haunts the cloisters. It is said that she appears in a particular place in the south wall of the nave, walks toward the church house and then disappears. She is said to walk with her head slightly bowed, completely ignoring all those who may be watching her. It is also said that a ghostly monk has been seen near Cathedral Close.

Exeter, Devon: Exeter Prison

A particular part of Exeter Prison is haunted by the figure of the last murderer to be kept on death row before hanging. The apparition is described as being a middle-aged man, who walks along the upper gallery before reaching a particular cell door and then vanishing. Two inmates were so affected by their encounter that they reported it to the prison governor. He examined the architectural plans of the building and discovered that this was once the site of death row. He arranged for the cell and the one below it to be cemented over and the end of the gallery to be sealed off. This has not prevented mysterious footsteps being heard in the immediate vicinity of the cell.

Exeter, Devon: Exeter University

Several witnesses have reported seeing the manifestation of a tall man in a long, white coat. It has been suggested that this is the phantom of a former decorator, who worked on the building several years ago. One of these decorators was so proud of the work that he had completed at the university that he often returned to look at it after the job had been completed. This may be his apparition, still making regular return trips to study his handiwork.

Exeter, Devon: Lord Haldon Hotel

Once owned by the Palk family, the hotel is all that remains of Haldon House. An 18th-century maidservant, who fell pregnant after an affair with the master of the house, haunts the building. When he discovered her condition he murdered her and dumped her body in the lake. This could explain why witnesses have seen the apparition wearing wet clothes.

Exeter, Devon: Ship Inn

Sir Frances Drake enjoyed the hospitality of this inn on many occasions. His ghost has been seen here by a number of witnesses. In addition to this, there is an aggressive spirit that tries to push people down the stairs.

Eyam, nr Bakewell, Derbyshire: St Lawrence's Churchyard

The apparition of 17th-century Catherine, wife of William Mompesson, Rector of Eyam, has been seen many times, dressed in white. In September 1665, the plague arrived in Eyam and wiped out over 300 of the population, including 50 children. It is believed that a bale of cotton, brought to the village by George Vicar, the local tailor, contained the plague virus. The cotton was bought to make a wedding gown, but the tailor and the bride-to-be were two of the first to die. The leaders of the village ordered that no one should leave and that there should be roadblocks to prevent the plague from spreading any further. William and Catherine worked tirelessly to help ease the suffering of the dying, until one morning Catherine commented that the air smelt sweet. William knew that she had the plague, as a sweet smell in the nostrils was one of the first symptoms. Catherine soon joined the other villagers in their graves.

Eynesbury, nr St Neots, Cambridgeshire

A witch called Nanny Izzard haunts the village by zooming around on her broomstick in the middle of the night. She is said to haunt this village because she was driven out of her home. The Old Rectory is haunted by strange noises in the middle of the night, but it is not known whether this is related to Nanny Izzard.

F

Falmouth to Fyvie Castle

Falmouth, Cornwall

The bay is haunted by the Cornish version of the Loch Ness monster. It is known as Morgawr, and has been seen on many occasions by locals and visitors to the area.

Fardel House, nr Cornwood, South Devon

Between the house, now a farm, and the bridge is a field. It is said that it cannot be cultivated. The spirit of a lady in dark and rustling silk clothes haunts it, and she is said to guard a buried treasure in the field. Witnesses have seen the apparition gliding up and down the road at night.

Faringdon, Berkshire

Sir Robert Pye, the Parliamentarian who besieged his own father's home, Faringdon House, appears as a headless ghost. He walks by the north wall of the church. The north wall is significant as it is the side of the churchyard traditionally left for the tainted, such as suicides. In nearby Oriel Cottage on Wicklesham Road, exorcisms have seemed to quieten down extensive poltergeist activity.

Farndon, nr Chester, Cheshire

On stormy nights, if you stand on the bridge spanning the River Dee, it is said that you can hear the sounds and cries of drowning children. In the 14th century Roger Mortimer ordered that the sons of Prince Madoc be pushed into the river and drowned.

Farnham, Surrey: Farnham Castle

The Norman keep and gateway are haunted by a strange, frightening figure which witnesses have not been able to fully describe. Some have claimed that it appears to be a woman dating from the 12th century, wearing a light-coloured gown and sporting a stern face. A ghostly monk haunts the Great Hall, and the stairway outside has the partially formed apparition of a dancing girl. It is said that she angered the owner of the castle, who made her dance until she collapsed. She crawled out onto the stairway and died. The ghost of Bishop Morley, who habitually slept in a coffin, has been both seen and heard in the Fox Tower. A tolling bell has also been heard here despite the fact that the tower does not have one. Phantom monks have been seen near the moat, and are described as being fully formed and solid.

Farnham, Surrey: Hop Bag Inn

This public house is said to be haunted by the sound of a coach and horses. This is a familiar tale as the Hop Bag Inn used to be a coaching inn.

Farnham, Surrey: Lion and Lamb Café

A grey lady haunts this place. She wears a grey habit and a large hat. Witnesses presume that she is a nun. Her haunting schedule is odd, as she has been seen by witnesses several times in one day, although she is sometimes absent for several months.

Farnham, Surrey: St Andrew's Church

Within the church witnesses have reported seeing what can only be described as a religious ceremony performed by ghosts. It is said that the ceremony replicates a pre-Reformation mass.

Farnworth, Greater Manchester: Dixon Green Labour Club

A ghost known as the blue lady, who has been regularly heard and seen in the club since it was built after the original manor house on the site was demolished in the 1930s, haunts Dixon Green Labour Club. She was even seen by one startled member as he was washing his hands in the gents' toilet. The blue lady, who is described as being very beautiful, has long golden hair and wears a blue silk dress with puffed sleeves. She is thought to be a victim of the Civil War. Before the old manor house was demolished, she was well known to the Tong family and their household, who lived there. One young man fell in love with the ghost and stated that he would have married her willingly, if only she had been real. However, beautiful or not, her appearances at the manor house were regarded as an ill-omen or prediction of some accident or misfortune that was about to afflict a member of the family.

Farringdon, Berkshire: Church of All Saints

In the graveyard, near to Farringdon House, the ghost of a headless man wearing a cloak has been seen walking slowly along the north wall of the church at dusk. He is believed to be Sir Robert Pye, a Parliamentarian who besieged Farringdon House, the local royalist stronghold owned by his father.

Farringdon, Berkshire: Winklesham Road

During the period 1963 to 1974, strong poltergeist activity was reported at Oriel Cottage in Winklesham Road. The police were called to investigate but said that they could do nothing about it. A spiritualist medium, called in to investigate, was able to contact the poltergeist and discover that it was the ghost of a lodger who had lived at the cottage and who had committed suicide there.

Fatfield, nr Sunderland, Tyne and Wear: Havelock Arms

A ghost that no one has been able to describe haunts this public house. Sometimes the manifestation is fully visible, but most of the time it seems to be more interested in moving objects around the building. This is a common form of ghost in a public house and a number of landlords from different inns have complained that their haunting takes this form.

Faulkbourne, Essex

The road from here to Witham is haunted. The key spot is beside Faulkbourne Hall. The spirit is that of a man in a hat, riding an old-fashioned bicycle. Witnesses suggest that the best time to catch him is at dusk. He will ride straight at you.

Faversham, Kent: Shipwright's Arms

Situated a mile north of the town of Faversham, the Shipwrights' Arms stands close to the tidal creek that flows into the River Swale. Accompanied by a rotting smell, the ghost of a sailor with glaring eyes, wearing an old-fashioned reefer jacket, haunts the pub.

Fawkham Green, Kent: Pennis Lane

The ghost that has been seen gliding down Pennis Lane is said to be that of a nun who was murdered there by would-be rapists. The sound of her screams and the thunder of horses' hooves have been heard from the lane at night. Her skull is kept at nearby Pennis House, and it is said that should it be removed from the attic, great misfortune will follow. Once the skull was removed to the village churchyard. Great disturbances then started to take place, which only ended when the skull was dug up and returned to the house.

Fawsley Park, nr Daventry, Northamptonshire

On New Year's Eve, clad in green, a ghostly huntsman appears near the ancient Dower House in the park. The building has not been inhabited since 1702. It is said that if he sees you then you will die a quick and painful death.

Featherstone Castle, nr Haltwhistle, Northumberland

Sir Reginald FitzUrse haunts this 13th-century castle. He starved to death in the dungeons. Abigail, the daughter of Lord Featherstone, fell in love with a young man of the Ridley family. The Ridleys were Catholic and the Featherstones Protestant. After much argument the two finally wed, and during the festivities they left to ride around the estate. On their ride they were set upon by the Ridleys and slaughtered, but a little later Lord Featherstone heard the drawbridge being lowered and the sounds of the party returning. As he went into the courtyard he saw the bridal entourage, but the newlyweds were deathly pale and their bodies were covered in wounds. The old man made the sign of the cross and the apparition disappeared. To this day the ghostly bridal party is seen at Pinkeyn Clough, the scene of the murder.

Felbrigg Hall, nr Cromer, Norfolk

William Windham haunts the library in the hall. He was a reclusive individual and a scholar who loved his books. His ghost replicates his behaviour and love of things scholarly. Windham died in 1810 at a friend's home. He perished trying to save his friend's books from the burning library.

Fife, Fife: St Andrew's Cathedral

A grey lady in a veil has often been seen by witnesses near the Round Tower that lies within the grounds of the ruined cathedral. Research has not uncovered who this woman is.

Fillingham, nr Lincoln, Lincolnshire: Fillingham Castle

A green lady is said to haunt the grounds of the castle, searching for her lover, who presumably died before she did. The castle also boasts the manifestation of a man on a white horse, who, it is said, committed suicide in the castle many years ago.

Flamborough Head, nr Bridlington, North Yorkshire

Flamborough has been a favourite haunt of smugglers for years, and it is unsurprising

that apparitions of them have been seen rolling barrels of alcohol around the north landing.

Flansham, West Sussex

Visitors to the Manor House have heard ghostly footsteps and the sound of something being dragged across the floor.

Flixton, nr Scarborough, North Yorkshire

During Saxon times there were wolves in this area. Consequently a hostel was built to provide shelter for travellers. It may be this connection that explains the present haunting, which takes the form of a red-eyed werewolf with huge fangs, accompanied by a deathly stench.

Flodden Field, nr Berwick-upon-Tweed, Northumberland

James IV fell on this battlefield, hacked to pieces by the English army under the command of the Earl of Surrey. Since 9 September 1513, several witnesses have claimed to have seen the moment of the king's death re-enacted by ghostly figures. The witnesses' descriptions accord with historical evidence in terms of heraldry and banners. On other occasions witnesses have heard the sound of fighting and have even seen 16th-century soldiers crossing the A697.

Folkestone, Kent: The Bayle, Priory Gardens

Several local witnesses have seen a cowled figure in the area. One couple saw the manifestation on the staircase of their home. An investigator discovered that witnesses have heard chanting in the front gardens of the houses in the street. Delivery men, postmen and milkmen claim to have heard religious hymns being sung, although they put this down to someone's radio. Another witness described a tall apparition, wearing a cape with a hood, which glided across the road. The area was the site of a former priory and some houses are built on land which belonged to the priory's grounds. The roadways cut across the land that also used to belong to the priory, which was built by Benedictine monks in 1530, to replace the religious community that had been established by the Normans in 1095. Some of the houses have original parts of the church wall as a part of their garden walls. Witnesses have reported seeing several monks working and making garden tools. They appeared to be oblivious to those watching them, and they wore brown habits, which may mean that they may date from the 13th century instead of the 16th century. They could be Franciscan or Dominican monks.

Folkestone, Kent: Leas Pavilion Theatre, The Leas

At the beginning of the 20th century an elderly caretaker hanged himself in the building. He was a gambler and had been in increasing amounts of debt for a number of years. He saw suicide as a way out. It is said that his spirit haunts the theatre, despite the fact that few people claim to have actually ever seen him. Staff have reported sensing the old man, watching doors close on their own and even bumping into invisible people. The ghost is now considered to be something of a good omen for the theatre and the staff generally agree that if the ghost of the old caretaker were to disappear it would mean the end of the theatre itself.

Forde Abbey, nr Chard, Somerset

A Cistercian abbey was founded here in 1138. The ghost, however, appears to date from around 1500 and is most likely to be Thomas Chard, the abbot at the time and the man credited with building the Great Hall and tower. Part of the cloisters is now known as

Monk's Walk, as several witnesses have seen the figure of a black monk there. Other witnesses have reported seeing the same apparition in the Great Hall.

Formby, nr Southport, Merseyside

A large, black dog is said to haunt the beach, but it never leaves footprints in order to mark its passing. A mediaeval house nearby, known as Tower Grange, was once a part of Whalley Abbey, and several witnesses have seen the ghost of a small monk there. It is said that the monk was in hiding at the time and preferred to starve to death in a priest hole rather than implicate the family that had hidden him. A skeleton was found in the priest hole when renovations were made. It is also said that animals can sense this ghost prior to its materialisation.

Fotheringhay, nr Oundle, Northamptonshire: St Mary the Virgin

Edward, Duke of York, grandson of Edward III, was buried in the church after being killed at the Battle of Agincourt. Mediaeval music has been heard coming from inside the church. The music may be associated in some way with the funeral that took place at that time.

Foulden, Norfolk: Foulden Church

On 14 November 1956, the local policeman was riding his bicycle through the village when he heard the church clock ring 25 times. The clock had permanently stopped at seven. He unlocked the church door and saw the rope swinging, but the church was empty. The time was 11pm. Later, talking to an old man that had worked at Foulden Hall, near to the church, he learned that a previous owner of the hall, who was buried in the graveyard, had died exactly ten years previously at 11pm on 14 November.

Fountains Abbey, nr Ripon, North Yorkshire

Once one of the wealthiest Cistercian abbeys in the country, built in 1132, ruined Fountains Abbey is haunted by a chanting male choir. You are most likely to hear the ghostly voices in the chapel of the Nine Altars.

Fountains Hall, nr Ripon, North Yorkshire

Built in 1611, the hall is haunted by the spirit of Sir Stephen Proctor. He was an unpleasant character who used all methods to extract fines from local Catholics. In the end one of them murdered him on his doorstep. His daughter, who witnessed the killing, appears as a ghostly blue lady. It is also believed that a man, dressed in Elizabethan costume, appears from the panelling in one of the rooms.

Fradley, nr Lichfield, Staffordshire

RAF Lichfield lies beneath an industrial estate. During World War Two it was used as a training centre for bomber crews. Several witnesses have reported seeing a headless man in period uniform walking around the area. The unfortunate man, in life, lost his head when he walked into the spinning propellers of a Lancaster Bomber. He was a tail gunner who sadly did not graduate from the training depot.

Freshwater, Isle of Wight: Golden Hill Fort

This huge hexagonal fort was built in the early 1800s as a precaution against possible invasion by Napoleon's French armies. It now has a more peaceful purpose, as it is a centre for small businesses and craftsmen of the area. A number of witnesses have reported seeing the manifestation of a soldier dressed in a World War One uniform, as well as a sailor of unspecified era who sits and watches

people work. Witnesses have reported that he is quite benign and simply smiles.

Friends' Burial Ground, nr Milverton, Somerset

This site is a decades-old Quaker burial ground. A number of witnesses have reported seeing a man dressed in old-fashioned Quaker costume. It is not clear who this man is or why he should haunt the site, but it is presumed that he is the ghost of someone who is buried there, or that he seeks to protect someone close to him in life.

Frithelstock, nr Great Torrington, Devon: St Mary and St Gregory's Church

A ruined priory stands next to the church and, during excavations in 1932, Barbara Carbonnell, a member of the Excavation Committee, visited the site with her daughter and her daughter's son. The small boy immediately exclaimed 'I love this place' and went on to say 'I have been here before. I have long, long ago, when I was a very old man.' As proof of this possible reincarnation the boy asked 'What have they done to my tower, my lovely tower, with the stairs that went windy up where I pulled the bell?' He was, at this point, standing where the tower used to be. Later excavations proved this to be true. Either the child was indeed the reincarnation of a former monk, or a monk's spirit temporarily entered the mind of the boy.

Frodingham, nr Driffield, East Yorkshire

A headless horseman is said to ride around the roads near here. Other witnesses have described the apparition as having a skull for a head, swathed in cloth or a cowl. On at least one occasion this manifestation has jumped onto the back of a horse ridden by an unwitting equestrian.

Frodsham, Cheshire: Heathercliffe Country House

Poltergeist activity was stimulated here during the 1970s, when attempts were made to contact spirits using a ouija board. As a result, guests and staff have reported items being moved around the kitchen and unseen hands pushing desserts off the sweet trolley.

Frostenden, nr Southwold, Suffolk

At the turning to this village along the Wangford to Reydon road, the phantom of a coach and four headless horses has been seen. They may carry the spirit of a wicked squire. Horses are terrified at this spot and one luckless rider lost his life at the beginning of the 19th century, when his horse reared up and threw him.

Fulmer, Buckinghamshire

Horses hoof beats can be heard here, accompanied by the sound of wheels crunching on gravel. This is a purely aural manifestation and nothing has ever been seen. Presumably this must be a haunting related to a coaching incident in the past, or the spirit of a long-dead coach driver who seeks to re-enact his favourite journeys.

Fyvie Castle, nr Aberdeen, Grampian

Many years ago, a trumpeter named Andrew Lammie fell in love with Agnes Smith. She was the daughter of the local miller and neither of her parents approved of the match. The local laird also had designs on the girl and had Andrew transported on a slaver to the West Indies. Andrew escaped and returned to Scotland, only to discover that Agnes had died shortly after his departure. It is said that Andrew died of shock, but on his deathbed he swore that his ghost would continually reappear to herald the imminent death of a lord of Fyvie. His apparition is described as being a tall man, clad in tartan, standing on the castle walls. If he is approached, he disappears. The castle also has a green lady, who is seen emerging from the haunted chamber. She glides through the corridors and then heads back to the room.

G

Gallow's Hill to Gypsy's Grave

Gallow's Hill, nr Little Gaddesden, Hertfordshire

A man in grey has been seen here. The sound of unexplained groaning and the clanking of chains accompanies his appearance. It is widely believed that he must be the apparition of a criminal sentenced to hang, as the spirit recreates a last walk to the gallows.

Gateshead, Tyne and Wear: W.H. Smith and Sons, Kirk Lane

Until 1912, this warehouse was a public house, which was finally forced to shut its doors owing to a decline in trade. However, the premises are still visited by one of the old regulars, who has been heard but never seen during the evening and also in the daytime. The times coincide with the old opening times of the pub. The ghost is thought to be that of a regular who collapsed and died outside the pub.

Gaulden Manor, Tolland, Somerset

James Turberville, Bishop of Exeter, was exiled here in 1563 following a spell in the Tower of London. Heavy footsteps, heard on the main staircase, may well be those of Turberville, who came to love the house. In the haunted Bishop's Garden, several ghost monks have been seen, which presumably relate to the time when Taunton Priory used it as a burial site in the 12th century. A ghostly grey lady has been seen on the right-hand side of the fireplace. A small woman haunts the front stairs and three blood-stained Cavaliers have been seen in a room called the Chapel, off the Great Hall, perhaps an echo of a Civil War battle nearby. Ghostly knuckles have rapped the front door and several servants have seen ghostly monks and a woman with dark hair and a blue dress.

Gawsworth, nr Macclesfield, Cheshire: Gawsworth Hall

Mary Fitton was the younger daughter of Sir Edward and Lady Alice Fitton. The ghost of Mary haunts her former home. She left Gawsworth in 1596, at the age of 17, to join the court of Queen Elizabeth as a Maid of Honour. In 1602, after an affair with the Earl of Pembroke, she fell pregnant. The queen was livid and sent both lovers to the Tower. In 1712, Lord Mohan and the Duke of Hamilton fought a ruinous duel that left them both dead; their spirits are believed to re-fight that last battle at Gawsworth. There is a strange smell of incense in one of the bedrooms, but this is believed to be related to the priest's hole above the room. During the 1920s, a sealed cupboard was opened to reveal a mouldering skeleton. It is thought that the discovery has a connection with the incense haunting.

Gidleigh, Dartmoor

A stone bridge crosses the Blackawton Brook, and not only are the sounds of a bloody fight heard here, but nearby the ghost of a woman who drowned herself appears. She has been seen on several occasions by a number of witnesses.

Gillamoor, North Yorkshire

In the 17th century, Kitty Garthwaite was deserted by her lover while she was preg-

nant. She preferred suicide in the River Dove to facing life alone. Her apparition is said to be dangerous to young men, whom she tries to lure into the water to join her in her wet grave.

Gilsland, Carlisle, Cumbria: Wardrew House

Now a guesthouse, this building was originally constructed as a watchtower against Scottish raiding parties. A green lady haunts it. Witnesses describe the apparition as being somewhat formless and making its presence felt as billowing green cloths or curtains.

Glamis Castle, nr Forfar, Angus

Glamis Castle was chosen by William Shakespeare as the setting for *Macbeth*. Indeed, King Malcolm II either died of his battle wounds here, or was murdered. His grandson, Duncan I, was also murdered within the castle. Macbeth succeeded him to the Scottish throne. Legend has it that the Strathmores, who now inhabit the castle, are cursed with the periodic birth of a vampire-type monster in the family. Numerous sightings of small 'monsters' have been recorded. As part of this tale, a workman making alterations to the castle encountered one such creature and was paid a large sum to emigrate to Australia and keep the family's secret. The unfortunate Lady Jayne Glamis, now called the grey lady, was hated by King James V, who imprisoned her in her own home and later burned her at the stake as a witch. Her glowing spirit can be seen floating above the clock tower, and at other times walking through the castle. Patrick, a Lord of Glamis in the 15th century, can also be seen, eternally playing cards with the bearded giant, Lord Crawford. They lost their souls to the devil in a card game. The spirits of several members of the Ogilvy family can still be heard thumping on doors to attract attention; they died of starvation while being sheltered by the Earl. Their skeletons were found in Victorian times. The ghost of a black servant can be seen in one of the sitting rooms. As a child, the Queen Mother was moved out of the Blue Room after being kept awake by hammering and banging.

Glasgow, Strathclyde: Shield's Road Underground Station

The apparition of a grey lady is all that remains of a woman who fell onto the tracks in 1922. She died, but a heroic stationmaster saved her daughter. It is presumed that the woman still seeks her child.

Glasgow, Strathclyde: Stobhill General Hospital

One witness, a nurse, saw the apparition of a woman in a white uniform moving into a side ward near the door in the area in which she was working. She knew that there was only one patient on that particular ward. The patient was due to be discharged the following morning and the vision of this white uniformed manifestation encouraged the nurse to check on the patient. She found her unconscious and doctors later said that she would have died if the nurse had not investigated. It is also interesting that the same witness would routinely talk to an unseen individual. When asked by her mother who she was talking to, the nurse replied 'Anne is my sister'. Her mother was amazed, as the girl had indeed had a sister called Anne, who had died at the age of 10 months, years before the second daughter was born.

Glasgow, Strathclyde: Theatre Royal

A former cleaning lady by the name of Nora haunts the Theatre Royal. She does not appear to cause any problems and is clearly very much at home in the theatre. Even after death she is reluctant to leave it.

Glasgow, Strathclyde: Western Infirmary

The same witness that was called inexplicably into a ward at Stobhill General Hospital encountered an apparition during her duties as a night sister at the Western Infirmary. She became aware of a tall, silver-haired male, wearing a blue dressing gown, standing in the doorway of the ward opposite. The apparition remained there for a few moments and then vanished. A ward nurse who had also seen the manifestation corroborated the description of the man. The ward nurse realised that it was a patient who had died two days before.

Glastonbury Abbey, Somerset

Not only are King Arthur and Guinevere said to be buried here, but the Holy Grail is also rumoured to be hidden in the Challis Well. Many regard Glastonbury as one of the most holy places in Europe, so it is unsurprising that this seems to be an important site for hauntings. Several individuals claim to have seen visions of King Arthur and his knights, as well as a host of monks and other apparitions.

Glastonbury, Somerset: George and Pilgrim Inn

This building was formerly used to house pilgrims en route to Glastonbury Abbey. Several people have seen a fat monk in what is now known as the Haunted Cell. Apparently the monk committed suicide in the room, but when he is seen he appears to be happy and cheerful. Other guests have been awoken by ghostly tapping and seen strange figures standing at the foot of their beds.

Glastonbury, Somerset: Lady Chapel

Around 30 years ago, a visitor to Glastonbury saw a column of white-robed figures that could either have been monks or nuns, apparently en route to a ceremony. As the visitor reached the ruins of the Lady Chapel, there was no sign of any of the figures. The man described the scene as being silent and still and could not explain what he had seen.

Glen Aray Castle, nr Inveraray, Strathclyde

The Duke of Montrose had a piper hanged nearby before the castle was built. Numerous witnesses have seen and heard the piper in various parts of the castle. Principle haunting sites include Archie's Room, the Blue Room and the Green Library.

Glencunie, Grampian: Christie Hill

Following the crushing of the rebels in 1746, Scotland became an occupied country with garrisons dotted around to disarm highlanders and enforce the ban on the wearing of the kilt. Sergeant Arthur Davies, of General Guise's Regiment of Foot, enjoyed wandering the hills by himself, fishing and hunting. He was also in charge of a party of eight men stationed at Dubrach, near Inverey. His comparative wealth meant that it was only a matter of time before someone robbed him. On 28 September 1749, he did not return from his walk. In June 1750, his ghost appeared for the first time. He manifested himself at the home of a shepherd, Alexander McPherson, and told him where his remains were hidden. McPherson took Donald Farquarson with him to help find them. The apparition also named his murderers as Duncan Clark and Alexander Bain MacDonald. The authorities were eventually informed and Clark and MacDonald were arrested and charged in September 1753, coming to trial at the Tollbooth, Edinburgh on 10 June 1754. Much of the evidence was circumstantial. Clark's wife had been seen with the sergeant's ring on her finger, and Clark himself had become a rich man, far from the poverty he was in

only a few years before. There were also two witnesses to the murder: the Cameron brothers, Angus and Donald. They had seen the two men with the sergeant and heard two shots, and then the accused were seen standing over the body. After 14 hours a not guilty verdict was reached, on account of the fact that the ghost had spoken to Alexander McPherson in Gaelic, a language Arthur Davies probably did not know. However, the sergeant's ghost had got its way, as the body was properly buried and the world knew who had killed him.

Glossop, Derbyshire

A grey lady is said to haunt the churchyard. She is described as such despite the fact that she is dressed in brown. The apparition may well be a vicar's wife who murdered her husband. It is also said that the vicarage itself is haunted, perhaps by the same ghost.

Gloucester, Gloucestershire: The Bishop's House

Strangely, the spirit that haunts this house has been known to assist visitors putting on their jackets and coats. It is presumed that it is the spirit of a former servant, who in life performed this task routinely.

Gloucester, Gloucestershire: Blackfriars Priory

Built in 1239, incorporating a church and extensive cloister, this Dominican priory is now largely in ruins. In 1530 the priory was already in considerable disrepair when a Mr Bell purchased it and turned it into a cap and cloth factory. Several new houses were built incorporating parts of the old priory, and are still residences. During restoration work in the 1980s the very old skeleton of a young child was discovered in a dungeon-like area beneath the old priory. Despite the fact that the remains were of a young child, many individuals associated the finding with sightings of a black monk, presumably an inhabitant of Blackfriars Priory in the past. Many of the workers involved in the renovations, and others who have worked there since, have reported seeing a monk near the underground room. They have also reported mysteriously locked doors and other happenings.

Gloucester, Gloucestershire: Gloucester Prison

One of Britain's oldest prisons, Gloucester gaol is haunted by the ghost of a 15th-century girl who was brutally murdered on the site of what is now landing A3. Cell 25 is particularly haunted and poltergeist activity has included books and utensils being hurled around the cell. On one occasion a disembodied hand was seen pointing at one of the prisoners. During a seance held in the cell in December 1969, with the use of a ouija board, the ghost described herself as Jenny Godfrey and said that she had been murdered by a drunken Irishman after an argument.

Glyder, nr Llanberis, Gwynedd

Between the two peaks of the Glyders, on a saddle in the mountain, lurks a strange manifestation that has been witnessed by a number of climbers over the past few years. Lying to the east of Snowdon, this area is still a strong challenge to the adventurous. However, many will not realise that they could encounter what has been described as a large opaque bear, which rushes toward you.

Godley, nr Hyde, Greater Manchester

A yellowish-brown phantom hound haunts this area. It has been described as being as big as a bull, with a ferocious appearance and the ability to appear or disappear at will. For a time people believed that it was an escaped feline from nearby Bellevue Zoo.

Godlingston Manor, nr Swanage, Dorset

This 12th-century house is reputed to be haunted by an unknown woman. The ghost has been seen walking in the garden beside an old wall, and on other occasions she has been seen looking in to the house through the windows. It is apparent that the ghost has been haunting the house for many years as previous occupants also reported seeing the figure. In more recent years the ghost has been seen on an upstairs landing. It is still unclear who she is, but it is presumed that she is a former inhabitant of the house.

Godolphin House, nr Penzance, Cornwall

Built in the early Tudor period, this building houses manifestations said to be related to Margaret, the wife of the 1st Earl of Godolphin. She is said to appear around the anniversary of her funeral, believed to be 9 September 1678. Margaret died outside Cornwall, and her lead coffin took two weeks to get back to Godolphin House. It is therefore difficult to be precise about the date of her funeral. She is said to emerge from a sealed closet and walk along a terrace in the house. The apparition of a ghostly funeral procession is perhaps related to her. The house has what they call a 'ghost path', which leads to the old family chapel. The path is one of five escape routes from the King's Room and the King's Garden, designed to allow Charles II to escape from the house if found there. It is also said that the face of Charles II has been seen looking out of a window of the room he occupied while he stayed at Godolphin prior to the Restoration of the monarchy. In nearby Jew's Lane a Jewish ghost appears. It is said that he hanged himself from a tree there and that he is buried beneath the road. He takes the form of a bull and a fiery chariot.

Gonalston, nr Nottingham, Nottinghamshire

The Old Mill is haunted by the sounds of cries and sobs that are probably related to the time when it was used as a place to send people from the workhouse to. They were virtual slaves and often ill treated. Those that died were buried in unmarked graves without the benefit of a service or a blessing. It is said that their graves are dotted around the local area in the woods and fields. As they are not buried in consecrated ground, their spirits remain restless.

Goodrich Castle, nr Pencraig, Herefordshire

Alice and Clifford haunt this castle. They were lovers, and were besieged in the castle in 1646 by Alice's Parliamentarian uncle, Colonel Birch. At the culmination of the siege, just as the Parliamentarians were about to storm the castle, the couple tried to escape. Unfortunately they were drowned in the River Wye and their restless spirits still haunt the area.

Goodwin Sands, off Deal, Kent

The sands mark part of King Harold's father's estate, now some 4 miles out to sea. The ghost ship *Lady Lovibund*, which was deliberately run aground on the sands while 50 guests on board were celebrating the marriage of Simon Peel, can be seen on the anniversary of the 1748 tragedy. The key date is 13 February.

Goonhilly Downs, nr Cadgwith, Cornwall

The Croft Pascoe Pool on the downs is said to be visited by a ghostly ship. It has a long sail but nothing else is known of it. It is thought that in the past the pool may have formed part of a series of waterways that were approached from the sea.

Goosnargh, nr Preston, Lancashire: Chingle Hall

Built in 1260 and said to be the birthplace of John Wall, a 17th-century saint, this hall is a small, moated manor house with a rich vein of history running through it. An unidentified apparition haunts it, and is widely believed to be John Wall, who was executed in Worcester in 1679. A grisly tale surrounds his corpse after the execution. One story claims that his head was smuggled into France in 1834, after nuns who had been protecting it returned there. In an alternative version, the head remains in Chingle Hall. Witnesses have reported tapping on walls, doors opening and closing and animals watching something unseen by humans. Footsteps are heard, particularly near the haunted room. Within the room itself, several witnesses have reported seeing a Franciscan monk. Others have reported seeing a strange light in the centre of the room, which is said to mark the place where another holy relic is buried.

Gosport, Hampshire: Blockhouse Point, HMS *Dolphin*

In 1777, Jack the Painter was executed for setting fire to the rope works in Portsmouth dockyard. Several witnesses have heard the creaking of the chains holding up the gibbet in which his body was placed after his death. It is said that his remains were kept in the gibbet for some years, as a grim reminder of the crime he had committed.

Grace Dieu Priory, nr Coalville, Leicestershire

A variant on the phantom hitch hiker story is associated with the A512 between Loughborough and Ashby. The ruins of the priory lie nearby, just off the road. A white lady not only walks around the ruins, but has also been seen on the road itself. Several motorists and bus drivers have stopped, believing that she wishes to be picked up. As they pull in, she vanishes. It is not known who she might be.

Grafty Green, nr Maidstone, Kent

A terrible coach crash of the early 19th century is re-enacted regularly at the village of Grafty Green. A coach and four set off from the Kings Head public house, bound for Lenham. After the driver had whipped the team up, the horses suddenly took fright and bolted. When the team reached the bend by the local church, instead of bearing left and following the road, the horses bore right, galloping up a driveway into the grounds of the old rectory and crashing into a tree. The impact killed the horses immediately and the coach was smashed to pieces. The driver was hurled toward a tree and decapitated. The passengers died in the wreckage.

Granard, Co. Longford, Republic of Ireland

The headless ghosts of a British Army officer and his horse have been seen at night in various parts of Co. Longford. The reports of the sightings are so well known in the district that people lock themselves in their houses at nightfall and refuse to leave again until daylight the following morning. The apparition is of Captain Blundell, who was attached to a cavalry unit in barracks near Granard in the early part of the 18th century. He was a gambler, drinker and womaniser. One morning, he failed to report for duty and his orderly discovered his headless body locked in his quarters. It appeared to be suicide as the door had been locked from the inside, but it was difficult to imagine a way in which a man could cut off his own head.

Blundell had made a fair few enemies, including a local landowner whose daughter had been badly treated by the officer. It is thought that his apparition appears in the hope that the truth of his death will one day become known.

Grantchester, nr Cambridge, Cambridgeshire: The Old Vicarage

Unexplained footsteps have been heard moving through the garden of the Old Vicarage, which are thought to be those of soldier-poet, Rupert Chawner Brooke. He lived in the house from 1911 until he died of illness while abroad on war service in 1915. He loved the house and made it the subject of one of his most famous poems, *The Old Vicarage, Grantchester*. Noises have also been heard coming from the top floor, as if someone is walking about. Books and other objects have been unaccountably moved.

Grantham, Lincolnshire: Angel and Royal, High Street

Originally built as a hostel for the Templars, the building is said to have been established as an inn as early as the 12th century. King John was a firm devotee of the place and established his court there in 1213. The apparition of a white lady haunts the corridors on the 2nd and 3rd floors, in the Georgian part of the building.

Granton, Lothian: Caroline Park

Built in the 17th century, this house not only boasts the manifestation of a green lady, but also plays host to a phantom cannon ball. The female apparition has been seen to emerge from a wall and walk through the front entrance; she then approaches the house from the east and heads for an old bell. She rings it and then vanishes. The bell itself is said to toll on its own at times. The incredible sight of a cannon ball crashing through the window of the Aurora Room has been seen on several occasions. It hits the floor and bounces across the room, but there is no visible damage to either the window or the room.

Grayingham, nr Gainsborough, Lincolnshire

It is said that the area is haunted by the manifestations of phantom black dogs. They are described as being huge and extremely frightening. Witnesses have seen them between Grayingham and the village of Hemswell, which is some three miles distant.

Great Addington, Northamptonshire

Tragic events during a house fire seem to be the basis for the sighting of a desperate-looking woman on the road between the village and Woodford. Unaware that her children's nurse had already led them to safety through the back of the house, the woman entered the blazing building to look for them. Unfortunately she lost her life.

Great Bealings, nr Woodbridge, Suffolk

Bealings House was the site of strange poltergeist activities in the mid-19th century. Between 2 February and 27 March 1834, the bells inside the house often rang without human aid. The bells were eventually disconnected and the phenomenon ceased.

Great Leighs, Essex: St Anne's Castle Inn

St Anne's Castle Inn is said to be haunted. The manifestation could either be that of a young girl who was murdered in front of her mother, or that of a witch who was burned at the stake.

Great Lumley, nr Chester-le-Street, Co. Durham

Christopher Walker, the uncle of 17-year-old Annie Walker, began a relationship with her that was to end both of their lives and leave a haunted legacy. By 1680, Annie was pregnant and after much gossip Walker arranged, through Dame Curie, for the girl to leave town. She moved in with Dame Curie for a week before a Lancashire coal-mining friend, Mark Sharpe, and Walker arrived to take her to Lancashire until the child was born. This was the last time that Annie was seen alive. Around a fortnight later James Graham, a fuller at a mill, saw a dishevelled woman, with five wounds in her head, badly bloodstained with her hair ragged and loose, standing in a room at his mill. The manifestation was clearly a ghost, and it told him that she was Anne Walker and that Mark Sharpe had killed her with his pick and thrown her body into a disused mineshaft. The apparition went on to say that the pick was hidden under a bank, and that Sharpe had unsuccessfully tried to clean his shoes before hiding those too. She also said that if Graham did not tell a magistrate immediately then she would continue to haunt him until he did. Graham was afraid, as Walker was a powerful and well-known local man, but after several more ghostly appearances he told the story to Thomas Liddell JP and Francis James JP. The body was found, as were the pick and the bloodstained shoes. In August 1681, Walker and Sharpe were tried at Durham Assizes, found guilty and hanged. It seems that the clinching point was when Annie's manifestation appeared to the judge, Sir Humphrey Davenport, swearing that her uncle was guilty.

Great Lumley, nr Chester-le-Street, Co. Durham: Lumley Castle

Built in the 15th century, the castle is haunted by Lady Lumley. It is said that, as a Catholic, she wished to become Protestant, but the priests in the castle conspired to murder her by throwing her into the moat. Her ghost is said to rise from its watery grave whenever the water level in the area rises.

Great Malvern, Worcestershire

A monk at Little Malvern Priory admitted to the prior that he had slept with a woman. Despite the fact that the prior was guilty of the same offence, he ordered the monk to crawl on his hands and knees up the rough side of Ragged Stone twice a day. After many such repetitions, the monk went mad and cursed the prior, the church and all those on whom the shadow of the two peaks should fall. He then fell down dead. The curse is said to have claimed the lives of Thomas Becket, Richard III, Cardinal Wolsey and Anne Boleyn, among others.

Great Melton, Norfolk

The ghosts of four bridesmaids who are periodically seen riding in a phantom coach haunt Great Melton. In life they had been returning from Norwich to Great Melton one dark night after a wedding, when the drunken coachman ran off the road into a deep pool, drowning himself and his four pretty passengers. Locals believe that if you see the girls' faces it is a sign of good fortune. To see their headless torsos is an omen of disaster.

Great Missenden, Buckinghamshire: Little Abbey Hotel

This hotel was once a school, linked with Missenden Abbey not only spiritually, but also physically, by an underground passageway. In the 1920s, servants were too frightened to enter the lounge because of the regular appearance of a monk-like figure. Fifty years later, in the early 1970s, a handyman was repairing a window when he became aware of a man walking toward

him. He watched him come up the stairs, wearing a brown hooded cloak. The manifestation held his hands together in front of him as if in prayer, and walked past the workman, ignoring him despite his greeting. At this point the workman believed the apparition to be a real person. After a few minutes, the workman became suspicious of the fact that the apparition had not reappeared. Only a toilet and staff quarters lay beyond where he was working. A search of the building revealed no sign of the strange figure.

Great Missenden, Buckinghamshire: Missenden Abbey

The Black Monks of Missenden were a notorious bunch, and it is not surprising that the abbey is said to be haunted by the apparitions of three ungodly brothers. Several witnesses have seen the manifestation of a monk carrying a sword. The 12th-century abbey is now used as a college, and is also haunted by a grey lady of unknown origin. She has been seen on the main staircase, wearing a grey Victorian dress. Others have described the dress as being a black crinoline, resembling a gown. Another sighting, perhaps of the same apparition, has occurred near the women's lavatories. The apparition is described as wearing a light grey dress. This second sighting has led some to believe that two female ghosts haunt the building.

Great Shefford, nr Hungerford, Berkshire

The ghost of Wild Darrell, a murderer, can be seen near Shefford Woodlands, where the new road crosses the old Roman road. The midwife who brought Darrell to trial after he murdered a newborn child lived in the village. Darrell was arrested, but bribed the judge to acquit him. He died 14 years later, when he fell from his horse and broke his neck. It is said that the horse panicked after seeing the ghost of the baby he had killed. Several witnesses have seen his ghost, with its head lolling at an odd angle.

Great Staughton, Cambridgeshire: Crown Inn

A former landlord, who was also a butcher, haunts the 18th-century coaching inn. He was known as 'Old Pork and Lard' by the regulars, but clearly had enough charm (some say money) to attract a young bride when he was in his 70s. She died in childbirth, and the apparition of the old man can be seen trying to do the domestic chores he would have done in the last few weeks of his wife's life. Clothes appear and disappear, footsteps have been heard going upstairs and crossing a first floor room and bottles have been heard clinking in the empty bar.

Great Wilbraham, Cambridgeshire: Carpenter's Arms

This 17th-century building suffers from strange noises. Echoing footsteps are heard making their way along an upstairs corridor. The sound always stops at a particular point. Investigations have revealed no sign of the unknown guest. On several occasions, the ghost has also knocked on the doors of bedrooms.

Great Yarmouth, Norfolk: The Gallon Pot

When German bombers hit a nearby church during World War Two, a man standing in the doorway of the pub was killed. The particular area of haunting seems to be the lower bar, where there is considerable poltergeist activity. Pictures are now screwed to the wall after the manifestation repeatedly strewed them around the room. The present publican insists that glasses are left face down, as the spirit has a habit of turning them over

himself. On several occasions the ghost has smashed glasses, leaving them shattered all over the floor.

Great Yarmouth, Norfolk: Seashore Camp

'Old Scarf' is a ghost who has haunted the coastal regions of Norfolk for some years, spending a great deal of his time at Great Yarmouth. Nothing is really known of this ghost, or why he haunts the area, but he has been very active. He specialises in prodding people in the ribs, and sometimes even bowls them over. He was very active on the caravan site at Seashore Camp on 5 June 1971, when he forced a holidaymaking family to vacate the caravan that they had rented for the week. One of the children was repeatedly prodded in the ribs, and finally had all his bedclothes off pulled before being thrown to the floor by the invisible ghost.

Greystoke Castle, nr Penrith, Cumbria

The history of Greystoke Castle began in the 12th century, when Ivo, grandson of local Saxon chieftain Llyulph, created the first stone structure on the site of the present castle in 1129. It is haunted by the ghost of a monk that was bricked up in the tunnel that led to the church.

Grindleford, nr Bakewell, Derbyshire: Stoke Hall

Built in 1755, the house is haunted by a headless ghost that seems to have a long history. Known as 'Fair Flora', she was murdered in the house many years ago. It is not known what her real name is, or why she was murdered.

Guildford, Surrey: AA Headquarters

The staff room is, apparently, the centre of a haunting experience. The sound of footsteps is heard, and the temperature of the room drops drastically. Staff have encountered the apparition of a woman dressed in a mauve skirt near the women's lavatory. This was followed by a separate incident, when staff heard a strange voice coming from the women's lavatory. On investigation, they could see nothing, save one of the cistern chains swinging. It is said that an old well still stands in the basement of the building, but it is not known whether this is linked in any way to the happenings upstairs.

Guildford, Surrey: Angel Hotel

Several witnesses claim to have seen the apparition of a man in the building. Perplexing though it may seem, it is said that the man is a military figure. The apparition has been described as dating from the early part of the 18th century, wearing what appears to be a Polish officer's uniform.

Guildford, Surrey: Loseley House

Both a brown and a grey lady are said to haunt this 16th-century house. The brown lady resembles one of the portraits that hangs in the building. The grey lady, although explanations are contradictory, also has strong connections with the house. She is either a mother who drowned her own offspring in the moat (which no longer exists), or she murdered her stepson so that her child would inherit Loseley House.

Gunby Hall, nr Skegness, Lincolnshire

The ghost of a murdered servant is said to haunt the pond and pathway in the grounds of Gunby Hall. The story of the servant's death varies, but it is believed that he was killed and dumped in the pond after Sir William Massingberd, the owner of the house, found out about his daughter's affair with the man. The servant is said to walk the path beside the pond, which has become

known as Ghost Walk. Another version of the story claims that both the daughter and the servant were killed, which would account for the image of a ghostly couple sometimes seen along the path.

Gunthorpe, nr Newark-on-Trent, Nottinghamshire

A ghostly cat, said to be as big as a large dog, haunts the road near the River Trent. There is great speculation as to whether this is, in fact, another sighting of one of the great cats of Great Britain. Sightings over a period of years suggest that it may be a genuine apparition.

Guy's Cliffe, nr Warwick, Warwickshire

This partly ruined house lies on the banks of the Avon, one mile to the north of Warwick. It dates from the 12th century, but was mainly rebuilt by Richard Beauchamp in around 1422. A stone and brick house in classical style now stands there, which was built in around 1750 for Samuel Greatheed. It was largely abandoned after World War Two. The adjacent chapel has a huge dungeon underneath the crypt, which has been used as a masonic lodge for many years. The ghostly links are to Piers Gaveston, who was beheaded on nearby Blacklow Hill in 1312. He was a favourite of Edward II. Cruelly, the horse that carried him to his execution was bedecked with bells and ribbons, apparently to mock Gaveston's unmanly appearance. The sound of these bells is still heard in the area, particularly near to the monument at the top of the hill.

Gwrych Castle, nr Abergele, Clwyd

Looks can be deceptive, as this castle only dates from 1820, but its stunning appearance could lead the casual observer to believe otherwise. A red lady and a white lady haunt it. Of the former we know very little, but the latter may be the apparition of the lady of the house, who died in a riding accident some years ago. This may explain her red clothing. In 1950, during preparation for a title fight, British boxer Bruce Woodcock encountered the red lady.

Gypsy's Grave, nr Newmarket, Suffolk

This spot, also known as the Boy's Grave, is the place where a young shepherd boy hanged himself after having been accused of stealing sheep. Others believe that a gypsy is buried here. Odd stories relate to the spot, including a strange figure that makes cyclists dismount.

H
Haddenham to Hyssington

Haddenham, Buckinghamshire

A murdered farmer, who was killed in 1848 as he returned from Thame market, haunts a road near here. The story is stranger than this; his wife saw her husband's ghost in a dream. He was clutching at his chest, which had been crushed with a hammer. From her descriptions, the authorities found the body and caught the footpads. They were hanged for their crimes.

Haddington, nr Edinburgh, Lothian: St Mary's Church

The Duke of Lauderdale died in 1682 and was buried in the family vault. He was not a much-liked man as he was a Covenanter, who ruthlessly enforced the laws in this district. After his body was embalmed and placed in the vault, it was found that his spirit was very restless. Every time that anyone entered it,

they found that the coffin had moved. His apparition has been seen in the churchyard.

Halesworth, Suffolk: Chediston Street

At various periods of the history of this road, there were fifteen pubs or taprooms and it was considered to be the more salubrious area of the market town. There is some talk of the ghost of a servant girl that is said to walk the street at night. There does not seem to be any particular incident that links a death or murder to this apparition.

Halesworth, Suffolk: Halesworth Cemetery

Many years ago, it was said that a man who had died under suspicious circumstances haunted a certain grave in this rather scary cemetery. If the particular grave were danced around, then the spirit would rise from the grave. On one particular occasion, just before World War Two, several local boys took a short cut through the cemetery at dusk, after scrumping apples near Holton. As they ascended the staircase to the newer part of the cemetery, they heard the clanking of chains and a low moan. To this day they do not know whether they unwittingly disturbed a ghost or whether it was just their imagination.

Halesworth, Suffolk: Market Place

Halesworth's Market Place has great charm and a wealth of history, but the haunting here dates back to the time when pilgrims used some of the houses en route to Walsingham. Behind the Georgian and later façades are much older houses, making it difficult to pinpoint the date of the haunting. Nevertheless, in one of the houses an attic bedroom is often pervaded by the smell of incense. One of the owners of the house also saw the shadowy outline of a male figure, rather like a priest, as she ascended the top floor stairs.

Hall-i-th'-Wood Museum, nr Bolton, Greater Manchester

This 15th-century building was extended in 1591 and further modified at several points over the years. Despite the fact that the building has changed significantly, both externally and internally, it is clear that it is haunted by three ghosts. The first moves freely through part of the wall, which used to contain a doorway. He is described as being small, dressed in green, with a lace tunic, breeches and buckled shoes. He is also spotted carrying a sack over his shoulder. The second apparition, seen on the upstairs landing, is a tall man in a black suit with a wing collar. In the kitchen area, several witnesses claim to have seen the ghost of a little old lady moving about. One characteristic that all three of the manifestations share is that they seem oblivious to humans and have never interacted with them in any way.

Hall Place, nr Rochester, Kent

After a stag in the courtyard gored Sir Thomas atte Hall, his distraught wife, Lady Constance, flung herself off the tower. Her ghost now haunts the house, along with a troubled maidservant in the attic. The house is also said to be haunted by the Black Prince.

Haltwhistle, Northumberland

Near the remains of the Roman wall, a phantom hunt used to be seen in the 19th century. It was said that the sight of the spectral hounds galloping past terrified the local dogs and cats so much that they would flee for miles. A phantom bridal party, wearing mediaeval clothes and walking in the direction of Alston, has also been seen at Haltwhistle. It is thought that this is the wedding party of a local girl, whose father had hastily arranged the match to prevent her marrying the man of her choice, who was in fact her illegitimate brother.

Ham House, Richmond, Surrey

A spaniel and a murderess are among those who haunt this imposing stately home. The dog is a King Charles spaniel, and has been seen in broad daylight. The murderess is Lady Dysart, who was seen next to a fireplace by a butler's child. Subsequently, papers were found that proved her conspiracy in the murder of her husband, carried out in order that she could marry the Duke of Lauderdale, who lived at Ham House. However, later research shows that her husband died in Paris in 1669, when she was either in London or at Ham House. However, she could still have ordered the murder.

Hampton Bishop, nr Hereford, Herefordshire

The ghost of Isobel Chandos, daughter of the governor of Hereford Castle during the reign of Edward II, haunts the River Wye at this point. Her lover was hanged for treason and she drowned while out in a rowing boat on the river. It is not known whether she fell, jumped or was pushed. The apparition takes the form of a ghostly boat, called the *Spectre's Voyage*, with a young woman on board. The ghostly woman gets out of the boat on the east bank of the river, and both she and the boat head for Hereford. About a mile from there, both apparitions vanish. It is interesting to note that the ghostly boat can move against the current and wind. Local fishermen and boatmen claim that if she or the boat is seen, it is an omen of death.

Handforth, nr Wilmslow, Cheshire: The Old Parsonage

This haunting dates back to 1745, when Bonnie Prince Charlie came a-visiting! A woman at the parsonage died of fright when he appeared and her restless spirit can be seen walking around the building.

Hanford House, nr Blandford Forum, Dorset

Built in 1603, this house is haunted by a woman in brown who has been seen to curtsy to visitors on the stairs and sit by the bed at night. At other times, there is a tremendous noise at night. A psychic visitor to the house believed that there were two ghosts.

Hanham Abbots, Gloucestershire

A church lies in the grounds of Hanham Court, which is said to be haunted by the spirit of a nun who used to visit the church regularly during her life. The area is often cold and clammy, even during warm, dry weather. At Court Farm Barn a shadowy figure has been seen entering the building, but when followed, he disappears.

Happisburgh, nr Cromer, Norfolk

At Cart Gap, in the middle of the 18th century, three smugglers had a serious argument that led to a murder and a haunting. Since 1765, a legless apparition has been seen moving toward the shore, carrying what appears to be a sack or bag. Brave souls have followed the manifestation to Well Corner. Once it gets to the old well, it climbs in and vanishes. Oddly, the locals decided to find out what was down the well and someone agreed to be lowered down. Near the bottom, on a ledge, was a sack similar to that which the apparition had been seen carrying. It was found to contain a pair of shoes and, sticking out of them, the legs of the legless ghost. It was decided to drain the well and search for more clues, which revealed a man's torso and a pistol, which was almost identical to one found in Cart Gap several years earlier. The discoveries do not seem to have stopped the hauntings, and the

ghost is still seen coming out of the sea and heading for the well.

Harbourne, nr Birmingham, West Midlands: The White Swan

John Wentworth (sometimes called Jack Harborne) haunts the pub. During the 19th century, he used the inn as a rendezvous with his lover, a local woman believed to be married. Unfortunately, she was fatally injured en route to the White Swan and died in John's arms. Grief stricken, he shot his dog and then himself.

Harbury, nr Leamington Spa, Warwickshire

The harvest moon signals the presence of a phantom woman and her child. Her husband, the father of the child, threw them both into the village pond. He stood there and watched them drown.

Hardwick Hall, nr Chesterfield, Derbyshire

Built in 1591 by Bess of Hardwick, the Countess of Shrewsbury, Hardwick Hall is a huge house with priest holes and secret rooms hidden in the massive chimneys and staircase. The countess's fourth husband was the custodian of Mary Queen of Scots during her imprisonment. It is this link that probably explains the sighting of what may be a phantom priest or monk. Witnesses have described the apparition as appearing to wear a black habit. It is also said that he has a brilliant white face. One day in 1976, no fewer than four different witnesses saw the same ghost within minutes of one another. Others, including two policemen, saw it during the period 31 December to 4 January. The same monk has also been seen on the outskirts of Sutton-in-Ashfield, about three miles away.

Harlow Wood, nr Mansfield, Nottinghamshire

Bessie Sheppard was murdered on 7 July 1817, and a memorial stone commemorates the place she fell. If the stone is moved, then her ghost will appear until it is replaced. Her ghost was seen on several occasions after road works meant that the stone had to be moved, and on another occasion when the stone was hit by a car and dislodged.

Harpham, nr Driffield, East Yorkshire

Close to Harpham Church there is a well, known as the Drumming Well because of the sound of the rolling of drums that emanates from its depths, thought to signify the imminent death of a member of the St Quentin family. A drummer called Thomas Hewson fell into the well many centuries ago. There are two versions of how he got down there: the first says that he accidentally fell after colliding with the lord of the manor in an archery contest held at the church, while the second version tells that he was pushed down there after being murdered by a member of the St Quentin family. Whatever the truth, his mother said that when a member of the St Quentin Family was about to die, the drum would roll. The drum has also been heard for recent deaths in the family.

Harrington, nr Kettering, Northamptonshire: Tollemanche Arms

The field behind this public house, now known as The Falls, was the former site of Harrington Manor. The ghost of Jane Stanhope, appearing as a white lady, has been seen in the field, which was once her much-loved terraced garden. Jane had an appalling temper and was hated and feared by all the servants. One day, the only person who ever stood up to her, an old gardener, was working on the terraces. She saw him standing on one of her favourite plants, grabbed a spade and hit him over the head with it. He died immediately, and her remorseful figure can be seen wringing her hands and crying. If you see the apparition of Jane Stanhope, beware, for it is said that you will die within a few months.

Harston, nr Cambridge, Cambridgeshire

On the road from Harston to Haslingfield, the figure of a woman in white has often been seen jumping from a bridge into the River Cam. The same spectre walks from the Queen's Head public house to Mill Road.

Hartland Abbey, nr Stoke, Devon

The road that runs beside the abbey and along the valley to the parish church at Stoke is haunted by a ghostly procession of monks. They have been seen at regular intervals and are, presumably, replaying a familiar scene from the time when they were active in this area.

Hartshill Castle, Hartshill, Warwickshire

This ruined Elizabethan mansion sits in the middle of the village, having slowly deteriorated over the past 200 years as part of the estate of the Moore family. Many local villagers will go nowhere near the place for fear of seeing the manifestation of a woman in a black, silk dress. Witnesses have reported that the apparition comes so close to them that they can hear her dress rustle. Just after World War Two, a member of the Moore family discovered an underground passageway leading to Merevale Hall. It is said that the skeleton of a man was found down there, seemingly the remains of an individual who attempted to walk along the passage in the dark. However, there is conjecture about whether this was in fact the skeleton of the woman whose ghost is so often seen.

Hartwell, Northamptonshire

If you cross the M1 here, you may encounter the ghostly apparition of a phantom coach and horses. Few have actually seen the coach, but it has been heard on a number of occasions, wildly careering through the trees and into the distance.

Harvington Hall, nr Kidderminster, Worcestershire

The ghost of Mistress Hicks, who was hanged, can be seen outside the porch. She was tried and convicted of being a witch. The house itself dates to the mediaeval period, and was once the home of Sir Peter Corbett. Returning home unexpectedly one day, he found his daughter in bed with her lover. He set his deerhounds on the man, and they chased him, killed him and ate nearly all of his corpse. The daughter threw herself into the moat and drowned, and Sir Peter died of grief soon after the violent events. You may see his tortured phantom leading his spectral deerhounds through the Wyre Forest.

Hassop, nr Bakewell, Derbyshire

A white lady appeared to Prince Arthur, the son and heir of Henry VII, in September 1501. She spoke to him and told him that he would soon enjoy his last pageant. Soon after this he married a Spanish noblewoman, but he died within weeks of the wedding. More recently a phantom stagecoach and the separate apparition of a ghostly Cavalier have been seen charging down the road.

Hastings, East Sussex: Hastings Castle

Dating back to 1069, when the Normans built it, Hastings Castle is haunted by the apparition of a nun who has been seen near the entrance to the dungeon. She is said to be digging in order to hide some of the church treasures from Parliamentarians. She is described as wearing a brown habit, and is also seen near the outer wall to the east of the castle. Another more frequent sighting is that of a female ghost dressed in a brown Victorian-style dress. She is described as being middle-aged, with a baby in her arms. She hesitates near the cliff edge, then moves toward it and vanishes. The local explanation is that a fisherman fathered the child and refused to acknowledge it, and in desperation the woman took her own life and that of the child.

Hatfield House, nr Colney Heath, Hertfordshire

A coach with four horses comes through the door and up the stairs at Hatfield House. A veiled woman is also seen here, who apparently has connections to Charles II. The spirit of Elizabeth I is said to haunt the Old Hall. This is where she was told of the death of her half-sister, Queen Mary, which opened the way for her to take the throne.

Hatfield Peverel, nr Chelmsford, Essex

A spectral hound called Shane's Shaggy Dog has been seen on the Chelmsford Road. It is said to be fairly harmless, but on one occasion a man was so frightened by its appearance that he tried to strike it with his whip. The man was struck down by a lightening bolt.

Hatherleigh, North Devon: The George Hotel

This hotel is haunted by a naked female phantom. People staying at the hotel have also experienced intense cold. Whether an incident occurred here in the past to leave the spirit of the nude apparition is unknown.

Hathersage, Derbyshire: Highlow Hall

A white lady, said to be the apparition of the lover of Nicholas Eyre, haunts this hall. In 1340 Eyre spurned the woman in favour of her younger sister. She committed suicide, but her ghost appeared to Eyre and told him that his family would prosper at the hall for just 14 generations. In 1842 the prophecy came true and the Eyres left the hall forever. A white man on a white horse has also been seen in the area.

Haughton Castle, nr Chollerton, Northumberland

During the 16th century, Sir John de Widdrington held the castle for the Crown and Lord Dacre of Gilsland was the rather ineffectual Lord Warden of the Marshes. The countryside was a dangerous place and robbers were everywhere. It was rumoured that Dacre was in league with them and profiting from the suffering of the population. Just before Sir John was to go to York to discuss the situation with Cardinal Wolsey, he managed to capture one of the more notorious criminals, Archie Armstrong. The man was incarcerated in the dungeons, but Sir John forgot about him and rode off to York with the only key in his pocket. He was in York before he realised his mistake and headed back as quickly as possible, but the man had died from starvation. Archie's screams can be heard emanating from the dungeon to this day.

Havant, Hampshire: Gypsies' Clump, Havant Forest

Alcoholic poacher Charlie Pearce's ghost can be seen here, complete with the damaged throat that caused his death. After a night's heavy drinking, he mounted his horse, still clutching a bottle of gin, and headed home to Rowland's Castle. In his drunken state, he failed to see an overhanging branch that struck his throat and ruptured his windpipe.

Haverhill, Suffolk

It is said that one of the shops suffers from unexplained banging noises and the sound of footsteps. The noises seem to emanate from the upper floors. The spirit seems more active when the shop is not in use. There is no apparent explanation for the haunting.

Haverholme Priory, nr Sleaford, Lincolnshire

Although most of the building was demolished in 1927, the bridge in the grounds is haunted by an odd manifestation that takes the form of a strange whizzing noise. Although it is not known what has caused the haunting, dogs will not cross the bridge.

Hawkesdale Hall, nr Carlisle, Cumbria

On Hallowe'en you may see the sad apparition of a young boy carrying a lantern. It is said that he can be seen walking from the front door of the hall down to the river. The river connection is confusing, as he apparently hanged himself in the hall many years ago.

Hawkham, East Sussex: Mill Hill Lane

In November 1976, a witness was returning home when she caught sight of the eccentric Mr Hawley walking toward his cottage. This was a common occurrence, despite the weather, as the old man would often walk around in the dark alone. It was a dreadful night, with a raging storm soaking the streets, but Mr Hawley was there in his green and pink pyjamas, brown dressing gown and carpet slippers. The witness could not mistake his large bald head. The only problem was, as the witness discovered the following day, that Mr Hawley had died three weeks earlier.

Haworth, West Yorkshire: Haworth Parsonage

The Brontë sisters lived at Haworth Parsonage for over 20 years. Top Withens, the house that *Wuthering Heights* was based on, is now ruined and stands down the pathway leading from the Parsonage. The apparition of Emily Brontë, who was regarded as the quietest of the sisters, has been seen on several occasions, wandering with her head down, as if in deep thought, along the pathway from the Parsonage to Top Withens. She tends to be seen in the second half of the year.

Hay-on-Wye, Powys

Mol Walbee, who is said to have built the castle in one night, haunts the fortress at Hay-on-Wye. She is also said to haunt Corfe Castle. Her family were staunch opponents of King John, and as a result, the temporary monarch used all his power to ensure that they died violent and painful deaths.

Helston, Cornwall: The Beehive, Coinage Hall Street

The ghost of a 30-year-old man has been seen on several occasions at around 10.30pm. When spoken to, he immediately vanishes. Despite the fact that he appears to be wearing modern clothing, many people seem to link the manifestation with two murders that occurred in the pub in the middle of the 18th century. The figure is also described as being a little indistinct.

Hemel Hempstead, Hertfordshire: King's Arms

In existence since the 16th century, the King's Arms was frequented by Henry VIII while he was courting Anne Boleyn. Edward VI, the son of Henry's third wife, Jane Seymour, also favoured this inn. A white lady, accompanied by a tall, fat man who has been heard laughing, haunts the pub. It is believed that the apparitions are those of Anne and Henry, reliving happier days together.

Hemel Hempstead, Hertfordshire: White Hart, High Street

Dating back to 1530, the pub has a spot near the stairs that seems to instil terror in customers and staff alike. The haunting that causes this dates back to the 18th century. During this period, a life in the ranks of the army or the navy was never a preferred occupation. Both sections sometimes had to rely on press gangs to fill the rolls. One night, a young local man was having a drink in the pub when he was approached by a group of drunken soldiers. They had decided that when they returned to the barracks that he was going to come with them and join up. The fight was brief and violent, occurring at the foot of the stairs. The local was killed in the brawl, leaving behind him the sense of terror that afflicts modern occupants of the pub. His apparition has also been seen at the foot of the stairs, with fright across his young face.

Henley-on-Thames, Buckinghamshire: Bull Inn

The air is permeated with the smell of burning candles, and a strange, cowled apparition has been seen in one of the bedrooms. Presumably the public house has religious connections from the past. Perhaps, as is the case in other locations, the explanation for the aural and visual manifestations rests with a link to pilgrims.

Henley-on-Thames, Buckinghamshire: Kenton Theatre

Mary Blandy was executed in Oxford in 1752 for poisoning her father. She, wrongly as it turned out, thought her father had killed her lover, Captain Cranstoun. There have been two productions of the story at Kenton Theatre. Witnesses report seeing an odd, ghostly figure, standing at the back of the stalls, watching the performances. Many witnesses believe that it was the spirit of Mary Blandy. The play is called *The Hanging Wood*.

Henllan, nr Denbigh, Clwyd: Llindir Inn

The public house was said to be haunted by Sylvia, a murder victim, but later sightings seem to disprove this notion. Her jealous husband, who committed the crime in a rage, killed Sylvia in the pub. Recent witnesses now claim that the manifestation is a male, possibly the murderer.

Heppel, nr Rothbury, Northumberland

Many local witnesses claim that they are forewarned of potential danger to the village, particularly flash floods, by a strange apparition. A mounted figure, sitting on a black horse and clutching his stomach, has been seen immediately preceding any such threat. It is not known who the man is or why he should look so kindly upon the village.

Hereford, Herefordshire: Hereford Cathedral

The ghost of a white monk has been seen at midnight, north-east of the cathedral, near the lady chapel. The monk was killed by a Welshman in 1055.

Hereford, Herefordshire: High Street

A 17th-century house, which was moved 100m in the 1960s to make way for a new development, is still haunted by the ghost of an apothecary who poisoned his apprentice

by mistake and then committed suicide. This could be 'Old Taylor', who wanders around the Morning Pit and White Cross.

Hergest Court, nr Kington, Herefordshire

Now a farm, Hergest Court was for centuries the home of the Vaughan family, and it was there that Sir Thomas Vaughan, popularly known as 'Black Vaughan', was taken prisoner and decapitated in 1483. It is said that at the time of his death his head fell to the ground and was seized by his bloodhound dog, which then ran off with it in the direction of Kington Church, some two miles away. The head has been seen many times, hovering above the moat, and both Black Vaughan and his bloodhound have been seen walking together in the direction of the church.

Hermitage Castle, nr Hawick, Borders

This dark and forbidding structure was built in the 13th century and is haunted by Lord 'Terrible' William de Soulis, who practiced occult magic in the castle. He and his assistant Robin Redcap abducted and murdered local children, whose horrible screams can still be heard around the castle. Local people eventually stormed the castle and threw them into a vat of boiling lead. Redcap has been seen on occasions, supposedly protecting his master's hidden treasure. His master's screams mingle with those of the ghostly children as he constantly relives his last bath. Numerous other events have occurred, including people experiencing the feeling of being pushed near the drowning pool, demons laughing and an attempt by a film crew to record strange noises and sights which led to their equipment being burnt out, despite the fact that it was not connected to a power source.

Herstmonceux Castle, nr Hailsham, East Sussex

This 15th-century castle, is said to be haunted by the ghost of a drummer. Two stories are attached to the haunting, both with a ring of truth about them. First, it is said that the drummer dates from the Battle of Agincourt and is the spirit of an Englishman who died in the conflict. The second explanation is more complicated and revolves around the strange behaviour of the elderly recluse, Lord Dacre. Although married, he instructed his wife and servants to treat him as if he were dead. Unfortunately, his wife took him at his word and began a series of affairs. In frustration the man beat a drum to scare off his wife's lovers. She retaliated by locking him in a cell to starve him to death. In the late 1970s, after the Royal Observatory had moved into the building in 1948, staff claimed to have seen the ghost of a woman near the moat. This may be the spirit of an heiress who was killed by her governess to prevent her from inheriting the family fortune. Yet another spirit is present, that of a sleepwalking man.

Heskin Hall, nr Chorley, Lancashire

During the English Civil War, a terrifying event, which must cast doubt upon the godliness of the priest involved, caused a haunting in the form of a white lady. A Catholic woman was sheltering a priest, and when Parliamentarian soldiers arrived to search the house they soon discovered his priest hole. Apparently the priest said that in return for not being carried away in chains, he would undertake to hang his woman benefactor for them. After he had committed the foul act, the Parliamentarian officer let the priest go and left the woman hanging from a beam in one of the rooms. The room concerned is the Scarlet Room, and the apparition of the woman has been seen there many times.

Hever Castle, nr Edenbridge, Kent

Construction of Hever Castle began in the late 13th century, continuing until around 1380. It was improved by a succession of owners. Henry VIII met Anne Boleyn at Hever. She was the grand-daughter of Henry, Lord Mayor of London. Her father, Sir Thomas Boleyn, continued to live in the castle after his daughter's execution for infidelity, but it was finally passed to Anne of Cleves, Henry's fourth wife. Several witnesses have seen the headless, blue robed apparition of Anne Boleyn at the castle. On one occasion a photograph was taken of the archways near the fountain, which when developed revealed the hazy image of Anne's spirit. There is also said to be the ghost of a farmer at Hever, who was murdered in the castle some years ago.

Hickleton, nr Doncaster, South Yorkshire

There are three skulls in the porch of the church, which are said to be the mortal remains of three highwaymen executed in the area. It is believed that one of the skulls is linked to a haunting that has been described as terrifying by the majority of witnesses who have seen it. A phantom highwayman approaches the church from the main road. On most occasions he is headless, hence the link with the skull. Other witnesses claim to have seen him with a head and a cloak, wearing a tricorne hat perched on his head.

Hickling Broad, nr Great Yarmouth, Norfolk

On frosty February nights, you may see the apparition of a ghostly Napoleonic drummer boy skating across the broad. He always skates, even when the broad is not frozen. The soldier had a lover across the broad and would skate across to see her. One night, the ice broke and he was drowned. It is said that the sound of drumming is heard at certain times of the year. The broad is also haunted by the manifestation of a woman in a white dress, punting across the water. Of this apparition nothing is known.

Highdown House, nr Pirton, Hertfordshire

On 15 June each year, the ghostly form of Goring, a Cavalier, can be seen riding to Highdown House from High Down. He was a royalist, sheltering at the house in order to evade capture by the Parliamentarians. When they searched the house, Goring fled, but was overtaken near an elm tree and killed. His apparition makes for Hitchin Priory, where it is believed that his lover was waiting for him.

Higher Filford Farm, nr Bettiscombe, Dorset

An old soldier appears in a room that was formerly used to ripen cheese. This is a very common sighting, and the ghost has been seen regularly over the past few years.

Highworth, nr Swindon, Wiltshire: King and Queen Inn, High Street

Part of this mainly 14th-century building was formerly a monastery, and there are some traces of a passageway that connected the cellars to St Michael's Church. During the 19th century, one of the upper rooms was used as a courtroom. A monk, said to be a hunchback and dressed in white robes, haunts the building. It is said that he had taken a lover and was discovered by the abbot and killed. His apparition has been seen in the yard, heading for the stables, and sometimes in the nearby church. On one night in 1968, the landlord's dog would not settle and eventually the two them went down stairs to investigate. They were con-fronted by the manifestation of a man standing in the yard. The landlord let the dog loose, but it refused to move, so he moved toward the monk-like figure. It glided through the wall and vanished. On other occasions, footsteps have been heard in the corridor outside the old courtroom, perhaps a ghostly memory of the many people that were sentenced to death there. When the staff investigated the corridor and the room, they found it empty.

Highworth, nr Swindon, Wiltshire: St Michael's Church

The ghost that haunts both the inside of the church and the churchyard has been seen during the daytime, as well as at night. It is described as having no discernible features and has deep, dark holes where you would expect to see eyes.

High Wycombe, Buckinghamshire: Hughenden Manor

Benjamin Disraeli, Earl of Beaconsfield, bought the manor in 1874, having it substantially rebuilt until his death in 1881. It is now a museum devoted to Disraeli. His ghost has been seen on numerous occasions on the main stairway, just beside a portrait of the man himself. He is said to stand there, holding papers, until someone approaches him, when he promptly disappears. Disraeli did not die at the manor, he passed away in London.

Hillside, nr Egham, Surrey

This is the site of a child murder in the early 20th century. A local farmer strangled a child, and it is said that the spirit of the child and other manifestations haunt the area.

Hinchingbrooke, Cambridgeshire: Hinchingbrooke Hall

The former home of the Earl of Sandwich,

who died at the Battle of Sole Bay in an indecisive fleet action against the Dutch on 28 May 1672, part of the house was formerly a convent. The area is haunted by a ghostly drummer of whom we know very little, apart from the fact that he tends to be heard in the middle of the night. There is a possibility that this is related to Oliver Cromwell, who was said to have played in the house when he was a boy.

Hinchingbrooke, Cambridgeshire: The Nun's Bridge

St Benedict is said to have fallen in love with a local girl, perhaps a nun, and met her near here to spend some time together by the banks of the river. They were discovered and both killed for breaking their vows. The apparition of the nun has been seen on a number of occasions. Some witnesses claim an older woman is also present, believed to be a nurse. Another version of the story tells that St Benedict's lover was not a nun but a local girl, who was murdered by her own brother.

Hintlesham, nr Ipswich, Suffolk: Hintlesham Hall

The second wife of Richard Savage Lloyd starved her stepson to death. It is her ghost that is seen in the library, around the south wing and on the stairs. The house appears to be in Queen Mary style, but is in fact an Elizabethan building. The Lloyd family purchased the estate in 1747.

Hinton Ampner, Hampshire

The manor here was so badly haunted that it was pulled down and rebuilt 50 yards away. Despite such drastic action, the hauntings continued. These include a man in a drab coat, a woman in rustling silk, banging doors and spectral screams. The ghosts are probably those of the 4th Lord Stawell and his sister-in-law, with whom he had a relationship after the death of his wife.

Hinton Martell, Dorset

The Old Rectory is said to be haunted. The ghost of a nun is also to be seen on the road toward Knowlton.

Hinxworth Place, nr Baldock, Hertfordshire

On stormy autumn evenings, strong thuds, screams and the crying of a baby can be heard at Hinxworth Place. Many years ago, a son of the household pulled a prank on a nursemaid. He dressed up as a ghost to scare her, but the prank back-fired when she attacked the 'manifestation' with a poker. The boy fell down the stairs and died.

Hitchin, Hertfordshire: Hitchin Priory

An unknown grey lady haunts the priory. For many years, she has been seen by a number of witnesses standing outside the building. She is described as wearing a grey robe and may be a nun. As Goring's ghost is seen in this area too, it has been assumed that the two apparitions may be linked in some way. It is believed that Goring's sweetheart witnessed his killing from an upstairs room in the priory.

Hoarwithy, nr Ross-on-Wye, Herefordshire

A white lady, a grey lady, a nun in a cowl and a female apparition in a boat that speedily sails down the River Wye can all be seen here.

Hob Stones Farm, nr Colne, Lancashire

During the 1950s, the hideous apparition of a hobgoblin, or evil dwarf, terrorised the farmer and his wife living here. On one occasion the farmer was having a quiet read in the outside lavatory when the door burst open to reveal the unpleasant apparition. He described it as being a squat, human-like creature with a vicious scowl on its face, but above all he noted that it had a damaged arm that was nearly severed at the elbow. After several more appearances, the farmer and his wife were forced to leave the farm forever.

Hockenhul Hall, nr Chester, Cheshire

Following the defeat of Charles I at Rowton Moor, Parliamentarian troops swarmed over the area, searching for royalists and their supporters. When they arrived at Hockenhul Hall, the only person there was an elderly housekeeper. The soldiers smashed their way into the house and began ransacking the building. Having found nothing of note they rounded on the housekeeper and demanded that she tell them where the family's treasures were hidden. She refused and one of the soldiers decapitated her. She now appears as a white lady and walks from the hall toward the pub, where she no doubt enjoyed the odd drink during her lifetime. Witnesses have clearly seen her, with her head tucked beneath her shoulder, its unblinking eyes staring forward.

Hoghton Tower, nr Blackburn, Lancashire

The haunting of Hoghton Tower bears all the hallmarks of a copy of a story behind the apparitions seen at Samlesbury. A green lady haunts the house, said to be the ghost of a woman called Ann. She was a Protestant and fell in love with a local Catholic. Carefully they planned to elope and leave behind their respective families, who had adamantly tried to keep them apart. As Ann waited near her home for her lover to arrive she saw him approaching, and as he dismounted her own father shot him dead. Whether Ann committed suicide or died soon after we do not know.

Holcombe, nr Teignmouth, Devon

The manifestation of a middle-aged man dressed in a long, grey coat carries a torch that he uses to flag down drivers just after dusk. The main area where the apparition is seen is around the Heatherton Grange Hotel. One witness claims to have struck the ghost, but on investigation found nothing. Several other motorists have had similar experiences.

Holford, Somerset: Plough Inn

A Spanish traveller was murdered here in 1555, en route to Bridgwater. In the middle of the night a murderer climbed up the stone stairs and strangled the Spaniard, stealing his money. The stone steps no longer exist, but the sound of footfalls on them is often heard. There are two explanations of the history of this story. The first casts the Spaniard as a spy involved in political activities prior to the marriage of Mary Tudor to the King of Spain, while the second story has him as a wealthy merchant with a sack of gold coins. The murderer who killed him never found his gold and hence his spirit returns to the scene of his death in order to see whether his gold is still safe.

Hollingbourne, Kent: Eyhorne Manor

Hollingbourne can trace its history back to 980, when Athelstan gave the estate to the church. The manor was probably built in around 1410 as a yeoman's hall. By the 1950s, the building was in a bad state of repair and had been converted into three cottages. The hauntings began with the sound of someone walking upstairs. A child that slept in the top of the building often saw a grey lady. Her mother often sensed a cold and clammy atmosphere in the corner of her bedroom, and heard a slithering sound. The child also claims to have seen the apparition of a small man in a black suit.

Hollingbourne, Kent: Hollingbourne House

A wild rider is seen at the house quite often. It is believed that he is a former lord of the manor, who was stupid enough to try to jump the wrought-iron gates on horseback. He died in the attempt.

Hollington, East Sussex: The Wishing Tree

The landlord and several customers have heard strange bumping sounds and unexplained footsteps coming from an empty room. In the kitchen, a witness reported feeling something brush past her, coupled with the swish of a woman's dress. An old woman with a 'funny face' awakened a youngster living in the house. The apparition of a middle-aged woman, dressed in Victorian clothes and pushing a pram has been seen outside the pub in the early hours of the morning. When challenged, she disappeared.

Holwell, nr Melton Mowbray, Leicestershire

The Black Shug, a phantom black dog, haunts the bluebell wood at Holwell Mouth. It is said that if you encounter it, you may lose someone close to you. The times to avoid are dawn and dusk.

Holyhead, Gwynedd

In 1743, a farmer and his ploughboy were hard at work in the field when they saw an amazing apparition. A sailing boat was heading toward them in the sky! It was approaching from the east with its sails billowing, and was surrounded by birds. They called other people to see the manifestation, by which time it was drifting back from whence it came. Perhaps this could be an early sighting of a UFO?

Holywell, nr Huntingdon, Cambridgeshire: Ye Olde Ferryboat

A white lady haunts the bar of this riverside public house. She is said to appear and point at her own grave. The public house was built over her burial site. She is the spirit of Juliet Tewsley, who committed suicide after the object of her love and devotion spurned her. The anniversary of her death and the date of her appearance is 17 March. After pointing at the grave, she drifts out of the building and vanishes near the river.

Honington, Warwickshire

On the road to Tredington, you may encounter the ghost of a witch sitting on a wall. She is thought to have been a local witch; perhaps she met her end near to the place where she is now seen in ghostly form.

Honk Green, nr Tunbridge Wells, Sussex

On the road to Bell's Yew Green, there is a phantom limousine that disappears when approaching cars are about 100m from it. There does not appear to be any logical reason why the car should appear at this point.

Hook, Hampshire

A ghostly Cavalier haunts the streets. The ghost, which has long hair, a loose cloak and a broad-rimmed hat, is thought to be that of a messenger who died in combat with Roundheads, while trying to deliver a message to the royalist garrison. It is also said that the White Hart pub is haunted.

Hope, nr Chapel-en-le-Frith, Derbyshire: The Travellers' Rest Inn

A black lady haunts this public house, and is particularly seen on Christmas Eve. The young woman in question fell down the stairs on

Christmas Eve while trying to avoid the attentions of an amorous drunken admirer. She has been seen gliding down the upstairs corridor.

Hopetoun House, nr Edinburgh, Lothian

A link with the Marquess of Linlithgow's family lies behind the menacing black-robed figure often seen on a particular path in the grounds. Witnesses have described the apparition as frightening, and it has a profound effect on dogs. It is said that the manifestation heralds a death in the Linlithgow family.

Hopton Castle, nr Ludlow, Shropshire

During the English Civil War, 31 Parliamentarians held the castle for three weeks against a royalist army of 500. When Colonel Samuel More, commander of the Parliamentarians, finally surrendered, the royalists shot all of his men. More was clapped in irons and taken to Ludlow. The ghostly apparitions of the murdered Parliamentarian soldiers can be seen leaving the castle, slowly disappearing as they walk until only their heads remain, floating in the air. These, too, disappear once they reach the pond.

Horning, Norfolk: Old Ferry Inn

A mead house belonging to the old abbey used to stand on this site. The building later became a pub, but was destroyed by a German bomb on 26 April 1941. Twenty-two people were killed when the bomb levelled the bar. The ghost, however, seems to be related to the earlier uses of the site and takes the form of a girl that appears every 20 years. The story runs that when the building was a mead house, several monks were sitting outside having a drink. A young local girl was walking along the riverbank and was spotted by the brothers. They grabbed her and took her into the house, where they raped and killed her, then dragged her body outside and threw it into the river. On 25 September 1936, the landlord and some of the customers saw her apparition. She is described as being a girl in her early twenties, with a deathly white face and wearing a greenish dress. The apparition glided away and walked through the front door. The ghost has also been seen near the ferry, where it vanishes into the water.

Horning, Norfolk: St Benet's Abbey

The ghost of a traitorous monk haunts this old abbey, which was built for the Benedictines in 816. In the days immediately following the Norman Conquest, the monk betrayed his brethren to soldiers of William the Conqueror, on the condition that he would be made abbot. True to their word, the Normans appointed him abbot before hanging him. The Normans had no love for traitors, even Saxon ones. His hauntings are limited to one day a year – 25 May.

Horseheath, Cambridgeshire

A mysterious character is said to have buried his gold near Money Lane. The spectre appears primarily on nights with a full moon, and attempts to entice the unwary to follow him to dig it up. No one has ever dared to do this – perhaps they fear that they may be digging their own grave.

Houghton Hall, nr Fakenham, Norfolk

Prime Minister Sir Robert Walpole built Houghton Hall in the 1730s on the site of the family ancestral home, and it is haunted by the ghost of his daughter, Dorothy Walpole, who spent the happiest part of her life there. After her marriage to the 2nd Viscount Townshend she moved to Raynham Hall, which she is also said to haunt.

Houndwood House, nr Eyemouth, Borders

The distinctly odd apparition of a male figure can be seen near Houndwood House in the north Back of the Eye. The manifestation, known as Chappie O'Houndswood, is only visible from the knees down.

Howick Hall, nr Alnwick, Northumberland

The apparition of a Victorian woman is said to disappear into the ground as a rainbow. This strange manifestation is described as being an old woman with a long skirt and a Victorian-style bonnet. It is not known who she is or the reason behind her strange disappearing act.

Hoylake, Merseyside: Royal Hotel

Built in the 1790s, the hotel is haunted by the ghost of a man seen wearing a Norfolk Tweed jacket, brown knickerbockers and a cloth cap. He has been seen walking down the corridor from the hall to the bathroom, and in the billiards room. He is also thought to be responsible for doors opening and closing of their own accord.

Huddington, nr Worcester, Worcestershire

On 31 January 1606, Thomas Winter, of Huddington, was beheaded for his involvement in the Gunpowder Plot. The apparition of his wife has been seen walking around the moat and through the oak trees on the anniversary of his death. What is most perplexing about this haunting is the fact that she appears headless.

Hulver Street, nr Beccles, Suffolk: Jay's Hill

A white lady has been seen standing on the hedgerow beside the road. Witnesses, while picnicking, felt as if they were being watched and even heard a low moan before they moved on. Later, a motorist reported seeing the apparition and suggested that the woman looked ill. In nearby Sotterly Hall, many years ago, a young woman was murdered by her lover after an argument. The spot where the motorist saw the ghost was the apparent site of the crime.

Hungerford, Berkshire

To the south of the town, a female ghost appears riding a grey horse. She is seen during the day. At night, however, the apparition is replaced by that of a coach and four. Whether the woman died near here or was killed is unknown. The coach and horses appear as the result of an accident that occurred many years ago.

Hunstanton, Norfolk: Hunstanton Hall

On the death of her brother, Sir Roger L'Estrange, in 1762, Hunstanton Hall passed to Armine L'Estrange, who had married Nicholas Styleman. She owned a magnificent Persian carpet that had been given to her by the Shah of Persia. When she died in 1766, she pleaded that the carpet should remain in the family forever; her servants duly obliged and put the carpet away in a trunk in the attic. It lay undisturbed for many years until one of her descendants found it and cut it up and gave pieces away to local villagers. As a result, Armine's ghost appeared and terrorised the household until someone remembered her deathbed plea and collected the pieces up again and sewed the carpet back into one. It now remains in the house, where she wanted it to stay.

Hunstanton, Norfolk: Hunstanton Railway Station

Local gossip links several accidents and

hauntings with a character known as Snotter the Spotter. Although the Great Eastern terminus at Hunstanton is now largely obliterated by a car park, the area is still said to be haunted by ghosts and events that happened many years ago. Snotter had been a train spotter and was involved in several pranks at the terminus. On one occasion he was implicated in the derailment of a runaway train that caused the death of Sam Larkins, the driver. Much later Snotter became a fireman and was employed to shunt trains around the yard. One Sunday he prepared a train that needed to leave the station at 6.45am. Having started the fire and got the steam pressure up, he applied the brakes and chocked the wheels of the train. He then dismounted the train and began to revolve the turntable so that the train could leave the engine shed on the right line. As he did so, something or somebody released the brake. Snotter was crushed and his broken body was found by the cleaners. It is believed that both Snotter and the ghost of Sam Larkins, his probable spectral murderer, still haunt the vicinity.

Huntingtower Castle, Perth, Perth and Kinross

Milady Greensleeves is said to be a ghost with a particular interest in saving lost causes. On one occasion she saved an old man from dying, while on another she cured a sick boy. She has also been known to warn people of their impending death.

Hurst Castle, nr Lynington, Hampshire

The castle is strategically positioned at the end of Hurst Spit and dominates the entrance to the western Solent. The crenellated triangular fort dates back to Henry VIII, and until the 20th century was a vital component of the region's defences. Hurst Castle was built between 1541 and 1544, and was constructed with stone taken from the ruins of Beaulieu Abbey. In 1648 King Charles I was imprisoned there on his way from Carisbrooke Castle on the Isle of Wight to London, where he was tried and executed. In 1700, during the purge on Roman Catholicism, Father Paul Atkinson was held prisoner here until he died 30 years later. It is said that his ghost haunts the old tower. The castle is now unoccupied. As a result of the haunting nobody sleeps there at night.

Hurst Green, nr Clitheroe, Lancashire: Punch Bowl Inn

18th-century highwayman Ned King, Knight of the High Toby, operated along the road between Longridge and Clitheroe. He habitually wore a white-ruffled shirt, a gold-trimmed scarlet coat, white breeches and knee-length black boots. The Punch Bowl was used as his headquarters, and as a place to check out his next victim. Eventually, the troopers found his hiding place and surrounded him in the hayloft. After a gun battle he was led away in chains. There was no trial, and he was immediately hanged in Gallows Lane. Ned's ghost can be heard clumping about in the middle of the night and moaning sounds emanate from the loft. He is described as being quite an ill-tempered apparition, throwing bottles around and other mischief. His spirit is a little calmer nowadays, after a partially successful exorcism in 1942. A priest from nearby Stoneyhurst College carried it out.

Husbands Bosworth, Bosworth Hall, nr Lutterworth, Leicestershire

Sir Frances Fortescue-Turville, the Catholic owner of the hall in 1881, was married to the Protestant Lady Lisgar. When one of her Catholic maidservants was lying on her deathbed she refused to call a priest to give the last rites. As a result the servant haunts the Bow Room. Some say that the apparition is actually Lady Lisgar. Shortly after the English Civil War a priest managed to evade Parliamentarian troops which had arrived in the middle of a mass. In his haste to make for his priest hole he knocked over his chalice, cut his hand and left a trail of blood and wine on the floor. It is said that the stain never dries.

Higher Huxley Hall, Huxley, Chester
The spirits of a ghostly horse and rider haunt the grounds of this old manor house. It is not known whether the rider and his mount were former inhabitants of the hall or whether their presence here marks a darker purpose altogether.

Hyde, Greater Manchester
A phantom convoy haunts the A57 between Hyde and Mottram-in-Longdendale. A number of fatal accidents during the late 1920s and early 1930s have been blamed on drivers swerving to avoid the oncoming truck.

Hylton Castle, nr Sunderland, Tyne and Wear
The Cauld Lad of Hylton, active for over 300 years, has haunted Hylton Castle. The Cauld Lad is Roger Skelton, a groom who was killed by his master, Robert Hylton, in 1605. Hylton threw the corpse into a pond and the remains were not discovered for several years. The apparition haunts the lower part of the castle, particularly the kitchen area. He likes to help kitchen staff tidy up, but becomes difficult if there is nothing to do. As a result, he is responsible for some destructive poltergeist activity. The castle is at present uninhabited, but the ghost was still around at the beginning of the 20th century.

Hyssington, nr Montgomery, Powys: St Etheldreda's Church
The apparition of a local wicked squire was

transformed into a large and unpleasant bull manifestation shortly after he died. Somehow the local priest managed to trap the ghost in an old boot that was then buried beneath a massive stone slab in the entrance hall to the church. It is said that if the stone is ever moved, then the ghost of the squire, in bull form, will rampage through the village once more.

I
Icklesham to Ivelet

Icklesham, nr Rye, East Sussex: The Queen's Head
Chewing a piece of straw and standing by the fireplace, the ghost of a former landlord can be seen in this public house. His name was Gutsell, and it is said that he enjoyed his own wake so much that his spirit is reluctant to leave the premises. Perhaps it was a mistake to bring his coffin into the bar while the guests toasted his departure?

Ightham Mote, nr Sevenoaks, Kent
There is an interesting Gunpowder Plot connection to the haunting here. The ghost is that of Dame Dorothy Selby, who warned Lord Monteagle to stay away from Parliament on 5 November 1605. This led directly to the discovery of the plot to blow up Parliament. Guy Fawkes, it is said, had Dame Selby bricked up in a secret room, and a skeleton was found at the house. Despite an exorcism, there is still a chill which marks the spot.

Ilfracombe, Devon: Chambercombe Manor
Built in the 14th century, the manor's dark secret was not discovered until 1865, when a

secret room was revealed. Within the room was a four-poster bed, surrounded by rotting curtains. Lying on what left of the bed itself was the skeleton of a young woman. After the burial of the remains in the local churchyard, enquiries failed to establish the identity of the girl. Her footsteps are frequently heard walking along the manor's corridors toward the chapel and the cobbled courtyard beyond. Moans can be heard emanating from the secret room, which is not used and can only be seen through a small window. The house also boasts a tunnel from the Manor Farm to Hele Beach, but it is not known whether this has any connection with the haunting.

Ilmington, nr Stratford-upon-Avon, Warwickshire: Parish Church

The middle-aged figure of Edward Golding, a former parish clerk, has been seen by a number of witnesses. He died several years ago and has been positively identified by the verger and volunteers who take care of the flowers in the church. One witness described the apparition as being of a solid nature, but as it approached her it seemed to fade away.

Ilmington, nr Stratford-upon-Avon, Warwickshire: Pig Lane

Pig Lane is the spot where a ghostly carriage and six headless horses clatter past. Locally, the apparition is known as the 'night coach', but it has been seen during daylight hours.

Ilkley Moor, West Yorkshire

Whether it is an apparition or folklore is unknown, but it is said that the phantom of a large black dog has been seen on the moor to the south of the town of Ilkley. Many say that the beast's lair is nearby, and numerous locals and visitors to the lonely moorland have seen it. Locally, it is known as Gytrash.

Inveraray, Strathclyde

The Duke of Argyll wrote the first account of the strange hauntings seen in the area, which he witnessed several times between 1746 and 1753. Marching from the Glen Shiray Bridge to Glen Aray castle, he saw a host of soldiers in red, accompanied by their women and camp followers. Two soldiers who witnessed the haunting described the multitude as being greater than the two armies that fought the bloody Battle of Culloden.

Inveraray, Strathclyde: Inveraray Castle

'The Harper of Inveraray', who was hanged by Montrose's men on the site of the castle before it was built, haunts Inveraray Castle, seat of the Dukes of Argyll. His music has been heard and he has been seen in various parts of the castle, including the Green Library and the stairs. He always wears the Campbell tartan and never seems to harm or frighten people who see him. He is normally seen and heard by women. Before the death of a chief of the Campbell clan, or a near relative, a ghostly galley, bearing a strong resemblance to the ship on the Campbell coat-of-arms, is seen on the loch, with three spectral figures on board.

Inverawe House, nr Taynuilt, Strathclyde

This large house boasts the manifestation of a young girl who is said to have drowned near the building many years ago. Locals refer to her as Green Jean, and her ghost has been seen by several people over the years. She only appears to members of the Campbell clan, and is said to be keen to help people with the housekeeping.

Inverness, Highlands: Eden Court Theatre

A green lady haunts the aptly named Green

Room in the theatre. Built in 1974, the theatre complex stands on the site of the Bishop's Palace and it is this connection that probably accounts for the sighting of the green lady. It is said that she was the wife of a bishop in the 1900s, and hanged herself in the chapel.

Inverurie, Grampian: Thainstone House Hotel and Country Club

A green lady, wearing a green cloak, has been seen in one of the bedrooms and in the restaurant. She moves items around and is strongly disliked by cats and dogs. It is said that she is the apparition of a woman who died while out hunting.

Iona, Strathclyde

Ghostly monks have been seen on the island, often accompanied by the tolling of bells and strange music. This was the site of St Columba's base, from which Christianity was established in Britain. Many other witnesses claim to have seen pagan and barbaric manifestations on the island, including the plunder of the monastery by Viking raiders.

Ipsden, Oxfordshire: Watch Folly

Near to Ipsden is an oak tree known as Watch Folly. A group of sheep thieves killed a shepherd there many years ago. The spot is now said to be haunted, but we do not know whether the ghost is the murdered man or one of his assailants.

Ipstones, nr Leek, Staffordshire

Indefont Well and Hermitage Farm are the two sites to avoid if you do not wish to see two phantom black dogs. As is typical of this type of manifestation, the history of the animals is unknown, but it is likely that they are the spirits of criminals or irreligious individuals whose spirits have been transformed.

Irby Dale Wood, nr Grimsby, Lincolnshire

Rosamund Guy was murdered by her fiancé at this spot on 1 November 1455. She has been seen by a number of locals and is commonly referred to as the Irby Boggle.

Ireby, nr Keswick, Cumbria: Overwater Hall

The apparition of a woman with no hands has been seen frantically tapping on the windows of the hall and walking through the door of room 3. Many years ago the then owner, Joseph Gillbanks, took his pregnant mistress out in a rowing boat onto Overwater Tarn. When he got to the middle he threw her in. As she tried to get back into the boat he chopped her hands off with an axe.

Ironbridge, Shropshire

Beneath the Ironbridge, shrouded in mist and heading toward Jackfield, a phantom boat resembling a Severn trow can be seen. During the 15th and 16th century, plague victims were transported along the river in boats in an attempt to prevent the disease from spreading. The boat is steered by a tall figure in a hood. Witnesses have not only seen bodies lying on the deck, but have also reported that ghostly figures unload the corpses at Jackfield.

Ironbridge, Shropshire: Bridge House Gallery

Referred to by the present inhabitants as the 'Lavender Lady', the gallery is haunted by the smell and presence of a female apparition. While the two witnesses were in the studio, they felt something brush past them, accompanied by the strong smell of lavender.

Ironbridge, Shropshire: Old Warehouse

This incredible Gothic folly of a building is more like a castle, with its towers and crennellations, than a loading bay for the Severn trows moving up and down the river. During the last century, small children were used to put blocks under the wheels of moving wagons. One young boy did not hear the shouts as he attempted to free a block and was crushed by the wheels. Several witnesses have seen his ghost pulling out an invisible block and then disappearing.

Ironbridge, Shropshire: Tontine Hotel

Fred is the ghost of a man who murdered a landlady in Ketley and took refuge in room 5 of the 200-year-old hotel. He was arrested at the hotel, tried for the murder and was one of the last men to be hanged in Shropshire. Several guests and staff have reported that lights turn on and off by themselves, water taps continue to run after being turned off, clocks in the room go backwards and there is a strange atmosphere in the room.

Itchells Manor, Hampshire

The source of the haunting here is confused by the fact that two murders have taken place in the building. It is also unclear whether the apparition is one of the victims or one of the murderers. In the early part of the 18th century, Squire Bathurst killed one of his manservants. The second murder is much better documented. One of the later owners of the house was an old miser, thought to have hidden away a vast treasure. His Italian valet, Guiseppe Mancini, killed him. Mancini then bricked up the body in a wall and headed for Southampton, where he had booked passage to France. He was arrested while trying to board the ship and tried at Winchester Assizes. They found him guilty and he was hanged. In 1818, the Lefroys bought the house and moved in five years later. They were continually disturbed by noises after 11pm. In 1840, with the aid of Captain Fraser, Mr Lefroy sat up and listened to all of the noises. They heard muffled blows coming from the wall, but the sounds seemed to come from a room beneath. This tallied with an experience Mr Lefroy had had when he slept there. He had been disturbed by the sound of a cart, laden with iron bars, passing below the window. He had looked out of the window, but no one was there. The sounds continue to this day and seem to follow the same pattern.

Ivelet, nr Richmond, North Yorkshire

A headless black dog is said to haunt the old bridge over the River Swale near Muker. The bridge forms part of what is known as the Corpse Way. There is a stone beside the bridge on which coffins being carried from remote farms were laid before the funeral procession moved on. Sighting the dog is said to bring tragedy to those who witness it.

J

Jackfield to Jenningsbury Farm

Jackfield, Shropshire: Boat Inn

Many years ago, the Devil paid a visit to the public house shortly before Christmas. He sat playing cards with some of the locals for a while until a card dropped to the ground. As one of the players stooped to pick up the card, he noticed that the stranger had a clubbed foot. With that, the Devil disappeared with a gust of wind. The ghostly figure of a young woman has also been seen in the building. The apparition awakened the landlady in the middle of the night, who saw the manifestation standing by her bed beckoning her. When the landlady went downstairs as she was instructed, she found nothing.

Jackfield, Shropshire: Ferry Road

The pitiful sound of crying twins can be heard coming from the house in which they lived before they drowned in the River Severn. They had been playing on the spoil tip of the Craven-Dunnhill tileworks when the bank gave way and pitched them into the river. Their bodies were found below the footbridge at Jackfield, caught in an overhanging branch, still holding hands.

Jackfield, Shropshire: Red Church

Lady Blithe left money to the parish to build a church on the top of the hill, but when construction began it was at the bottom of the hill. It is said that odd noises were heard and the foundations mysteriously moved to the top of the hill. The workmen realised that they had no option but to continue the construction there. Whether the young woman in a long flowing gown and a bonnet, carrying a lantern, who slowly crosses the field near the church, is Lady Blithe is unknown.

Jedburgh Castle, Borders

King Alexander III first saw the apparition at Jedburgh Castle in 1285. It appears as a hooded monk-like figure, with a dark cloak and mask. Alexander III's feast was ruined by its appearance, but it purpose was far more sinister. Within six months the king was dead: his horse fell and threw him into the Firth of Forth, where he drowned. James I similarly saw and ignored the doom signalled by the manifestation shortly before the Battle of Flodden Field. He met defeat and died on the battlefield.

Jenningsbury Farm, nr Ware, Hertfordshire

The spirit of a man said to have drowned himself nearby haunts the farm. He has been seen on several occasions, but there is no evidence of his name or the period when the events may have occurred.

K

Kemsing to Kylesku Hotel

Kemsing, nr Sevenoaks, Kent

One of the knights that murdered Thomas Becket in Canterbury Cathedral in 1170 is said to haunt the church at Kemsing. The manifestation appears on 29 December, galloping up to the church in full armour. It dismounts, ties up its horse and enters the church. Once inside, the ghostly knight walks down the aisle and kneels before the altar. It then disappears for another year.

Kenchester, nr Hereford, Herefordshire

On nights with a full moon, you may be fortunate enough to see a glimmer of England's ancient past. It is said that a cohort of Roman legionaries marches through the village in full combat order. Clearly this is a reflection of some long-forgotten incident during the Roman occupation.

Kendal, Cumbria: The Copper Kettle

A poltergeist is extremely active in the restaurant. It has tried to push people down the stairs and lights have been switched on and off. On one occasion, when the poltergeist pushed someone, the victim felt the force of the hand for a full two hours after the incident.

Kenovay, Isle of Tiree

A seaman was drowned in the waters off the island. Witnesses claim to have seen his ghost in the local churchyard both before and after his body was found washed up on the beach and subsequently buried.

Kensworth, nr Dunstable, Bedfordshire

From the church a path leads over Bury Hill, which is the haunting place of two ghosts. The first is that of a witch, who presumably lived or was killed nearby. The other is far more puzzling, and takes the form of a headless milkmaid.

Kentisbeare, nr Cullompton, Devon

At midnight every night, so it is said, you may encounter a strange manifestation on the Bradfield Hall Estate. Driving a traditional horse-drawn roller, a ghostly farm labourer works the same field for eternity.

Kessingland, nr Lowestoft, Suffolk

Accounts of a strange phantom beast off the coast here date from the 1850s, 1912, 1923 and 1978. The 1912 sighting was by none other than Kessingland's main claim to fame, author Rider Haggard. He reported seeing a ghostly creature moving off the coast, which was about 60ft long with a series of spikes along its back. He likened the monster to Nessie.

Kettleness, nr Whitby, North Yorkshire

The publication of Bram Stoker's *Dracula* may be partly to blame for the sightings of enormous black dogs on the beach here. In the book, Dracula leaves a doomed ship and swims ashore as a black dog. Was Bram Stoker influenced by the tale of black dogs, or are the sightings the result of the influence of his writings?

Kidderminster, Worcestershire: Harveys of Bristol, Swan Street

The wine bar that once stood in Swan Street has now been demolished. The Tudor building boasted a brown lady, described as wearing a long, brown dress and a white ruff. She was seen to walk through the bar and straight through the cash till. When the building was finally demolished to make way for the Swan Centre, two skeletons were found in the cellar. They are believed to date from the reign of either Henry VIII or Elizabeth I. These may have been the cause of the haunting. Workmen also discovered a tunnel running from the cellar to St Mary's Church.

Kidderminster, Worcestershire: Ye Olde Seven Stars

Throughout the 20th century, witnesses reported seeing the apparition of a middle-aged woman wearing a white dress or a white apron. First seen in around 1910, she appeared to be wearing clothing of the latter half of the 19th century. Customers have seen the white lady in the bar, where she appeared for a minute or so before fading away.

Kidsgrove, nr Stoke-on-Trent, Staffordshire

The gruesome vision of the ghost of Kit Crewbucket has been seen stalking the canal tunnels in this area. She is described as being hideous to behold, hunched and gnarled in appearance. You are particularly likely to encounter her in the Hardcastle Tunnel, where she was murdered and dumped in the canal.

Kidwelly, nr Llanelli, Dyfed

A headless grey lady, the spirit of the wife of a 12th-century Welsh prince, haunts Mynydd-y-Garreg, which overlooks Kidwelly.

It is said that she was Gwenillan, whose husband joined an alliance against the Normans when they came to Wales. He was killed and the Norman soldiers beheaded Gwenillan and her children. Gwenillan still searches forlornly for her lost head and family.

Kilkea Castle, nr Castledermott, Co. Kildare, Republic of Ireland

The Wizard Earl Garrett Ogg, the 11th Earl of Kildare, practised magic here in the 16th century. Ogg was demonstrating his magical abilities to his wife, and told her that he would turn himself into a bird before her very eyes. The only condition was that she was to show no sign of fear, as this would prove fatal to him and he would vanish forever. After transforming into a bird, a cat entered the room. Ogg's wife screamed in terror and her husband vanished in a puff of smoke. His apparition appears in that fateful room every seven years, before galloping off to Mullaghmast. Room 222 is the key site of the haunting. Bedclothes have been scattered around the room and footsteps and female voices have been heard on the roof over the bedroom.

Kilkenny, Co. Kilkenny, Republic of Ireland

The ghost of a tall thin woman with long flowing hair, hobbling on crutches and wearing a long coat, has been seen walking in the vicinity of St John's Parochial Hall. In May 1969, a young nurse and her boyfriend saw the figure while they were in a parked car after spending an evening at the local dance. Other people have seen the apparition too, including a local priest.

Killiecrankie, nr Pitlochry, Tayside

On the anniversary of the Scots victory over the English on 27 July 1689, strange lights appear over the battlefield at dusk. At the northern end of the pass is the terrifying apparition of the ghost of Mrs Hays. Murdered here over 200 years ago, her head, separated from the rest of her body, emanates a green light before rejoining her body. It is said that the body appears to be rather misty, but once the head has joined it, it promptly disappears. A phantom monk has also been seen in the pass. He wears a white robe and it is said locally that if he touches you, you will die within a year.

Kilmington, nr Warminster, Wiltshire

The churchyard is haunted by the 8th Baron Stourton's band of ghostly thugs. He was hanged at Salisbury in 1557 for the murder of his father's steward, William Hartgill. His ghost has also been seen in the church. Stourton and his men have been seen around the village. In nearby Bull Lane, a headless horse sometimes appears.

Kimbolton Castle, Cambridgeshire

The Queen's Chamber is said to be haunted by Catherine of Aragon. She was Henry VIII's first wife, and spent two years imprisoned here while her husband decided her fate. During her stay she was constantly under threat of being poisoned by one of her husband's agents. It is also said that the ghost of a small child haunts the castle. Legend has it that the child was thrown from the castle battlements.

Kings Langley, Priory Orchard, Hertfordshire

The Priory Orchard is, rather predictably, haunted by phantom monks. The apparitions are said to be rather hazy and indistinct. It is not known specifically why the monks have chosen to haunt this place, but the religious connections are clear.

Kings Lynn, Norfolk: The Duke's Head

The pub dates from 1683 and was a coaching

inn during the 18th century, on the routes to Yarmouth, Norwich and London. The ghost of a maidservant that used to work there haunts the building. She was hanged in the Market Square for poisoning and murdering her mistress. Several witnesses have seen her in the pub, the site of the crime.

Kings Lynn, Norfolk: Tudor Rose Hotel

Parts of this old hotel date back to the 15th century, when the building was a nunnery. A sinister tale concerning the fate of a witch is attached to the building. Augustinian monks handed over Margaret Read, a supposed witch, to the nuns. She was tried and subsequently burned alive in the market place. This may explain the sighting of a small woman in a grey gown in the hotel. The manifestation has been seen on the stairway, accompanied by the sound of footsteps. When seen by staff the apparition gradually faded into a mist and disappeared. Rooms 7 and 9 may be the centre of this haunting, as several guests have complained about unexplained draughts and cold spots in the rooms.

Kingston St Mary, nr Taunton, Somerset

The ghost of Squire Surtees haunts the drive of Tainfield House on old Christmas Eve (5 January). He rides a grey horse and is accompanied by the sounds of rattling chains.

Kinlet, nr Ludlow, Shropshire: Kinlet Church

The tomb of Sir George Blount is one of the most impressive Elizabethan monuments in the country. His stone image kneels, with his wife by his side. Between them kneel their daughter and son; the latter choked to death while eating an apple. George was a warrior knight nicknamed the Terror of Scotland, and

even after his death in 1581 he did not rest. It was said that his spirit would rise from a pool in the grounds of Kinlet Hall. His daughter's marriage was a great trial to him, causing him to disinherit her and vow that he would haunt her and her descendants. Villagers saw his spirit rising from the pool, an occurence which eventually forced the family to abandon Kinlet Hall and build a new house in 1720. George, being a resourceful character, has taken to haunting this site too. Following an exorcism his spirit was trapped in a glass bottle and according to varying stories, either hidden in the church or thrown into the sea. Certainly, the bottle was in the tomb in the church in 1886. Strangely, it disappeared sometime between 1890 and 1893. In recent years George has not been seen.

Kinsale, Fort Kinsale, Co. Cork, Republic of Ireland

The ghost of a white lady haunts Fort Kinsale, which was built in 1677. The fort was the home of Colonel Warrender, who was a strict disciplinarian. He christened his daughter Wilful. She married Sir Trevor Ashurst, and on the day of their marriage they were walking along the battlements when the new Lady Ashurst saw some flowers growing on the rocks below. She asked her husband to get some for her so he asked a sentry to climb down and collect a bunch. To avoid Colonel Warrender being angry at finding a sentry out of position, Sir Trevor took the sentry's place, putting on his tunic while the soldier went to collect the flowers. It was a cold night and Wilful went inside. Sir Trevor was tired and drunk, and fell asleep at the sentry's station. When Colonel Warrender made his round he saw what he thought was a sentry sound asleep on duty. He drew his pistol and shot the man through the heart. It was only when the body was brought inside that he realised, to his horror, that he had killed his new son-in-law. Lady Ashurst, distraught, threw herself over the battlements, and later that night Colonel Warrender blew his own brains out. In the summer of 1815 Major Black, who was serving in the castle, saw the apparition of a woman walk through a doorway and then ascend the staircase. He was intrigued as the woman was wearing a very old-fashioned dress, so he followed her into the room where she had disappeared, only to find it empty. Two of Major Black's men had their children with them and they had both seen a white lady smiling at them. In the 1870s, two officers, Captain Marvell Hull and Lieutenant Hartland, were walking upstairs when they both saw the white lady. She looked at them and then disappeared through a locked door. In later years the apparition seems to have had a detrimental affect on men that have seen her. On two occasions witnesses have been left lying senseless at the bottom of the stairs where the apparition appears. Whether this is simply shock or some new variation in the haunting is unknown.

Kinver, Staffordshire

The phantoms of George Grey, the 7th Earl of Stanford, and his second wife, have been seen holding hands and walking along Kinver Edge, near Kidderminster on summer nights. George Grey met his second wife when she was working as a stable hand in 1850. She was an orphaned gypsy girl, but by all accounts they were a very happy couple.

Kippax, nr Leeds, West Yorkshire: The Old Tree Inn

The spirit of a former landlord is said to haunt this public house. He has been known to turn off the gas taps for the beer, so it seems that he still has a healthy interest in the running of the pub. Witnesses have reported seeing the apparition with a smiling white face.

Kirkby Stephen, Cumbria

The blind ghost of Lord Wharton is said to haunt the road to Ravenstonedale. His stumbling spirit can be seen making its way along the road. In life he was a thoroughly unpleasant individual, and was struck blind one day as he rode home to Ravenstonedale. Although completely visible, both rider and horse appear to be transparent.

Kirknewton, nr Edinburgh, West Lothian: Dalmahoy Hotel and Country Club Resort

Built by the Dalrymple family in 1725, the building was later acquired by Lord Aberdour, who became the Earl of Morton. One of his five children, in the form of a white lady, haunts the hotel. She is specifically seen in some of the bedrooms and in the corridors. For identification purposes, her portrait still hangs in the hotel.

Kit's Grave, borders of Dorset, Hampshire and Wiltshire

The ghost of a young female suicide victim haunts this site. She was buried on the spot. No birds sing along the avenue leading to it. Some witnesses report having seen a forlorn-looking phantom on or around the supposed gravesite.

Klive, Somerset: The Hood Arms

Set at the foot of the Quantock Hills, this 17th-century coaching inn is haunted by a former landlord's mother. She has often been seen sitting in the corner of the bar in a rocking chair. It appears that she is uncommunicative and does not seem to be interested in anything going on around her.

Knaresborough, North Yorkshire

Murderer Eugene Aram is said to haunt the area surrounding St Robert's Chapel, which stands on the north bank of the River Nidd. He committed the murder of William Houseman in 1744 and hid his body in a cave, which is now aptly named Eugene Aram's Cave.

Knebworth, nr Stevenage, Hertfordshire: Knebworth House

The spirit of the Victorian novelist, Edward Bulwer-Lytton, of the Lytton family, haunts his former home. He was a close friend of Charles Dickens, obsessed with the occult, and very much devoted to his gargoyle-infested home. It is said that an impending death is foretold by the sight and sound of the phantom spinner, Jenny. Part of the house dates back to the Tudor period and it is suspected that the apparition dates from that time. She can be heard at work in the top of the East Tower.

Knepp Castle, Sussex

The manifestation of a 13th-century girl can be seen around the castle. Her spirit has been transformed into the apparition of a white deer. Perhaps the girl had a sad end at the castle, but nothing is known of the history or the purpose of the haunting.

Knutsford, Cheshire: The Royal George Hotel

A wonderful story of a double life lies at the heart of the haunting of this traditional coaching inn. The gentleman in question was a burglar and highwayman by night, but a solid pillar of the establishment by day. Edward Higgins paid for his crimes and deception in 1767, after having been caught committing a robbery. He was executed, but his spirit lives on in the Round Room of the inn.

Kylesku Hotel, nr Ullapool, Highlands

Formerly known as the Old Ferry House Inn,

this building has two equally plausible stories to account for the sighting of the ghost of a man. The first revolves around a barrel of whisky that fortuitously appears on the beach near to the inn. Several locals enjoyed the contents for some time, but one tried to bring it up the ladder from the hidden room in which they were drinking. He slipped and broke his neck. The other story tells of the McKays, a brother and sister partnership who ran the pub in the 1890s. The brother so enjoyed the liquid benefits of running the inn that his spirit is loathe to leave. He can be seen in the former snug.

L

Lakenheath to Lytchett Maltravers

Lakenheath, nr Mildenhall, Suffolk

Witnesses have reported seeing what may be the ghost of an Australian pilot near the Brandon Road side of the airbase. The pilot was one of many Australians who flew Stirling bombers out of the base during World War Two.

Lanark, Strathclyde: The Cartland Bridge Hotel

A pale blue lady has been seen by several people in this Georgian building that now operates as a hotel. She is described as being old, and is wearing a veil and a light blue dress. It is supposed that she is one of the former occupiers of the house, whose spirit feels unable to leave the building. The hotel also has the ghost of Annie Farle, a seven-year-old girl who died in a riding accident. Her apparition often makes an appearance in the room that was once her bedroom.

Lanark, Strathclyde: Clydesdale Hotel

The hotel was built in 1792 on the site of a Greyfriars monastery. Just below the floor of the basement are the remains of the monks' sleeping quarters. It should come as no surprise that the grey abbot, whose appearance is said to signal good luck for the hotel, haunts the building. In the 1800s there was a fire in the attic that claimed the life of a child. As a result, the cries of a child can be heard in the rooms near that part of the building.

Lancaster, Lancashire: Grand Theatre

A grey lady haunts the auditorium of the theatre, but it is the apparition of the actress Sarah Siddons that attracts most attention to this building. Her brother was once the theatre manager here and she performed on the stage on a number of occasions.

Langenhoe, Essex

Although the church was pulled down in 1962, its site and the nearby manor house are the location of several notable hauntings. Just before World War Two, the vicar encountered numerous examples of poltergeist activity. Ghostly figures appeared, the house was pervaded by the smell of violets in September and the vicar was even embraced by the figure of a naked female ghost.

Langford Budville, Somerset

The ghosts of Squire Fitzwarren and his horse haunt the drive leading to the site of this square home, just to the west of Taunton. It is also said that the squire encountered the Devil and the Wild Hunt, whose hounds frightened the horse and caused the accident that killed them both. The Wild Hunt dates back to Norse mythology. Odin and his pack of hounds were supposed to tear across the sky at night in search of the souls of the damned. This piece of folklore was adapted, and after the Reformation the hunt became the Devil hunting for souls of non-baptised children whose bodies had were not buried in consecrated ground. Witches were entwined with the story and were said to follow the Wild Hunt on their brooms. Around the country the hunt has slightly different guises. In the West Country the hounds are called the Whisht Hounds, and in Yorkshire they are known as the Gabriel Hounds. Usually the appearance of the Wild Hunt heralds a personal, local or national disaster.

Langley Castle, Langley, Northumberland

Lying just four miles south of Hadrian's Wall, Langley Castle, built in the 14th century as a border defence against the Scots, is haunted by the ghost of a woman dressed in white. She has been seen walking up the driveway to the front door, where she vanishes. Also seen on the driveway is a phantom coach pulled by four horses, whipped on by a headless coachman. Several people have complained of being pushed while standing on the battlements, and the sound of singing has been heard from within the castle when it has been known to be empty. Yet another mysterious happening at Langley Castle is the sound of a door opening and closing, when in fact no door, or doorway, exists at the spot.

Langley Park, Durham, Co. Durham

Set to the north of the A691 is the ruin of an impressive Tudor mansion. Witnesses have reported sighting a phantom hearse drawn by a headless horse and driven by a headless man. It is said that if you stand near to the drive at Coalpark Gill at midnight, you will encounter this terrifying apparition.

Lanreath, nr Lostwithiel, Cornwall: Punch Bowl Inn

A strange story of murder and mythology is

attached to this pub. Many years ago, a young curate fell in love with the old rector's young and beautiful wife. The curate was invited for a meal and the old rector went downstairs to the cellar to fetch a bottle of wine. Whether he was pushed or fell down the staircase we will never know, but his soul was somehow transferred into the apparition of a rather combative black cockerel. It attacked everyone on sight and presently made for the pub, where it flew in through an open window. It came to rest inside an earthenware oven, where a kitchen maid trapped it and a mason sealed it in forever. It is said that the spirit of the old rector, in the form of the cockerel, still rages in the wall of the pub.

Langstone, nr Havant, Hampshire: The Royal Oak

A white lady has been seen in the corner of one of the bedrooms of this 14th or 15th-century inn. The apparition is visible for a few moments and then fades into the wall. Other witnesses have heard scraping noises, but it is not known whether this is related to the same manifestation. Explanations relate to the fact that the inn is sited on the old harbour walls and may have a maritime connection, or the haunting may originate from the time when the building was a bakery. Other witnesses claim to have seen a man dressed in 18th-century clothing crossing the main road in the vicinity of the inn.

Lapford, nr Exeter, Devon

The spirit of Thomas Becket gallops through the village at midnight on St John's Eve (27 December). He is en route to Nymet Tracey and the church which one of his murderers (Sir William de Tracy) built as part of his penance. Lapford has a second ghost, John Bedford, a rector of the church who murdered his curate. He was acquitted at trial, but on his death left instructions that he was to be buried in the chancel. The authorities refused permission and he was buried outside the door. The cross on his grave cannot be kept straight and there is supposed to be a hole in the grave through which his ghost escapes.

Larkfield, Kent: Larkfield Priory Hotel, London Road

Originally built in 1890, the old wing of the hotel is haunted by the ghost of a woman. She is popularly called Charlotte and has been seen on many occasions by staff and guests. It is also thought that the hotel is haunted by another unseen spirit, which is said to be involved in poltergeist activity. It is not thought that this second manifestation is related to Charlotte.

Larkhall, nr Lanark, Strathclyde: Applebank Hotel

It seems that only a fragment of a building is sufficient to leave a ghostly imprint on the landscape. Such is the case at this public house, which contains a lintel from the home of the McNeil family. Their house burnt down many years ago, but the spirit of one of the family haunts the building to this day. One of the sons married an Indian princess, who inexplicably disappeared one day. She was desperately homesick and hated living in Scotland. Whether she was murdered or died later, her tortured time in Scotland was such that she haunts the area she loathed in life.

Laugharne, nr Carmarthen, Dyfed: Boat House

The Boat House is a former home of Dylan Thomas, and is said to be haunted by the literary figure himself. He is also said to haunt the Shepherd's Bush Theatre in London. There is a pit nearby at Pant-y-Madog, which several witnesses claim is the stalking place of a black dog, but it has never attacked or menaced anyone.

Launceston, Cornwall

The bizarre apparition of a ghoul, also known as a Kergrim, is said to stalk the churchyard here. It is presumed that the ghoul is the malevolent spirit of someone who was buried in the cemetery. Whether the ghoul actually eats human flesh, as ghouls are said to do, is not known.

Lauriston Castle, nr Edinburgh, Lothian

The spirit of a former butler haunts this magnificent castle. Although some witnesses claim to have seen him, many more have just heard the shuffling of his slippered feet proceeding along the corridors and across the rooms of the castle where he was formerly employed.

Layer Marney Tower, nr Tolleshunt Knights, Essex

The unfortunate Lord Marney did not live to see the completion of his tower, as he died in 1523. As if to compensate himself for the poor timing of his death, his spirit is said to haunt the tower and its precincts.

Leamington Spa, Warwickshire: Manor House Hotel

The apparition of a former housekeeper, dressed in a grey uniform, has been seen for many years. She is said to wander the corridors of the hotel and guests have reported that the temperature of the area in which she is seen drops dramatically.

Leasowe Castle, nr Wallasey, Merseyside

Built by the Earl of Derby in 1593, the castle fell on hard times and acquired the unflattering title Mockbeggar Hall. The castle now operates as a hotel. In one of the bedrooms the ghosts of a man and his son appear. The man murdered his son and then committed suicide.

Leatherhead, Surrey: Church of St Mary and Nicholas

At some unspecified time in the past a monk or priest was confined in a small room within the church. Whether the man was in hiding or whether he had been imprisoned is unknown. Nevertheless, his spirit still haunts the church.

Leeds, West Yorkshire: Kirkstall Abbey

It is said that the indistinct manifestation of a former abbot of the abbey can be seen lurking near the gatehouse. Several witnesses claim to have seen this figure during their visit to the abbey gatehouse museum.

Leeds, West Yorkshire: Queen's Hotel

Karen Fleet was a housekeeper at the Queen's Hotel in 1916 and received the terrible news that her son had been killed at the Somme. After some considerable time she arranged to have her son's body returned to England. Unfortunately the ship carrying the body was sunk off the French coast. Mrs Fleet had attended a number of meetings at the hotel with the General Manager and even after the time had passed when the body should have arrived, she continued to appear at 11am each morning for news. After three weeks, after much self-neglect, she collapsed and died in the hotel. Her ghost still visits the hotel at 11am each day. She is often seen in the boiler house area and is described as a white figure that indulges in some poltergeist activity at the hotel.

Leeds Castle, nr Maidstone, Kent

In the 15th century the Duchess of Gloucester

was imprisoned at Leeds Castle for witchcraft. It is presumed that sightings of the black dog of Leeds are connected to her in some way. The dog could be an apparition of her familiar. Unlike many black dogs, this one appears not to be malevolent. On one occasion the black dog saved a woman's life. She was sitting in one of the Tudor bay windows that overhang the moat when the black dog appeared. The woman mistook the dog for one of her pets and rose to approach it, only to see it disappear through a wall. As she did so the seat she had been sitting on crashed into the moat, pulling masonry away with it. The woman would have certainly been injured, or even killed, had she remained seated.

Leedstown, Cornwall

A ghost 'runs up and down the stairs, and sits and weeps and sleeks her hair'. This is the spirit of a woman whose lover refused to marry her until she gave him the title deeds to her property. When she did, he sold them and went off to America.

Leeming, nr Northallerton, North Yorkshire

Bombers used this airfield beside the Great North Road during World War Two. Ghostly activity seems to emanate from a former bomb store on the southern edge of the airfield. Concealed beneath a mound of earth lies the wreckage of several aircraft that crashed on landing at Leeming. Witnesses have reported seeing a ghostly flying crew, dressed in full flying kit and accompanied by ghostly voices.

Leicester, Leicestershire: Ashfordby Police Station

Although this building is now a police station, it was once a fire station. Several officers and other witnesses have reported the manifestation of a chief fire officer dressed in a Victorian uniform.

Leicester, Leicestershire: Blackfriars Hall

This building, now in at least its third reincarnation, has been both a Dominican monastery and the Holy Cross Church. With such a rich and varied history it is not surprising that the building has two religion-related apparitions. The first is a former prior of the monastery, while the second, more recognisable ghost is that of Father Norbert, who was a priest at the church in around 1918. Witnesses have seen him near the altar.

Leicester, Leicestershire: Leicester Castle

William Napier Reeve, who was a Victorian historian, was a great lover of Leicester Castle. His ghost has been seen on several occasions, presumably revisiting the building that gave him so much pleasure during his lifetime. He haunts the courtyard of the castle and can be seen resplendent in his top hat. It is also said that the ghost of John of Gaunt haunts the castle.

Leicester, Leicestershire: Leicester Cathedral

Visitors to the cathedral should be particularly cautious if they encounter a strange, hooded figure in the churchyard. It is said that if the apparition touches you then you will die within the year. Particularly noticeable about this ghost is the fact that it is often seen kneeling down with its ear on the ground, and it has unusually long arms.

Leigh, Greater Manchester

A 19th-century bombardier either fell or jumped into one of the ponds near Hooten Lane. Whether his death was deliberate or an accident is unknown, but it is said that his spirit, in full uniform, has been known to stalk people and run up behind them.

Leigh, Kent: Ramhurst Manor

Originally, Ramhurst was a manor house owned by the Culpepper family. In 1857, an Indian army officer bought the place. His wife, her brother and the cook all heard voices, footsteps and rustling silk in the house. The brother even thought that he heard his sister crying for help in the middle of the night, so he came to her rescue with a shotgun. She was sleeping peacefully. The visit of a friend, who happened to be a medium, began to unravel the mystery. The medium actually saw the ghosts, who informed her that their names were Dame and Richard Children, husband and wife. Richard had died there in 1753. They had loved the house so much that they could not bear to leave it. They were determined to haunt the place until the manor house came back into the hands of the Children family. Perhaps they changed their minds, as shortly after this, the ghosts were heard no more.

Leith Hall, nr Huntly, Grampian

The ghost of John Leith, who died after being shot in the head by Abernethy of Mayen in 1763, has been seen in his former home. The incident occurred during a dinner party in Aberdeen. Further evidence that this is John Leith is provided by the fact that the apparition is of a large man with a black, bushy beard and a bandaged head.

Lenchwick, nr Evesham, Worcestershire

The horrific manifestation of a spectral coach has been seen on the road running from Lenchwick to Evesham. Witnesses report that the horses snort fire from their noses and that more flames spurt out of their eyes. The coach driver's whip flashes in the night like lightning bolts. It is also said that the coach carries the ghost of the murderer John Wybon, who murdered Gabriel Bigge in 1615. Those that have seen the phantom passenger state that he has red marks around his neck from the hangman's noose.

Leominster, Herefordshire: Talbot Hotel

The ghost of a monk, believed to be Cadwallader, who was hung, drawn and quartered by a local butcher, has been seen in one of the bedrooms. The apparition is described as wearing a grey habit with a hood.

Letchworth Corner, Scudamore, Letchworth, Hertfordshire

During the 1950s several witnesses reported hearing ghostly footsteps and thuds in the late evening, emanating from an empty room. The owner's dog refused to enter the room but the sounds seemed to stop as abruptly as they had started. It is believed that the sounds are caused by the spirit of a man who converted three 400-year-old cottages into the present dwelling.

Leven, nr Beverley, East Yorkshire: White Cross

Equestrians should beware of the ghost of a headless lady if they are riding near White Cross. It is said that the apparition jumps onto the horse behind the rider and flicks their ears with her bony fingers.

Levens Hall, nr Kendal, Cumbria

This fascinating 16th-century hall, incorporating earlier buildings, boasts two interesting manifestations. The most celebrated is the phantom black dog, which rushes down the staircase and has been seen by the owners and visitors alike. A pink lady has also been seen, making her way through the hall and then into the gardens. Nearby, Levens Bridge boasts the apparition of a grey lady, who stands on the bridge leading to the house. On one occasion, she nearly caused a fatal accident when she walked out in front of a car and forced the driver to swerve to avoid her.

Lewes, East Sussex: Lewes Prison

On several occasions, inmates and warders of the prison have seen the manifestation of a woman dressed in Victorian clothing. It is supposed that she is the spirit of a prison visitor or relative of one of the prisoners.

Lewes, East Sussex: Offhan Hill

The Battle of Lewes in 1264 settled the outcome of the Baron's War against the king. Henry III was defeated here and some 3,000 men perished, the bones of whom have been found in the nearby chalk pits. May is the month to witness the cries and screams of men and horses, mingled with the sounds of battle. Due to changes in the calendar since the 13th century, the key date is 25 May and not 14 May, which is the anniversary of the battle.

Lewes, East Sussex: Shelley's Hotel

Room 26 is said to be the centre of intense poltergeist activity, during which witnesses have reported that their beds levitate and clothes and other personal effects are tossed around the room. This is all associated with a suicide that did not actually occur on the premises. During the 1930s, a man stayed in the room, leaving early in the morning but failing to take his belongings. He went to the house of a nearby relative and gassed himself. The staircase at the centre of the original 16th-century building is the site of the manifestation of a ghostly Cavalier. Staff and guests alike have also seen the form of an old lady in a blue and white dress walking along one of the upper corridors.

Lewtrenchard House (The Manor Hotel), nr Lydford, Devon

The spirit of Margaret Belfield, known locally as Old Madam, haunts the former manor house of the Baring-Gould family. The manor house is now a hotel. Her spirit protects the house and the family treasure. During her life Margaret Belfield maintained the family fortune despite the best efforts of her spendthrift son. Witnesses have reported seeing her in the Long Gallery. Other witnesses have also reported seeing a white lady, the apparition of Susannah Gould, who died of a heart attack on 19 March 1729, shortly after her marriage.

Lidgate, nr Bury St Edmunds, Suffolk

A house known as John o' Lydgate's was once a guesthouse for travelling monks, particularly a monk from nearby St Edmundsbury Abbey, a one-time pupil of Chaucer. Occupants of the house have reported smelling strong cooking odours emanating from an old fireplace that may have been the monks' refectory. Other witnesses have reported smelling baking bread, cooking meat and incense.

Lidwell, nr Teignmouth, Devon

The ghost of a mad monk is said to haunt this small hamlet. The hermit monk lived in the 14th century and lured unsuspecting folk into his cell near a holy well to confess. He murdered them, robbed them and disposed of their bodies.

Lilleshall Abbey, nr Telford, Shropshire

Witnesses have reported being approached by the strange manifestation of an elderly Augustinian monk clad in a black robe. Almost uniquely this ghost is said to talk. He asks witnesses whether they have found the hidden treasure of Lilleshall Abbey.

Lillington, nr Leamington Spa, Warwickshire: Jack and Jill Inn, Newland Road

Graham Boulton used to be the landlord of the pub. He would spend his spare time during the summer months sitting on the patio with his dog. In 1970, long after his death, the then landlord looked out of the window one June morning and saw his apparition standing in the roof garden, along with his dog. The witness described the apparition's appearance as like a reflection in a mirror, and the description fitted Graham Boulton. A barmaid working in the cellar was stunned to see Boulton walking around some beer barrels. She could clearly see the outline of the barrels through the apparition. The probable explanation for the haunting is the popular story that Boulton was buried in the wrong grave.

Lincoln, Lincolnshire: Greestone Steps

These steps lead up to the cathedral, so it is not surprising that the spirit of a 17th-century cleric, perhaps a monk, haunts this area. Nothing is known of this character or why he should choose to haunt the steps rather than the cathedral itself.

Lincoln, Lincolnshire: White Hart Inn

Now a Forte Hotel, this old inn is the site of hauntings that have been featured on national television. The young female victim of a ratcatcher murderer has been seen on the first floor. She was a maid at the inn when she was killed. A faceless highwayman is said to haunt the Orangery. His ghastly appearance relates to the fact that he had a branding iron pushed into his face. More recently, staff and guests have reported the sighting of a well-turned out ghost, dressed in a smoking jacket and wearing a cravat.

Lindholme, nr Doncaster, South Yorkshire

This cultivated area served as an airfield during World War Two and lies within an area of barren marshland. Lindholme seems to have an affinity with spirits called William. Many years ago the area was renowned for its manifestation of the ghostly hermit William de Lindholme. More recently, during World War Two, a Polish Lancaster bomber pilot crashed on Hatfield Moors. Paradoxically, his name was also Willy and his spirit now seems to have replaced the older William.

Lindisfarne: Lindisfarne Priory

St Cuthbert came to Holy Island in 664, and it is thought that the grey-clad monk that is seen wandering among the rocks and walking down to the narrow causeway is him.

Lingfield, Surrey: Greyhound Inn

Originally registered in 1584, this pub once had a hidden room, frequented by smugglers, behind an inglenook. Large enough for two or three people, its entrance is hidden behind a panel in the circular skittle room. Catering staff have complained of being touched by unseen hands and suffering from the disappearance of various kitchen items. Dogs are terrified of going near the cellar door or the top of the stairs. Witnesses have also reported seeing the ghostly figure of a young boy, about eight years old, standing in the corner of the skittle room, accompanied by a sudden drop in temperature, which fades away.

Linley, nr Bridgnorth, Shropshire

Strange illuminations light up the skies around Linley during the night, often described as balls of light. Although some attribute this to geological fault lines beneath the village, others believe that there is a more supernatural explanation. Certainly, witnesses have reported seeing a black monk and a white lady, together with descriptions of various poltergeist activities.

Linlithgow Palace, nr Edinburgh, Lothian

Shortly before the Battle of Flodden, James IV of Scotland was confronted by the manifestation of an elderly man clad in a long blue gown. He warned James that his death was near. The Scottish king died on the battlefield. James's wife, Margaret Tudor, has also been seen near the palace entrance, again dressed in blue. Witnesses report that she is best seen in April, near the church, at around 9am.

Linslade, Bedfordshire: The Buckingham Arms

Although nobody has ever seen the ghost that haunts this pub, it has caused a great deal of consternation over the years. At 5am each morning, the front gate is pulled open and then slammed shut. An enormous amount of noise has been heard from the cellar and staff and customers have felt an icy blast of air.

Liphook, Hampshire: The Royal Anchor

Captain Jack, a highwayman, was tracked down to this coaching inn and shot in one of the bedrooms. His ghost still haunts the public house. In the lanes to the north of the town, leading to Bramshott, the spirit of a fair-haired boy playing pipes is said to lead lost travellers to safety.

Lissett, nr Bridlington, East Yorkshire

The phantom of a Halifax bomber, known as Reaper's Bomber, was last seen on 16 August 1944. RAF Lissett was used as a bomber base from 1943–44. The appearance of Reaper's Bomber was said to foretell the imminent loss of a bomber crew if it left on a mission the same day as a sighting. On that last fateful day in 1944, a Halifax crewed by Canadians crashed at Foston. Although the airbase no longer exists, several local witnesses have stated that they have heard the phantom bomber's engines overhead.

Little Compton, nr Shipston on Stour, Warwickshire

The ghost of Mr Drane, who was a curate at St Denis's Church, haunts the church and surrounding area. He was hopelessly in love with Miss Fielding, who sang in the church choir. She, however, was in love with Captain Brandon, who lived at the nearby Grange. Subsequently Miss Fielding and Captain Brandon became engaged and asked Mr Drane to perform the wedding ceremony. He fulfilled his duties, kissed the bride and then hanged himself in the belfry.

Littlecote House, Wiltshire

This Tudor manor house has a ghost dating back to a 16th-century murder. William Darrell murdered his own newborn child in one of the bedrooms. Several witnesses have reported seeing the shadowy form of a midwife holding a child, beside the four-poster in the fateful room. An individual living in the house and acting as a tour guide witnessed a blue lady walking up the stairs on the third floor. The figure walked through a rope tied across the banisters.

Little Davley, nr Ironbridge, Shropshire: Holly Road

14A Holly Road was recently demolished, but its cruck-frame is to be erected at Blists Hall Open Air Museum. The building is a good example of a timber-framed hall of its period. A young child, with large, sad eyes, haunted the house. The spirit is said to have been seen sitting at the top of the stairs. During the demolition, several toys were found near the spot where the child sat crying so mournfully. The phantom of what may have been the last tenant of 14A was also often seen staring out of one of the windows before the demolition. Witnesses described him as 'a stooped old man'.

Littledean Tower, nr Melrose, Borders

A local laird was said to have murdered a stable boy at the tower and is now cursed to ride a spectral horse around the area on stormy nights.

Little Gaddesden, Hertfordshire: The Manor House

A 17th-century suicide victim, Jarman, haunts the manor house and village pond. He chose to take his own life after the daughter of Lord Bridgewater of Ashridge Park spurned his advances.

Little Haven, nr Haverfordwest, Dyfed: Castle Hotel

The manifestation of a white lady, presumed to be the ghost of a woman who was found dead on the beach opposite, has been seen on several occasions. A hunch-backed apparition has also been reported, as well as the phantoms of two men, apparently in relatively modern clothing. One of these spirits slowly appears from the feet up. Another invisible manifestation pushes down on the bed in one of the bedrooms when people are in it.

Little Lawford Hall, nr Rugby, Warwickshire

This is the site of an exorcism. In 1752 12 clergymen managed to conjure the spirit of the Elizabethan ghost 'One-handed Broughton' into a bottle. One-handed Broughton had been terrorising the area with his spectral coach and horses for several years. In life he was struck by lightning and lost his hand, an event which altered his personality from meek and mild to violent and aggressive. As part of the exorcism, Parson Hall managed to extinguish 11 of the candles held by the clergymen and complete the ritual. He allowed the spirit the freedom to roam for a short while each night, and it has been seen by several witnesses over the years. The family kept the bottle containing the ghost when they left the hall, and it is said that it has been sealed into a block of concrete and hidden somewhere known only to the family.

Little Malvern, nr Great Malvern, Worcestershire

The vague shape of a woman can be seen resting her head in her hands as she sits on a large rock on a small spur of the Malvern Hills. The site is known as 'Mrs Dee's Rock'. Mrs Dee lived in a cottage near the rock with her 13-year-old daughter and a cruel husband. On her deathbed, she threatened to return and haunt the man if he mistreated her daughter. Within months, he had made the girl's life such a misery that she resolved to drown herself in the pond. Her mother's ghost is said to have risen from the water, simultaneously terrorising her husband and thwarting the suicide attempt. The ghost plagued the husband for several months until a priest exorcised the spirit. Her ghost is now restricted to the rock overlooking the cottage.

Little Shelsey, Worcestershire: Court House

Lady Lightfoot was imprisoned and murdered here in the 16th century, because of her opposition to Henry VIII and his serial monogamy. A phantom coach and four horses have also been seen. This is a reflection of a poorly-organised rescue attempt during her imprisonment. The coach with her would-be rescuers in pulled up, but the driver was too drunk to control the coach and the whole party was pitched into the moat and drowned. Ironically, the rescue was futile, as Lady Lightfoot was already dead. Several witnesses have seen the phantom coach bolting across the lawn toward the moat, where it and its ghostly passengers disappear into the water.

Little Wymondley, nr Hitchin, Hertfordshire

The priory is said to have not only a chestnut tree planted by Julius Caesar, but also the manifestations of ghostly monks.

Litton Cheney, Dorset

At Baglake House, the spirit of William Light, who committed suicide in 1748, can be seen. Sometimes he is accompanied by another ghost in rustling silk, either in the drawing room or the summer house.

Liverpool, Merseyside: The Adelphi Hotel

Staff at this city centre hotel call their frequent ghostly guest George. George has been seen in several of the bedrooms, particularly in the evenings, but does not appear to be menacing or frightening in any way.

Liverpool, Merseyside: Aintree Racecourse

Home of the Grand National since 1839, the racecourse is haunted by Lottery, the winner of the first Grand National. His rider, Jem Mason, accompanies him as they retrace the steps that brought them victory. Witnesses have said that the ghostly duo leap over 30ft into the air

before disappearing. Lottery was so good in his day that he was barred from participating and ended his days as a plough horse.

Liverpool, Merseyside: Albert Dock

When a new café opened in March 1992, it seemed to trigger a host of slumbering ghosts. Customers and staff alike have reported hearing chattering voices, accompanied by doors swinging open and closed. One waitress challenged the ghosts to 'come out, come out, whoever you are'. The following morning they found writing on a napkin that had been placed on the till. It said 'I come out but you gone'. Of a more identifiable nature is the ghost of James Jones, a drunken night watchman. He fell into Salthouse Dock after a drinking bout in 1817. He has been seen near the Tate Gallery, dressed in 19th-century clothing.

Liverpool, Merseyside: Cathedral Church of Christ

The largest cathedral in Great Britain took 74 years to build. However, it was not until 1973 that ghosts were reported in the vicinity. A tramp called Bob found he was locked in the cemetery after having fallen asleep. With or without the influence of alcohol, he reported seeing the shadowy figure of a man wearing a top hat and a long, flowing cape. The figure limped toward him, and Bob fled. Bob encountered the phantom near a domed, circular monument in the middle of the cemetery. This is where one William Huskisson lay entombed. He died in September 1830 after falling under the wheels of George Stephenson's *Rocket*. The train crushed one of his legs and Huskisson subsequently died. Perhaps this explains the ghost's limp?

Liverpool, Merseyside: Lawrence Gardens

The ghost of a World War Two police officer

is said to have been seen, still walking his beat, tapping windows through which light can be seen in order to enforce the blackout. Older residents claim that the officer was killed in May 1941, shortly after carrying a disabled child to an air raid shelter. Others, however, believe that this apparition is of a policeman from the 1930s.

Liverpool, Merseyside: Leveson Street, Toxteth

In 1849 John Wilson butchered his lodger, the pregnant Ann Hinrichson, and her two sons, Henry and John. He also all but killed Mary Parr, the maidservant. It was she who survived long enough to tell the authorities how Wilson had wiped out the whole family. Meanwhile, Wilson returned to his former wife in Tranmere, but on three occasions a ghostly apparition appeared at his window, pointing an accusing finger at the murderer. When Wilson fled the house and tried to pawn some of the jewellery he had stolen after the murder he was recognised, arrested and hanged in September. It is believed that the house in which Wilson lived in Tranmere was once the home of a judge, whose ghost it was that spooked him. Wilson's apparition is said to stalk the area where he committed his foul crimes.

Liverpool, Merseyside: Liverpool Prison

Cell G2 in Walton Jail is haunted by William Kennedy, who was hanged there for the murder of an Essex policeman. After his execution in 1927, prison warders reported seeing William Kennedy a week after he had died. Inmates unlucky enough to have been allocated this cell have said that they have felt ghostly hands strangling them in their beds and seen a ghostly black shadow standing over them at night.

Liverpool, Merseyside: Maghull

At the southern end of Maghull the sound of galloping horses and the clatter of soldiers' accoutrements have been heard at dusk, and on several occasions the ghosts of headless soldiers have been seen against the background of a grey-stone wall. These are thought to be the ghostly remnants of a royalist army fleeing south in 1648, after being routed by the Parliamentarians. However, some feel that they could be Jacobite soldiers trying to escape in 1715, when Preston was recaptured by English troops.

Liverpool, Merseyside: Penny Lane

Poltergeist activity during the night is so noisy that several local residents are unable to sleep. It seems to emanate from No.44, which in 1945, when the activity began, was a shop hit by a bomb during a wartime raid. After a period of quiet, the poltergeist activity resumed in the 1970s, when the building was once more a shop. Despite extensive investigations, including pulling up floorboards, nothing could be discovered. The owners decided to set up a tape recorder and try to capture the sounds of the ghosts. They were successful in obtaining some evidence of supernatural activity. Over the years the ghostly noises gradually diminished, although many residents expect the poltergeists to return at some point.

Liverpool, Merseyside: Philharmonic Hall

The present hall, opened just before World War Two, replaced the old one, which opened in 1849 and burned down in 1933. A night watchman reported seeing a chair moving across the floor toward him, and on another occasion, in the Green Room, he heard knocking noises. Others have reported footsteps on the roof and an unseen spirit descending the stairway toward the

Projection Room. Many people believe that these activities are related to the opera singer Grace Moore, who died in the 1960s. In 1987 two witnesses reported seeing a young woman standing on a balcony in the hall. The apparition waved at them and then disappeared.

Liverpool, Merseyside: Rodney Street

The ruins of St Andrew's Church seem to be the centre of activity of a ghostly apparition dressed in a cape and top hat. He has approached witnesses and then inexplicably disappeared through solid brick walls. It is believed that he is the spirit of a Scotsman called McKenzie, who was involved in the railways and science. His remains are housed in a pyramid-shaped tomb in the cemetery. Apparently the corpse was propped up on a chair in front of a card table, with a winning hand of cards pressed between his stiff fingers.

Liverpool, Merseyside: West Derby Road Fire Station

During the 1990s several firemen reported seeing the apparitions of one or two Victorian male ghosts, often accompanied by a group of children. These spirits would visit the rest room and rouse the firemen during their sleep. A medium identified one of the ghosts, who wore a top hat, as Edward Wilson. It is said that Wilson lived on the site of the fire station during the Victorian period.

Llanafan, nr Aberystwyth, Dyfed

The cave of Craig-y-Rogof is said to be the hiding place of a great treasure seized by pirates in the past. It is therefore quite understandable that ghostly pirates have been seen in the area, presumably protecting their hidden loot.

Llanbadrig, nr Holyhead, Gwynedd: Galan Ddu

This house was once the home of Rosina Buckman, the New Zealand opera singer. Her ashes were buried in the garden until 1964, when the construction of the Wylfa nuclear power station prompted them to be moved. Since then, witnesses have reported seeing her spirit in the form of a white lady, humming beautifully, in the area.

Llandysul, nr Cardigan, Dyfed

Many years ago, a harpist was drowned in the Pool of Harper on the River Teifi. It is said that on cool summer nights you can hear his plaintive music wafting through the still air.

Llanfaglan, nr Caernarvon, Gwynedd

During June you may be fortunate enough to see a ghostly procession of people dressed in 18th or 19th-century clothing approaching the churchyard. It is said that the ghosts enter the churchyard, walk toward their graves, raise their arms and jump back into their coffins. They are thought to be the phantoms of people who were drowned at sea and buried in the churchyard.

Llangadog, Carmarthenshire: Red Lion Hotel

This old coaching inn dates from the early part of the 16th century. The spirits of a woman and her child haunt the building. It is believed that they were murdered there during the reign of Queen Victoria.

Llangathen, Dyfed: Aberglasney House

The spirits of six young girls who were suffocated in the Blue Room are said to stalk the building and the grounds. Other witnesses have reported hearing various odd noises, including fighting, clinking coins and furniture being moved. These noises are not believed to be related to the girls.

Llangefni, nr Bangor, Gwynedd

A phantom coach runs along the Penmymydd Road. It is believed to be related to an incident in the past, when a highwayman held up a coach and robbed and then murdered all the passengers.

Llangoed, Anglesey, Gwynedd: Parc Terrace

A ghostly white dog was seen on several occasions during the 1970s, running along the lane in this small village. It is assumed that this is the phantom of a local pet that was knocked down by a car several years ago.

Llangollen, Clwyd: Plas Newydd

This was the former home of Lady Eleanor Butler and the Honourable Sarah Ponsonby. They lived there over 200 years ago and it is said that they were rather eccentric. Known as the Ladies of Llangollen, they entertained a number of distinguished guests, including Byron, Wordsworth and Shelley. The women would habitually wear traditional Welsh costume. Their spirits have been seen on a number of occasions, often accompanied by a ghost called Molly the Basher, who was, in fact, their maid, Mary Carryll.

Llanhilleth, nr Abertillery, Gwent

To the east of the village is Llanhilleth mountain, which is haunted by the ghost of an old woman. She may have been a local witch and is seen carrying a pot and wearing a four-cornered hat. Her appearance often encourages witnesses to stray from their path and end up way off normal tracks near the mountain's summit.

Llanrhidian, nr Swansea, West Glamorgan: Welcome To Town Inn

The Regency ghost, Henry, a phantom coachman, has been seen sitting in the pub. It is believed that in life he loved to visit this inn. Nearby several witnesses have seen a white lady, perhaps related to the village of Llanellan, which was wiped out by the plague.

Llanrwst, Gwynedd: Gwydir Castle

The ghost of a man dressed in an Edwardian-style suit has been seen on several occasions. It is not known who he is or why he should choose to haunt the former country seat of the Wynn family.

Llanvihangel Court, nr Abergavenny, Gwent

A white lady has been seen walking from the hall of the court to nearby Lady Wood. Witnesses have said that once she reaches the trees she disappears. Other witnesses have reported seeing the ghost of a green man who appears to be very small.

Llanvihangel Crucorney, nr Abergavenny, Gwent: The Skirrid Inn

Judge Jeffreys used this building as an execution place following the Monmouth rebellion. Not only is it said to be the oldest public house in Wales, but it was also the site of no fewer than 182 executions. Convicted rebels were hanged from the stairwell and presumably buried nearby. On one occasion a woman felt ill at the pub and when someone loosened her clothing they found that she had what looked like a noose mark around her neck. Other witnesses have seen figures wearing helmets passing by the windows outside.

Llyn Cwm Bychan, nr Harlech, Gwynedd

The Roman steps at the north end of the lake

are said to be the place where you may encounter ghostly Roman miners and soldiers. There was indeed a Roman mine here, and witnesses have reported seeing a procession of the former workers accompanied by a legionary guard.

Llyn Cynwch, nr Dolgellau, Gwynedd

A monstrous human-shaped figure emerges from the lake and is said to drag unsuspecting victims into the murky waters if they are unwary.

Loch Morlich, nr Aviemore, Highlands

A giant, fierce warrior, known as Big Donald of the Ghosts or Red Hand, is said to haunt the sandy beach of the loch.

Loch Mullardoch, nr Kyle Of Lochalsh, Highlands

During the 1980s two people walking in the area saw a cottage on the bank of this remote loch. They consulted their map and saw that it was not featured. As they walked toward the cottage they went down into a depression and when they emerged from the other side it had vanished. Local people claim that the cottage was a hunting lodge that had been under water for some 30 years following a change in the level of the loch's water.

Locking, nr Weston-super-Mare, Somerset: Locking Manor

After the Battle of Sedgemoor, Monmouth's officers were hunted down. John Plomley and his two sons were not only sympathetic to Monmouth, but had actually taken part in the battle. The two sons were captured and hanged, but the father hid for some time in Cheddar. He returned home, but was spotted by royalist spies. When the soldiers arrived, an innocent Lady Plomley, clutching her dog, feigned no knowledge. The dog wriggled free and ran straight to John Plomley's hiding place. The soldiers slid back a wall panel and entered the secret passage. Plomley was captured hiding in a coppice and taken away with his wife. John was hung, drawn and quartered, with Lady Plomley looking on. She returned home and threw herself down a well, along with her dog. Servants, owners and guests have regularly seen the ghosts of all four members of the Plomley family, as well as the little white dog.

London Colney, Hertfordshire: Salsbury Hall

This distinctive manor house is surrounded by its original Norman moat. Various witnesses have reported seeing the figure of a man in one of the corridors and when challenged he disappears. It is not known who this spirit is.

Long Compton, Warwickshire: Harrow Hill

In 1879 a local farm worker called James Hayward stood trial for the murder of Anne Tennant. He claimed that she was a witch and had cast a spell on him. Baron Bramwell, at Warwick Assizes in January 1880, found that Hayward was mad and therefore unfit to plead. Only five years earlier, William Davis had killed another so-called witch by the name of Nanny Morgan on nearby Westwood Common. He had committed the murder with an eel spear. Much later, in 1945, Charles Walton was killed with a pitchfork, apparently a tried and tested method of killing witches. Even in 1949 witchcraft was rife in the area and a black mass was supposed to have been held at the Rollright Stones. In November 1949 two furniture delivery men encountered the ghostly apparition of an old woman with grey, matted hair, wearing a dirty black shawl. She appeared in front of the van and glided past the vehicle. It is believed that it was the ghost of Anne Tennant. Many other witnesses claim to have seen this strange old woman.

Longham, Dorset: Berrans Avenue

A grey lady has been seen walking through the back gardens of the houses on this avenue. The figure disappears from sight for a few seconds and then reappears, having walked through a fence. She leaves no trace behind her and unfortunately her identity is unknown. Also near Longham is an old cottage, haunted by a woman with long, black hair. She has been seen sitting in one of the rooms.

Longleat House, nr Warminster, Wiltshire

The ghost of a green lady, believed to be Lady Louisa Careret, wife of Viscount Weymouth, has been seen by a number of different witnesses. Weymouth discovered her with her lover and fought a duel with him. He succeeded in killing the man and buried his body in the cellar. The area you are most likely to see Louisa in is now known as Green Lady's Walk. The Red Library is also haunted and there are other ghosts, including one who knocks at bedroom doors at night. When the central heating was being installed the remains of Louisa's lover were discovered under the flagstones of the cellar floor.

Long Marston, nr York, North Yorkshire

Oliver Cromwell used the Old Hall as his headquarters during the Battle of Marston Moor in 1644. Many witnesses, notably several motorists in 1932, have seen phantom royalist soldiers running along the road.

Long Melford, Suffolk: The Bull Hotel

The hotel has been the site of poltergeist activity. Footsteps have been heard and numerous objects have been moved by telekinesis. It is said that dogs are terrified of the place. In July 1648, as a result of an argument, a man called Roger Greene murdered a farmer, Richard Everard, in the hallway of the inn. The ghost of the murdered man returns periodically to the Bull Hotel, the scene of his tragic death.

Longnor, Shropshire: Bridge Street

The figure of a young girl has been seen standing on the bridge. She has been described by witnesses as wearing a wedding dress. The figure stands there for a few seconds and then floats over the bridge and into the stream. It is believed that she is the ghost of an abandoned bride who committed suicide after being jilted at the altar.

Longridge, nr Blackburn, Lancashire

The ghost of an old lady, carrying a basket and wearing a long skirt, has been seen on numerous occasions. She wears a bonnet that conceals her face, but if you approach too closely, she will turn to face you and reveal that she has no head. Her head is, in fact, in the basket, as she will then proceed to show you. Once she has done this it is said that she will chase you, shouting and laughing.

Long Stratton, Norfolk

Old Hunch, who died in 1647, is said to drive the phantom coach and four horses that have been seen in this area. For some reason the coach is also related to Judge Reeve and his wife, who are buried in Long Stratton church.

Long Wittenham, Oxfordshire

The Co-op in the main street is said to be the centre of extensive poltergeist activity. It is believed that the manifestations must relate to a much earlier period, although nobody seems to have any further information.

Looe, Cornwall: Jolly Tar Inn

A white hare is said to haunt this old pub. The apparition is thought to be the spirit of a girl who committed suicide in the building. The hare runs down the hill at Talland and vanishes at the door of the pub. The apparition is said to be a sign of impending misfortune.

Loseley, nr Guildford, Surrey

One of the houses here is haunted, but it is unclear what is causing the problem. The manifestation must be very frightening as it caused the swift departure of an American tenant. The family packed their bags and left overnight, such was their fear of the haunting.

Loughton, nr Milton Keynes, Buckinghamshire

On Traps Hill Dick Turpin's ghost can be seen. His spirit drags a woman behind his horse and it is said that this re-enacts an incident when he tried to force a woman to tell him where she had hidden her jewels. The spirit is seen about three times a year. The area was familiar to Turpin, who often used it as a base from which to rob coaches on Watling Street.

Louth, Lincolnshire: Thorpe Hall

Thorpe Hall was once the home of John Bolle, who accompanied Raleigh at the Siege of Cadiz in 1596. There he met Donna Leonora Ovido. Attracted to the dashing Englishman, she set her heart on marrying him. He refused, but took away with him a portrait of her. Bolle always laid a place for her at his dinner table. It is said that she eventually did come to England in order to try and convince Bolle to marry her; he refused again and she committed suicide in the gardens. The hall is haunted by a green lady, and in her portrait Donna Ovido wears a green dress.

Louth, Lincolnshire: Ye Olde White Swanne, Eastgate

The apparition of a tall man in a white cape haunts this 14th-century pub. Witnesses report seeing the manifestation at around midnight. Unfortunately the identity of the ghost is unknown, but he may also be responsible for considerable poltergeist activity in the building. On several occasions crates of beer have been cast onto the ground and noises have been heard emanating from an upstairs room.

Loveden, Lincolnshire: Stragglethorpe Hall

A nearby monastery once owned the hall. It is said that a ghostly coach rattles along the road outside, en route to an unknown location. Witnesses have also reported that the attic houses unseen spirits that hammer metal and drag chains.

Lowestoft, Suffolk: Anchor Hotel

Now abandoned for economic reasons rather than supernatural ones, this hotel is said to be on the site of an underground chapel of St Bartholomew's Priory, which was demolished in the 15th century. Shortly after 1900, builders revealed that the chapel had tunnels leading to the Parish Church. It may be reasonable to assume that the hooded figures seen in the cellar and other parts of the building have a religious connection. Individuals have also reported feeling cold blasts of air in the building, but this may have more to do with the fact that Lowestoft is the most eastern town in the country than with any supernatural phenomena.

Lowther Castle, nr Penrith, Cumbria

By all accounts James Lowther, the 1st Earl of Lonsdale, was a thoroughly unpleasant landlord. His ghost has been seen in and around the ruined castle and Haweswater.

Lowton Common, nr Warrington, Cheshire

In 1883 Joshua Rigby was murdered at Cheetham Fold Farm. Unfortunately the man arrested for his murder was acquitted. As a result, Rigby's restless spirit still haunts the area, taking the form of a misty and indistinct figure.

Loxley, nr Sheffield, South Yorkshire

The tortured spirit of Mary Revill has been seen stalking the common. She was murdered there on 31 December 1812. Her murderer was never caught, which may explain why her spirit remains restlessly active.

Lubenham, nr Market Harborough, Leicestershire

Papillon Hall was built by David Papillon, who apparently had a Spanish mistress kept locked away in the house. It is said that she died in mysterious circumstances in 1715. Papillon married shortly after the incident. However, the Spanish mistress left behind a curse on the house in the shape of her shoes. It is said that if they leave the building, then a disaster will befall those living there. During World War Two American pilots used the hall as a base and on two occasions the shoes were removed and pilots did not return from their missions. When Lutyens rebuilt the house in 1903, the builders discovered the skeleton of a woman.

Ludham, nr Norwich, Norfolk: St Benet's Abbey

At the junctions of the rivers Bure and Thurne lies St Benet's Abbey. The ghost of a monk who was said to have betrayed the abbey to the Normans haunts the remote ruin.

Ludlow, Shropshire: Broad Street

A grey-haired lady wearing a dressing gown has been seen in the churchyard and rectory. This may or may not be a slightly different version of the apparition of Catherine of Aragon, who many claim haunts the area. Alternatively the apparition could be Marion de la Bruyère, who married into the Lloyd family. Her husband was very cruel to her and kept her locked up in a four-foot square room under the stairs.

Ludlow, Shropshire: Corve Street

A Greyfriars Priory was once sited in this area and had associations with the existing St Leonard's Chapel. Despite this, there are no ghostly monks, but there is the manifestation of a man who looks like John Bull, a cartoon figure of the typical Englishman common in print until World War One. He has been seen running toward the chapel and then disappearing near the burial ground. The figure may be William Owen, who was a portrait painter to the Prince Regent. He died a very gruesome death when a chemist's assistant gave him a bottle of poison instead of medicine.

Ludlow, Shropshire: Feathers Hotel

The apparition seen by several individuals, particularly during the 1970s, is somewhat out of the ordinary. Witnesses reported seeing a girl aged about 16 years old wearing a mini-skirt and a see-through blouse. The apparition has been seen to walk through cars and glide across the pavement before disappearing. Notably, the sightings tend to occur at around midday. A researcher discovered a strange explanation for the apparition. The girl, called Carol, used to visit her aunt once a week until her aunt suddenly died. Carol then moved to Birmingham where she still lives. The apparition apparently appears when Carol visualises herself walking along the road toward her aunt's house.

Ludlow, Shropshire: Ludlow Castle

The manifestation of Marion de la Bruyère

that may or may not haunt Broad Street is very much associated with Ludlow Castle. Her lover regularly visited her even during a siege of the castle during the reign of Henry II. She would leave a rope hanging out of a window at the appropriate time so that he could join her in her bedchamber. On one occasion he arrived, accompanied by soldiers of the besieging force. Immediately she grabbed his sword, ran him through and then jumped out of the window. As a result, witnesses have reported hearing strange grunts, gasps and snoring sounds from the Hanging Tower. The name of the tower gives a clue to its original purpose. It was used for executions, so an alternative explanation for the sounds may be that they are the last gasps of men who died at the end of a rope.

Ludlow, Shropshire: St Lawrence Church

This area may be the haunting place of Catherine of Aragon or Marion de la Bruyère, but the grey/blue lady appears to be far older than either of these two women were when they died. It is said that the apparition walks through the graveyard and disappears at the church door. The best time to witness the manifestation is on summer evenings.

Lulworth Cove, Dorset

To the east of the cove lies Bindon Hill. Several witnesses claim to have seen Roman soldiers marching in the area. This was one of the first areas to be occupied by the Romans after their invasion.

Lustleigh, nr Newton Abbot, Devon

A spectacular haunting here may be related to an event in 1240 called the Perambulation of Dartmoor, or a Royal Hunt. Certainly a number of witnesses have seen what are locally referred to as the Knights of Dartmoor. A number of mediaeval noblemen, guarded by foot soldiers and dogs, appear near Lustleigh Cleave and disappear into nearby woodland. Strangely, the woodland no longer exists and has become part of the haunting.

Luxulyan, Cornwall

The vicarage garden is said to be haunted by the ghost of an 18th-century vicar called Cole. He presumably loved the vicarage so much that his spirit is unable to leave the area.

Lych Way, west of Devil's Tor, Dartmoor, Devon

Funeral processions took this route from the moorland homesteads to Lydford church. Monks in white and a phantom funeral entourage have been seen at regular intervals.

Lydford, Devon

The spirit of Judge Jeffreys, the Hanging Judge, haunts the castle. Lady Howard, whose ghost takes the form of a black hound, accompanies him. Nearby Lydford Gorge has a haunted pool called Kitty's Steps, where the ghost of an old woman with a red headscarf is seen.

Lydiard Millicent, nr Swindon, Wiltshire

On 30 October each year Lady Blunt can be seen in the garden of the manor house. She married the curate and witnessed his savage murder in the 17th century. The date she appears is the anniversary of the crime. She subsequently married Sir Ferdinando Blunt.

Lyme Hall, nr Bollington, Cheshire

Sir Piers Legh, who died in Paris on 16 June 1422 after being fatally wounded at the Battle of Meaux, is the source of the haunting at Lyme Park. His body was brought back to Cheshire but before burial spent some time on Knight's Law, a small hill near his home. Consequently, a phantom funeral procession has been seen in the area, accompanied by a white lady. She is his mistress, Blanche, and not his widow, Joan. Poor Blanche died of grief after hearing that her lover had died. She was buried in a meadow now known as Lady's Grave. Her apparition has also been seen in the hall. Many years ago a skeleton was found in the hall, under the floorboards of a secret room. They are the remains of a Jesuit priest, whose ghost has also been seen walking along a corridor outside the room, accompanied by the sound of bells.

Lyme Regis, Dorset: Angel Inn

The eccentric Mrs Langton owned the pub from 1926. She had the habit of wearing clothes to make her look like Queen Victoria. She died at some point in the 1930s and from then on her ghost has been habitually mistaken for Queen Victoria. The apparition has been seen coming out of a cupboard, which may once have been the door to her daughter's bedroom. One particular witness claimed to have seen the ghost of Queen Victoria standing over him while he was in bed. The owners of the pub told him that it was Mrs Langton and that he had been sleeping in her daughter's bed.

Lyme Regis, Dorset: Royal Lion Hotel

Opposite the hotel is the old courthouse, which still has its dungeons. It was the site of several 17th-century public hangings. On one of the upper floors of the hotel several witnesses have heard moaning and footsteps and claim to have seen a strange, misty shape floating around. Others have reported feeling a cold sensation. It is said that the manifestation is none other than Judge Jeffreys, as some claim that he wears his wig and black cap and carries a bloody bone in his hand.

Lymington, Hampshire: The Angel

The hotel is over 200 years old and was used in the past as a stopping off point for sailors en route to Southampton. Staff and customers claim to have seen the ghost of a grey-haired man dressed in a naval uniform, complete with brass buttons fastened up to the neck. Popular belief has it that this is the ghost of a naval officer who was due to appear in a naval court but chose to kill himself in one of the bedrooms rather than face the ordeal.

Lympne Castle, nr Hythe, Kent

Six Saxon soldiers who were killed by the Normans haunt the castle. There is also the spirit of a Roman soldier who fell to his death while on duty. He is heard to mount a flight of steps, but not to come down again.

Lyonesse, Cornwall

The legendary land of Lyonesse was said to have linked Cornwall and the Scilly Isles, so the Scillies themselves are the hills and mountains of that land. Gradually over the years the sea claimed the lower-lying land and after 1967 the *Torrey Canyon,* which came to grief on Seven Stones Reef, was said to mark where a major city once lay. Fishermen have continually reported seeing the roofs of churches and houses deep beneath the water. In 1584 Richard Carew in his *Survey of Cornwall* wrote: 'the encroaching sea hath ravined from it the whole country of Lyonesse together with the divers other parcels of no little circuit and that such a Lyonesse there was these proofs are yet remaining'. When the Portuguese suffered an earthquake in 1755 that killed 3,000 people, the seas off the west coast of Cornwall rose by 10ft. It is popularly believed that a similar incident occurred many, many years ago that caused the seas to cover Lyonesse. Lyonesse once had 140 parish churches, but was flooded forever and now lies under the sea. In many respects the apparition of Lyonesse beneath the waves is a very similar vast manifestation to that of Dunwich in Suffolk.

Lytchett-Matravers, nr Poole, Dorset: St Mary the Virgin

Sir John Matravers, who was deeply implicated in the murder of King Edward II, is buried in the churchyard. Although his apparition has not been seen, it is believed that it is his spirit that is responsible for the strange, whispering voices heard on a pathway that runs from the village to the church. At one particular part of the path, called Whispering Corner, many witnesses have heard faint voices at various times of the day and night. They are described as being very animated, but unfortunately nobody has been able to decipher the content of their conversation. It is believed that the conversation revolves around the plot to kill the king.

London
Acton to Wilton Row

Acton, W3: St Dunstan's Church

This site has had religious connections since the monks of the Order of St Bartholomew lived here in the Middle Ages. Monks have been seen walking up the central aisle, as many as 10 or 12 at a time. It thought that their appearances come in four-yearly cycles, always accompanied by beautiful chanting and music of a bygone age.

Addington Palace, Addington, nr Croydon

Archbishop Edward Benson is said to haunt Addington Palace, although very little is

known of the specifics of the apparition. The surrounding countryside has a much later ghost. During World War Two a German pilot was killed when he bailed out of his aircraft, and his apparition haunts the area. 'Digger Harry' haunts nearby Beare's Wood. Harry was brought to trial for the murder of his wife, although she had died of old age. He had buried her close to his run-down cottage so that he could still be with her. He served six months in prison, but by the time he returned home he had forgotten where he had buried her and he died of a broken heart. His apparition has been seen on many occasions, presumably still searching for the site of his wife's burial.

Aldgate Station, EC3: Aldgate High Street

The present-day railway track crosses a much older one here. Witnesses say that they have heard footsteps walking toward the old control room door. They have also heard a strange whistling noise. Several years ago an engineer saw the figure of a woman gently stroking the head of one of his colleagues. The man was unaware of her presence. He had been involved in an accident with high voltage equipment and should have been killed. Instead, he was knocked unconscious after having 22,000 volts course through his body.

Aldwych, The Lyceum Theatre

A most macabre apparition appears from time to time in one of the former stalls seats. The haunting seems to relate to a man whose family owned the land on which the original theatre was built in 1772. This land was owned by the 1st Duke of Exeter, who was executed in 1400 for conspiring against Henry IV, but it is believed that the haunting is of a later member of the family, Henry Courtenay, who was executed in 1538. Alternatively, the ghost could be a family member beheaded at

LYTCHETT-MATRAVERS–BELLINGHAM

the behest of Cromwell. On certain occasions, looking down from one of the boxes, you may see a woman calmly sitting in one of the seats with a severed head on her lap. On other occasions the woman discreetly pulls a shawl over her lap to hide the hideous manifestation.

Argyll Street, W1: The London Palladium

The apparition of a beautiful woman dressed in a crinoline gown haunts the old crimson staircase. She is said to be the ghost of Helen Campbell, who lived here when the site was, in fact, Argyll House. Many other people believe that she is more likely to be the apparition of a former actress, as the staircase was only built as part of the theatre and did not exist in Argyll House.

Baker Street, W1: No.228

Sarah Siddons, the 18th-century actress, lived here, but the site now houses an electric sub-station used by the tube lines. The Inspection Gallery on the top floor is the approximate location of her bedroom. Several engineers have seen her at this spot. Her ghost seems to be active during the day and has been seen walking through walls and rooms.

Baker Street, NW1: The Volunteer

The ghost of Richard Neville, a Cavalier, has been seen in the cellar. Strangely, the door of an alcove opened to reveal a phantom wearing a coat, breeches and stockings. The manifestations seem to have their root in 1963, when major structural work was undertaken. Since then, lights have been turned on and off and footsteps have been heard. Neville was a royalist and fought at the Battle of Naseby in 1645. The pub itself was built in 1794 on the site of his family's farm. The farm and his family were wiped out in a fire in 1654.

Bank of England, EC2

Sarah Whitehead's brother was employed by the bank but was said to be a forger. He was arrested, convicted and hanged in 1811. The events seemed to unhinge Sarah's mind, and every day for the next 25 years, until she died in 1836, she made a visit to the Bank of England to enquire after her brother. She haunts the small garden in the middle of the building. Another bizarre haunting is linked with this building. Many years ago a truly enormous giant of a man worked as a cashier. He seemed to have some morbid fear that his body would be taken by resurrectionists after he had died. Prior to his death he convinced the governors of the bank to allow his body to be buried within the building in order to protect it. They acceded to his wishes and when alteration work was done years after his death, workmen discovered a lead coffin, said to be eight feet long, with a large iron chain wrapped around it. His apparition has been seen and is described as being eight feet tall.

Barnes Common, SW13: Common Road

The common is said to be haunted by a ghost dressed in 19th-century prisoner's clothing, complete with broad arrows. The apparition is said to walk out of a pond and pass people out walking at night. The haunting may be related to the tale of an escaped convict who was being treated at nearby Putney Hospital. He took an opportunity to escape, but drowned in the pond after a chase.

Bellingham, SE6

On 2 September 1898 Alice Grant was killed when her bicycle was hit by a brewer's dray. Her apparition can still be seen cycling around the area and is clearly distinguishable. She wears a long, black skirt and a white blouse with puffed sleeves.

179

Berkeley Square, W1

The ghost of a little girl dressed in Scots plaid haunts No.50, built in the 18th century. She was said to have been either tortured or frightened to death by a wicked nanny. She has been seen wringing her hands in despair and sobbing on the upper floors of the house. Another ghost here is Adeline, who lived at the house with her uncle in the 18th century. Her screaming ghost has been seen hanging from the window ledge, replaying her last moments as she tried to escape the attention of her uncle. At the end of the 18th century a Mr Dupré locked his mad brother in a room (the Haunted Room) at the top of the stairs. The man was fed through a hatch in the door. The apparition of a white-faced man with a gaping jaw is still seen.

Bermondsey, SE1: The Anchor Tap, Horseley Down Lane

A ghost called Charlie is said to haunt the pub. Over the years, several licensees have reported that items have disappeared and then reappeared in strange places. On one particular occasion, a woman's watch disappeared for two months from its normal place on a dressing room table, to appear again in the laundry basket. Despite its long disappearance, it was still working and showing the correct time.

Bermondsey, SE1: The Horn Inn, Crucifix Lane

The ghost of an eight-year-old Victorian girl called Mary Isaac haunts the pub. Her spirit has been heard to cry and call for her mother, who died shortly before her. The inn is also haunted by the manifestation of an old woman. She bangs on the floors and walls and moves furniture about.

Bethlehem Hospital (Bedlam), Liverpool Street, Moorfields and Lambeth Road

The Hospital of the Star of Bethlehem was the first mental asylum in London. Originally it was situated on the site of what is now Liverpool Street Station, but from 1675 to 1815 it was sited at Moorfields, before being moved to ground on which the Imperial War Museum now stands. During World War Two a barrage balloon unit was stationed in the grounds of the museum, and the crew complained that they heard groans and the rattling of chains. One of the many stories that may explain some of the hauntings relates to 1780. A servant girl called Rebecca fell in love with her master. One day, he decided to move away, and he thanked her for her services and slipped a golden guinea into her hand. This slight sent the girl insane and she was admitted to Bedlam. She spent the rest of her life there, holding the coin and wishing to be buried with it. An attendant prised it from her still-warm fingers when she died. Rebecca's ghost was seen with wild-looking eyes searching for the stolen coin. On more than one occasion attendants and patients were confronted with Rebecca's ghost screaming 'Give me back my guinea!' When the asylum was transferred to Lambeth Road in 1815 the ghost of Rebecca moved with it, still searching for her coin.

Bexley, Hall Place

The building dates from 1537, but its ghosts seem to predate the manor house that was built here. A white lady, said to have been the wife of a man who was gored by a stag, haunts it. The Black Prince also appears in his black armour. His apparition is said to be of particular significance as it foretells a terrible tragedy for the British Army. On four occasions between 1917 and 1943 sightings of his apparition coincided with defeat for Britain. The link with the Black Prince is through his wife Joan, who was born near here. Prior to leaving for France and Crécy, the Black Prince actually stayed here. Finally, the ghost of a maidservant who is said to have died or have been murdered here haunts the attic area.

Blackheath, SE10: Hare and Billet Road

The shadowy manifestation of a Victorian is thought to have been a woman who had just left her husband and was waiting for her lover, who never arrived. She hanged herself from a nearby elm tree when she realised that she had been stood up.

Blackheath, SE3: Public Library, St John's Park

Elsie Marshall lived here in 1874 during her father's term as a local vicar. She became a missionary and was killed in 1895 by Chinese bandits. However, it seems that she had a particular affinity with the building as her ghost has returned here. The building is now a library and various witnesses have felt her presence brush past them while they browse the books.

Blackheath, SE18: Shooters Hill

In January 1844, a labourer here unearthed a skeleton with a skull fracture. The body had not been buried long. It was surmised that there was a connection with the manifestation of a white lady that had been seen in the area. The Old Bull Hotel stood near here and when it was demolished they found an old pistol. The theory is that the woman was clubbed to death with the pistol and left to die. Witnesses passing this spot continue to hear a woman's cries for help.

Blackwall Tunnel, E14

The tunnel was opened on 22 May 1897 and was at the time the longest underwater tunnel in the world. During construction, which took six years, 641 people living in Greenwich had to be rehoused because their homes were demolished. The cost of this, plus the building of the tunnel itself, provision of lighting and purchase of land, came to £1,400,000. One of the houses demolished was once owned by Sir Walter Raleigh; it was said that the first pipe smoked in England was lit there. Later, the same house was inhabited by Sir John de Pulteney (four times Lord Mayor of London) and Sebastian Cabot. When the tunnel was built Brunel had only recently invented the shield tunnelling method, and had used it on an earlier Thames tunnel, now used by the Underground. The safety record was good. A tunnel was built under the Hudson River just before Blackwall and there were reports of one man a month being killed. There were only seven fatalities in the six years of construction at Blackwall. As traffic through the tunnel increased, it was apparent that a second tunnel was needed. The second bore took seven years to construct. In October 1972, a motorcyclist offered a lift to a boy from Essex whom he saw hitch hiking on the Greenwich side of the tunnel. By the time they reached the end of the tunnel, the boy had gone. The biker sped back to see if he had fallen off, but could find nothing. He went to the boy's house to tell them what had happened and was told that their son had died in the tunnel several years earlier, while riding pillion on a motorbike.

Bow Road, E3: Black Swan

A bomb dropped from a Zeppelin in 1916 destroyed the original public house. The landlord's mother, two of his daughters and the eldest daughter's baby were killed in the blast. It is no great surprise that Sylvia and Cissie Reynolds, the two daughters, haunt the site of their untimely death. Not only have they been seen in several rooms, especially the cellar, but they may also be responsible for a number of strange incidents. Beer taps have been turned on during the night, causing floods of beer, and a German Shepherd dog kept by the landlord will not go down the stairs to the cellar.

Bow Road, E3: The Bow Bells

Classically original, this public house boasts a 'phantom flusher' in the women's lavatory. Several witnesses have reported that the locked lavatory door has been flung open and an unseen hand has flushed the toilet's cistern. After the landlord had experienced icy cold conditions when all of the doors were closed, and seen a strange mist rising from the floor, a séance was organised. All that was achieved by this was that the spirit was provoked to storm the door and break a pane of glass in a window.

British Museum, WC1

Given the vast number of exhibits in the museum, it is rather surprising that there are only two major hauntings. The first relates to exhibit 22542, an Egyptian mummy case of the Amen-Ra period. It was discovered in the 1880s and is said to have been linked to at least 13 deaths. In its entirety, it is said to be wholly evil. Attendants are very reluctant to stay in the room and when the body was removed to America it was said to have caused the sinking of the *Empress of Ireland* in the St Lawrence River. In 1921 two psychics attempted to exorcise the case. They described the apparition that emerged from it as having a flat face and a jelly-like body. The second manifestation relates to an African mask that is said to be able to cause deep wounds in anyone that touches it. There does not appear to be any apparent reason why the mask should do this, as it has no sharp edges. It is believed that the object is cursed.

Buckingham Palace, SW1

Built by the Duke of Buckingham during the reign of Queen Anne, the palace is haunted by the ghost of a monk who died in a punishment cell of the priory that had stood on the site until 1539. It is said to appear at Christmas, walking in irons on the rear terrace. The palace is also haunted by Major John Gwynne, private secretary to King Edward VII, who committed suicide at the beginning of the 20th century after a divorce scandal.

Buckingham Street, WC2

Two houses in the street are haunted. No.12 boasts the spirit of none other than Samuel Pepys. He lived here during the Jacobean period (1603-1625). No.14, although the house of the Victorian painter William Etty, is not haunted by him but by one of his models, who spent countless hours posing for him.

Camberwell, SE5: Churchyard Passage

St Giles's Church was built in the middle of the 19th century, but is just the latest of five churches on this site. There is a passage that used to lead to the old Clergy House, but this is now demolished. The ghost of an old clergyman has been seen walking along the passageway; he is thought to be a former vicar.

Charlton House, SE7

Sir William Langhorne, a wealthy merchant, died at the age of 85 in 1714. Despite two marriages he failed to produce a son and heir. As a consequence, his apparition haunts this house, which was designed by Inigo Jones. He seems to be a particularly troublesome spirit and even in death seems to wish to produce an heir. On one occasion his ghost was accused of raping a girl. There is another apparition in this house with an equally unpleasant story to tell. Following damage to the house renovation work was undertaken that revealed a horrible secret in a chimney breast in the north wing. Carefully placed on a ledge inside the chimney, partially preserved by the heat and smoke of countless fires, was found the body of a baby. This may have a link with the ghost of a servant seen holding a baby in various parts of the house.

Cheam, Greater London: Century Cinema

Many years ago, during the building of the cinema, one of the workmen vanished without a trace. His lunch bag was found hanging near the stage area and his wages were never collected. There is no indication of why he disappeared or what happened to him. Many people believe that the haunting must relate to him and that his body lies somewhere in the vicinity. Strange, shuffling footsteps have been heard in the stage area and this was experienced by three local newspapermen who decided to stand vigil there one night.

Chelsea, SW3: Cheyne Walk

In Tudor times, the area where Cheyne Walk now stands was part of a Royal estate. The ghost of a bear harks back to the cruel days of bear-baiting. The phantom animal was seen in the garden of one of the houses in Cheyne Walk as late as the mid-1920s. It is believed that there was a bear pit here until the 16th century.

Chelsea, SW3: Elystan Street

In the 1820s a policeman was lynched on this street. The haunting relates to this, but involves not only the apparition of the murdered man, but also that of the baying crowd that killed him. The house, outside which the apparitions appear, was a former tomb maker's yard, although it had to be rebuilt after World War Two when it was flattened by German bombs.

Chelsea: Markham Square

A pig-faced lady whose real name was Tamakin Skinker, born in 1618 in Germany, once lived in Windsor. Her body was perfectly normal, but her nose resembled that of a pig and her eyes were small and swine-like. Apparently she could speak no English and communicated in either Dutch or French. At one point £40,000 was offered to any man who would marry her, according to Elliott O'Donnell in his pamphlet *A Certain Relation of the Hog-faced Gentlewoman*. At some point she lived in Chelsea, but her movements are confused, as her other residences include Blackfriars and Covent Garden. The actor William Barrett and his wife encountered the ghost of this unfortunate woman, which caused the lady to faint, whereupon the pig-faced apparition disappeared. It seems that she originally haunted a house in Blackfriars but her ghost has moved to Markham Square.

Chiswick House and Walpole House, Chiswick, W4

Built in the 17th century, Walpole House, in Chiswick Mall, was the home of Barbara Villiers, Duchess of Cleveland and mistress of King Charles II. In her old age she became haggard and obese. She spent hours pacing up and down in front of her drawing-room window, praying for her beauty to be restored to her. She died in 1709 from dropsy. Her ghost has been seen many times at the house, accompanied by the sounds of the tapping of her high-heeled shoes. She wrings her hands in despair as she stands in front of the window. Her ghost has also been seen in Chiswick House, which was built some 50 years after her death.

Clapham Common, SW4: The Plough Inn

The apparition of a ghost known as Sarah has

been seen in the form of a white lady, with her long black hair hanging loosely over her shoulders. The pub was built in the early part of the 19th century, but a sealed room was discovered only recently. The top floor had three outside windows, but only two doors leading to rooms. Strangely, the window of the third room was sometimes open. The landlord and staff have often seen Sarah, but there are no clues as to why she has chosen to haunt this pub. In 1970 a landlord was sacked for spending too much time trying to find out Sarah's identity.

Cleopatra's Needle, WC2

A strange, silent apparition, thought to be the ghost of one of the many people who have chosen this spot to commit suicide, has been seen on numerous occasions. The ghost is described as being male, tall and naked. Witnesses have seen him jump from the parapet beside the needle and hit the water but create no splash. Other witnesses have clearly heard strange laughing and moans in the vicinity.

Clerkenwell, WC1: Dougherty Street

Charles Dickens lived at No.29 in the 1830s and his ghost has been seen walking in and out of the house and, on some occasions, standing in the street. He has been described by witnesses as being a short, well-dressed man in a dark suit and coat, with a stovepipe hat on his head.

Cockfosters

Geoffrey de Mandeville, Earl of Essex, seems to have been a wholly unpleasant individual who built up his fortune by preying on the very people that he had been charged to protect by the king. He was killed at Mildenhall in Suffolk in 1144, but his ghost has been seen here and at many other places around Christmas time. He haunts Trent Park, Cockfosters and East Barnet. Witnesses

describe him as being a fully-armed knight, with a red cloak and a red plume in his helmet. When the king discovered that he was a bandit and extortionist he had him outlawed. The Earl fled to the Fenlands, where he continued his activities until his death.

Colindale, NW9

An extremely vicious and unpleasant apparition is said to haunt the area of the Hyde. It is the ghost of a haymaker who was pitchforked to death by one of his colleagues. The apparition now seems to take pleasure in attempting to use his own pitchfork on unfortunate victims that may encounter him. There is also some talk of a strange manifestation of a multi-coloured donkey. It is said to have the ability to temporarily blind witnesses who look at it.

Connaught Road, E16: The Connaught Arms

The top floor of the pub is haunted by the ghost of an old woman who is said to have been mad and committed suicide. After she died, the room in which she slept could not be kept tidy and no one would sleep in there. At 6am one morning, a barman discovered the manifestation of the old woman with an evil look in her eyes. The two dogs that the man had with him were terrified.

Covent Garden, WC2: Covent Garden Underground Station

William Terris, who was murdered outside the stage door of the Adelphi Theatre in December 1897, has been seen many times at Covent Garden Underground Station. He used the station while travelling between the theatre and his home in Putney. He is seen wearing his white gloves, an old-fashioned suit and a Homburg hat. It was impossible to track down any commuters that claim to have seen him, but various members of the station staff, particularly near the staff restroom, have seen him.

Covent Garden, WC2: King Street

In 1674, the eldest son of Lord Mohun was involved in an argument with Prince Griffin. They agreed to fight a duel with swords on horseback at Chelsea Fields. At 10am on the morning of the duel, Mohun passed Ebury Farm, and was waylaid by a party of men who picked a fight with him and shot him dead. At exactly the same time, his lover was lying in bed in her King Street home when Mohun opened the curtains of her bed and looked in at her in complete silence. He then left, although she pleaded with him to stay.

Cranford Park, nr Hounslow: Cranford House

Two apparitions haunt what little remains of this former home of the Berkeleys. One is the apparition of a man who has been seen in the area of the stables, and the other is a female ghost that was seen in the kitchen before that portion of the house was demolished. The entire area is said to be rather forbidding, but this may be due to the fact that it is often shrouded in fog from the river.

Crouch Hill, N8: Mountview Theatre School and Art Centre

The apparition of a little girl, perhaps around 12 years old, dressed in a late 19th-century pinafore smock, has been seen several times. It is believed that she was either the victim or the murderer involved in a scandal that led to the school being closed down in the 1890s. On a couple of occasions the apparition has been known to hold the hand of someone standing on the stage late at night.

Croydon Airport

The ghost of a Dutch pilot, killed shortly after the airport was opened, has been seen still wearing his flying kit. His presence is said to foretell the imminent closure of the airport by fog. The unfortunate pilot crashed just after take off in thick fog and on several occasions has actually warned other pilots that the conditions will soon be very similar to those he encountered when he died. In 1940 a perfume factory on the site was hit in one of the first air raids on the city. Sixty people were also killed when a bomb hit an air raid shelter. Many witnesses have heard wartime communal singing emanating from this area. In January 1947 12 passengers died after their aircraft crashed and burst into flames during a snowstorm. Three of the dead were nuns, and they can be seen walking around the airfield. They were Mother Superior Eugene Jousselot, and Sisters Helen Lester and Eugene Martin of the Congregation des Filles de la Sagasse, who were all travelling on the Spencer Airways Dakota bound for Salisbury. It collided with an aircraft flying in from Czechoslovakia.

Croydon, Roundshaw Estate

A wartime fighter pilot riding a motor cycle has been seen in this area, much of which stands on the former airfield. The apparition wears clearly identifiable flying gear and is believed to be one of the many pilots that failed to return home after a sortie.

Crystal Palace, SE19

An unfortunate platelayer, working on the track in the tunnel that runs from Crystal Palace to Gypsy Hill, was decapitated in an accident and can still be seen wandering through the tunnel. There is also said to be a train bricked up in an abandoned tunnel. This may be the source of a haunting experienced by several witnesses in 1978, which immediately followed the discovery of the train after a girl had fallen down a lift shaft. The official explanation behind the train is that it was an experimental vehicle that proved to be something of a failure and was consequently bricked up and forgotten for many years.

Dean Street, W1: The Gargoyle Club

Nell Gwynne was said to have lived here while she worked as a barmaid in Drury Lane. The haunting may not be that of Nell, but could be the same ghost that haunts the site of the Royalty Theatre next door. The apparition has been described as being a grey shadowy figure. She wears a high-waisted dress and a large flowered hat, and walks across the floor and disappears into an old lift shaft. Whenever she appears, she is accompanied by an overpowering smell of gardenias. A tall cowled and shrouded figure has been seen outside the club, but disappears when approached.

Dean Street, W1: Royalty Theatre

The Royalty Theatre stood in Dean Street, but has now been demolished. Built in 1840, it was on the site of a Queen Anne period house. The white lady that haunted the theatre was said to date from this period and was often seen walking down the stairway leading to the vestibule. At the bottom she would let out a piercing scream and then vanish. In the basement, to add credence to the story, the skeleton of a murdered 18th-century woman was found. Another ghost was that of a gypsy girl dressed in green and scarlet, who walked down a non-existent staircase and through the offices. Again, she was a murder victim and when the theatre was built, her body was found encased in plaster of paris. The ghost of a grey lady, thought to have been Fanny Kelly, also haunted the building. She was an actress who became manager of the theatre when it was built. After she committed suicide, she was seen sitting in her favourite box on a number of occasions.

Docklands, E14: The Gun Inn, Coldharbour

This was a favoured meeting place of Horatio Nelson and Lady Hamilton. Nelson's ghost has been seen here on a number of occasions.

Downing Street, SW1

No.10 has been haunted for many years. The apparition, dressed in Regency-style clothes, has been seen in various parts of the house, both inside and out. Workmen reported that they had seen a misty-white old-fashioned figure, crossing the garden to the rear of the building. It is said that the manifestation only visits the property when Britain faces a crisis.

Drury Lane, Theatre Royal, WC2

A man in grey haunts the theatre and is said to be the ghost of a slim man, thought to be Arnold Woodruff, who was very handsome with a powerful chin. Descriptions seem to date him to the 1770s, as he is dressed in a grey riding cloak, white wig and riding boots, and the tip of his sword can be seen from under his cloak. The ghost had an actress girlfriend, but the theatre manager wanted her attentions, so he stabbed the man and walled the body up in a passageway near the stage. In 1848, a small room was discovered, containing the skeleton of a young man. The ghost has been seen by literally hundreds of people, and on one occasion he was witnessed by 50 people at the same time. The appearance of the man in grey is regarded as a sign of a successful production. The Green Room at the theatre was the scene of a vicious killing in 1735, when Charles Macklin murdered another actor, Thomas Hallam, after an argument over a wig. Macklin's ghost has been seen near the orchestra pit, usually in the early evening. Other ghosts include the comedian Dan Leno in his favourite dressing room, and a white-painted clown who sits in one of the boxes. He is thought to be the clown, Joe Grimaldi.

Ealing, W5: Amherst Lodge

Ghostly footsteps have been heard at Amherst Lodge, perhaps those of a nun that has been seen in the building. One particular witness saw a nun bending over a patient, only to see her slowly vanish. At one stage the building was used as an orphanage run by a group of nuns.

Ealing, W5: Ealing Common

An old-fashioned blue coach, perhaps from the 18th century, has been seen crossing the common, pulled by two mottled, grey horses. As it approaches the Uxbridge Road, the apparition is said to vanish. This was a route taken by coaches during the 1700s, and the apparition has appeared, complete with driver, on a number of occasions.

Ealing, W5: Montpelier Road

It is thought that 21 people died in No.16, a Victorian house, which claimed its first victim in 1887. Anne Hinchfield was just 12 when she jumped 70ft to her doom from the tower of the building. In 1934 a double death occurred when a nursemaid jumped to her death holding a young child in her arms. The house was described as having an evil atmosphere and a strange smell every 28 days. It is believed that some malevolent spirit convinced the 'suicides' that they were walking into the garden and not to their deaths. Thankfully, the house was demolished just after World War Two.

Eaton Place, SW1

On 22 June 1893, Lady Tryon was giving a party at Eaton Place and the cream of Victorian society was in attendance. Suddenly, a haggard-faced figure in full naval uniform entered the room. It was Admiral Sir George Tryon, and at the moment of his appearance, his body was lying in the wreckage of his flagship, HMS *Victoria*, at the bottom of the Mediterranean. Sir George's squadron was taking part in manoeuvres off the coast of Tripoli. He ordered that both columns turn toward one another. His ship collided with HMS *Victoria* and sank with a great loss of life. His apparition was seen just after the ship had settled beneath the waves.

Edmonton, Edmonton Church

Several witnesses have seen the apparition of a phantom white dog at the church. It remains apparently harmless provided it is ignored. The ghost of a labourer killed by a bullock has also been seen. The labourer died at a place known as Wire Hall, now demolished. This building was the site of a murder that left the place so badly haunted that it was bricked up for 50 years before being pulled down. A cook working at the hall murdered another member of the staff, leaving an indelible mark of the deed on the building.

Enfield, Bell Lane

The phantom stagecoach called the *Enfield Flyer* has often been seen travelling at speed some five or six feet above the road surface. The *Enfield Flyer* is a black coach, with two female passengers wearing large hats on board. It seems to have a connection with the nearby River Lea. In the past, the ground near the river was higher (accounting for the 'floating' of the coach), and a coach resembling the manifestation crashed off the road and into the flooded river, presumably killing all the passengers.

Enfield, Crown and Horses

The pub has been the site of at least two sudden deaths, one in 1816 and the second in 1832. On one occasion witnesses saw the apparition of an old woman pass one of the windows. Another time the ghost was seen inside the pub, despite the fact that the building was closed and locked. It is unfortunately not known who the apparition is, but it is assumed that she had something to do with one of the two deaths.

Enfield, Royal British Legion Headquarters

The apparition of a man wearing black trousers, a white shirt and a black tie has been seen standing in the corner of the cellar. When approached by a barman on one occasion the apparition vanished. Since then several other staff and customers have seen the ghost and heard footsteps walking across the floor of the upstairs bar. There also seems to be poltergeist activity here in the form of smashed glasses. Before becoming the property of the British Legion, this building was a fire station. It is believed that a fireman was crushed to death by his own tender in the building, and that a woman, trying out the fireman's pole, fatally injured herself and later died.

Fish Street Hill, EC3: St Magnus the Martyr

Built by Sir Christopher Wren in 1676, the church is haunted by the manifestation of a black-haired priest, believed to be Miles Coverdale, who produced the first English edition of the Bible in 1535. He is accompanied by a feeling of sadness. A former verger's wife said that she had twice seen the figure of a short, black-haired priest kneeling at the same spot. Miles Coverdale was rector of St Magnus's church before becoming Bishop of Exeter.

Forest Hill, SE23: Horniman Museum

A ghostly couple have been seen on the terrace, clad in evening dress, dancing on the brick balcony beside the greenhouse. From the description they appear to date from the 1920s. The man has heavily greased hair and the woman is wearing a red dress. They are not accompanied by music but after their dance they disappear into the trees.

Garlick Hill, EC4: St James's Church

Built by Richard Rothing in 1326, St James's was rebuilt by Sir Christopher Wren in 1682 in the aftermath of the Great Fire of London. It contains a mummified body thought to be at least 500 years old; its ghost has been seen on several occasions. It was found in 1839 when excavations took place, and has acquired the name of 'Jimmy Garlick', who may have been one of the Lord Mayors of London buried in the church. The apparition is described as being tall, swathed in white and with a face like a dried-out corpse.

Gower Street, NW1

Gower Street is haunted by the figure of a man who is said to have his head swathed in bandages. He is dressed in clothes of the pre-World War Two period and is said to be enveloped in his own light. It is thought that the ghost is that of a man who stayed at a boarding house in Gower Street and used a local teashop. He is thought to have died in 1936.

Gower Street, NW1: University College

Built in 1828, the builiding houses the preserved body of Jeremy Bentham, co-founder of the college. Bentham's ghost has been seen several times in the corridors, tapping with his favourite stick and wearing his white gloves. It is thought that his apparition, and the tapping of his stick on the glass front of the case which houses his remains, is an attempt to force the college officials to give his body over for a proper burial.

Gower Street, NW1: University College Hospital

The ghost of Lizzie Church, an early 20th-century nurse, is said to haunt the hospital. It is said that she accidentally gave an overdose of morphine to her fiancé, a patient, who died as a result. Overcome by remorse, she also died. Witnesses have seen her apparition, dressed in an old-fashioned uniform, supervising morphine injections to help ensure that no further mistakes are made.

Greenwich, SE10: Royal Naval College, Queen Anne's House

A photograph of the Tulip Staircase in Queen Anne's House revealed the figure of a cowled monk climbing the staircase, accompanied by a less-clear figure. A ring could be clearly seen on the hand of one of the figures. There was once an abbot's house at Greenwich, and perhaps the cowled figures were monks from that period. In 1756, Admiral Byng was defeated in a sea battle against the French while attempting to relieve the British garrison at Minorca, and he was brought back to stand trial by court-martial at Greenwich. He stayed in the house until he was executed. Door handles move on their own and doors have been thrown open. Footsteps have also been heard in the corridors, leading people to believe that Byng's spirit is attempting to make the injustice of his death known.

Guy's Hospital, St Thomas Street, SE1

Built in the 1720s, the hospital is haunted by a ghostly sister. She has been seen to put her arms around patients in need of reassurance. Another manifestation is present, which is heard and not seen. Three members of staff were talking outside a ward in which there was a dying elderly female patient. They heard footsteps walking toward the ward, through the doors and down toward the old lady's bed. The doctor and the two nurses could also hear the creaking of new boots. The sounds came back and then disappeared. When they checked the old lady, she had died.

Hackney Road, E2: The Nag's Head

After a series of strange sounds and odd happenings, one of the cellar men encountered the probable cause of the problems. The witness described the ghost as appearing to be an old woman in a long, Victorian dress with a grey shawl wrapped around her shoulders. After a séance the spirit of the old woman seems calmer than she was in the past.

Hammersmith, W6: St Paul's Churchyard

A ghost appears in the churchyard every 50 years, and in 1955, on the appropriate day, a large crowd of people gathered to wait for its appearance. After the appointed hour had passed, most of the crowd gave up and went home, but they had not taken account of British Summer Time. Those that did wait saw the ghost come out of the church porch and head for a tomb, whereupon it vanished. In 1804, after a spate of hoaxes in the churchyard, some individuals lay in wait for the ghost. Obviously confused in some way, they shot a local man who had pretended to be the apparition.

Hampstead, NW3: Church Row

A rather unsavoury crime involving the death of a child occurred in Church Row. A housemaid, left in charge of a child, murdered it and took the body out of the house in a carpetbag. The red-haired apparition of the murderess can often be seen leaving the house in a furtive manner.

Hampstead, NW3: Spaniards Inn

Mounted on Black Bess, the ghost of the infamous highwayman Dick Turpin can be seen around the Vale of Heath. Turpin's spirit will gallop toward you and, at the last minute, vanish. Several witnesses near the public house have heard hoof beats. Turpin used to lodge here. At the nearby Turpin's Restaurant, guests dining in the restaurant have seen the ghost of a strangled girl, apparently murdered in the 1700s, on several occasions.

Hampstead, NW3: William IV

The manifestation of a girl in a white shroud, with long, plaited hair, can be seen peering mournfully in through the windows of the pub. It is said that she committed suicide in the dentist's surgery that was once located opposite.

Hampton Court, Old Court House

There are two ghosts here. The first is an eight-year-old boy, dressed as a 17th-century page, with long hair. More significant is Christopher Wren, who is said to appear on 26 February, the anniversary of his death.

Hampton Court Palace, Hampton Court

There are numerous ghosts at this historical site, all connected to famous individuals that have some connection with this place. Cardinal Wolsey, who actually built the palace, was seen at a performance held there in 1966. Catherine Howard also haunts the building. After Henry VIII's discovery of her infidelity, she begged him to forgive her and spent many hours in the chapel praying for forgiveness. She was said to have been physically held down on the execution block. As a result, witnesses have heard her fists banging on the door of the chapel and her screams. Jane Seymour appears as a white lady walking through the Silver Stick Gallery. She died of an infection caught in childbirth after providing Henry with a son and heir, the future Edward VI. The apparition of Mrs Sibell Penn, who died in 1562 of smallpox and was buried in the old church, has also been seen. She was King Edward VI's nurse until he died aged 16 in 1553. She did not begin to haunt the building until her tomb was moved in 1821. She is responsible for the noise of a ghostly spinning wheel, which emanates from a wall in the southwest wing. Toward the end of the last century, two skeletons were discovered in a shallow grave under a door, following a number of disturbances at night. During World War One, the policeman on duty saw two men and eight women, all phantoms, by the front gate.

Haymarket, SW1: Her Majesty's Theatre

The actor John Baldwin Buckstone was manager of the theatre from 1853–1878. He haunts his favourite dressing room and witnesses report seeing him entering the room, crossing to a certain cupboard, rummaging through it and then walking out through the door again. His voice has also been heard rehearsing lines. The actress Margaret Rutherford was one of those who claimed to have seen the apparition. His appearance usually signifies a long run of the show.

Heathrow Airport, Runway 1

On 2 March 1948, 21 people died when a DC3 aircraft crashed and caught fire. It is believed that the ghost of one of these passengers now walks on Runway 1. In 1970 radar picked up that someone was walking on the runway. Three police cars and a fire engine were sent to the site and directed to the exact spot. When they arrived they could see nothing. The operator could see the vehicles and the rogue blip and continually gave the police instructions as to where the figure was. As they turned around, they were told that they had actually driven through the figure. On this occasion the apparition chose to be invisible, but on other occasions he has actually been seen. He is described as being a tall man, wearing a bowler hat and a pair of cavalry twill trousers. Apparently, shortly after the crash, some of the rescue workers were asked by a man fitting this description whether they had found his briefcase.

Highgate N6/N19: Highgate Cemetery

Several ghosts can be seen in one of the most ornate and strangely forbidding cemeteries in the country. The spirit of a mad woman searches the graves for the children that she murdered. Near the main entrance a ghost with bony fingers lies in wait, and the spirit of a man in a black hat can be seen near the cemetery walls at Swain's Lane.

Highgate N6/N19: Pond Square

In 1626, Sir Francis Bacon was being driven through Pond Square in his coach. It was snowing and the pond was frozen. He had the coachman stop and buy a chicken, which he then ordered to be killed. Bacon stuffed snow into the bird and created the first frozen chicken. However, as a result of the experiment, Bacon caught a chill and died of bronchitis at the home of Lord Arundel in Highgate. Many witnesses claim to have seen the partially plucked chicken flapping around the square. It eventually disappears through a brick wall.

Highgate Hill, N6: Ye Olde Gate House

Dating back to 1310, this used to be a favoured stopping point for drovers en route to Smithfield. The ghost of an old woman haunts the building, appearing as a black-robed figure. This is the spirit of Mother Marnes, who was murdered, along with her cat, by a robber. The apparition does not appear if children or animals are present.

Holland House, Holland Park

Built in 1607 by Sir William Cope, Holland House was once the home of the royalist Sir William Rich, Earl of Holland. It has now been substantially rebuilt, following its near destruction during the Blitz. Rich was executed at Palace Yard in 1649 and Oliver Cromwell gave the house to General Fairfax. Rich's ghost haunts the house, and is seen holding his head in his hand. Three spots of blood are said to mark where his manifestation appears, and efforts to remove the bloodstains have met with failure.

Honor Oak Park, Honor Oak Road, Dulwich

In September 1948, two witnesses saw the figure of a woman dancing around the trees. They described her as being about 20 years old and wearing a black coat with a white apron underneath. The ground was uneven and covered in twigs and fallen leaves, yet the woman made no sound as she danced. The apparition has been seen on several other occasions, but no one seems to know who she is.

Hyde Park, The Devil's Elm

Also known as 'Black Sally's Tree', vagrants avoid sleeping here, as they are likely to be found dead in the morning. In the 1920s, a woman called 'Black Sally' was murdered under the tree by her husband, and it is said that moaning sounds have been heard coming from the spot where her body was found. In all respects, the tree is considered to be evil.

Ickenham, nr Uxbridge: Railway Station

The apparition of a middle-aged woman with a red scarf haunts the station. Several years ago she fell onto the electrified rails and was killed.

Ilford Broadway, Ilford: The Old Fire Station

Geoffrey Netherwood, a fireman in Victorian

times, was obsessed with the supernatural. It is not therefore surprising that after his ceremonial burial, he returned to the station to haunt the building. He was seen by several of his former colleagues and other witnesses have seen him since. He appears in his full uniform, despite the fact that the fire station has moved to Romford.

Isleworth, Osterley Park House

The apparition of a white lady has been seen on many occasions, usually at 4.30pm, standing near the left-hand arch under the main staircase, near the entrance hall. She appears in her fine, flowing gown, stands in position for a few seconds and then moves toward the doorway and vanishes. It is believed that she was a former mistress of the house.

Islington, N1: Bride's Street

Michael Faraday, who discovered the principle of electro-magnetic induction, was an elder of the Sandemanian sect that once occupied No.113. There is a plate on the floor that marks the position of his pew when it was a chapel. On several occasions Faraday's ghost has been seen walking through the building.

Islington, N1: Old Queen's Head, Essex Road

Although the original building was pulled down in 1829, this site has been a public house since the reign of Elizabeth I. She herself used the public house, whose license was granted by Sir Walter Raleigh. One of the upper rooms was sealed after child victims of the plague died there in 1665. On the first Sunday of each month, doors swing inexplicably open and then close, and the sound of footsteps coming down the stairs can be heard. Landlords and customers claim to have seen a sad-looking little girl and a woman dressed in Elizabethan costume, accompanied by footsteps and the swish of a dress. It is also said that there is a tunnel from the Queen's Head to Cannonbury Tower, which enabled Elizabeth I to visit her lover, the Earl of Essex.

Islington Green, N1: Collins Music Hall

The building was demolished in 1963 following a fire, but it was haunted by its founder, a man called Vagg. He opened the theatre in the 1860s. Witnesses saw doors slam shut and felts icy fingers on their faces. Dan Leno was also seen there after his death, sitting in the same seat near the front of the stalls.

Kenley, nr Croydon

A grey lady, carrying a baby, haunts the area and has been seen in many different locations. She is said to have some connection with the lost village of Watendone.

Kensington, W8/W11: Kensington Palace

Queen Victoria was born here, William III, Queen Anne and George II all died here, but it is George II who has actually been seen here. His ashen-faced ghost has been seen many times, looking out of his bedroom window toward the weather vane.

Kensington W8/W11: St Mark's Road

First reported in June 1934, a phantom bus has been seen here. On that fateful morning in 1934 the ghostly No.7 bus caused the death of a motorist whose car burst into flames after having swerved off the road to avoid the apparition. On numerous occasions the coach has sped toward motorists and vanished just before impact. Research has not uncovered any reason why a No.7 bus should haunt the area, as it seems that they never passed through St Mark's Road.

Kentish Town, N7: Hilldrop Crescent

Doctor Hawley Harvey Crippen was hanged for the murder of his wife in November 1910. He was arrested mid-Atlantic, en route to America with his mistress. Supernatural interest, however, revolves around some wasteland near to Crippen's home in Hilldrop Crescent. Just before the murder, Crippen spent several nights walking around on the waste ground, perhaps plotting the deed. When the body was found, the head and other parts were never discovered. It is thought that he may have buried them here. Crippen's ghost has been seen walking around the wasteland with a parcel, heading toward a pond. As the manifestation moves away from the water, he no longer has the parcel.

Kidbrook Lane, Kidbrook

In 1871, Edmund Pook was tried and acquitted for the murder of Jane Maria Clouson. Her head had been battered with a hammer. They had been having an affair and Jane was pregnant, but Edmund had no intention of angering his father by marrying the girl. Despite finding the bloodstained hammer, blood on Edmund's clothing and the fact that Jane accused him on her deathbed, he got off. Her ghost appears as a white lady with her face covered in blood. Witnesses have heard her cries for help and groans.

King Street, SW1: St James's Theatre

St James's Theatre was opened in 1835. Before that it was Nerot's Hotel, and it is now an office block. Two ghosts haunt the site. The first is a woman dressed in 18th-century clothes, possibly dating back to its time as a hotel. The other ghost is that of a former dresser, who helped actors on with their costumes and brushed them down before they went on stage.

Knightsbridge, SW1: The Grenadier

Many years ago an officer was caught cheating at cards and was taken into the cellar and flogged. He died as a result of his injuries. In September the pub experiences an enormous amount of poltergeist activity and on several occasions a figure has been seen standing beside the beds of those sleeping upstairs. The pub is also said to be haunted by a man who committed suicide by electrocuting himself in the bathroom. It is not known whether the figure is the flogged soldier or the suicide victim.

Ladbroke Grove, W10: Cambridge Gardens

The phantom bus that operates down St Mark's Road enters Cambridge Gardens at one o'clock in the morning. One local garage owner reported having to repair many cars that had been damaged as a result of evasive action taken by their drivers in Cambridge Gardens, a situation that was taken so seriously by the local borough council that they widened the road. It was suggested that the bus could have been a late-staff bus returning duty crews to their homes after work, but witnesses were adamant that although the bus was fully lit there was no sign of a driver or passengers.

Lambeth Palace Road, SE1: St Thomas's Hospital

Originally built in the 13th century and dedicated to Thomas Becket, the hospital is haunted by a grey lady. She is described as being middle-aged and dressed in a grey uniform. She is believed to be the harbinger of death and has been seen in Block 8. The apparition can only be seen from the knees up, which tallies with the fact that the floors have been raised by 18in. She is thought to be the ghost of a 19th-century nurse, who committed suicide after accidentally killing a newborn child.

Lambeth Palace, SE1

Anne Boleyn was held here and tried for adultery before her execution in the Tower of London. Her ghost can be seen getting into a boat at the river's edge for her last journey to the tower. Other witnesses have heard her voice crying and sobbing near the door where Archbishop Cranmer presided over the trial in Undercroft. Part of the palace that was formerly Lollards Prison has a door that locks and unlocks itself. The prison was used to hold individuals, usually Catholics, who were to be burned at the stake.

Langham Place, W1: The Langham

On several occasions the figure of a bearded butler has been seen limping down the third floor corridor carrying an empty tray. Another apparition has disturbed several occupants of Room 33. It is believed that he was a World War One German officer who leaped to his death from the fourth floor.

Lewisham

Along one of the main streets, mournful voices are heard coming out of the sky in the early hours of the morning. The only possible explanation seems to relate to the time when the plague was particularly active in this part of the country, and it may be that the spirits of those buried in mass graves around the edges of the city are still restless here.

Lincoln's Inn Fields, The Royal College of Surgeons

A man called Forster murdered his wife and child and after his execution his body was given to the college for dissection. During the experiments the body quivered and one eye opened. The corpse's right hand was seen to rise and clench. By all accounts the man was still alive. Not only is he said to haunt this building, which was his ultimate place of death, but his body's movements also caused a second death. The beadle, Mr Pass, watched the experiments and died of fright on his way home. He, too, is said to stalk the building.

London Bridge, E14: The Horns, Crucifix Lane

Sited under the railway arches, this pub is haunted by the manifestation of an old lady. It is not known who she is, but she is thought to have been murdered nearby. The Horns also used to house the apparition of a young girl searching for her mother, but most people do not believe that the two ghosts are linked in any way.

Mayfair, Hill Street: Hill House

On 24 November 1779, Lord Lyttleton was asleep in his room. He was awoken by a strange fluttering noise. Standing by his bed, he saw the figure of a white lady. He recognised her as one of the Amphlet girls. He had seduced them, deserted them and then they had committed suicide. The spirit told him that he had would be dead before midnight on the third day after the sighting. When the fateful hour approached, with a slight gasp, he dropped his hands to his side and died in the arms of his valet, aged 35. Lyttleton's ghost itself appeared just as he died, wearing a dressing gown and standing at the foot of his friend's bed, in Dartford. The apparition said 'It is all over with me'.

Mayfair: Lansdowne Passage

Although this was closed and replaced by Lansdowne Row in the 1930s, it is still a very haunted place. Highwaymen used it as an escape route after holding people up in Piccadilly. Witnesses have suggested that they have heard running feet, moans and the occasional pistol shot.

Mayfair: Sheppey's Restaurant, Shepherd Market

Edward Shepherd built Shepherd Market as a

cattle market in 1735, and he built his house in Mayfair on the site of an old fair that had been held there since the 13th century. During the middle of the 18th century the ground floor of the building was converted into a coffee house and was frequented by Boswell and Dr Johnson. In 1860, the house was demolished and a new coffee house was built. The ghost of a highwayman, who lived there during the 18th century and was hanged at Tyburn, haunts the present restaurant. He has been described as being tall and thin and wearing a black cloak.

Mill Hill, Lawrence Street

In 1963, workmen digging in the grounds of St Joseph's Nursing College discovered the coffin of a nun buried in the 19th century. Shortly after this incident, several witnesses reported seeing a cloaked figure in the street. The apparition disappeared when approached. Others reported hearing hymns being sung in the vicinity. It is interesting to note that Lawrence Street was haunted by a cloaked figure during the 1920s. Perhaps, whatever the connection with the disturbed nun, the apparition has chosen to recommence its hauntings.

Neasden Lane, NW10: St Mary's Church

The church is Victorian, but still retains a significant part of its former 13th-century structure. The church itself is haunted by the spirit of a priest, accompanied by the smell of incense. He has a tendency to rattle the door handles in the vestry. The grounds of the vicarage are haunted by the figure of a rotund monk in a black habit. He is said to be happy-looking, enjoys walking around the garden and tends to be seen near the site of a well that was once used by the household.

Newgate, EC1: Amen Court

In 1783, the new Newgate Prison was built

and a new system of hanging, dropping the prisoner through the floor of the scaffold, was introduced. A new scaffold was built outside the prison so that 12 men could be executed at the same time. Between Newgate and the Old Bailey was a small passageway, completely caged in, called Birdcage Walk (or Dead Man's Walk), which was also the location of the lime pits in which the remains of the executed prisoners were buried. Jack Shepherd, the cat burglar, was hanged in November 1724 after having escaped custody three times. Witnesses have seen a dark shape in Dead Man's Walk late at night and have heard the sounds of chains and heavy footfalls. It is believed to be the phantom of Shepherd.

Newgate Street, EC1: Greyfriars Churchyard

Standing beside the ruined Christ Church, founded by Franciscan monks in 1228, it was said that no matter how evil you may have been in life, burial in Greyfriars would protect you from the devil. Queen Isabella 'the she-wolf of France', wife of Edward II and mother of Edward III, left her husband for Piers Gaveston and absconded to France. She returned with an army, defeated Edward II and then imprisoned and murdered him. She ruled for just four years until she was defeated by her own son and held 'in protective custody' for the rest of her life. She is buried in the churchyard with her husband's heart on her chest. Two other known ghosts join Isabella; Elizabeth Barton (The Holy Maid of Kent), executed for high treason at Tyburn in 1534, and Lady Alice Hungerford, who was executed at Tyburn in 1523 for poisoning her husband. They appear together and are often involved in violent arguments between themselves.

New Scotland Yard, Parliament Street, SW1

Once the headquarters of the Metropolitan

Police, this building now houses the Black Museum, a collection of gruesome criminal exhibits. When it was being built in 1888, a workman found the mutilated remains of a woman; a search of the area produced a foot and other parts of the body. The head was never found, but a silver crucifix engraved with the name of a convent made the police believe that she may have been a nun. Several officers and civilians have seen the dark figure of a headless nun in the basement of the building, which disappears if approached.

Norwood, St Joseph's College

In 1864 Daniel Philpot, Mr Prior's senior groom, bet his life savings on one of the stable's horses. Prior was a well-known racehorse breeder and Philpot was convinced that this particular horse had all the winning qualities. Philpot lost his life savings on the horse and hanged himself. His ghost appears every five years in the Oak Room. It is said that he will next appear in 2003.

Notting Hill Gate, Coronet Theatre

The ghost of an actor/manager is said to stalk this theatre, particularly the stairs to the circle. It is believed that the man committed suicide and is probably of the Edwardian era. On the few occasions he has actually been seen, he has been described as being middle-aged. The haunting tends to take the form of an uneasy and oppressive atmosphere in that particular area of the theatre.

Park Royal, NW10: Central Middlesex Hospital

The ghost of a young girl, said to be the apparition of a youngster who was taken into the hospital for a minor operation but given the wrong anaesthetic, has been seen here. She died in theatre but has been seen on the ward in which she stayed prior to the operation. She is said to be responsible for strange clinking noises that have been heard in the ward. It is also believed that the lift that takes patients to the surgical ward moves up and down of its own free will. This may, of course, be linked to the same haunting.

Peckham, The Old Tower Cinema

The ghost of a middle-aged man has been seen to walk across the stage about 10ft in the air and then disappear into a bricked-up recess that once held the organ. In 1953, two people working late saw the same ghost and refused to enter the building again. It was seen again in 1954, by a group of workmen. A number of other strange events have taken place here, including bags of cement being ripped open and water dripping through the ceiling, despite the fact that there was no leak. The most probable explanation is that the building was the site of a chapel in the early part of the 19th century. According to a map dating from around 1819, the ground floor used to be about 10ft higher than it is today.

Peckham Rye, SE15: The King's Arms

The King's Arms is built on the site of a 17th-century pub that was destroyed by a direct hit during the Blitz. The bomb smashed through the pub and exploded in the cellar, which was being used as an air-raid shelter, killing 11 people. Footsteps have been heard, objects moved, dogs are petrified and voices singing wartime songs accompanied by a piano have been heard. A female apparition has been seen, who is thought to be one of the regulars killed on that fateful night.

Pentonville Prison, N7

Strange and unaccountable footsteps, coupled with an unpleasant atmosphere, are said to be related to the suicide of a prisoner here many years ago. The prison is said to be haunted by the ghosts of several prisoners who were held and executed here, as it was used as a place of hanging almost until capital punishment was abolished.

Piccadilly, W1: Naval and Military Club

Major Henry Braddell, known as Perky, was killed in an air raid in 1941 and has been seen in the Egremont Room of the club. He has been easily identified by his uniform and ankle-length greatcoat. There is another ghost in the club that is somewhat more frightening and dangerous. It often jumps out and scares people. Many years ago a man went into a fit just after visiting the club and died. It is believed that this is his apparition.

Piccadilly, W1: Vine Street Police Station

In the early part of the 20th century, a sergeant committed suicide on the premises. As a result, his ghost haunts the police station in the form of heavy footsteps in the corridors. It is believed that the sounds are made by his ghostly hobnailed boots.

Queen Caroline Street, W6: St Paul's Churchyard

The Hammersmith ghost was first seen in 1805 when it chased a woman through the churchyard. It is described as being a tall, white male phantom, believed to be a suicide victim. In 1855, 50 years after the first haunting, a group of vigilantes staked out the churchyard and lay in wait for the mani-festation. Unfortunately, they mistook a man in a white smock for the phantom and shot him. The blunderbuss owner was sentenced to death for the killing, but this was later commuted to one year in prison after the courts took account of the circumstances.

Ratcliff Wharf, Regents Canal Dock, Stepney, E8

The 19th-century vicar of Ratcliff Cross opened a lodging house for seamen. It is now widely believed that he was a serial murderer, killing his lodgers in their sleep for their money. The apparition of a grey or white haired vicar has been seen on a regular basis for around a hundred years. He wears clerical clothes, with gaiters that button at the sides, and he carries a walking stick.

Sadlers Wells Theatre, EC1

Joe Grimaldi, the stage clown, died in 1837. It was this theatre that helped establish his act and popularity. His ghost has been seen in one of the boxes in the theatre, sometimes sitting behind members of the audience. He is clearly identifiable by his white face paint.

St James's Palace, Pall Mall, SW1

The Duchess of Mazarin and Madame de Beauclair were the mistresses of Charles II and James II, and were given a suite of apartments at the palace for their retirement. Both had an abiding interest in the afterlife. Mazarin died first, but for many years did not contact de Beauclair. Mazarin died first, having accurately predicted her death to the minute. Within hours of her death she managed to make contact with the surviving de Beauclair. In 1810, Ernest Augustus, Duke of Cumberland and fifth son of George III, was said to have murdered a servant called Sellis. Cumberland had seduced Sellis's daughter and made her pregnant. In a rage and to cover up the scandal, he slit Sellis's throat and injured himself to make it appear that Sellis had tried to assassinate him and then committed suicide. Sellis's ghost can still be seen walking around the palace, his throat cut from ear to ear.

St James's Park, SW1: Birdcage Walk

The headless figure of a woman, dressed in a red and white striped gown, has been seen walking from the Cockpit Steps down to the canal. For some years, only officers and men of the Coldstream Guards saw the apparition, although today she seems to be happy for anyone to see her. She is thought to be the ghost of the wife of a sergeant in the Coldstreamers, who was murdered by her husband. He had thrown her body into a canal that ran through the park and buried her head nearby.

19 St James' Place, SW1

Ann Pearson died in 1858, and her sister Harriet followed her in 1864. In November 1864 Harriet had become very ill and was being nursed by her servant, Eliza Quintin. Harriet's nieces were also on hand to help. On 23 December, they all saw a woman going into Harriet's room, wearing a shawl and a black cap. They rushed into the room to see who it was, only to find Harriet alone. She told them, just before she died the following evening, that it had been her sister coming to take her away.

St Martin's Lane, Coliseum Theatre, WC2

The manifestation of a World War One British officer has been seen walking down into the dress circle area and heading for the second row, just as the performance is about to start. It is said that he died on 3 October 1918. The night before he returned to the front, he had spent the evening at the theatre.

St Martin's Lane, Duke of York's Theatre, WC2

In 1949, the actress Thora Hird was using a short-backed bolero jacket as part of her costume. To begin with it fitted well, but the more she wore it the tighter it became. Erica Foyle was her understudy and felt the same tightness around the chest and arms. She even saw the apparition of a young woman in the mirror, wearing the same jacket. Others tried it on too; the wife of the play's director was left with red weals on the side of her throat. A medium related the story to them; the jacket belonged to a Victorian girl called Edith Merryweather, who was murdered by a man who had held her head in a water butt until she drowned.

St Paul's Cathedral, EC1

The Kitchener Memorial Chapel, formerly the All Souls' Chapel, commemorates those lost during World War One. A whistling clergyman who appears for a few seconds and then disappears into the wall haunts it. The point of disappearance was solved when a hidden doorway was found, leading to a staircase and the dome. The Deanery of St Paul's is also haunted by strange footsteps and other noises in the middle of the night.

St Thomas' Church, off Regent Street, W1

In 1921 Revd Clarence May, the assistant priest at the church, arrived to prepare to say mass. He saw another priest, wearing a black cassock, at prayer in front of the altar. He went over to greet the priest, only to find that the sacristy was locked. When he unlocked the door, the sacristy was empty. Three other witnesses concurred with May's description and it was later discovered that this was the manifestation of a 19th-century priest.

Shepherd's Bush, W12: The Bush Theatre

The ghost of Dylan Thomas has been seen standing at the back of the auditorium with a drink in his hand. This was once a BBC rehearsal room on the top floor of the Shepherd's Bush Hotel and was much used by Dylan Thomas during his life when he worked for the BBC.

Smithfield, EC1: Cock Lane

The ghost of No.33 Cock Lane is known as

'Scratching Fanny'. In 1759, Richard Parsons, his wife and their two daughters occupied the house. They let part of the house to William Kent, whose wife Elizabeth had died two years before, and he shared the accommodation with his sister-in-law Frances. They lived together as man and wife. Following a row, Kent and Fanny moved to Clerkenwell, where Fanny died of smallpox in 1760. Noises then began waking the Parsons in the night. Mary Frazer, a servant, suggested that the knockings and tappings were a simple code and that it was Fanny and that she had been poisoned by William Kent. The latter took the Parsons to court in protest against the allegations that they made, and won. However, in 1845 Fanny's coffin was opened and the corpse showed all the signs of death by arsenic poisoning.

Stanmore, Old Church Farm

This was a former rectory and is haunted by the ghost of a parson. He has been seen to rise from his grave opposite the farm, walk toward the farm, enter the house and then make the return trip. Witnesses report hearing knocking and other noises and the ghost seems particularly interested if there is an ill person in the house. In nearby Honeypot Lane, witnesses have spoken of a rushing sound and the feeling that something has brushed past them. It could be that this is related to a battle that took place here between the Romans and the Britons shortly after Caesar's invasion.

Stepney: Hanbury Street

Annie Chapman was murdered and mutilated by the 19th-century serial killer Jack the Ripper, and appears here in phantom form. It is interesting to note that she has been positively identified. Extensive news coverage made her face very familiar to the public for several years.

Strand, WC2: The Adelphi Theatre

William Terris, whose ghost also appears at Covent Garden Underground Station, was actually murdered here by a bit actor who was jealous of his success. His apparition appears bathed in green light and clad in a grey suit with an old-fashioned collar and white gloves. Electricians have seen him walking through a whole row of seats and disappearing through a wall. His former dressing room is said to reverberate with rapping noises but they may not be made by William. It is remembered, however, that Terris used to tap on the door of his leading lady's dressing room to let her know that he was going elsewhere.

Strand WC2, Coutts Bank

This was the site where Elizabeth I had the 4th Duke of Norfolk beheaded for treason on 2 June 1572. An exorcism was carried out in 1993 to calm the restless spirit that has appeared headless and moaning on numerous occasions.

Strand WC2, Somerset House

This building was formerly the Admiralty and is haunted by none other than Horatio Nelson. His ghost appears in full uniform, but it is interesting that the apparition does not have an arm and Nelson appears to look frail. This is unlike some of his more hearty hauntings elsewhere. There is also a strange cloud manifestation above the apparition's head.

Temple, EC4: Fleet Street

Originally built by the Knights Templar, who remained there from 1184 until their order was disbanded in 1312, the building was leased to Aymerde de Valence, Earl of Pembroke. In 1608, King James I gave the property to the Inner and Middle Temples. The ghost that haunts the Temple is Sir Henry Hawkins, a barrister later to become Lord

Brampton. He is seen dressed in wig and gown, gliding through the cloisters with papers under his arm. Some years ago, a perfectly preserved skeleton was found in a wall near the roof, which is believed to be over 200 years old.

Thamesmead, SE28

During the Battle of Britain, a Spitfire pilot was shot down and crashed on Erith Marshes. The manifestation of the pilot, dressed in his RAF uniform, walks around the Tavey Bridge area. He is described as being tall and dark. The apparition is known to make banging noises in the local butcher's shop and has even made an appearance in a neighbour's bedroom.

Tottenham, N15: Bruce Castle

This is the former home of Rowland Hill, founder of the Post Office and the Penny Post. The building dates back to Elizabethan times, and is on the site of an older house constructed by the father of Robert Bruce. In the 17th century, Lord Coleraine imprisoned his beautiful wife Constantia in a chamber above the entrance. At her wits end, she took her child in her arms and jumped from the balustrade on 3 November 1680. Constantia's screams can be heard on the anniversary of her death. Strange ghostly figures in 18th-century costume have also been seen in the grounds, disappearing into the wall of the building.

Tower Hill, EC3

The aftermath of a full execution seems to be the manifestation that has appeared here on a number of occasions, particularly once during World War Two. A sentry, guarding the area at the time, watched a procession of men pass by. The figures were later identified as being mediaeval Sherrif of London's guards and priests. They were carrying a stretcher with a corpse on it. The head looked

as if it had been severed. Since then the manifestation has regularly appeared in this location.

Tower of London, EC3

Steeped in history, this magnificent structure teems with ghosts that mirror the royal heritage of this country. At Traitor's Gate Thomas Becket's ghost is said to have struck the structure twice, reducing it to rubble. In the Bloody Tower the ghosts of King Edward V and his brother Richard, Duke of York, possibly murdered by Richard III, have been seen standing hand-in-hand, clad in nightgowns. Skeletons believed to be the remains of the two princes were discovered in 1674 and are now buried in Westminster Abbey. A face has been seen looking out of one of the windows of St Thomas's Tower by staff and visitors. In the Martin Tower Edmund Swifte saw a glass tube, which phased from white to blue, on one occasion in 1817. The Tower also boasts the ghost of a bear. Northumberland's Walk is the home of the ghost of the Earl of Northumberland, who exercised here prior to his execution. Anne Boleyn haunts the Queen's House, where she has been seen by several different people, including sentries who have attempted to attack her apparition with bayonets. Guildford Dudley's ghost has been seen both in the Beauchamp Tower and on Tower Hill. Lady Jane Grey has also been seen in the Beauchamp Tower. Sir Walter Raleigh walks around the battlements. Ghostly choirs have been heard and numerous other poltergeist activities have been reported.

Twickenham, St Margaret's Churchyard

Alexander Pope was buried here, but did not haunt the site until 1830 when someone stole his skull. Following this incident his hunchbacked ghost has been seen walking around the churchyard and church. What is odd about it is that he talks to himself and coughs a lot. When he has not been seen, witnesses have reported hearing the slightly uneven sound of footsteps inside the church.

Vauxhall, SE1: The Morpeth Arms

The pub is on the site of the former Millbank Prison and it is believed that prisoners were once housed in what is now the cellar area of the pub. They waited there until they were transported to Australia. One of the prisoners, clearly unable to cope mentally with the prospect of imprisonment and transportation, took his own life down there by hanging himself. The cellars have strange cold spots and smells that may also be related to the haunting. Although nothing has been seen, a strange presence is definitely at work in this place.

Wandsworth Prison, Heathfield Street, SW18

Built in 1851, the prison is haunted by 'Wandsworth Annie', who was employed there as a cook and died in the 1870s. She is described as appearing to be middle-aged, with grey hair. She wears a Victorian grey dress, and staff and prisoners have seen her walking down the corridors.

Wanstead, E11

The terrifying apparitions of a man and woman have been seen in the churchyard. The manifestation begins with a ghostly skeleton emerging, pushing a coffin cart. It approaches an ornate tomb in the middle of the cemetery, where it is joined by a man in white. The man walks over to the skeleton and puts his arms around it. The pair are husband and wife, and continue to embrace one another even in death.

West Drayton, nr Uxbridge: West Drayton Church

Strange noises have been heard from the vaults under the church that hold the remains of the Pagets and the de Burghs. It is believed that two of the corpses either murdered one another or committed suicide together. Screams and knocking noises have been heard, and on one occasion a large black raven was seen sitting on one of the coffins. People with lanterns and sticks and stones scared it off. When it fell, exhausted, onto the ground, it vanished.

Westminster, WC1: Red Lion Square

The ghosts of Oliver Cromwell, his son-in-law Henry Ireton and John Bradshaw (president of the court that sentenced Charles I) have been seen walking abreast across the square from south to north, deep in conversation. Their bodies were taken out of Westminster Abbey after the Restoration and hanged at Tyburn. After the disinterment, their corpses were first taken to Red Lion Square (then Field) as there were gallows there. It is believed that their bodies were desecrated before being taken to Tyburn, hence the haunting.

Westminster Abbey, SW1

Father Benedictus can be seen walking in the cloisters between 5 and 6pm. However, he does not actually walk, he glides. The flagstones are somewhat lower than they were in his time. He is described as being a tall, lean and cowled figure. He was killed during the reign of Henry VIII at the Chapel of Pyx. The ghost of the Unknown Soldier has been seen near the tomb with its head bowed, dressed in the uniform of a World War One infantryman.

Westminster Cathedral, SW1

Although officially denied by the Catholic Church, this cathedral in Victoria is haunted by a black-robed figure that is said to disappear near the High Altar. On one particular occasion when the cathedral was locked in July 1966, a sacristan on night duty saw it stand there and then fade into nothing.

Whitechapel, E1

The ghost of Jack the Ripper's first victim, Polly Nicholls, has been seen lying in the gutter near Whitechapel Station in Durward Street. She is described as lying huddled and surrounded by a strange aura.

M
Macclesfield to Murrow

Macclesfield, Cheshire: Capesthorne Hall

Two Members of Parliament witnessed the apparition of a grey lady some years ago. Charles Taylor and Walter Bromley-Davenport both saw the manifestation as they approached the stairs of the west wing. The latter had also encountered the ghost near the chapel. A former butler, in a newspaper story, stated that the woman in the grey gown was thought to be a family ghost.

Macroom, Munster, Republic of Ireland: Macroom Castle

The gateway is all that remains of this once magnificent castle overlooking the market town and the River Sullane. An unseen spirit, thought to be a former owner of the castle, haunts it. Admiral Sir William Penn, whose son founded Pennsylvania, also once owned the town.

Maddington, nr Salisbury, Wiltshire: Shrewton

The ghost of a young woman dressed in white is said to be particularly active in the village, at the public house near where the gibbet once stood, at the church and outside some of the cottages on the outskirts of the village. A former vicar believed that she was a novice from the former seminary in Maddington Manor, and perhaps met an untimely death.

Madeley, Shropshire: St Michael's Church

The ghost of an old lady leaves flowers on one of the graves. She tends to be seen at first light, moving about the gravestones. In the nearby Madeley Court House, an Elizabethan manor house, monkish figures not only haunt the building, but have also been said to sit on the crossbeam of the Great Hall. Close to the hall, in a hollow, a terrace of cottages once stood, and their long-dead inhabitants have been seen returning to the area.

Madingley, nr Cambridge, Cambridgeshire: Madingley Hall

Lord Hyde built a house here in 1543, but the manifestation is that of his wife, Lady Ursula Hyde. Her husband furnished their house with items looted from various churches and monasteries, a sacrilege of which she thoroughly disapproved. Consequently, as if in penance, her spirit has been seen to roam the area. In the upper terrace of the hall, witnesses have also reported seeing the ghost of a young man with a green face. It is also said that he has a loathing expression on his face.

Maes y Neuadd, nr Harlech, Gwynedd

This hotel was first built in the 14th century. The author Robert Graves stayed at the place and was convinced that it was the most haunted hotel that he had ever slept in. It is said that some of the ghosts can even be seen in mirrors. Not all of them are malevolent. The spirit of a nanny will visit sick children staying at the hotel. On bright mornings, you may see a phantom yellow dog prowling around the lawn.

Maghull, nr Liverpool, Merseyside

The Siege of Preston in 1715 has left its mark on the landscape near here. Witnesses have reported hearing the sounds of battle, including gunshots, horses and cries, although there is nothing to be seen. The site most affected seems to be to the south of Maghull at around dusk.

Maidenhead, Berkshire: The Hobgoblin

A poltergeist moves clothing and money, as well as turning beer taps on and off. The pub also suffers from ghostly footsteps in the night. On many occasions doors will refuse to open and each year, just before Christmas, the landlord hears glasses clinking together in the bar, despite the fact that it is empty.

Maidstone, Kent: West Kent General Hospital

Founded in the 18th century, this hospital boasts the presence of a female ghost who cries. In the distant past, it is said, she was also visible, but now staff and patients merely hear her pitiful sobbing. Despite extensive investigations, including past medical records, it has been impossible to identify the woman.

Mallwyd, nr Machynlleth, Gwynedd

In 1554, Sir John Wynne of Gwydir led a punitive expedition against the lawless brigands occupying the upper Dovey Valley. The group were said to be tall and copper-haired, with an appalling reputation for robbery and other crimes. Sir John succeeded in rounding up some 80 of the band, and Baron Owen at the Montgomery Assizes

sentenced them to death. The judge was cursed by the mother of one of the men, who said 'these yellow breasts have given suck to those who will wash their hands in your blood'. True to her word, the judge and his party were ambushed on Christmas Day and some 30 arrows were found in his mutilated body. It is said that his cries of agony can still be heard some two miles from Mallwyd where the road passes through a ravine.

Malmesbury, Wiltshire: The Old Bell Hotel

Built in the 13th century as a hostelry for the Abbott of Malmesbury, the Old Bell Hotel is haunted by the apparition of a grey lady. She has been seen in the building and in the garden area. Her identity is unknown.

Manchester Airport, Greater Manchester

The buildings at Manchester Aiport leased by Messrs Claridge and Co. were formerly barracks for No.613 (City of Manchester) Squadron, Royal Air Force. They are haunted by the apparition of an old man. The ghost tends to be seen late at night or in the early hours of the morning, walking through the offices in bare feet. If approached, the apparition will disappear. On one occasion, the police were called in to investigate noises emanating from the empty building and found that although the building was secure, equipment had been scattered around. Screams have been heard and footsteps reported in the corridor. Despite the fact that the police have investigated and the company have checked all of their records, the identity of the barefoot phantom intruder is still unknown.

Manchester: Birchen Bower, Hollinwood

Madame Hannah Beswick haunts the

industrial estate that now occupies the site of Birchen Bower. Hannah was buried at Harpurhey Cemetery on 22 July 1868, although she had been dead since 1758. The story behind this is complicated, but begins in 1745 when Bonnie Prince Charlie and his highlanders were marching south before turning back at Derby. By this time, Hannah was quite old and infirm and had retired and moved into a small cottage in the grounds of the manor. She was still a rich woman and, what with the rampaging Scots heading her way, she was determined that they would not get their hands on her wealth. She systematically converted all of her wealth into gold and hid it in the grounds of the manor. The Scots never reached her, and she lived another 13 years. It is supposed that her gold was still safely hidden underground. Her brother John Beswick 'died' in around 1745, but as his coffin lid was being screwed on, his eyes flickered and he was saved from being buried alive. He had been in a deep coma for some days. This spooked Hannah so much that she declared that on her death, she must not be buried. While her body remained unburied, her brother and descendants could enjoy the income from her estate. On her deathbed, she repeated this pledge and also offered to show the family where the gold was hidden, but she deteriorated before she was able to carry this out. Hannah's body was embalmed and wrapped in bandages and was a prize exhibit at the Natural History Museum. Every 21 years, according to her will, her body was taken back to the estate. Each time, strange things happened. Animals got loose and on one occasion a cow was found in the hayloft. Hannah's ghost was seen on numerous occasions, as a black lady, walking through her old parlour. She would disappear when she reached a particular flagstone. Joe the Tamer was a poor hand-loomer who moved into Birchen Bower, whereupon his luck seemed to change. While digging a treadle hole he discovered a hoard

of gold bars. Significantly, this was at the exact spot at which Hannah's ghost would disappear. He sold the bars to a gold dealer. Hannah's ghost still haunts the area, despite the fact that Birchen Bower is no more. She was seen in 1956, 1968 and 1972. In the early part of the 20th century, she was also seen standing beside an old well, and on the site of a barn that was used to house her body when it returned every 21 years. Perhaps she had hidden part of her hoard there as well.

Manchester Cathedral, Manchester

A headless dog is said to have haunted the streets of central Manchester in the early part of the 19th century. It was seen many times in the area of the Old Church, which is now Manchester Cathedral. In 1825, it terrified a local tradesman by placing its paws on his shoulders. It is recorded that the tradesman, a man called Drabble, ran very quickly back to his house, followed by the dog.

Manchester: Great Western Hotel

This vast hotel in the Moss Side district of Manchester has a ghost whose activities seem to be confined to the cellar. The male ghost, dressed in a grey jumper, has been seen on numerous occasions by members of staff. He is described as having black hair and is thought to be in his thirties. The witnesses also experience a measurable drop in temperature. It is believed that the ghost was a former worker in the hotel.

Manchester: Shakespeare Hotel

This is another Manchester hotel that is haunted by the spirit of a former employee. The apparition has mostly been seen by members of staff. Apparently the girl, who was working as a maid at the hotel, had a tragic accident. Somehow her clothes caught fire and she was burnt to death. It is believed that this occurred around 50 years ago.

Mannington, nr Aylsham, Norfolk: Mannington Church

The ghost of a female member of the Scalmers family haunted Mannington Church until the 19th century. The family owned Mannington Hall before it was taken over by the Orfords. The 2nd Lord Orford is said to have destroyed the Scalmers tomb at the church. The ghost was seen many times, especially during the 18th century. In an attempt to rid the family of the curse of the phantom lady, the Orford family hearse, containing each subsequent dead member of the family, was driven three times round the church before the burial service.

Mannington, nr Aylsham, Norfolk: Mannington Hall

On 10 October 1979, Doctor Jessop was staying at the hall as a guest of Lord Orford. After a meal, he went into the library to read by candlelight. After some time, he was startled to see a large man standing behind him. Jessop described the man as appearing to be a monk, with veiny white hands. Doctor Jessop was not frightened and had the presence of mind to try to quickly draw a sketch of the apparition, but it soon disappeared. After five minutes the figure returned. Jessop tried to talk to it, but again it disappeared. He waited, but the figure never appeared again.

Manningtree, Essex

Matthew Hopkins was the Witchfinder General of the 17th century, and he began his career at Manningtree by condemning a coven of witches. The descendants of the supposed witches are still to be found locally. Hopkins was paid 20 shillings for each witch he managed to discover, and suspects were tested by being bound and thrown into a river. If they sank and were drowned they were innocent, if they floated and survived they were witches. Those found to be witches were hanged or burned at the stake. Hopkins is buried at Mistley Heath.

Manorbier Castle, nr Pembroke, Dyfed

The manifestation of a tall woman is said to haunt the path and gateway to the castle. She appears as a black lady part way along the path, and walks toward the gateway, disappearing a few feet from it. Several visitors to the castle, as well as a number of locals, have seen her.

Mapledurham, Oxfordshire

This impressive mansion near Reading is home to the grisly manifestation of a murder that is replayed on a regular basis. Some years ago, the master of the house murdered one of his servants in a fit of rage. Not only have witnesses seen the unfortunate murder victim, but some also report that they have seen the immediate aftermath of the murder. Some witnesses claim to have seen the murderer dragging the corpse across the floor of one of the rooms.

Marazion, Cornwall

It is said that the manifestation of a woman will jump onto your horse and ride with you as far as the Red River. This white lady materialises near Marazion Green and disappears as suddenly as she appears. It is thought that she tends to make her presence known late at night.

Marchants Cross, Dartmoor

This point marks a branch of the Abbot's Way. For many years, people have believed that this place is one of the sites haunted by Sir Francis Drake. Drake is said to take the place of the Devil as the leader of the Wish Pack, or Wild Hunt, and roam the area with the ghostly hounds. It may be that two separate stories have become merged over the years.

Marford, nr Wrexham, Clwyd

In 1713, Margaret Blackbourne lived at Rofft Hall (later Rofft Castle) with her husband. By all accounts, he was not a faithful man and his affairs ended in Margaret's death. He was tried for the murder, but escaped a guilty verdict. Soon after, he remarried and set up home in Rofft Hall. It was then that Margaret's ghost made an appearance. The manifestation would walk through the village, peering into the windows of the houses, bent on finding her murderous husband. Eventually, the hauntings became so frequent that he was forced to move out of the house, only to discover that the spirit followed and tormented him for the rest of his life.

Margam Castle, nr Port Talbot, West Glamorgan

A white lady haunts this ruined castle (in fact a mansion dating from around 1840). It is presumed that she was a former owner of the house. Nearby is a ruined Cistercian abbey that has ghostly monks walking around its grounds.

Margate, Kent: Theatre Royal

The ghost of an actor who committed suicide in a stage box and fell on to the boards haunts the former Theatre Royal. Even after extensive renovations, including the bricking up of the box, mysterious lights can still be seen. The second ghost is that of Sarah Thorne, who died in 1899. She had formed a well-respected theatre company and school at the theatre, and is seen walking down the central aisle and up on to the stage.

Market Bosworth, nr Hinckley, Leicestershire

Dating from 1680, Bosworth Hall was once the residence of Sir Wolstan Dixie. In 1758, he discovered that his daughter Anne was hav-ing an affair with the son of his gardener. Sir Wolstan was an unpleasant, bad-tempered and arrogant man and he was determined to put a stop to this liaison. Consequently, he placed mantraps around the grounds in the hope that he would snare his daughter's lover. Unfortunately, he snared his daughter instead. Horribly crippled by the mantrap, she bled to death in her room. Her tortured spirit now takes the form of a grey lady. It is also said that an indelible bloodstain remains on one of the ceilings in the shape of a woman's hand.

Market Drayton, Shropshire: Old Colehurst Manor

A ghost now known as Fred is a short man in old-fashioned clothing with long, curly hair and a smile on his face. He seems to be quite friendly. Three other ghosts also haunt the manor house and are seen sitting under the window of one of the rooms on the ground floor. They are a man and a woman comforting a young child.

Market Harborough, Leicestershire

It is said that a flat above shops in the High Street is haunted by a presence that makes itself felt by means of smell and a strange atmosphere. Witnesses have suggested that the smell can be likened to cigar smoke. They also sense a presence, but are unsure what it might be.

Markyate, Hertfordshire: Markyate Cell

This was the former home of a notorious highwayman. The 'Wicked Lady Ferrers' operated in the 17th century. She used a secret stairwell from the house and would lie in wait for unsuspecting travellers. Often, she would climb into a tree and stand on a branch overhanging the road, before dropping on to her victims. One night, however, she was shot and died as she reached Markyate Cell. Her ghost has been seen riding wildly across the countryside, in the branches of a tree and in the gardens of her former home. Her treasure was never found.

Markyate, Hertfordshire: Pack Horse Inn

The apparition of a tall cricketer has been seen on several occasions on the road near the Pack Horse Inn on the road from Markyate to Dunstable. In 1958, the Kenwood Manufacturing Co. Ltd cricket team was returning to Surrey from a game at Milton Bryan. The driver, swerving to overtake a car, crashed the mini-bus, killing two and seriously injuring another three of the team. Sidney Moulder and Jerry Rycham were the two fatalities and it is thought that it is the ghost of one of them which scared the life out of a taxi driver near the spot in the 1970s. Several other motorists have seen the ghost since.

Marnhull, nr Shaftesbury, Dorset

Two ghosts cross the Sackmore Lane carrying a coffin. Their faces are hidden. They are said to walk toward Todber, the site of a battlefield. Perhaps they are a distant echo of the past when many fell here. Large numbers of bones were dug up in the area in 1870.

Marple Hall, Marple, nr Stockport, Greater Manchester

The date of the original house on the Marple Hall site is uncertain, but the Vernons of Haddon Hall probably built it during the reign of Henry VII. At the top of the house is a room leading to the roof. Below is a curious passage, or chamber, which may have been used as a priests' hiding place. During some repairs made at the beginning of the 19th century, two skeletons were found here, the origins of which are unknown. Nevertheless, it is believed that the skeletons may be the source of the haunting here.

Marsden Grotto, nr Sunderland, Tyne and Wear

A public house now occupies a cave that was used by smugglers. The ghost that is said to haunt the pub and the surrounding area is that of Jack the Blaster. He was one of the smugglers, but turned the rest of the gang in to the customs officers. One of the tankards behind the bar supposedly belongs to him, and if it is moved it initiates a period of poltergeist activity.

Marston Moor, Long Marston, North Yorkshire

Since around 1968, various tourists have reported seeing the manifestation of a group of men, dressed in 17th-century clothing, making their way along a ditch beside the road. The apparitions seem to be oblivious to the fact that they are being watched. Witnesses say that once they have passed the ghosts, the spirits disappear. It is very likely that these manifestations are related to the nearby battlefield of Marston Moor (1644).

Marwell Hall, nr Fishers Pond, Hampshire

This place is said to be haunted by the spirit of Jane Seymour, who was married to Henry VIII. She died after giving birth to the future Edward VI. Her apparition has been seen on several occasions. Jane was Henry's third wife, whom he married after the execution of Anne Boleyn.

Mayfield, East Sussex: Middle House

Like many places in the area, Mayfield prospered at the height of the iron industry, and much of its finest architecture dates from that time. Middle House, in the High Street, is a splendid oak-beamed Tudor inn. The date 1575 is carved into the bargeboards. Twenty-five years before the inn was built, four Protestants were burned at the stake here. Their ghosts are said to haunt the ground on which their pyres were stacked before the building of the inn.

Meggernie Castle, nr Killin, Tayside

This 15th-century former clan stronghold houses a frightening manifestation with a plausible explanation. Either during the 15th century, or perhaps at a later date (some suggest 1862), a murder took place here. Taking the earlier date, we are led to believe that the head of Clan Menzies, during a raging fit, killed his wife. To hide the body, he cut it in half. The bottom half was buried in the churchyard and the upper half under the floor of the North Tower. The apparition, which takes the form of a beautiful woman, appears in two halves. The top half favours the top floors and the North Tower. The lower part of the apparition haunts the Lime Avenue approach to the castle and the ground floor. The lower half, skirted, is covered, not surprisingly, in blood. If the apparition touches you, you will feel a sense of burning but your skin will be undamaged.

Melling, nr Liverpool, Merseyside

Now a hotel, Melling Hall was once the home of Lady Darlington, who lived there during World War One. She now appears as a purple lady, but another apparition beggars all explanation. Witnesses have seen a dwarf-like figure, with bird legs, which appears in a very excited state. The ghost of a former pet dog also haunts the hotel, walking around with its collar and name disc on.

Melrose Abbey, Borders

A monk haunts this ruined old abbey, but has a strange way of moving around that may have a link with devil worship or a curse laid on it as a result of misdemeanours in life. The manifestation slithers along the ground, rather like a snake. It is likely that the ghost is that of Michael Scot, a mediaeval scholar. He was believed to be a wizard by the locals as he had a great interest in science. Other locals believe, to this day, that the apparition is the ghost of a vampire.

Meopham, Kent: Dean Manor

The psychic Harry Price investigated and laid traps for the ghost that haunted this old house. He experienced paranormal activity near the cellar door, always finding it open even though he had closed it. The temperature in the area dropped considerably and footsteps were heard in the early hours of the morning. Later the haunting was further investigated and it was discovered that a servant girl had hanged herself from a beam in the granary after she had been falsely accused by her mistress of stealing a gold sovereign. Apparently she had also been involved in a disastrous love affair with a local man. Other witnesses have reported hearing tapping noises and the sound of an axe being used on wood. Intermittent sounds, such as footsteps on gravel, twigs snapping and metal clicking noises have also been heard.

Meopham, Kent: Steel Lane

During the Napoleonic Wars Madamoiselle Pinard became the mistress of a British soldier. She followed him home but was not well received by either him or his family. She hanged herself, but her ghost can still be seen, dressed in orange silk. There is also talk locally of a headless man, thought to be a monk, who walks between the Georgian pub and the church. Another suicide victim, this time a miller, who hanged himself from a beam in a nearby building, is also said to stalk the area.

Mersea Island, nr Colchester, Essex

On 23 September (the autumn equinox), you may encounter the manifestation of a Roman soldier patrolling the causeway to the island and the Peldon Rose Inn. Local archaeology suggests that there was a substantial Roman presence on the island during the occupation, centred in a 20ft high tumulus called The Mount. Romano-British lead coffins and glass bowls containing human ashes have been unearthed. A taxi driver, taking a fare from a pub in West Mersea, encountered a patrol of Roman soldiers standing in the middle of the road. He drove straight through them and then looked back to discover that they had disappeared.

Mersey Tunnel, Merseyside

The ghost of a girl that died in the 1960s sometimes appears on the back of motorcycles travelling through the tunnel. This phantom hitch hiker is said to suddenly appear, riding pillion, and then disappear when the biker realises that she is there.

Metheringham, nr Lincoln, Lincolnshire

The modern equivalent of a green lady appears on this former RAF airbase, to drivers crossing the site. The apparition is probably that of a WRAF who died in a motorcycle accident. Witnesses have suggested that she does have an RAF badge on the lapel of her coat. When she first appears, requesting a lift, witnesses have said that she smells of lavender. Suddenly she vanishes and leaves a putrid, rotten smell behind.

Mevagissey, nr Truro, Cornwall

The apparition of Walter Cross, a smuggler who introduced a stagecoach service to Cornwall in 1796, has been seen at the reins of a phantom coach on the quiet country lanes in this area. The coach is described as being bright red, with small doors and windows and a sloping back. It is a correct description of the kind of vehicle used to deliver mail in the area at that time. The coachman wears a greatcoat with wide blue lapels and is accompanied by a guard, clad in a scarlet coat and black hat, blowing a post horn.

Michelham Priory, nr Hailsham, East Sussex

Boasting England's longest mediaeval water-filled moat, the house dates back to 1229, when the priory was founded. It was lived in by Augustinian canons until the Dissolution in 1537. After this time, the Church of the Holy Trinity was destroyed and the house underwent various transformations, including the addition of an extensive Tudor wing. A grey lady haunts the gatehouse, said to be the ghost of a woman that drowned in the moat. In the Tudor Room, there are two more ghosts, a blue lady and a monk.

Mickleover, nr Derby, Derbyshire: Woodlands Orthopaedic Hospital

A ward sister was killed here during World War Two when the Germans bombed the hospital. In 1948, a witness reported seeing a ward sister, with an unusual 'butterfly' style cap. Some of the ward sister's colleagues were still at the hospital and the description given matched her perfectly. She had appeared on her favourite ward. Since then, the ghost has appeared to several patients and nursing staff.

Mickleton, nr Stratford-upon-Avon, Warwickshire

On still nights, you may hear the terrifying cries of the Mickleton Hooter. It is said to be a ghostly cow or goblin. Others suggest that it is just a legend, invented by local landowners wishing to scare off poachers.

Certainly, Meon Hill has ghostly connections with a huntsman and his hellhounds that tear around the area.

Middle Claydon, nr Winslow, Buckinghamshire: Claydon House

A grey lady, thought to be Florence Nightingale, haunts the Rose Room and the bedroom in which she is said to have slept on a number of occasions. Florence Nightingale was the sister of the owner of the house, Lady Parthenope Verney. The apparition is said to wear a long grey gown.

Middleton, nr Manchester, Greater Manchester: Ring o' Bells

During the English Civil War, royalist supporters would meet here, using a tunnel leading from the cellar to pass unnoticed to the exit in the nearby churchyard. Lord Stannycliffe's son was one of the royalists, who one day found a group of Roundhead soldiers waiting for him in the churchyard. Mortally wounded in the ensuing fight, he crawled back along the tunnel and died (perhaps in the Cavalier's Seat) in the pub. His ghost now haunts the pub, sharing the place with the manifestation of a man dressed in a grey suit.

Middleton, nr Manchester, Greater Manchester: St Leonard's Church

A photograph was taken of one of the two ghosts that are said to haunt this church. The picture showed the indistinct figure of a woman. The apparition of a slim clergyman also haunts the church. Witnesses have reported seeing the manifestation for a second or so, before it moves behind one of the pillars and disappears.

Milford, nr Stafford, Staffordshire

On Weetman's Bridge, on the road to Rugeley, you may encounter the manifest-

ation of a ghostly cyclist. It is believed that the cyclist was killed in a road accident here some years ago.

Minehead, Somerset

Mrs Leakey's ghost is known as the 'Whistling Spectre', and appears in the streets, on the shore and out to sea. It is said that she was a witch who sold fair wind charms to sailors. The ghost was particularly active during the 17th century.

Minsden Chapel, nr Hitchin, Hertfordshire

Famously, the phantom of a monk was photographed in 1907. The site is said to be very eerie with a strange atmosphere. Reginald Hine, the ghostwriter, is also said to haunt this chapel after predicting he would do so in one of his books.

Minsterley, nr Shrewsbury, Shropshire

The ancient ghostly spirits of Wild Edric and his warriors are said to issue forth from the old lead mines here if Britain is in danger. They are said to fly across the sky, their mission to wake the dead to come to support the country in its hour of need. If a mortal sees them, then they will be made blind or mad.

Minster Lovell Hall, nr Witney, Oxfordshire

The ghost of Lord Lovell, who supported Lambert Simnel in 1487, haunts these ruins. After the Battle of Stoke, looked after by one faithful servant, he locked himself up in a secret room. When the servant died, he starved to death. A vault was found in 1718, in which the skeleton of a man sitting at a table was found, with a dog at his feet.

Miterdale, nr Broughton-in-Furness, Cumbria

The particularly unpleasant sight of a robber with a shapeless white face is said to haunt the area. Many years ago, the robber, perhaps disguised as a woman, was given shelter in a local farm. He fell asleep and the farmer's wife suddenly realised that this was no simple traveller. She poured hot tallow down his throat and killed him. His ghost can be seen making horrible choking noises.

Monkstown, nr Dublin, Republic of Ireland

The singer, Sir Valentine Grace, once owned a house in the area. In his will he stipulated that his trees be left untouched. Following the felling of one of the trees, his plaintive singing can be heard, following a call for help.

Monmouth, Gwent

The spirit of a highwayman or an ancient battle that took place here probably explains the haunting near to Chippenham House. In the autumn, late in the afternoon, you may hear the sound of horses' hooves clattering along the road and disappearing near the house. There are also phantom coaches, phantom soldiers, animals and crying children.

Montgomery, Powys: Montgomery Churchyard

In 1821, John Newton Davies was hanged for robbery. He had been accused by two local men, one of whom had hoped to marry Jane Davies, John's wife. The other man had been negotiating to purchase Jane's mother's farm. John protested his innocence to the end, and vowed that no grass would grow on the spot where he was buried. He spoke the truth, and the plot remains bare to this day. It is said that if anyone tries to seed grass here then they will come to regret it.

Montrose Old Aerodrome, Tayside

Lieutenant Desmond Arthur, who died in an aircraft crash in 1913, is said to haunt the area. He appears in full pre-World War One flying kit. He shares the airfield with another phantom pilot, an RAF man who crashed there in 1942. It is said that he haunts the airfield because the circumstances of the crash were suspicious.

Moresby Hall, nr Whitehaven, Cumbria

During the Jacobite rebellion, the Fletcher family supported the Stuarts. The ghost, however, is not that of a Fletcher, but that of another Jacobite. The head of the Fletcher family had hidden the man in the house, but when Fletcher was taken to London for interrogation, the man died. His spirit is still seen in the house.

Morley, nr Batley, West Yorkshire: Howley Hall Golf Club

Originally built in the 16th century by Sir John Saville, Howley Hall was largely destroyed by the Duke of Newcastle in 1643. What remained of the hall was then let out to various tenants, who included the Villiers family. Witnesses have seen the ghost of a woman and other figures, dressed in 17th-century clothing, in the area. One such sighting described the woman as wearing a long dress with a dark top and a red veil over her face and shoulders. After a few seconds, the apparition fades and vanishes.

Morley, nr Norwich, Norfolk: Morley Old Hall

In 1965, the small, bearded ghostly monk that haunts the building actually appeared on television during an interview in the hall about the hauntings. Prior to this, over 20 people had claimed to have seen the apparition.

211

Mortham Tower, nr Barnard Castle, Co. Durham

This mediaeval tower was once owned by the Rokeby family and was the site of a murder. A husband murdered his unfaithful wife by cutting her head off. He disposed of the corpse by throwing it into the river. As a result, the manifestation of a headless woman can be encountered here. Interestingly, an 18th-century cleric met the ghost near the bridge over the River Greta and spoke with her in Latin. He did not comment on how the ghost managed to talk to him without a head. A spiral staircase in the tower still had the indelible marks of blood on some of the steps.

Morville, nr Bridgnorth, Shropshire: Acton Arms

The ghost of Richard Manners, the last prior of Morville, is said to appear on a regular basis in the pub. Manners saw the priory dissolved in the 16th century. It is said that his apparition can make several visits in one day. On the outskirts of the village is a hill upon which once stood a large Victorian house. Many years ago it burned down and the family perished in the flames. Some motorists claim to have seen the house with people in Victorian clothes clustered around it.

Mosborough Hall, Mosborough, Sheffield, South Yorkshire

It is said that this hall, now a hotel, has several underground passages leading to a number of different places around the estate. Whether these are related in some way to the manifestation of a former maid is not known. She was murdered in the hall many years ago.

Mount Craig Hotel, nr Pencraig, Herefordshire

Now known as Pencraig Court, this is a fine Georgian country house hotel set in three and a half acres of its own gardens and secluded woodland, standing high above the banks of the River Wye. It is said to be haunted, but no one has been able to describe the exact nature of the manifestation.

Moyles Court, nr Ringwood, Hampshire

The spirit of Dame Alice Lisle haunts this place. She was allowed to be beheaded rather than face the prospect of being burned at the stake by Judge Jeffreys. Her crime was harbouring a supporter of Monmouth.

Muchalls Castle, nr Stonehaven, Grampian

A green lady haunts the drawing room of this 17th-century stronghold of the Burnetts of Leys. It is said that she was drowned in an underground sea cave beneath the castle as she went to meet her lover, a sailor. The apparition is known as Green Jean, but more recent witnesses claim to have seen her appear in a yellow dress in one of the bedrooms. Perhaps this is another apparition.

Mullion, nr Helston, Cornwall: Bochym Manor

A pink lady, said to be less than 5ft tall, haunts the manor. Her father supposedly killed her lover in a duel. The Royal Naval Balloon Corps used the manor as a base during World War One. One of the officers stationed there experienced the apparitions of two men fighting a duel in a field beside the driveway. One of them was run through and the other figure dropped to his knees and beckoned six other phantoms, carrying a coffin toward him. At this point, the surviving duellist noticed that he was being watched and levelled his sword toward the officer. The officer fainted and when he recovered, all of the ghosts had disappeared.

Muncaster Castle, nr Whitehaven, Cumbria

Sir Ferdinand Pennington lived in the castle during the 17th century. In 1600, his jester, Thomas Skelton, died. Skelton was not just a fool; he was Pennington's right hand man. On one occasion, he killed a servant that his master suspected of being rather too familiar with his daughter. He brought the head of the hapless man to Pennington as a sign of his loyalty. Skelton and the headless servant now haunt the Tapestry Room of the castle.

Mundesley, nr Cromer, Norfolk

The manifestation of a ghostly coastguard, known as the Long Coastguardsman, is said to haunt the coast here. Generally, he is seen at around midnight, on moonless nights, shouting and challenging storm clouds.

Murrow, nr Wisbech, Cambridgeshire

Ghost Hill is, predictably, a haunted site. The ghost is said to be that of Oliver Cromwell, presumably haunting this place because it is the only high elevation in an otherwise flat area of fenland.

N
Nafferton to Nyetimber

Nafferton, nr Driffield, East Yorkshire: Wold House

Many years ago one of the rooms was used as a Catholic chapel, and it may be this that provides the key to the hauntings. On several occasions strange noises have been heard in the middle of the night, including doors opening and footsteps along the corridor. Guests staying in a particular room have also noted that their watches have stopped in the middle of the night.

Nailsworth, Gloucestershire: Gatcombe Park

This haunting, on the face of it, may have more to do with gamekeepers trying to prevent poachers from entering the estate than a genuine manifestation. Gatcombe Park is the home of Princess Anne, and it boasts the apparition of a headless dog, perhaps a Labrador. It is said to brush up against people, after moving quickly and silently toward you. The phantom dog has been seen on several occasions by a variety of different witnesses.

Nannau, nr Dolgellau, Gwynedd

In 1402, Owain Glyndwr visited his cousin, Hywel Sele, in an attempt to persuade him to join him in his revolt against Henry V. They disappeared to talk and plot in the Deer Park, but it is believed that Glyndwr murdered his cousin and hid the body in a hollow oak tree. Some 40 years later, a skeleton said to be Sele's was found in the tree. In 1813, the oak was felled and it is said that this ended Sele's haunting, but some say that his spirit is still active here. A former lady of the house and her pet dog, who were murdered by the Lord of Nannau, haunt the crossroads where the road to Dolgellau meets the way to the Deer Park. The ghosts of a groom and a horse can be heard at the Mules Well (at Ffynnon-y-mulod). The stallion trampled the groom to death after being spooked by the wind.

Nannerch, nr Mold, Clwyd

A black lady haunts a lane that leads to Afonwen. She is a Victorian lady who was killed in an accident while on her way to the chapel. The manifestation often appears in front of on-coming cars and has caused a number of new accidents. It then crosses the road and disappears into the hedgerow.

Nanteos, nr Aberystwyth, Dyfed

A female member of the Powell family, who built the Georgian house in around 1739, is said to haunt this house in the form of a grey lady. She appears to warn of the death of the head of the family living there, and she carries a candelabra for dramatic effect. A phantom horseman is said to haunt the drive to the house, he can be seen late at night. Another ghost is that of a woman who is said to have got out of her deathbed to hide her jewellery. She is seen in several places around the house, presumably still searching for the jewellery that has never been found.

Nantgarw, nr Cardiff, South Glamorgan

Cwn Annwn is a phantom black hound, which is said to be an omen of death. It haunts the surrounding area. You may dissuade it from devouring your soul by brandishing a crucifix. Alternatively, for the multilingual, you can say, in Welsh, 'the blood, the blood which flowed from Jesus' side one afternoon'. Following that, it will trot away and bother someone else.

Nantwich, Cheshire: The Bear Inn

In 1583 the inn caught fire and rapidly became an inferno. The innkeeper, John Seckerton, kept four bears and was as worried about them as the rest of his business, as he had built up a thriving trade of locals and passing travellers alike. In the midst of the flames and chaos, he let the bears out from their cages beside the stables. The people throwing water into the fire had to save themselves from the panic-stricken animals. The apparitions of the four bears can still be seen roaming about the streets. They look scared, just as they would have done all those years ago when they were let out during the fire.

Nantwich, Cheshire: The Red Cow

A 1730s plague victim and her unfortunate child haunt this public house. Although few have seen the manifestation itself, many people have witnessed the sounds of footsteps pacing up and down, accompanied by the rattling of doors.

Napton-on-the-Hill, nr Southam, Warwickshire: St Lawrence's Church

The manifestations of two women dressed in Elizabethan clothing are regular worshippers at this parish church. A number of witnesses have seen them kneeling in prayer in the front pew.

Narborough, Leicestershire: Narborough Arms, Coventry Road

Dating from around 1600, this public house was once used as a church. It is perhaps this that explains the haunting. On a number of occasions, patrons and staff have seen the 'shrouded' figure of a man. It appears, then walks a few paces and disappears through a wall. It is thought that the disappearing point was once a doorway.

Naseby, nr Market Harborough, Northamptonshire

The English Civil War Battle of Naseby in 1645 has caused hauntings of the area. Sadly, one of the main manifestations has ended before our time. In the past this involved a ghostly re-fight of the conflict in the skies over the battlefield, but the spectacle has not been witnessed for many years.

Nechtansmere, nr Letham, Angus

It is said that a battle took place here in 685

between the Picts and the Northumbrians. The smaller Pictish force defeated the Northumbrians. The battlefield, which is the scene of a ghostly re-enactment of the conflict, is now partially covered by the lake. As a result only part of the phantom battle can now be seen along the shoreline.

Nether Stowey, Somerset

The ghost of a monk walks from the church to the house near St Peter's Well for Vespers. At the Over Stowey crossroads is the spirit of 'galley beggar', who sits on a hurdle and laughs, then takes his head in his hand and slides it downhill toward Bincombe and Nether Stowey, bathed in a strange glowing light.

Netherton, nr Dudley, West Midlands

Theopillus Dunn, who died in 1851, was a specialist in recovering lost or stolen items. His ghost is said to haunt a site called Bumble Hole, one of the many places that he frequented during his life.

Netley, nr Southampton, Hampshire: Netley Abbey

The abbey was built by the Cistercians in the 13th century, and two witnesses report having seen a pink lady with a dog at the site. The apparition appeared to have some kind of tapestry behind it, described as pastel in colouring. This manifestation appeared on the chapel wall and for some reason, has been linked to Florence Nightingale. Beware of straying into the abbey ruins on Hallowe'en night, as you may encounter the phantom known as Blind Peter, the ghost of a Cistercian monk that is said to be guarding the hidden treasures of the abbey, which have lain undiscovered since the Dissolution. Legend has it that there is a long tunnel hidden under the abbey ruins, at the end of which lies the treasure itself. A treasure hunter, by the name of Slown, was frightened to death down there.

Netley, nr Southampton, Hampshire: Royal Victoria Military Hospital

The majority of the ruins were demolished in 1966 and may be one of the haunting sites of Florence Nightingale. There were, apparently, several other ghosts walking around the place. The grey lady may be Florence Nightingale, although she tended to appear when a patient was about to die.

Newark, nr Selkirk, Borders: Newark Castle

Fifteenth-century Newark Castle's ruined rectangular tower and wall stands on a mound, but it has strong connections with the 17th century. Following the Battle of Philliphaugh in 1645, the victorious Covenanters murdered around 500 Montrose survivors here. Despite the fact that the massacre was supposed to have taken place on the moor outside the castle, there is a feeling of death and despair in the building, together with the occasional sound of screams. Later research has revealed that the killings did actually take place in the castle courtyard.

Newbury, Berkshire

During the first Battle of Newbury in 1643, Lord Falkland, the Secretary of State, fell from his horse while trying to jump a hedge. Whether he was alive or dead after the fall, he was taken to a nearby farmhouse. It is presumed that he died there as his ghost as been positively identified as haunting the building.

Newcastle-upon-Tyne, Tyne and Wear: St Nicholas Cathedral Church

The manifestation of a knight in full armour

has been seen on several occasions clanking around the church. It is believed that he is the apparition of one of the knights buried in the church, as he tends to appear near a crusader's tomb.

Newchurch, Isle of Wight: Wisteria Cottage

Wisteria Cottage is around 300 years old. At various times it has served as a slaughterhouse and a bakery, and it is now a post office. The old kitchen, which has sat disused for over 100 years, is the centre of the olfactory haunting that pervades the building. The occupants have reported strong smells of frying eggs and bacon and baking cakes and bread.

New Galloway, Dumfries and Galloway: Glenlee House

A grey lady haunts Glenlee House. She is the ghost of Lady Ashburton, who murdered her husband because she could not stand his constant infestation of lice. Soon after she had committed the crime, she in turn was murdered by the butler. Witnesses have seen the grey lady several times, dressed in a rustling, grey silk dress.

Newmarket, Suffolk: Hamilton Stud Lane

Fred Archer, the famous jockey who died in 1886, is said to still ride in ghostly form on the racecourse. His presence has spooked several horses. His ghost is also to be seen at Hamilton Stud Lane. On the heath itself, you may be unfortunate to encounter the Black Shuck, a large phantom dog, although it is unclear whether this is the same creature that haunts Bungay and involves Hugh Bigod.

Newport, Gwent: Newport Castle

Built by the Normans, this castle still has phantom vestiges of its earlier life in the form of an apparition of its first owner. Robert FitzHamon founded the castle here and his spirit is said to appear as a phantom giant. Witnesses report that the manifestation quickly fades if you look straight at it.

Newstead, nr Melrose, Borders

Trimontium was a Roman camp based on the banks of the River Tweed, named after the nearby three peaks of the Eildons. Witnesses report hearing marching soldiers in the area, accompanied by bugle calls and the sounds of soldiers building a camp.

Newstead Abbey, Ravenshead, nr Nottingham, Nottinghamshire

After some 400 years as a priory of the Augustine order, Henry VIII passed the property over to the Byron family as part of his dissolution policy. Unsurprisingly, the manifestation of an evil friar, described as being malicious, cold and dark, has often been seen gloating over the death of a member of the Byron family. The 'Black Friar' has also made appearances at happy occasions to bring the festivities to a close. Notably, he attended the marriage of Lord Byron to Annabella Milbanke. In later years, an electrician working at the abbey was said to have died after seeing the Black Friar. Sophia Hyatt, who was a deaf mute and supposedly fell deeply in love with Byron, haunts the abbey after being killed in a coaching accident. Byron's dog Boatswain has been seen by several staff, particularly in the grounds and on the abbey roof. Other manifestations include heavy footsteps in the Great Hall, the smell of perfume, and women's voices emanating from Lord Byron's bedroom. The famed Ghost Room features an apparition that wraps victims in a cloak and pulls them to the ground.

Newton Aycliffe, Co. Durham: Redworth Hall Hotel

This hotel is said to have a number of different ghosts, including the manifestation of Lady Catherine, now seen as a grey lady. Witnesses have also heard ghostly footsteps and the sounds of a 'phantom party'.

Newton Burgoland, Leicestershire: The Belpher Arms

An unpleasant and potentially dangerous manifestation seems to haunt this pub. Although nothing has actually been seen by either landlords or their customers, several strange and disturbing events have taken place here. The site of the old fireplace experiences sudden drops in temperature, several people have complained of feeling that they were being suffocated by unseen hands and one of the landlord's family felt the sensation of something jumping on to their bed.

Newton-le-Willows, nr St Helens, Merseyside

In August 1648, Oliver Cromwell rode into the village and rounded up all the royalist sympathisers in the area. He had them hanged on the spot. For many years, on August nights, witnesses have reported hearing the sounds of marching feet. On Castle Hill, on the road to Golborne, several people have suggested that they have seen a white lady, or perhaps a monk. The figure certainly wears white.

Newton Toney, Wiltshire

It is said that there are strange noises to be heard here at night. Locals suggest that this may be related to the ghost of a parson that has reportedly been seen.

Nomansland, nr Dodington, Somerset

At midnight on Christmas Eve you may encounter the manifestation of a phantom coach and four black horses. Witnesses state that it drives up to the village, turns around and then drives away again. Perhaps related to this haunting in some way is the ghost of a white lady who walks from nearby Holford to Nether Stowey. On other occasions, presumably when she gets tired of the walk, she catches the phantom coach.

North Allington, nr Bridport, Dorset: The Boot Inn

On the left-hand side of the bar, two figures have been seen sitting at a table. One is dressed in khaki uniform, while the other is a more vague shape. In the late 1870s a man entered the public house with a loaded gun. It went off in the bar, hitting a regular customer in the head. He died the next day, but his spirit, wearing period clothing and hobnail boots, haunts the other side of the bar. Upstairs the ghost of a grey lady, thought to be a former landlady of the King's Arms just down the road, only appears to customers who have fallen ill inside the bar and have been taken upstairs. It is said that her spirit remains in the area in order to seek revenge on the Cavalier who killed her, who was staying at The Boot Inn.

Northampton, Northamptonshire: The Shipman's

Over 100 years ago, Harry Franklin, the then manager of the pub, committed suicide by cutting his own throat. The unfortunate man took a week to die. Since then a ghostly figure has been seen standing near the fruit machine in the bar, glasses jump off the bar onto the floor and footsteps are heard on the stairs.

Northampton, Northamptonshire: The Wig and Pen

The cellar seems to be at the centre of the

poltergeist activity that is extremely active in this pub. Lights switch on and off, objects are moved around and dogs will not enter several of the rooms.

North Benfleet, nr Southend-on-Sea, Essex: Screeching Boy's Wood

Two different and equally plausible stories account for the strange name given to the woods near Fanton Hall and the A13. Both of the explanations are said to date to around 1734. The first is the tale of a young plough-boy who had his head cut off by a woods-man, and the second is a similar story which states that the murder was actually perpetrated by the boy's master. Whichever is the case, the sounds are said to be his cries just at the point of his death.

Northfleet, Kent

A 1930s council house, 16 Waterdales, is home to the ghosts of a young girl with fair hair and a headless man. There does not appear to be a reason for the hauntings, so we can only surmise that the ghosts pre-date the present building.

North Huish, Devon

The former manor house, now a rectory, is said to be haunted by a monk. Witnesses have suggested that the manifestation is bearded and has brown hair. The haunting may be related to the presence of priest holes in the house.

Northiam, Sussex: Hayes Hotel

This 16th-century building has a Georgian façade and is haunted by a ghostly spinner. There was a spinning wheel in an alcove of the main bar, and on a number of occasions witnesses saw a little old lady actually working the wheel. She is described as being rather wizened. There is another ghost in the hotel, believed to be a baker's daughter who

was murdered in one of the bedrooms. In the late 1970s, the landlady encountered the ghost when it appeared in her bedroom. She described the apparition as being young, aged around 30, wearing a white hat and a grey dress or gown. After a few seconds, the manifestation disappeared.

North Petherton, Somerset

For many years a ghostly corpse and coffin have been seen in a hollow in the roadway. Many horse riders have reported that their steeds have stopped here and refused to move. Others have reported a coffin with a corpse sitting on top of it. Many years ago, a horse fell at the hollow and broke its back. Whether this, or the ghostly corpse, affects the horses is unknown.

North Tidworth, Wiltshire

There is a well-authenticated apparition here. However, some describe it as a high-lander, while others contend that it is a Roman soldier. The latter is more likely as a Roman pavement was excavated here.

Norton Fitzwarren, nr Taunton, Somerset

The haunting here is more folklore than a haunting. Many years ago, there was a battle at Norton Camp, a nearby hill fort. After the battle was over and the bodies were piled up, the bones transformed themselves into a dragon that proceeded to terrorise the area. As can be seen on a screen in the church, the dragon was slain by Fulk Fitzwarren.

Norwich, Norfolk: The Adam and Eve

This 14th-century inn, standing on St Martin's Plain, was the place where Lord Sheffield met his maker during Robert Kett's Peasant Revolt. On 1 August 1549, Robert Kett met Lord Sheffield in battle. At the crucial point,

Sheffield took off his helmet to encourage his troops and a local butcher called Fulke bashed him over the head. Sheffield was taken into the pub, where he died. Fulke met his end dangling from a hangman's rope after the Battle of Dussindale. Sheffield, meanwhile, haunts the pub to this day. Regulars call him Sam.

Norwich, Norfolk: The Bridge House Inn

During the 16th century, the cellars of this pub were used as dungeons to hold the followers of Wycliffe. After being held here, they took the short walk to Lollards Pit, where they were burned at the stake. It is one of Wycliffe's followers that is said to still haunt the inn.

Norwich, Norfolk: The Curate's House

This Tudor building is said to be haunted by strange footsteps walking along a corridor. The site was a former synagogue, which was burned down with much of the surrounding area many years ago. There were no reports of a haunting here until the skeleton of a woman was found in the cellar. It is believed that she may have died as a result of the fire.

Norwich, Norfolk: The Maddermarket Theatre

This building was once, during the 18th century, a Roman Catholic church. As a result, it seems that the haunting has both a religious and an 18th-century feel about it. Witnesses have reported seeing the ghost of a monk or a priest, dressed in a black robe, performing mass.

Norwich, Norfolk: Magdalen Square

In around 1873, a woman was murdered in this building. At the time it was a pub, but it is now a charity shop. The murder, it is said,

occurred in one of the upstairs rooms. Consequently, the volunteers in the shop have reported hearing footsteps on the stairs, draughts, cold spots and the feeling that they are not alone. On a couple of occasions, the apparition of a woman has even been seen on the staircase.

Norwich, Norfolk: Norwich Castle

Dating back to around 1067, the castle now resembles a keep rather than a conventional fortification. It has served various functions over the years, including time as the county jail, but now houses a museum. Among the numerous ghosts said to haunt the structure are a floating skull and the spirit of Mrs Bulwer. Although she was a great benefactor to the museum, she now enjoys scaring the wits out of people. She appears as an old woman in a black, Victorian-style dress. In 1820, three men awaiting transportation to Australia were nearly scared to death by something supernatural, prompting an investigation by the local magistrates.

Norwich, Norfolk: Norwich Railway Station

In September 1874 a railway accident occurred between Norwich and Great Yarmouth, claiming the lives of 23 people. Two trains met on a single track. Ghostly activity continues in the form of a hideous apparition with sharp fangs and foetid breath, appearing to be something like a rat, which has been seen in the area. Whether this is in any way related to the train crash is unknown.

Nottingham, Nottinghamshire: AA Headquarters, Derby Road

The ghost of an AA Area Supervisor haunts the building at around one in the morning. The unfortunate man died of a heart attack in his office at around 5.30pm, after having worked too many shifts without a break. He is described as wearing a grey suit and has been positively identified by some of his co-workers at the time. The apparition also has a tendency to crash around some nights making quite a noise.

Nottingham, Nottinghamshire: Colwick Hall

Dating from around 1776, this former hall is now a hotel. It has a white lady that is said to haunt the east wing and the grounds. The explanation has a particularly sad conclusion, in that the ghost is said to be Mary Ann Chaworth-Musters, who died after catching pneumonia. Byron much admired her as a girl and called her the 'Morning Star of Annesley'. In 1831, Reform Bill protesters attacked Colwick Hall and Mary Ann fled into the gardens to hide. It was here that she caught the cold that subsequently killed her.

Nottingham, Nottinghamshire: Hippo Restaurant, Bridlesmith Gate

The basement of this building seems to hold the clues to the hauntings that have terrified staff and customers for a number of years. The hauntings were triggered off by the discovery of a hidden basement during renovations in 1969. It is said that the basement connects with some ancient caves that lie beneath the city. Witnesses have reported extensive poltergeist activity, footsteps and even the manifestation of a ghostly figure. The manager in 1971 described the apparition as appearing to be a male Quaker, complete with a dark coat and large hat. It was seen sitting at one of the tables in the newly refurbished basement.

Nottingham, Nottinghamshire: North Wilford Power Station

Old George haunts the Screen Room and the Turbine Room of this power station. By all accounts, George is the ghost of a man who worked at the station for over 25 years. He is described as being short, wearing a checked shirt, a blue overall and a cap. He also has thick lips and wide eyes. He has been seen by several of the workers at the station and is said to only be visible for a few moments before smiling and then disappearing.

Nottingham, Nottinghamshire: Nottingham Castle

The Countess of Nottingham haunts the Long Gallery, and it is said that if you encounter the apparition then you will be dead within a year. Beneath the castle is a series of underground passageways that are the favoured haunt of Queen Isabella. After she and Roger Mortimer murdered her husband, Edward II, at Berkeley Castle, she was captured in 1330 and held here. Mortimer was put to death almost immediately, but Isabella remained incarcerated in a variety of places for 30 years. She is also said to haunt Castle Rising. The final ghost here has not been described, but apparently haunts the Bonnington Room. It is prone to setting off the alarms in the middle of the night.

Nottingham, Nottinghamshire: The Trip to Jerusalem

Crusaders used the pub as they travelled from the north to join King Richard I. The haunting of the inn goes back to the early 14th century, when Edward II was overthrown by his wife, Queen Isabella, and her lover Roger Mortimer. Prince Edward was offered the crown, but refused it until his father officially abdicated. After some persuasion, Edward II agreed, and his son became King Edward III on 24 January 1327. The real power behind the thrown was still vested in his mother and Mortimer. When his father was murdered at Berkeley Castle on 21 September 1327 by Sir Thomas Gurney and Sir John Maltravers, under instruction from Mortimer, Edward III realised that he could soon find himself in the same position. He bided his time and waited to strike and on 19 October 1330, while Isabella and Mortimer were staying at Nottingham Castle, Edward and his best men arrived at the Trip to Jerusalem. They used the secret underground tunnel to gain access to the well-guarded castle. By midnight they were poised outside Isabella's room. They burst in and Edward seized Mortimer. To his mother's cries of 'Fair son, have pity on the gentle Mortimer', Mortimer was dragged from the room and thrown into a dungeon. It is still known as Mortimer's Hole, where he spent many hours pacing up and down, pondering his fate. Some time later, he was taken to London and tried for murdering Edward II. After being incarcerated in the Tower, he was hanged at Tyburn on 29 November 1330. Isabella, meanwhile, was imprisoned for the rest of her life. Mortimer's ghost has been heard pacing up and down in Mortimer's Hole. This cell is next door to the inn. During World War Two, a group of American servicemen were leaving the inn when they heard a woman screaming in a 'foreign' language. They claim to have heard, in French, the same phrase uttered by Isabella on that fateful night when her son took control: 'bel fitz, eiez pitie du gentile Mortimer'.

Nottingham, Nottinghamshire: Wilford Ambulance Station

The manifestation of a male ghost has been seen and heard around the station for a number of years. One of the ambulance crew reported seeing a stranger heading for the toilets, but when he checked, there was no one to be seen. On another occasion, crew claimed to have seen a shadow moving around to the side of them. Doors have opened and closed without explanation and footsteps have been heard.

Nottingham, Nottinghamshire: Wollaton Hall

Built between 1580 and 1588 by Sir Francis Willoughby, the hall now houses a museum. Lord and Lady Middleton were the last owners before the City of Nottingham purchased it in 1925. Lady Middleton had sustained serious injuries after a fall down the stairs, and spent the last years of her life downstairs in what is now Room 19. As a result, the room is haunted by her and it is said that she makes her presence felt at night. If viewed from outside, the room is bathed in candlelight despite the fact that all of the lights are off and there is no one in the building.

Nottingham, Nottinghamshire: Ye Olde Salutation Inn

Built in the 15th century, this pub has two ghosts. The first is a former landlord who accidentally poisoned himself; the second has a far more forbidding appearance. This is the ghost of a highwayman, who appears with a pair of pistols in his hands.

Nunney, nr Frome, Somerset: The George Inn

This was the site of a hanging place dating from the period of the Monmouth Rebellion. Following the Battle of Sedgemoor in 1685, numerous rebels were hanged and then put in gibbets outside the pub. To this day you can hear the ghostly gibbets swinging in the breeze.

Nunney, nr Frome, Somerset: Nunney Castle

Built in 1373, this castle suffered very badly during the English Civil War, but it is a much later apparition that haunts the area near here. A ghostly hitch hiker haunts the road to Frome. He has been seen thumbing a lift, but also, more frighteningly, he has appeared on the back seat of passing cars, visible just long enough to scare the living daylights out of the driver. The hitch hiker is described as being about 35 years old, wearing a sports jacket and flannel trousers. His favoured hitching spot is at the end of the lane leading to the castle.

Nutwell Court, nr Exton, Devon

This was the home of the Drake family after the death of Sir Francis. The ghost of Elliot Drake haunts the main road nearby. He challenged a friend to a horse race along the road, but both he and his horse fell and broke their necks. His spirit is said to appear on the anniversary of his death.

Nyetimber, West Sussex: The Lion Hotel

A grey lady has been seen and heard wandering around the ground floor and in one of the bedrooms in this 14th-century building. In bedroom No.5, there is a bricked-up doorway leading to an inner room where the grey lady has been seen several times. It is thought that she was the mistress of a 17th-century smuggler who frequented the hotel. She was killed because she knew too many of the smuggler's secrets.

O

Oakley to Oystermouth Castle

Oakley, Hampshire

A female manifestation is said to walk around here, as if she is lost or has misplaced something. She peers at anyone for a second or two before disappearing, perhaps in the hope that they can help her.

Oare, nr Lynmouth, Devon

The former parish priest haunts the church. It is said that he will greet a new priest by ringing the church bells. He will then appear to them when they come to investigate.

Offord Cluny, nr Huntingdon, Cambridgeshire

Four generations of new wives establishing themselves in this old manor house have witnessed the apparition of an old woman very soon after they have moved into the house. It is believed that she may be one of the first women to have lived here.

Ogmore Castle, nr Bridgend, Mid Glamorgan

A white lady is said to guard treasure buried here. On one occasion in the past she showed a man the treasure and allowed him to take half of it. When he returned to claim the remainder, she drove him away, but not before scratching him with her fingernails. He died of blood poisoning.

Okehampton, Devon: King's Way

Wicked Lady Howard and her Coach of Bones can be seen along the old road, the King's Way. The 17th-century coach is said to be built from the bones of her four husbands, all of whom, it is said, she murdered. A skeletal animal, probably a dog, follows the coach. She has also been seen sitting on a stone near the castle, combing her hair.

Okehampton, Devon: The White Hart Hotel

The manifestation of a young boy called Peter haunts this hotel sited in the centre of the town. Numerous children have complained that he hides their toys and insists that they play hide and seek with him.

Oldbury, nr Hartshill, Warwickshire: The Blue Bell Inn

Built in the 18th century, although substantially modernised over the years, this pub is haunted by an old man whose face is often seen peering through the window. It is believed that the face belongs to William Parker, who was a servant of the Turton family of Brades Hall. He was a regular at the pub and met his end when a chimney fell on him. Other witnesses have seen a large blue shape in one of the bedrooms but it is not known whether or not this is related to William Parker.

Old Cleeve, nr Minehead, Somerset: Bardon House

The Bardon Coach, a headless dog and the ghost of Robert Leigh haunt the grounds of the house. In the past, the phantom coach was actually seen, but now witnesses only hear the sound of a coach passing by. The headless black dog is supposed to signal the imminent death of a member of the Leigh family. The manifestation of Robert Leigh is confused, as he appears headless, but carrying a head that is not his own. More strangely, when the building was known as Old Cleeve House, stories surrounded the white dove of Bardon, which was supposed to have been the spirit of Mary Queen of Scots. It was at Bardon House that the Bardon papers were faked that led to her execution.

Oldham, Greater Manchester: Colosseum Theatre

The actor Harold Norman, who was killed on stage in 1947, haunts the theatre. The accident occurred when he was involved in a stage fight as part of a performance of *Macbeth*. Witnesses suggest that he tends to appear on Thursday, the day that he was killed.

Old Hunstanton, Norfolk: The Lodge Hotel

This 400-year-old building was in an area much frequented by 18th-century smugglers. There is said to be a smugglers' tunnel leading from the hotel to the beach. Two customs men were shot and killed and buried in the local churchyard, and they are said to haunt the area still. An elderly grey lady has also been seen in some of the corridors of the hotel, passing freely through locked doors. It is believed that the haunting has its centre in a small attic room at the top of the building.

Oldmeldrum, Aberdeenshire: Meldrum House Hotel

A white lady has been seen on many occasions and seems to be particularly good with children. If they are left to play alone in a room, she will come in and look after them. She also gave a guest an icy kiss in 1985. It is believed that she is the apparition of a former nanny.

Otterburn, nr Hexham, Northumberland

The Scots defeated the English in a battle here in 1388. As with many other battlefield hauntings, witnesses have reported seeing apparitions fighting in the sky above the site.

Oulton, nr Lowestoft, Suffolk: Oulton House

Not only can you spot the Wild Hunt here at around midnight, but there is also a manifestation of a lady bearing a poison cup. The apparent explanation goes back to the reign of George II. The squire of Oulton House returned from hunting to find his wife with her lover. The man killed the husband and the couple fled. She left her daughter, who later became engaged to a local farmer. On the eve of her wedding a black carriage drew up, within which was her mother, who offered her a poison cup, which she unknowingly drank from. The mother carried out the evil deed to prevent her daughter from relaying the story of her husband's death and implicating her in the murder.

Oulton Broad, nr Lowestoft, Suffolk

The *Mayfly* set sail from Great Yarmouth bearing a treasure chest containing £4,000 and a young woman. Presumably the temptation was too much for the wherry's captain; he made for foreign parts. The voyage ended in tragedy. The sole survivor of the crew and passengers was the cabin boy, who escaped in a dinghy. Witnesses have seen the *Mayfly* making its way across Oulton Broad. The writer George Burrows, who lived in a cottage overlooking the broad, also haunts the area. Several witnesses have seen him walking around in a wide-brimmed hat and long cloak.

Oundle, Northamptonshire: Nene Cottage

Originally a 17th-century cottage and former inn, Nene Cottage was the site of a number of hauntings when new owners moved in during the 1970s. Door handles rattled in the late afternoon, and one of the rooms was said to have a particularly odd and forbidding atmosphere. Soon after, footsteps were heard and shadows were seen on the walls. Finally, they began to see full apparitions appearing. The first was a young girl with long black hair. She was encountered sitting in the outhouse, crouching down. She was wearing a nightdress. The second ghost was a boy with long fair hair, with what appeared to be early 20th-century clothing. He haunted the garden and was seen leaping around the grass and then disappearing into the garden wall.

Oundle, Northamptonshire: The Ship Inn

Several years ago one of the landlords committed suicide by jumping from one of the upstairs windows. To this day, several landlords, staff and customers have felt something push past them on the staircase. Certainly the bedroom from which he jumped has a strange, disturbing atmosphere.

Oundle, Northamptonshire: The Talbot Hotel

A phantom, believed to be Mary Queen of Scots, is said to haunt two of the bedrooms and the staircase. It is believed that the staircase was taken from Fotheringhay Castle, the very steps that Mary trod on the day she lost her head.

Owlpen, nr Stroud, Gloucestershire

Margaret of Anjou, who was the Queen Consort of Henry VI, haunts Owlpen Manor. She stayed here before the Battle of Tewksbury in 1471. She is described as being very serene and wearing beautiful clothing. She particularly appears in the room in which she stayed.

Owmby, nr Lincoln, Lincolnshire

Tiddy Mun is a horrific apparition said to live on the marshes. It is described as being childlike in size, but with the appearance of an old man. During the 17th century the creature was blamed for the murder of several Dutch engineers who were working on the drainage canals in the area.

Oxford, Oxfordshire: Exeter College

A headless Elizabethan phantom, dressed in a gown, brown breeches and a yellow jacket, is said to haunt this college. It is believed that he is the manifestation of John Crocker, a scholar, who is buried in the chapel.

Oxford, Oxfordshire: Magpie Lane

A brown lady, said to be Prudence Burcote, haunts a Tudor building on the corner of this road. Although the Burcotes were Parliamentarians, Prudence took a Cavalier lover. It is not certain whether the man died or ran away, but her family disowned her and she died of a broken heart.

Oxford, Oxfordshire: Merton College

Cromwell shot Colonel Frances Windebank here in 1645. He had just surrendered to the Parliamentarians before his death. His spirit can be seen walking around the Fellow's Garden.

Oxford, Oxfordshire: St Giles's Church

A grey lady haunts the churchyard. Legend has it that she left all of her money to the church but her relatives spirited the cash away before her executors could act on her wishes.

Oxford, Oxfordshire: St John's College

The amazing manifestation of Archbishop Laud has been seen by witnesses bowling his head toward them. On other occasions Laud will walk several inches above the ground, matching the old level of the floor. The Archbishop was beheaded in 1645 for his stand against Parliament and is buried underneath the altar of the chapel.

Oxford, Oxfordshire: University College

Obadiah Walker, who was master of the college during the reign of James II, haunts Room 1 on Staircase 8. This was the room that he occupied during his tenure.

Oxford, Oxfordshire: Westgate

Executed in 1752 for the murder of her father, Mary Blandy haunts the area. Some say that a bird landed on the scaffold as she was being hanged and as a consequence no birds sing in this spot.

Oxney Bottom, nr Dover, Kent

A grey lady is said to walk across the road, and has caused several fatal accidents. In the woods to the left of the road are the ruins of a church with an underground stream, but it is not known whether this has any connection to the apparition. On one occasion a bus conductor stopped to pick her up and swears that she went upstairs. When he went to collect the fare nobody was there.

Oxwich, nr Swansea, West Glamorgan

A white stallion that appears to be walking on its back legs haunts the churchyard. Witnesses also state that they have seen an indistinct shape that seems to glide between the gravestones.

Oystermouth Castle, nr Swansea, West Glamorgan

This 11th-century castle, now in ruins, is haunted by a white lady. Although we do not know who she is, witnesses have reported seeing a bleeding wound on her back and have also said that the apparition appears to be crying.

P

Park Farm to Pyecombe

Park Farm, nr Taunton, Devon

The ghost of Sir John Popham (d.1607) makes

its way from the copse above the farm to the family vault in Wellington Church. On one occasion he caused so many problems that a farmer employed a white witch to get rid of him. The copse has a muddy pool that was thought to be an entrance to Hell, from which Popham had escaped.

Peasdown St John, Somerset: The Waggon and Horses

The manifestation of a tall man, wearing a strange black hat, has been seen both in and around the pub. Landlords and staff also report significant poltergeist activity in the building.

Peebles, Borders: Cross Keys

Built in 1693 as a coaching inn, the Cross Keys featured extensively in Sir Walter Scott's *Waverley* novels. A former landlady, Meg Odds, haunts it. She has been seen in and around the pub for many years.

Peel Castle, Peel, Isle of Man

Sax Rohmer, writer of such classics as *Fu Manchu*, spent a night in the castle. He reported hearing a dog howling in the passageway outside his room. Rohmer believed that the noise must have pagan connections. Other sightings of the Moddey Dhoo (or Mauthe Dhoog), as the spectral dog is known, are linked with deaths. A Methodist parson died within a week of seeing the manifestation, and a drunken soldier who went out to hunt the dog, saw it and died within minutes screaming 'the black dog, the ghost dog!'

Pembroke, Dyfed: The Port Hotel

A former maid, who is said to exude the strong smell of lavender, haunts the hotel. The building became a hotel in 1947 after the nearby dockyard closed.

Penally, nr Tenby, Dyfed

An eerie phantom funeral procession has been seen taking a cross-country route in this area. The manifestation was particularly common in the 19th century, although some claim to have seen it more recently.

Pendragon Castle, nr Kirkby Stephen, Cumbria

Sir Hugh de Morville, one of the knights who murdered Thomas Becket, is said to haunt his former home. Legend has it that there is also the ghost of a black hen at the castle, whose purpose is to conceal the burial site of a hidden treasure.

Penfound Manor, Cornwall

Kate Penfound's ghost can be seen on 26 April. Kate was in love with a neighbour, John Trebarfoot, but his family were Parliamentarians and hers were staunch royalists. Her father, Arthur Penfound, caught them trying to elope and killed John. Arthur Penfound's ghost also haunts the house. He was a famous smuggler in these parts and killed more than one customs officer.

Pengersick Castle, nr Penzance, Cornwall

The 13th-century Henry de Pengersick was excommunicated for evil deeds and now haunts the castle. The castle is also haunted by the ghost of Mr Millington, who bought the property during the reign of Henry VIII. He tried to murder his wife by poisoning her, but she exchanged the goblets and they were both carried off by the devil.

Pengethley Manor, nr Ross-on-Wye, Herefordshire

A ghost known as Harriet is said to have been a maid at the time when a fire gutted the building in the late 1800s. It is believed that she died as a result of her injuries from the fire. Several people have reported sensing her presence beside their beds and have also heard a noise coming from an empty room. On other occasions her presence has been felt in the reception area, and sometimes doors will close by themselves.

Penhow Castle, nr Newport, Gwent

A blue or grey lady haunts the castle, and is described as being a young girl, possibly a maid. Witnesses have seen her in the Great Hall and it is believed that her appearance may have something to do with restoration work that took place in the 1970s.

Penhurst Place, nr Tonbridge, Kent

Sir Philip Sidney, who was born at Penhurst in 1559, is said to haunt this place. He is not alone, as it is also said that the Black Prince, Henry VIII (who feasts here) and Queen Elizabeth I (who dances here) are all in spectral attendance.

Penkaet Castle (Fountainhall House), nr Tranent, Lothian

John Cockburn once owned the house and still haunts it, as does the apparition of a beggar called Alexander Hamilton, who was hanged for witchcraft. Strangest of all is a haunted bed that was once slept in by King Charles I. The bed-related manifestations began in 1923 when the four-poster, sporting a death mask, was moved into the house. It was a present from some the students of Professor Holbourn, who owned the house then. The following year, a guest was given the room and found that the bedclothes were in a state of disarray, despite the fact that the housekeeper had just tidied the room. The housekeeper said that this had happened on several occasions in the past year. Various noises have been heard coming out of the room, including the sounds of someone moving around, someone using the bed and moving furniture and even someone falling out of the bed. When a female guest stayed in the room, people ran to her aid when they clearly heard her fall out of bed. When they reached the room she was sound asleep. The story surrounding Alexander Hamilton is also odd. He was sent on his way when he begged for food and shelter one night. His response was to bind the gates with blue thread, an act of witchcraft. Two days later Lady Ormiston, the lady of the house, and her eldest daughter died as a result of a mysterious illness. Hamilton was captured and admitted the two murders and numerous other crimes that the local authorities were keen to clear up. He was hanged at Castle Hill, Edinburgh. His ghost still returns to Penkaet, repeating the gate-binding trick. The ghost of John Cockburn, who murdered a man called Deton, has acquired the name 'Gentleman John' and actually stops banging about if someone tells him to do so.

Penn Common, nr Wolverhampton, West Midlands: The Stag's Head

The apparition of a Victorian lady, said to be the wife of a local vicar, has been seen sitting on a beer barrel in the corner of the bar. Apparently, the lady and her husband enjoyed visiting the pub for a drink, which must have caused quite a stir in those days, and she is unable to break the habit, even after death.

Penrith, Cumbria: Beacon Hill

The ghost of Thomas Nicholson, who was hanged and gibbeted here in 1767 for committing murder, haunts the area in the form of a skeleton.

Penrith, Cumbria: Blakehills

On Midsummer's Eve, 23 June 1735, a farm labourer was working on William Lancaster's farm when he saw a column of troops marching from the north across the eastern side of the Fell. Given the fact that there is a 1000ft drop on either side of the Fell, he took it to be a genuine troop of soldiers. He told Lancaster and others, but no one believed him. On Midsummer's Eve two years later, Lancaster himself saw it. A great host of men, marching five abreast, following the same route as the man had said. He saw a mounted officer in front of each of the companies; presently he called his whole family, who also witnessed the event. By nightfall, the troops were still marching although the marching was more ragged, and eventually darkness obscured them. Lancaster was not believed either, and the phantom army was not seen again until 1745. By then, Lancaster had assembled some 30 people and this time the apparitions were all the more impressive. Carriages could now be seen among the troops. The following morning, the Fell was investigated and not a single footprint or hoof mark was found.

Penryn, Cornwall

In the last few days before Christmas, a phantom coach drawn by headless horses haunts the town. If the coachman makes eye contact with you, it is said that you will die. The campanologist, Captain Martin, haunts St Gluvias's Church; he drowned in the 1880s after his ship was wrecked.

Pentre Meyrick, nr Cowbridge, South Glamorgan

In what may be a manifestation created by the devil, a short, fat man has been seen to roll down the hill and fall into the old quarry in a shower of sparks.

Penzance, Cornwall: Chapel Street

The town is haunted by the apparition of a phantom coach and headless horses, and also by the apparition of Mrs Baines. She had employed a guard to protect her orchard.

However, she believed that he was sleeping on the job. She crept up on him one night and he promptly shot her.

Penzance, Cornwall: The Dolphin Inn

Sir John Hawkins, when enlisting local Cornishmen to fight the Spanish Armada in 1588, used this inn. Judge Jeffreys is said to have held one of his courts here, and in the cellars there are still reminders of the prisoners that were held in custody before attending his Bloody Assizes. Smugglers also used it as a hiding place for illicit spirits and wines. In the 1960s, two casks of brandy were found hidden in the cellars, still in good condition. Penzance was the first port of call for ships making their way from the New World to England, and it is almost certain that the first pipe of tobacco to be smoked in this country was smoked at the Dolphin. There are believed to be two ghosts at the pub. The first is that of an old English sea captain. He is said to wear lace ruffles and a three-cornered hat, and it is believed that he died here. The second is the ghost of a fair-haired young man, who fell to his death from the loft to the cellars in February 1873. Both have been seen, but their manifestations are more often heard than seen.

Penzance, Cornwall: Kenegie

The Bolitho family lived here until the 1920s and it is the manifestation of one of their housekeepers that haunts the house. She has been described as being tall and having a large bunch of keys dangling from the belt around her black dress. Whether the other haunting is related to this housekeeper is unknown, but a girl's laughter has been heard and young women who have visited the house have experienced a ghostly hand stroking their faces.

Perranzabuloe, nr St Agnes, Cornwall

Walking in Perranzabuloe churchyard one day, an old woman was said to have spotted a pair of false teeth protruding from the soil. Thinking that she might have a use for them, and feeling sure that the previous owner would not, she dug them up and took them home. That night the poor old woman was terrified to be awoken by an unearthly noise outside her cottage. 'Give me back my teeth', came the unearthly wail, 'give me back my teeth'. Shivering with fear and not daring to look outside, she hurled the false teeth out of the cottage window and the noise ceased. She heard the faint sound of footsteps retreating in the direction of the churchyard. Next morning, when she fearfully ventured outside the cottage, the old woman could find no sign of footprints, and there was no sign of the false teeth.

Petworth, West Sussex: The Angel Hotel

A sad tale of two old ladies seems to be the explanation for the haunting of this pub. The two women were guests at the hotel and one came downstairs and sat by the inglenook fire, waiting for her friend. Unfortunately, the other lady fell down the stairs and died. Grief-stricken, the surviving woman died a few days later, but her ghost can still be seen sitting in the chair, waiting for her friend.

Pevensey Castle, Pevensey, East Sussex

Fourteenth-century Lady Pelham haunts the remains of this Roman fort. Her apparition has been seen on the ramparts and this may be related to the reports of an army being seen massing on the marshes below the castle. Lady Pelham was a supporter of Bolingbroke, and she held the castle and died defending it.

Pimperne, Dorset: Pimperne Church

A former soldier became a notorious poacher in the 1780s, and on one fatal occasion several gamekeepers surrounded him. He managed to kill one of them before he was over-powered. In the struggle he had one of his hands chopped off. After a period in Dorchester prison he was released and moved to London, where he died. However, his severed hand was buried in the churchyard at Pimperne. It is this ghostly hand that has been seen both in the church and at the spot where the fight took place at Bussey Stool Farm.

Pinkworth(y) Pond, nr Challacombe, Devon

This man-made pond lies near the treacherous bog called The Chains. The ghost of farmer Gammon haunts it. He was from Bowley Barton, and drowned himself after a rebuffed marriage proposal in 1889.

Plas Pren, nr Denbigh, Clwyd

A ghostly Roman soldier is said to stand guard on the bridge here. If he sees you, then it is said that you will die. The ruined hunting lodge near the Sportsman's Arms is also said to be haunted by a skeleton.

Plas Teg, nr Wrexham, Clwyd

The house was built in 1610 and owned by Sir John Trevor. A white lady, said to be the ghost of a 16th-century girl who drowned in the well, haunts the house. Her lover, who committed suicide after he heard of her death, accompanies her.

Plaxtol, Kent: Old Soar Manor

Built in 1290, Old Soar Manor consists of just six rooms and a chapel, and was originally owned by the Colpepper family. Edward II's men murdered William Colpepper's son at Leeds Castle in 1326. It is believed that the Colpeppers had not endeared themselves to the monarch after Queen Isabella was refused entry into the castle in 1321. During the 18th century, the Geary family owned the manor.

One of their dairymaids was called Jenny, and at 17 she fell in love with Ted, a farm worker. The Gearys had a huge dinner that Christmas in 1775, and one of the guests was the family priest. He was drunk and went into the kitchen after more ale. He found Jenny there and dragged her into the barn and raped her. Jenny fell pregnant as a result but was too scared to say what had happened. As the pregnancy became more obvious, her father and Ted wanted nothing to do with her, and she could not tell Master Geary as he would not believe her. She was left with the prospect of confronting the rapist priest. What happened next is open to different interpretations, but the gist of the story is this. Jenny found the priest in the chapel and he told her that he could not marry her as he was a Roman Catholic priest. He was perturbed that Ted wanted nothing to do with her and realised that if the scandal were ever made public then he would be defrocked. He suggested that she find another man willing to marry her. At that point he may have left, but the next incident may prove that he did not. Perhaps hungry and faint, Jenny passed out and hit her head on the piscina, and the priest 'found' her dead in two inches of holy water. It was assumed that Jenny had committed suicide and she was buried in unconsecrated ground. Since then, manifestations may have the answer to the puzzle of how a young girl managed to fall with her face ending up in so little water. Witnesses have reported sudden drops of temperature in the chapel and the feeling of a ghostly presence, coupled with the sound of unearthly music. One witness actually saw the crime being re-enacted when a phantom figure of a priest was seen bending over the piscina. Another, older witness, who had worked on the farm in the early part of the 20th century, frequently heard the sound of a woman's footsteps pacing the floor of the empty room upstairs. The room above is the chapel and the month was June, around the time that Jenny met her end.

Pluckley, nr Ashford, Kent: Black Horse Inn

The Black Horse Inn became a pub in the early 19th century, although the building is nearly 700 years old. It is not known who the ghost of the Black Horse is but he seems to take great delight in making things disappear, only to make them reappear again in another part of the pub, at times varying from one day to two years. He is not fussy what he takes: keys, clothing and paperwork have all disappeared and it is most inconvenient for the landlord and his staff.

Pluckley, nr Ashford, Kent: Blacksmith's Arms

At the crossroads near the pub, appropriately called 'Fright Corner', an old gypsy woman, huddled in a shawl, has often been seen sitting against the wall of the bridge that crosses Pinnock Stream. It was at this spot that the old woman, who earned her living selling bundles of watercress, accidentally burned herself to a gruesome death when she fell asleep smoking her old clay pipe, which set fire to her shawl. Of late, only a small pink glow has been seen at dusk, coming from the side of the bridge. Just a few yards away, the stump of an old tree is all that remains of the scene where a highwayman had his last fight. Having been finally cornered, he stood with his back to the tree and his attacker plunged his sword through the man's body, embedding the blade in the bark of the tree. On bright moonlit nights, the whole scene is silently re-enacted by the phantom participants.

Pluckley, nr Ashford, Kent: Dering Chapel

Lady Dering, who died several centuries ago, lies buried in the Dering Chapel. It is said that in life she was as wicked as she was beautiful. When she died, her husband ordered that she be laid to rest in three lead coffins, each fitting inside the other, these to be placed in an oak casket, which was then to be put in the family vault. His last act, before she was interred, was to place a red rose on her breast. Lady Dering, complete with the red rose she was interred with, has been seen many times in the churchyard. There have been unexplained knocking noises heard coming from the direction of the Dering Chapel, as well as unexplained lights that have been seen to shine through the stained-glass windows. The ghost of a woman in modern dress also haunts the church, although who she is and what her connection with the church is, is not known.

Pluckley, nr Ashford, Kent: Dering Woods

Until Dering Woods was flattened in the 1960s, the ghost of a suicide, an 18th-century Army colonel who hanged himself in the woods, was seen dangling from one of the trees. The figure of a soldier has also been seen many times walking along a footpath through the park wood, and it is thought that these two may be connected, if they are not the same ghost.

Pluckley, nr Ashford, Kent: Dicky Buss's Lane

Close to the Black Horse lies Dicky Buss's Lane, where a schoolmaster hanged himself from a tree at the beginning of the 19th century. The ghostly form of this man has been seen many times, swinging from one of the overhanging branches. He has been described as wearing a frock coat and dark-striped trousers.

Pluckley, nr Ashford, Kent: Elvey Farm

Originally built as a barn in the 15th century, the building is now a house and is haunted by an unseen walker. He has been known to bolt the door and throw hay around. On one occasion, the manifestation moved a large bowl of milk from the table to the floor in the old dairy. Witnesses have also reported smelling burning wool in the house. On another occasion, the owner's wife was brushing her hair in front of a mirror. In the reflection behind her she saw the apparition of a young man, aged about 20, lying on the bed with his head propped up on her pillows. She described him as being pale with a closely cropped beard. When she turned around, he was gone. According to records, a young tenant farmer in the middle of the 19th century shot himself in the old dairy after his wife had died.

Pluckley, nr Ashford, Kent: High Street

The noise of a coach and horses can still be heard driving through the village, down the High Street in the direction of Smarden. In earlier days this scene was often visually witnessed and the driver was described as being headless. The ruined mill at Pluckley contains the ghost of a miller who hanged himself there after losing his sweetheart. He is still trying to find her again. There have been many reports of witnesses hearing the screams of a man coming from the direction of the old brickworks. In the 19th century a man fell to his death down a deep clay pit at the brickworks, which is near the railway station.

Pluckley, nr Ashford, Kent: Rose Farm

Rose Farm lies on the Smarden Road, not far from the church. In the olden days the farmhouse was two separate cottages and each of the original dwellings has a ghost. The phantom of the Greystone Monk has been seen from time to time, certainly as late as 1971, walking in the area around his cottage, and a young woman who died next door after eating poisoned berries has also been seen and often heard, calling her dog in. On several occasions both ghosts have been seen together.

Pluckley, nr Ashford, Kent: St Nicholas's Church

St Nicholas's Church is haunted by at least four ghosts, including the Red Lady, one of the three Lady Derings who haunt the village. She is said to be searching for her dead baby's grave and has been seen walking through the churchyard in her grief-stricken state. She has also been seen inside the church, but her main activities seem to centre on the outside, among the gravestones.

Pluckley, nr Ashford, Kent: Surrenden Dering

Yet another Lady Dering has been seen wandering around the blackened ruins of the old manor house that was destroyed by fire in 1952. When she died, her husband had her body embalmed, in order that her beauty would be everlasting. So convincing was the ghostly figure, that one visitor to Surrenden Dering, before it was destroyed, actually fired two shots at her with a revolver. That area of the house is still subject to poltergeist activity.

Plymouth, Devon

The exploits of Sir Francis Drake were thought to be so miraculous that people believed he was in league with the Devil. The most southern point of the city is known as Devil's Point. It is here that Sir Francis and his fellow 'magicians' can be seen and heard muttering their incantations.

Plympton, nr Plymouth, Devon

The Hairy Hands are said to haunt both this spot and Postbridge. Several drivers have reported seeing clawed hands scratching their windscreens.

Plynlimon, nr Llanidloes, Dyfed

A malevolent spirit that has the ability to kill is said to haunt this mountain. It is believed to be something akin to a Will o' the Wisp.

Pocklington, East Yorkshire: Feathers Hotel

An unseen spirit is said to haunt the corridors of this former coaching inn situated in the centre of the town. A highwayman was hanged for murder on the gallows that used to stand in the hotel car park, and his ghost is reputed to haunt the hotel. The haunted room is supposed to be Room 7, where the ghostly sound of someone pulling something heavy down the corridor kept two guests awake all night.

Polesden Lacey, nr Leatherhead, Surrey

A monk-like apparition, dressed in a brown, hooded cloak has been seen on the bridge on the drive to the house. In Nun's Walk, a trail in the woodland, a ghostly, whistling sound has been heard.

Poling, East Sussex

The former site of St John's Priory now has a house built on it. The sound of chanting can be heard, and there are more frightening occurrences, such as intense poltergeist activity.

Polstead, Suffolk: Polstead Rectory

This 16th-century rectory has been the subject of two failed exorcisms, once in the early part of the 19th century and another in the late 20th century. When the Reverend Hayden Foster and his wife Margo moved in they were undisturbed for the first three nights, but when they changed bedrooms to make way for a guest, they woke up to find that the newly decorated room was covered in old-fashioned damp and peeling wallpaper. They heard a child scream and had the sensation of being strangled. They left immediately. A previous vicar's wife, who had lived in the house for 15 years until 1976, had heard only ghostly footsteps. It is also believed that a procession of ghostly monks walks outside the rectory gates at six feet above the ground. The most probable explanation is that a small boy was murdered in the house during the 18th century. Local legend also has it that a mad monk used to live on the site at some point in the distant past.

Pontefract, West Yorks: Rogerthorpe Manor

This seems to be a very haunted place, with tales of Cavaliers and ghosts of old women who abruptly disappear. Of a more sinister nature, witnesses have also reported seeing the apparitions of young pale-faced children, who rattle the doorknobs of the doors to attract attention.

Pontypool, nr Newport, Gwent

A pre-historic camp called Tym Barlwm is said to act rather like the Pied Piper. Its eerie music is said to attract children. Alternatively, this may have been the site of a house that was lost in a landslide many years ago. It appears that a relative of the lady of the house cursed the site after she refused to give food to a starving relative.

Poole, Dorset: The Crown Hotel

During the 19th century, a landlord murdered his two crippled children by sealing them up in a room above the stables. Licensees have complained of poltergeist activity and the sounds of children screaming and running around the stables. In the 1960s a small room in the roof of the hotel was discovered. It contained a fireplace and a window, but no door. The hotel also suffers from a phantom piano player and the noise of a body being dragged across the floor.

Poole, Dorset: Guildhall

Now a museum, this building is haunted by the ghost of a Victorian clerk. He hanged himself from one of the rafters in the building and his apparition has been seen on numerous occasions by a variety of people.

Poole, Dorset: Scaplens Court

In 1598, an attempted robbery led to the murder of the lady of the house and her maidservant. This Tudor building is now haunted by Agnes Bear, the maidservant.

Porlock, Somerset: Porlock Hill

Multiple hauntings that must be related to the innumerable accidents that have occurred on this 1 in 7 gradient hill have been witnessed by many people over the years. These include a phantom coach and horses, a hearse and an old man on a bicycle. Most of the manifestations appear to vanish as they reach the hedgerow.

Porlock, Somerset: Porlock Weir

The bodies of three sailors were washed ashore here and buried in the Marsh Field. Several people have seen their ghosts. Interestingly, one of the sailors is black and another is a boy. They have both been seen on the beach.

Portland, Dorset: Isle of Portland

The Tow Dog haunts the island and has been described as a phantom hound with large, blazing eyes. A number of witnesses have found it difficult to get past the creature as it seems to want to block their way.

Portlaw, Co. Waterford, Republic of Ireland: Gill House

Nicola Hamilton and John, 2nd Earl of Tyrone, entered into a pact to contact one another from beyond the grave, no matter who was to die first. Lord Tyrone left school and lived the life of a recluse, while Nicola Hamilton married Sir Tristram Beresford. In October 1693, Sir Tristram and Lady Beresford were visiting Lady Beresford's sister at Gill House. Leaving Lady Beresford asleep one morning, Sir Tristram rose early and went for a walk before breakfast. When he returned there was some consternation regarding a mark on Lady Beresford's wrist, as she had it covered with a black ribbon. Lady Beresford refused to explain and simply said that she would wear it forever. A letter arrived a few days later from Lord Tyrone's steward, informing her that his master had died in Dublin the previous Tuesday, 14 October 1693, at 4pm. Lady Beresford now explained to her husband that Lord Tyrone had appeared to her soon after his death, while Sir Tristram was taking his pre-breakfast walk. The apparition had placed his finger on her wrist to prove that he was there and it was not a dream. The skin that he had touched left a black mark on her skin and shrivelled the joint. The manifestation of her friend said that she would bear a son and would marry a second time, adding that she would die at the age of 47. Lord Tyrone was right on every count and Lady Beresford bore the mark of his touch for the rest of her life.

Portreath, Cornwall: Smugglers Cottage Guest House

Built in the 16th century, this building is haunted by an 18th-century man, described as being small and in his twenties. He is said to emerge from the wood panelling on the first floor corridor. He then walks toward the staircase and disappears. The panel is said to be the entrance to a smugglers' tunnel that was sealed up at some point in the early part of the 20th century. During the 1950s a secret room was discovered, which revealed a skeleton, a seat and a table. The bones were propped up as if the man had been sitting on the chair. The remains of a black cloak were found around the seated frame. In the corner of the room

was found an antique sea chest and a rusting sword. It is believed that the man was sealed up in the room as a result of some smugglers falling out over the division of loot.

Portsmouth, Hampshire

Before German bombers flattened much of Portsmouth, there were several haunted inns, notably The Spotted Dog, where John Felton murdered the Duke of Buckingham in 1628. King's Bastion is believed to be haunted by grey ladies and bearded sailors.

Portsmouth, Hampshire: The Blue Posts Inn

Following the decisive Battle of Trafalgar, Mr Hamilton arrived in Portsmouth to join his ship, the *Euryalus*. His ship had not arrived and the town was packed with sailors who had just paid off their crews. There were also local elections on and it was very difficult to find anywhere to stay. Eventually he found a double room at the pub, and he even paid double to ensure that he had the room to himself. He locked the door and settled down for the night and was later awoken by drunken sailors carousing in the street. As he turned over, he saw a partially dressed sailor in the bed next to him. He was half-sitting and half-lying, with a pair of trousers on and a red-spotted belcher handkerchief, tied round his head like a nightcap. He was sound asleep. In the morning the man was still there and Hamilton could see his dark complexion and bushy whiskers. The spotted handkerchief was not as it had appeared earlier. Hamilton could see it was white and saturated with blood. There was also blood on the man's cheek and on the pillow. In the morning Hamilton was furious with the landlady and told her that she had broken her promise that she would not sub-rent the room. She told him that he had the only key, but he replied by telling her what he had seen. The landlady went pale and told him that three nights previously a party of sailors were drinking at the inn. A fight broke out between them and a party of Marines, and she herself had tried to break it up by hitting a young sailor on the forehead with a pewter tankard. She had knocked him out and his friends had taken him upstairs. Despite their attentions, he had died. To hush up the whole affair the landlady agreed to the body being buried in the garden. The current building on the site replaced the old one, which was demolished in 1870.

Portsmouth, Hampshire: Theatre Royal

One of the dressing rooms is said to be haunted by the frightening apparition of a ghostly actor. He appears in period costume with a terrible gash beneath his chin. He committed suicide by cutting his own throat in the 1880s.

Portsmouth, Hampshire: The White Swan

The apparition of a Victorian barmaid is said to haunt this pub in Guildhall Walk. It is said that her husband, who was a sailor home on leave, murdered her.

Postbridge, nr Moretonhampstead, Devon

The Hairy Hands that also haunt the A38 at Plympton are active on the road to Two Bridges. Although there is no explanation for the nature of this haunting, it was responsible for a death in 1921 and has caused several other near fatalities since. The hands seem to be particularly attracted to motorcyclists and seem keen to grab the handlebars and force the drivers off the road.

Potter Heigham, Norfolk

Sir Godfrey Haslitt married the beautiful Lady Evelyn Carew on 31 May 1742. At midnight, during the course of the wedding celebrations, the bride was seized from the hall and carried out screaming to a waiting coach. The coach tore down the drive and headed along the road toward Potter Heigham. Arriving at the bridge, the coach, which was travelling too fast, smashed into the wall and was flung, with its occupants, into the River Thurne below. At midnight, on the anniversary of the fatal wedding night, the phantom coach repeats the journey. It was certainly seen as late as 1930.

Poulaphuca, nr Ballyvaughan, Co. Clare, Republic of Ireland

Poulaphuca means the 'cave of spirits' and *phuca* is a generic term to describe fairies. An apparition that takes the form of a black goat, near over 50 wedge tombs, haunts the enormous limestone dolmen here. The manifestation, it is said, has the ability to give the unwary a hunched back.

Poundstock, Cornwall: St Neot's Church

A relative of Kate Penfound haunts the church. The ghost is reputed to be the ghost of William Penfound, a 16th-century priest of the parish, who was murdered there in December 1536. During a mass on 27 December 1357, locals who had decided to take the law into their own hands murdered him, along with several barons who had been pillaging the area. It is not believed that they meant to murder Penfound, but they probably thought that it would be imprudent to trust him not to reveal their identities to the authorities.

Powderham, nr Exeter, Devon

St Clement's churchyard seems to be haunted by a grey man who has been seen walking through the gate and in between the gravestones. It is believed that this haunting may have its history in a death during World War Two, as witnesses have only reported it since then.

Poyntington, Somerset

The ghost of Baldwin Mallet and his headless, royalist soldiers, accompanied by a girl, can be seen here. They died in 1646. The soldiers were buried in a meadow by the stream and Mallet was interred in the churchyard.

Prestbury, nr Cheltenham, Gloucestershire: Clever (or Cleeve) Corner

At a 17th-century farmhouse at Clever Corner, the unseen ghost of a murderer has been sensed and felt in one of the bedrooms. People who have slept in the bedroom have described a feeling of evil and several have reported a sensation of fingers grasping their throats. It is thought that the ghost is that of a man who strangled a newly-wed bride in that room.

Prestbury, nr Cheltenham, Gloucestershire: Prestbury House Hotel and Restaurant

The headless ghost of a royalist soldier haunts this 300-year-old Georgian house. As he galloped with despatches from Sudeley Castle he failed to notice a wire strung between two trees, which decapitated him. There is also the apparition of a serving girl who appears to pre-date the building. She is often seen in the garden.

Prestbury, nr Cheltenham, Gloucestershire: St Mary's Church

The 16th-century Old Priory is the haunt of a monk known as 'the black abbot'. His footsteps have been heard regularly at Christmas, Easter and All Souls' Day, and appear to start at the front door and continue up to the attic. The black abbot also haunts St Mary's parish church, where he has been seen walking down the centre aisle to the west door with his head bowed and his hands tucked in his sleeves. He has also been seen walking in the High Street.

Prestbury, nr Cheltenham, Gloucestershire: Shaw Green Lane

By far the most famous ghost of Prestbury is the un-named courier who was killed while carrying news of the Battle of Tewkesbury on 4 May 1471. While galloping down Shaw Green Lane he was struck in the chest by an arrow, and his ghost is seen riding furiously down Bow Bridge Lane into Shaw Green Lane, where he vanishes. In the early part of the 20th century, road repairs were being carried out in the lane and a skeleton was discovered. Firmly stuck between the ribs was an arrowhead.

Prestbury, nr Cheltenham, Gloucestershire: Sundial Cottage

At the end of the 19th century and up until World War One, the figure of a girl was seen on several occasions playing a spinet in the garden of Sundial Cottage. Although she has not been seen since the beginning of World War One, occasionally the sound of her music can still be heard, especially on warm summer evenings. At Walnut Cottage the ghost of an old horse-trainer, called Old Moses, was seen as late as 1961. There is also a knight in armour, an old woman who looks through windows and a phantom shepherd and herd in Swindon Lane, all of whom contribute to the claim that Prestbury is one of the most haunted villages in England.

Preston, nr Alnwick, Northumberland

A phantom hound, said to be as big as a

horse, haunts this village. It was specifically bred many years ago for its size and ferocity. When its owner realised he could no longer control the animal, he attempted to poison it. Unfortunately, the poison only succeeded in making the creature stronger, whereupon it escaped from its cage, ripped its keeper to pieces and then died.

Preston on Stour, nr Stratford-upon-Avon, Warwickshire

A weird apparition has been seen in the fields and woodlands near to this village. It is something like a ghostly centaur, but is half man and half cow.

Preston Park, nr Brighton, East Sussex: St Peter's Church

The graveyard of St Peter's Church adjoins Preston Manor and boasts the manifestation of a middle-aged woman in mediaeval costume. She has been seen to approach a large terracotta tomb and then simply fade away. It is also believed that the churchyard is the haunt of Sir Charles Stanford, who died in the 1920s – his ashes were buried here.

Princethorpe, nr Leamington Spa, Warwickshire

Princethorpe Wood is haunted by the manifestations of both a priest and a nun. It is possible that if the apparitions are contemporary, then they may have been lovers who chose to end their lives here amid the bluebells.

Purse Caundle, nr Sherborne, Dorset

Chanting plainsong can be heard at the manor, and a ghostly huntsman's horn, accompanied by the baying phantom hounds of King John's pack, can be heard on Midsummer's Eve at Bowling Green.

Puttenden Manor, nr Lingfield, Surrey

A ghostly couple haunt this place, leaving the scent of perfume and tobacco in the air. The couple are probably a pair of previous owners of the property.

Pwyllywrach Manor, nr Bridgend, South Glamorgan

Many years ago a huntsman left his hounds for three days while he enjoyed a drinking binge. When he finally went to the kennels, he heard hounds baying from above. He sounded his horn and his own dogs broke from the kennel and ripped him to pieces. The airborne hounds are said to have been the Cwn Annwn, or Hell Hounds. Obviously his spirit has joined them, as it is said that on the first Monday of August you can hear him screaming in the sky.

Pyecombe, West Sussex

Now replaced by a new road, the route past the village near Brighton is still said to be haunted by a young girl who died in a fatal car accident. Sightings of her have diminished since the new road was constructed.

Q

Quantock Hills to Quothquan

Quantock Hills, Somerset

Myth and legend may be more appropriate explanations for the manifestations seen in this area. Both the Wild Rider and the Woman of the Mist have been seen. The former will kill you if he sees you and the latter just walks around with a bundle of sticks.

Quarr Abbey, nr Ryde, Isle of Wight

Eleanor of Aquitaine, mother of King Richard I and King John and wife of King Henry II, is said to haunt the ruins of the monastery that lie a little way from the more modern Benedictine abbey. Although Eleanor died in France in 1204 she still walks the ruins here. She spent time at Quarr after being banished by her husband. Some say that her restless spirit protects the gold coffin in which she was buried.

Quothquan, Lanarkshire: Shieldhill Hotel

This stone manor house can trace its history back to 1169. During the 14th century, the daughter of the master of the house fell pregnant to the gamekeeper's son. Unfortunately, not only was the baby stillborn, but it was also buried without the mother's permission while she was recovering. It is said that she never knew where the baby was laid to rest and that her spirit still searches for it.

R

Raby Castle to Rye

Raby Castle, nr Barnard Castle, Durham

The apparition of Lady Barnard, known as Old Hell Cat, can be seen on the battlements of the castle. She is said to knit at such a furious pace that the knitting needles are red hot. The murder victims of Maria Cotton, an early serial killer who was executed in Durham in 1873, have also been seen running around the fields near to the castle.

Raglan Castle, nr Monmouth, Gwent

The ruins of this 15th-century castle were once a well-respected bardic centre. Unsurprisingly, therefore, a bard haunts the ruins. Whether he met a sticky end here or whether he simply enjoyed festivals held at the castle 500 years ago is unknown. However, it is interesting to note that visitors to the castle who are unaware of its past still claim to have seen the apparition.

Ragley Hall, nr Alcester, Warwickshire

A white lady, or perhaps three, haunt the house. In the 19th century the skeleton of an Anglo-Saxon woman was found in the parkland. Her remains bore all the signs that she was a rich noblewoman of the period. The brooches, rings, other jewellery and iron dagger all combine to give the impression that she could, indeed, be the source of the haunting. There does not appear to be any other particular reason why three ghosts should haunt this Palladian mansion.

Rainford, nr Liverpool, Merseyside: The Golden Lion

A farmhouse and girls' boarding school before becoming a public house, this building has two ghosts. The first is a soldier who was the son of the landlady, killed during World War Two, and the second is that of a 19th-century schoolgirl who was raped and murdered.

Rainham, Essex: Rainham Hall, New Road

The friendly spirit of Colonel Mulliner, an Edwardian owner of the hall, can be seen during daylight hours, dressed in his grey tweeds. Apparently he loved the house so much that even after his death he could not bear to leave it.

Rait Castle, nr Nairn, Highlands

The manifestation of a female ghost in a bloodstained dress, with no hands, walks ceaselessly around the tower of the castle and has its origins in an inter-clan war. The castle belonged to the Comyns Clan, who invited the Mackintoshes to a meal. They intended to murder them all. Unfortunately for the Comyns Clan, the daughter of the chief of the Comyns was in love with a Mackintosh and she warned them of what her father had planned. In retribution, her father cut off her hands. This drove her mad and she threw herself from the tower.

Ranworth, Norfolk: Old Hall

The Honourable Colonel Thomas Sydney lived at Old Hall and was a hard-drinking, boisterous huntsman who did not enjoy losing bets. On 31 December 1770, at the biggest meet of the season, he challenged a neighbour to a race. When he found that he was well behind, and obviously going to lose, he pulled out his pistol and shot his opponent's horse, causing the rider to be thrown and break his neck. That evening the Devil and the Wild Hunt took the colonel's soul, and they were seen galloping across the broad in a cloud of steam. This scene is re-enacted every year.

Ranworth Broad, nr Norwich, Norfolk

Ranworth Broad is haunted by the ghost of Brother Pacificus, who is occasionally seen in the dawn light wearing a black habit, rowing a small boat with a dog sitting in the bow. Brother Pacificus was a monk at St Benet's Abbey in the 16th century, and every day at dawn he rowed himself and his small dog across the broad to his place of work. In the 1530s he was restoring the rood screen in Ranworth Church, and one summer's evening, his work almost completed, he rowed back across the broad to the abbey to

find that the king's troopers had pillaged it and left many of his brother monks dead. For many years afterwards he lived the life of a hermit in the ruins of the abbey and eventually died there. Knowing of his love for Ranworth Church, the villagers buried him in the churchyard, on the far side of the broad from his beloved St Benet's.

Ratlinghope, nr Shrewsbury, Shropshire

The road to Church Stretton is haunted by a phantom funeral procession. Wild Edric and Lady Godda, his wife, are also said to ride from this point to the aid of Britain. Apparently they were seen as recently as 1982. Edric was a local landowner and as a loyal Saxon, fought against the Normans.

Ravensden, nr Bedford, Bedfordshire

A black lady has been seen on the lane to Buckden. Unusually, she has been seen in daylight and is said to have long, flowing, black garments. It is most probable that this apparition is that of a witch who was driven from her home in the 16th or 17th century. Witnesses claim that she has an evil look about her.

Raynham Hall, nr Fakenham, Norfolk

This 16th-century building is haunted by a brown lady that has been seen on the staircase and in the corridors, wearing a brown brocade dress. This is the apparition of Dorothy Walpole, positively identified from the portrait of her that still hangs on the wall. Dorothy was the daughter of Robert Walpole, MP for Houghton, and the sister of Sir Robert Walpole, the Prime Minister. She fell in love with the 2nd Viscount Townshend, but her father was the young man's guardian and would not consent to the marriage for fear of people believing that he had manipulated the situation in order to profit from the match. In due course Lord Townshend married the daughter of Baron Pelham of Laughton, who died in 1711. Dorothy had become the mistress of Lord Wharton, but he left the country in ruin and disgrace. When Townshend eventually married Dorothy as his second wife, he was disgusted by some of the stories that he heard about her time with Wharton, and also believed that she was still sleeping with him. He had Dorothy locked up in her apartments, where she died on 29 March 1726, a broken woman. Whether she died (as is officially stated) of smallpox or (as is more likely) of a broken neck after being pushed down the Grand Staircase, is unclear. Her apparition is said to return to the hall in search of the children that her husband refused to allow her to see. Captain Marryat and two others saw her apparition in 1836, and they actually fired a shot at it. The bullet went straight through the figure, which disappeared just after the shot was fired, and was later found embedded in a door behind the spot where she had been seen. In 1849, Major Loftus pointed to the figure of a woman standing by one of the doors in the corridor as he was saying good night to his friend. He also mentioned that the manifestation's eye sockets were empty. In November 1926, Lady Townshend saw the brown lady on the staircase. In September 1936, Captain Provand took the now world-famous picture of the brown lady. Interestingly, the apparition was spotted by his assistant Indre Shira, but did not appear in the viewfinder of the camera. There are also said to be the ghosts of two children at the hall, and a phantom cocker spaniel, although it is not known whether these are in any way related to the brown lady.

Reading, Berkshire: Broad Street

The apparition of a woman who first ap-peared when she was not yet dead, but in a coma, has been seen on this street. A woman was holidaying in Italy when she fell ill and was flown back to Reading Hospital for treatment. She lapsed into a coma and while in that state began haunting the area. She has been seen on other occasions since.

Reading, Berkshire: The Roebuck Hotel

The Roebuck Hotel is haunted by the sound of footsteps that pace corridors at night, hammering on doors and the mysterious opening of locked doors and windows. All these happenings are thought to be caused by the unseen ghost of a naval officer who died at the Roebuck in the 18th century.

Reculver, nr Margate, Kent

A Roman fort stood on the site of this Saxon church. Following an archaeological excavation, during which the bones of young children were found, witnesses have reported hearing the sounds of crying children. On the cliff edge, you may be lucky enough to see a ghostly excise man by the name of Gill, fighting a smuggler. Gill was killed in the struggle.

Redbrook, Gloucestershire: Swan Pool, Newland Road

A short distance from the Welsh Border lies the village of Redbrook, and on the right-hand side of Newland Road, just outside the village, is a large pond called Swan Pool. The pond is haunted by a lady wearing a white gown, who has been seen many times rising from the water carrying a baby in her arms. A black dog accompanies them. The story concerning the haunting is that the woman and child were the victims of a murder in the 18th century and that the dog was killed at the same time, while attempting to protect them.

Redhill, nr Stratford-upon-Avon, Warwickshire: The Stag at Redhill

Originally built as a post house in the 16th century, part of the building was used by travelling circuit judges and as cells. Prisoners were hanged at the crossroads nearby. The ghost of an old woman has been seen on Midsummer Night, which is said to be the anniversary of her son's execution. The hotel also has a haunted bedroom, believed to contain the apparition of a Parliamentarian officer.

Reigate, Surrey: St Mary's Church

A ghostly choir sings here at night after the church has been locked up. Witnesses have reported seeing the apparition of a white lady in what may be a wedding dress, walking down the path to the church. If approached, the manifestation simply fades away.

Renishaw, nr Chesterfield, Derbyshire

The Kissing Ghost, or the Boy in Pink, is said to kiss female visitors three times on their lips. The touch is described as being very cold. It is said that this is the spirit of Henry Sacheverell, who died in 1716. There are a number of other notable apparitions, including that of a young woman in a crinoline dress, who is described as having dark hair and a habit of appearing during the day.

Renwick, nr Penrith, Cumbria

When the old church was being pulled down in the 18th century, a strange creature that may have been a dragon or a vampire flew out of the building. It is still said to haunt the area.

Reston Hall, nr Windermere, Cumbria

Built in 1743 by Robert Bateman, this hall has a ghost that is often seen near the entrance gates. It is believed that the apparition is Bateman, although he died and was buried abroad. Over the years women who have lived there have found the place to be very forbidding. Bateman hated women and his spirit may be there to drive them away.

Rettendon, Essex

On the road to East Hanningfield you may encounter the ghosts of a farmer and his pony and trap walking along the lane.

Rhossili, nr Swansea, West Glamorgan: The Old Rectory

A man called Mansel drives a phantom coach across the sands here on stormy nights. In the 16th century he was the first to find and loot a Spanish treasure galleon, and he absconded with the gold that by rights belonged to the Lord of the Manor. The sea itself is said to be haunted by an unseen sea creature that crawls along the sand and enters the house.

Richborough Castle, nr Sandwich, Kent

This fortification was originally built by the Romans as they began their 500-year occupation of Britain. The site is said to be haunted by several Roman soldiers.

Richmond, North Yorkshire: Richmond Castle

Alan the Red of Brittany built the 100ft keep in 1071. The ghost, however, dates from the 18th century, and is connected with a tragic accident. Some soldiers found a passageway under the keep, and, keen to investigate it, they tried to get in. They were all too broad-shouldered to get through the entrance and then their eyes fell on the drummer boy. He was pushed into the hole and told to constantly drum so that the others could follow his progress above the ground. They followed the drumbeats as far as the Market

Place and Frenchgate. The drumming eventually stopped by the River Swale near to Easby Abbey. The soldiers could never find the boy again, and it is presumed that he either fell into the river and drowned, or that there was a well hidden in the darkness of the tunnel. His drumbeats can still be heard emanating from the tunnel below.

Riding Mill, Northumberland: Wellington Hotel

The Wellington Hotel is haunted by the ghost of Anne Armstrong, a local girl who was the victim of a terrible revenge attack carried out by a witches' coven. She had given evidence against them in court on 5 February 1672, and five of the coven had been convicted of witchcraft, for which a death sentence was mandatory. Annie was lured into the kitchen of their house, then a private dwelling, and hanged. When the house became a pub in 1822, several of the staff and customers began to complain of an eerie atmosphere and the fact that they would occasionally see Annie's apparition.

Ringstead, nr Kettering, Northamptonshire

The spirit of a murder victim haunts the gates of the church at night. A local farmer and butcher, William Weekly Ball, made Lydia Atley pregnant and then murdered her. Her body was never found. It is said that her phantom seeks to show where her bones are hidden so that she can be buried in holy ground.

Ripley, nr Harrogate, North Yorkshire: Ripley Castle

A ghostly nun haunts the Castle and is said to knock on guest's bedroom doors. She will not enter the room unless she is invited. She is said to be Lizabeth Ingleby, who was to become the Nun of Ghent. Her portrait hangs on the main staircase.

Ripon, North Yorkshire: The Unicorn Hotel

Tom Crudd, or Old Boots, was a boot boy at the hotel until he died in 1762. It is said that he had a particularly ugly face that resembled Mr Punch. He earned extra money by balancing a coin between his chin and his nose. He still haunts the hotel and the market place.

Rivington, Lancashire: Rivington Castle

These ruins are said to be haunted by strange white figures that move around the grounds of the castle. Witnesses, including workmen on the M61, have described shapes moving around the bushes beside the castle ruins. One figure gave the impression that it was patrolling the walls of the castle like a sentry. Paradoxically, the figures are described as being at least 10–12ft tall.

Robertsbridge, East Sussex: Battle Road

A police officer followed what appeared to be a drunken cyclist late one evening. He had decided to stop the rider as he had no lights. The officer overtook the cyclist, parked to stop him and was astounded to find that the rider and cycle had vanished. This occurrence had happened on several other occasions and the rider has now been identified as a man who was killed in the mid-1960s while cycling home to his nearby cottage.

Robertsbridge, East Sussex: The George Inn

A ghost known as Georgina haunts this pub. Although she has never been seen, the licensees, staff and customers have experienced a number of strange happenings. Doors will open of their own accord, room temperatures will suddenly drop, banging and crashing is heard upstairs and dogs refuse to go into one of the bedrooms. The manifestations seem to take place after a wedding reception or at lunch times.

Robertsbridge, East Sussex: High Street

Just after World War Two, a young girl went fishing during a storm. Over the course of the day the water level continued to rise and culminated in the village being surrounded by the flood. The parents of the child had expected their daughter to go to friends, but instead they heard something bump against the back door. It was the body of their drowned daughter. Her ghost has been seen in a grey dress, carrying her fishing rod, standing on the riverbank.

Robertsbridge, East Sussex: The Seven Stars

This pub is haunted by strange footsteps near the bathroom and on the stairs. One guest in particular claims to have seen a monk walking along the upstairs corridor in the early hours of the morning. The manifestation seems to be particularly active from just after closing time until dawn.

Roch Castle, nr Haverfordwest, Dyfed

A white lady has been seen on numerous occasions, floating along corridors within the castle and passing through locked doors. The apparition is believed to be Lucy Walter, who was born in the castle in around 1630 and later became the mistress of Charles II. Running footsteps have also been heard in the castle, but it is not known if these are related to Lucy.

Rochdale, Greater Manchester: Rochdale Market

The market is built on an old graveyard, but the hauntings here seem to be linked to ground disturbances during the construction of St Mary's Church in 1909. Several people claim to have seen the indistinct form of a male ghost floating across the market toward Baum.

Roche Chapel, Roche, nr St Austell, Cornwall

This near inaccessible ruin is something of a tourist magnet, despite the reluctance of many locals to visit it. A 'fleeting shadow' of an unseen inhabitant of the chapel has been seen in a corner of the building. Others say that they sense something moving around the ruins. Legend has it that the ghost is either that of a leper, a smuggler or a miner. The former used it as a place to die and the others used it as a sanctuary from demons.

Rochester, Kent

In 1264, Simon de Montfort besieged Ralph de Capo in Rochester Castle. During the battle Capo's wife, Lady Blanche de Warenne, was killed. Her ghost appears on the anniversary of her death with an arrow stuck in her chest. The moat of the castle boasts the spirit of a white-bearded man. He is often seen near to where the old burial ground was located, and is also seen under the Corn Exchange clock. Locals believe it to be Charles Dickens, who expressed a wish to be buried here.

Rochester, nr Jedbergh, Northumberland

Some of the houses in this village include masonry from the Roman settlement of Bremenium. Whether the haunting is related to this fact is unknown. Nevertheless, the apparition of a partly nude woman has been seen on summer evenings, sitting and crying gently.

Rochford, Essex: Rochford Hall

The ghost of a headless woman haunts Rochford Hall, said to be the birthplace of Anne Boleyn and now an exclusive golf club. It is unlikely that the apparition is Anne herself. The figure has been seen inside the house at the foot of the stairs and in the grounds outside, and is a regular visitor on the 12 nights before Christmas.

Rockfield, Gwent: Ancre Hill

In 1850 a major coach crash occurred five miles to the north-west of Monmouth. On a dark stormy night, a coach and four returning a party to Monmouth crashed into a brick wall, killing three of the occupants. On several occasions, in similar weather conditions, the vague form of a coach and four has been seen once again approaching the bend at Ancre Hill, where the horses are seen to go out of control. The whole apparition hits the brick wall, bodies are flung over into a field on the other side and the coach disintegrates. When the shattered vehicle comes to a rest on the ground the apparition simply disappears.

Rock Hall, nr Alnwick, Northumberland

A grey lady is said to appear on 15 August each year, walking from South Charlton to Rock. It is said that this is the anniversary of her husband's death. The hall is also said to contain the apparition of a phantom Cavalier.

Rodbourne Cheney, nr Swindon, Wiltshire

Mrs Dyer was hanged in 1896 but can still be seen walking from her former home, a cottage, toward the churchyard. Witnesses have claimed that she carries a baby in her arms.

Rodhuish, Somerset

The ghost of a red-haired butcher's boy who was killed by a friend during a prank can be seen here. The boy dressed up as the devil, with horns and animal skins. He jumped out to scare his friend, who attacked the 'devil', then ran back to the village. When others came to investigate, the body was gone. It is said that the devil had claimed his own. The boy's ghost can often be seen riding behind the devil on Croydon Hill, accompanied by screams and groans of agony.

Romsey, Hampshire: Palmerston Restaurant

Charlie, a white-haired old man, haunts the upper floors of the Palmerston Restaurant, named after the statue sited in the market place of the former prime minister who lived in Romsey. The nearby Swan Inn seems to be haunted as a result of hangings that took place there during the English Civil War. Two Roundhead soldiers were hanged from the pub's sign and can still be heard gurgling.

Romsey, Hampshire: The White Horse, Market Place

The sad apparition of a young ostler boy, murdered in the stable block behind the hotel, haunts the building to this day. The hotel is Elizabethan, with strong links to the abbey, but there are signs of phantom monks here.

Roslin Chapel, nr Edinburgh, Lothian

Closely linked with the St Clair Erskin family, the Earls of Roslin, the building appears to be on fire if a member of one of the families is about to die.

Rosset, nr Chester, Cheshire: Llyndir Hall Hotel

First licensed in 1494, this old hotel boasts the manifestation of a distraught female ghost dated to around the period of the English Civil War. The spirit's name is Henrietta, and she committed suicide after the death of her royalist lover, who fell in the Battle of Rowton Heath on 24 September 1645.

Rossett, nr Wrexham, Clwyd: The Golden Lion

Old Jeffrey is the ghost of a 17th-century ploughman turned murderer. He was hanged at Ruthin and his corpse was sent back to Rossett Green, where the murder had been committed. The local blacksmith could not produce an iron gibbet, so his body was simply fixed to a wood plank board fitted with iron staples. After his body had rotted away, the board was used in the construction of one of the Golden Lion's outbuildings. Consequently, Old Jeffrey can be seen on the upstairs landing and in Room 2, still dressed in his ploughman's smock.

Rossington, nr Doncaster, South Yorkshire

A former owner of the estate, a Victorian gentleman, dressed in a frock coat and top hat, has been seen in and around the stable area.

Rothbury, nr Alnwick, Northumberland

The haunting place of a phantom black cat is said to be on the river's edge, beside the bridge that spans the River Cocquet. Witnesses have only ever caught sight of the beast out of the corner of their eyes. When they turn to face it, it disappears.

Rotherfield, nr Crowborough, East Sussex

In June, the King's Arms is haunted by the sound of footsteps rushing up and down the stairs and along the passages. The building was originally a tithe house, after which it became a bakery, where legend has it that an unhappy miller ended his life by hanging himself from one of the rafters.

Rotherham, South Yorkshire: Hellaby Hall Hotel

Gutted by fire in 1980, this building boasts three ghosts that have been particularly active on the site since the disaster. Witnesses claim to have seen the manifestations of an old woman, a young boy and a strange unknown presence.

Rothley, nr Leicester, Leicestershire

The apparition of a former stationmaster predictably haunts Great Central Station. He shares the site with the manifestations of a farmer and his dog, who died in an accident on the line sometime during World War Two.

Rougham Green, nr Bury St Edmunds, Suffolk

Teacher Ruth Wynnard and one of her pupils, Miss Allington, encountered a strange phantom house in 1926. They were walking along the path to Bradfield St George, when they came to a park wall. They looked through the wrought iron gates and saw a large Georgian house. Passing this way again some months later, they found no sign of the house. Parish records show that no house was ever built there.

Rough Tor, nr Camelford, Cornwall

In 1844, widowed Philippa Peter ran a farm near here with the aid of her son John and three employees: John Stevens, Matthew Weeks and Charlotte Dymond. Matthew was clearly interested in the 18-year-old Charlotte. She used to tease him and in time a deep jealousy brooded in his mind. On Sunday 14 April 1844, Charlotte and Matthew went for a walk across the Tor. She did not know was that he was carrying a knife in his jacket. As they reached the foot of the Tor, he picked a fight with her and Charlotte told him that things had gone too far. Matthew returned to the farm alone, telling Mrs Peters that Charlotte was at a farm in nearby Brown Willy. The local constable found her body, covered in stab wounds that she could not have inflicted on herself. Weeks was arrested in Plymouth, attempting to board a ship. On 4 August 1844, he was tried and found guilty of murder at Bodmin. He was hanged on 12 August. A stone monument marks the spot where Charlotte's body was found, and several locals and visitors have seen her ghost walking down the path from the Tor. During a séance, her spirit told the spiritualist that Matthew Weeks did not kill her. Perhaps this is why she is still seen in the area?

Rowarth, nr Glossop, Derbyshire

A white lady haunts Long Lee Farm. She is said to be the ghost of a penny-pinching old woman who kept the body of a child in one of the rooms in order to avoid paying the 17th-century shroud tax.

Rufford Abbey, nr Ollerton, Nottinghamshire

This Cistercian monastery is haunted by the manifestation of a monk dressed in a black cowl, which partially covers his grinning skull. It is said that a man who encountered the apparition died of fright in the early 20th century.

Rufford Old Hall, nr Leyland, Lancashire

A grey lady, thought to be a bride, haunts this place. Her wedding dress is grey, rather than white, as a result of the fact that her husband left to go to war straight after their marriage. She vowed that she would not remove it until he returned. He did not and

her spirit is still waiting. It is also said that the hall boasts the motionless figure of Elizabeth I, who sits for a while and then disappears.

The Rufus Stone, nr East Wellow, Hampshire

There are three haunted places near to this spot, all of them related to William Rufus, who was murdered in 1100. His ghost follows the route of the cart that took his body to Winchester. The nearby site of Castle Malwood, which was used by Rufus as his hunting lodge, is also haunted. To the west of the stone is Ocknell Pond, which is said to be red with the blood from the hands of Rufus's murderer.

Rugeley, Staffordshire: Ravenhill

The ghost of a little grey lady has been seen in the drawing room, sitting by the fireside. Despite the fact that the building, thought to be nearly 150 years old, has been used for a variety of purposes over the years and that the fireplace is now sealed up, witnesses still report seeing the old woman, although none can shed light on who she may be.

Runcorn, Cheshire: Norton Priory

Two phantom monks and a ghostly choir haunt this monastic building, thought to date from the 12th century. A poacher witnessed two monks, about 5ft tall, wearing small crucifixes on what appeared to be shrouds. Augustinians were not buried with shrouds and crucifixes but it is plausible that these were two members of another religious order that happened to be buried here.

Rushbrooke, nr Bury St Edmunds, Suffolk

Agnes de Rushbrooke haunts her former home in the guise of a white lady. Her purpose may be either revenge or remorse.

Rushyford, Co. Durham: The Eden Arms

A grey lady haunts room 19. Her appearance is said to signal a severe drop in the temperature in the room. Witnesses have seen the vague outlines of ghostly children in one of the corridors.

Ruswarp, nr Whitby, North Yorkshire

Goosey was the village idiot, so called because he could eat a whole goose in one sitting. The unfortunate character was murdered, but haunts the road out of the village. He has often caused accidents as motorists have swerved to avoid his presence.

Ruthin Castle, Clwyd

Owain Glyndwr besieged the castle in 1400. It was defended by English troops commanded by Reginald de Grey. De Grey was a cruel and vicious Governor of North Wales, and is said to haunt the drowning pit, part of the dungeon that could be filled with water from the moat. A grey lady also haunts the castle, probably dating back to the period of Edward I. She killed her husband's lover by chopping off her head and then had the favour returned on her execution.

Ruthven Castle, nr Kingussie, Highlands

A green lady haunts the castle and is said to be a harbinger of death. Alexander the Wolf of Banenoch, Robert II's son, is also said to haunt the place. His soul was taken by the Devil when he lost a game of chess with him.

Rycote Chapel, nr Thame, Oxfordshire

A grey lady in Tudor costume, called Arabella, can be seen just outside this building, standing beneath a giant yew tree. Robert Dudley, Earl of Leicester, who is said to have murdered his wife, Amy Robsart, also haunts the chapel. Thomas More and Giles Heron, who were executed together, have both been seen here.

Rydal Mount, nr Ambleside, Cumbria

In 1850, William Wordsworth died here. His ghost has often been seen on the first floor, in the corner room that used to be the bedroom of his sister, Dorothy.

Rye, East Sussex

This walled town seems to be overwhelmed with phantom monks. As many as seven monks have been seen at the same time. Monastery Hall was a former Augustinian friary, and there also seems to be a link with Watch Bell Street, where another ghostly brother has been seen.

Rye, East Sussex: Mermaid Hotel, Mermaid Street

The Mermaid may be one of England's oldest public houses, but the hauntings seem to date from the 16th or 17th century. Many staff and guests over the years have witnessed the apparitions of two men sword fighting, as if in a duel, in one of the upstairs bedrooms.

S

Saddell Abbey and Castle to Sykes Lumb Farm

Saddell Abbey and Castle, nr Campbeltown, Strathclyde

Many say that the very fabric of the castle contains the spirits of monks that are also said to haunt the abbey. The castle was constructed using masonry and headstones from the grounds of the religious site. The apparitions have been seen in both structures and along the shoreline.

Saddleworth Moor, nr Oldham, Greater Manchester

It is not surprising that the moors are haunted by the victims of Myra Hindley and Ian Brady, but other hauntings here are said to date back much further than the 20th century. Strange apparitions have been seen on the moors after dusk, including large glowing shapes and indistinct figures.

St Albans, Hertfordshire: Battlefield House

This house in Chequers Street resounds with the chanting of monks and the clash of arms in battle. The sounds of fighting are easily explained, as this was the site of a battle during the Wars of the Roses. The reason for the chanting is not so clear. There is also talk of the fact that St Albans may be the haunting place of 'Mother Haggy'.

St Albans, Hertfordshire: Mallinson House

This mansion in St Peter's Street is haunted by the ghost of a butler who committed suicide after having been caught drinking his master's brandy. He appears in one of the upstairs windows, complete with a tunic with silver buttons and a powdered wig.

St Albans, Hertfordshire: St Albans Abbey

In the 1930s, Canon George Glossop was working late on a sermon when he heard monks singing. Only three months later, he heard music composed by Robert Fayrfax (d. 1521), who is buried in the abbey. Another witness, again in the 1930s, heard music emanating from the

Lady Chapel at 2am. During World War Two, the Fayrfax music was heard again. The keys of the organ were being depressed by invisible hands, and in the flickering candlelight the figures of monks were seen. After the war, further witnesses saw a procession of ghostly Benedictine monks walking toward them through a wall. They are said to have been seen near the Great Gateway.

St Albans, Hertfordshire: Salisbury Hall

This was the former home of Nell Gwyn, mistress of Charles II. She has appeared wearing a blue dress. Winston Churchill's mother, while living there, saw the ghost of her second husband. Another ghost, that of a Cavalier, has been seen walking along with a sword through his body. In recent years, a wall through which some of the ghosts pass was investigated. A blocked up door beside the fireplace in the bedroom above the porch was discovered.

St Albans, Hertfordshire: The Wicked Lady

The pub is named after Lady Katherine Ferrers, the notorious highwaywoman. She is said to have used the pub to plot her escapades. The manifestation of a woman haunts the pub, but she has never been seen, and it is difficult to assume that it is Ferrers. Nevertheless, the ghost has been heard by several people, who describe a woman crying in one of the upper rooms.

St Andrew's, Fife

The cathedral was consecrated in 1318, but in the 1700s a monk was brutally murdered by a jealous rival in one of the towers. His apparition has been seen on several occasions, usually around the time of a full moon. The same tower is haunted by the manifestation of a young woman, dressed in white and wearing elbow-length gloves. She has been seen on stormy nights, and it is believed that she is one of the 14th-century nobles buried in the cathedral. A phantom coach and four horses also haunt the town. They are often seen clattering down Crail Road before disappearing into St Andrew's Bay.

St Athan, nr Barry, South Glamorgan

Lady de Clare, in the form of a white lady, haunts the former site of West Orchard Castle. Lady de Clare's husband returned from the Crusades and accused her of being unfaithful. To punish her he used a Saracen method of chastisement, burying her up to her neck in sand. After ten days she died, but her spirit can still be seen here.

St Audrie's Bay, nr Watchet, Somerset

A black dog haunts the stretch of road from St Andrie's Farm to Penny Farm. It is also said that a 'grey shapeless thing' can be seen here, as well as a coffin lying beside the road.

St Blazey, nr St Austell, Cornwall

A bizarre manifestation that is said to look like a bear but walk like a horse is said to haunt the village. Several witnesses claim to have seen this creature over the years.

St Boswells, Borders: Dryburgh Abbey Hotel

Built in 1845 on the site of a former house and abbey, the hotel is haunted by the apparition of a grey lady who committed suicide in the nearby river. She had been having an affair with one of the monks and the abbot was informed of the wrongdoings. He had the man killed and she ended her own life. Her apparition is also seen walking across the chain bridge.

St Brelade, Jersey

A small hut on Mont Nicolle is said to produce the greatest headache anyone can possibly imagine, and being inside the hut is so oppressive that you must leave immediately. During the latter part of the 1800s a man hanged himself there, and it is said that it is his spirit that causes these sensations.

St Buryan, nr Penzance, Cornwall

At the Quaker burial ground, you may encounter the Wild Hunt. It is also haunted by Kenegie, whose spirit is condemned to count every blade of grass at Castle-an-Dinas. A parson, it is said, laid his spirit here.

St Clement, Jersey

Work was undertaken to replace an old staircase in one of the houses here. The workmen had hardly begun when they saw a grey lady on the stairway. Investigations revealed that a woman had fallen down the stairs and died.

St David's, Dyfed

This ruined chapel was dedicated to the mother of St David, St Non. It still stands, overlooking the bay, and on St David's Day (1 March), you may hear voices singing hymns emanating from the chapel ruins.

St Donat's Castle, nr Llantwit Major, South Glamorgan

William Randolph Hearst once owned the castle, but the hauntings predate this period. The manifestation of Lady Stradling, wearing high-heeled shoes and a long dress, has been seen in the Long Gallery. She tends to be seen just before a disaster will hit Britain. An ugly witch haunts the armoury, a phantom panther or big cat has been seen in the corridors and invisible hands play the piano, even when the lid is shut.

St Helier, Jersey

In the past the punishment for stealing anything worth more than a shilling was hanging. The executioner always received the clothes of the criminal as part of his pay. The Mount of Hanging, or Gallows Hill, is said to be heavily haunted by those that met their end here.

St Hilary, nr Marazion, Cornwall

The ghost of the Revd John Penneck, the 18th-century Chancellor of Exeter, flies into rages and causes great storms here.

St Ives, Cambridgeshire: The Ferryboat Inn

Juliette Tewsley committed suicide after having been continually spurned by a local woodcutter, Thomas Roul. She was found hanging from a willow tree near to the inn. Her tombstone is inside the pub and on the anniversary of her death, 17 March, she can be seen walking restlessly around.

St Ives, Cambridgeshire: The Golden Lion Hotel

A green lady and a Cavalier haunt this pub, and they were investigated by a team from Cambridge University. The green lady occupies room 12 and is prone to pull the bedclothes off beds, open doors and ring bells. The Cavalier moves along the corridor, through a wall and seems to be at home in room 15.

St Ives, Cornwall

The apparition of a shipwreck victim has been seen on the beach and in the cobbled streets. She is looking for her baby by the light of a lantern. She was rescued from the sinking ship, but her child was lost. She died of shock and her ghost was first seen on the beach during her funeral. It is believed that to see the lady with the lantern is a warning of an impending shipwreck.

St Ives, Cornwall: Skidden House Hotel

A blue lady has been seen walking past the kitchen, through the dining room and into the reception area of the hotel. On many occasions guests or new members of staff who are unaware of the haunting have spotted her. The figure of a ghostly gentleman with a grey beard, wearing a long, frocked coat, has been seen on the first floor of the hotel. Poltergeist activity has also been reported, particularly during the period when the hotel was being renovated. Workmen constantly complained that unseen hands moved their tools.

St Ives Head, Cornwall

Distress rockets were seen to the west of St Ives Head and local fishermen went to the aid of the ship, only to see it disappear when they pulled alongside. No sooner had they reached the shore than they saw the rockets again. This time the ship in distress was the *Neptune*, identical to the phantom ship, but real. The phantom ship has been seen since at St Ives Head, always before a local sea disaster.

St Just, nr Penzance, Cornwall

The notorious local drunk, John Thomas, fell 30ft into a clay-pit in the middle of a drinking bout. The following Sunday, James Thethewy was looking for some of his sheep. He noticed an odd figure near the clay-pit. As he got closer, the figure disappeared, but he heard a voice from below and discovered a weak and filthy John. Others had also seen the strange figure, but had taken no notice of it.

St Lawrence, Jersey

The ghostly apparition of a coach and six horses can be seen approaching the church once a year at midnight, accompanied by the pealing of bells. The story runs that a girl arrived for her wedding to find that the bridegroom had vanished. She is described as wearing her bridal gown, and the coach is driven by a coachman with white ribbons on his whip. If you stare too closely at her, the white veil will be moved to reveal a grinning skull.

St Leonards, nr Wendover, Buckinghamshire: Dundridge Manor

Margaret Pole, the Countess of Salisbury, has haunted this building since her execution for treason in 1541. She tends to be seen late in the afternoon between August and October. The ghostly footsteps of two boys are also heard near to the staircase. It is said that one of the boys killed the other with a ploughshare.

St Leonard's Forest, nr Horsham, West Sussex

The Devil is said to appear along with the ghost of Squire Paulet, who joins him on a horse. It is presumed that the squire made a deal with the Devil during his life and that his spirit is left to regret that decision.

St Leven, Cornwall

A ghost ship has been seen sailing straight toward the shore. It then crosses the beach and continues for almost half a mile inland before disappearing. It is believed that in the distant past, the water level was very different. There may even have been an estuary and river.

St Martin, Jersey

Many years ago a criminal called Geoffroy was convicted of murder and taken to the cliffs to be thrown off. The executioner pushed the man over and he was seen to land in the water near the rocks and then swim away. Baying for blood, the assembled crowd demanded that he be thrown in again. This time Geoffroy offered to jump himself, having been promised that if he survived he

would be set free. Unfortunately he hit his head on a rock on the way down and was killed. His ghostly apparition can be seen continually jumping from the cliff edge.

St Mary's Loch, nr Selkirk, Borders: Tibbie Shiels Inn

In 1878, the former owner and namesake of this historic coaching inn on the shores of the loch died, aged 96. His ghost has been seen on regular occasions, keeping an eye on the business and the area that he loved so much.

St Neots, Cambridgeshire: The New Inn

The ghost of the Earl of Holland haunts this pub. He was captured by the Parliamentarians and imprisoned here before being taken to London for his eventual execution. Although some of the other royalists were executed near the New Inn, only the apparition of the Earl has been seen. He is described as being tall and thin and wearing an ankle-length coat, and is seen in the bar before walking through a closed door and into the courtyard.

St Ouen, Jersey

White ladies haunt the lanes in this area, particularly in Rue à la Pendue (Hanged Man's Lane). They are described as appearing as a standard white lady and are known as *les blanches femmes*.

St Saviour, Jersey

Phantom horses have been heard in the courtyard of the manor here. They may be related either to the death of Athelstan Riley's daughter-in-law, who died after falling from a horse, or to that of a lawyer who was thrown by his horse and died in a ditch by the roadside. On another occasion a completely different ghost has been seen in a small cottage here. It was the apparition of an old man floating above a couple's bed at night.

Salisbury, Wiltshire: The Haunch of Venison

A grey lady haunts this pub, which is sited in Minster Street beside a graveyard. Witnesses have seen the apparition in and near the pub, and some say that it is the spirit of a woman buried in the cemetery.

Salisbury, Wiltshire: Salisbury Cathedral

White, swan-like birds have been seen flying around the spire of the cathedral to signify the death of the bishop or one of the clergy attached to the cathedral. In 1885, the daughter of the bishop at the time saw the apparition on the day her father died. In 1911, another witness saw the same manifestation when the bishop died on 16 August.

Saltburn-by-the-Sea, Yorkshire: Coastguard Cottages

The ghost of an 1860s murderer or his victim haunts the Coastguard Cottages. One witness reported feeling the touch of an invisible hand, a sensation shared by several people who have stayed there over the years.

Saltergate Inn, nr Pickering, North Yorkshire

Superstitions die hard, and in this pub a fire has been kept burning for 200 years. It is said that a man died in a skirmish between smugglers and customs men and that the body is buried beneath the hearth. If the fire goes out, the spirit of the man will be released to haunt the pub.

Saltwood, nr Hythe, Kent

The road leading to Sanding, particularly near Slaybrook Farm, is haunted. Balls of fire have been seen, which gradually transform into a man carrying a lantern. The apparition is said to be either a Roman solider or the spirit of a local, rather eccentric, farmer.

Samiesbury Old Hall, nr Preston, Lancashire

A white lady with a greenish tinge to her face haunts the hall. She is Dorothy, daughter of Sir John Southworth, a Catholic during the reign of Elizabeth I. Dorothy had fallen in love with a Protestant, but her brother discovered her affair with him and both men died in the ensuing fight. The white lady can be seen in the house, in the grounds and on the road nearby.

Sampford Peverell, nr Tiverton, Devon

In 1810, the Revd Caleb Colton published details of this haunting in his *Plain and Authentic Narrative of the Sampford Ghost*. Strange noises were heard in various parts of the house and people walking around the rooms would find that their footsteps were being imitated. In May 1810, six female servants in the Chave household were attacked and beaten as they lay in bed. Other activity including loud knockings, violent rappings and rattling noises and the sound of a man's slippered feet coming downstairs and passing through a wall has been witnessed. On one occasion a Bible was flung 7ft through the air and a sword was seen suspended in mid-air.

Sandford Orcas Manor House, nr Yeovil, Dorset

The manor boasts 14 ghosts. These include a lady in green in the south bedroom, the lady in red silk on the stairs (who appears just before noon), a dog, a monk, a local man (who hanged himself in the gatehouse), Sir

Hubert Medlycotts (an ancestor of the owners), an Elizabethan lady in the courtyard and the sound of a spinet. The ghost of a 7ft tall highwayman and rapist also appears if there is a virgin the house.

Sandhurst, Kent: Bodiam Road

Two ponds, the Chapel Pond and the Brick House Pond, were the chosen places for two suicides separated by some 80 years. The apparition that haunts the road near these ponds could either be a woman or a man, but certainly something has been seen on a number of occasions. One witness claims to have seen a male ghost, described as being around 30 years old with a smile on his face. The figure followed the witness for a few yards and then disappeared.

Sand Hutton, nr Thirsk, North Yorkshire: Busby Stoop Inn

In 1702, Tom Busby murdered his father-in-law with a hammer. He was hanged and gibbeted outside the pub. His ghost tends to be seen on moonless nights, still with the noose around his neck and his head bent at an odd angle.

Sandquar Castle, near Thornhill, Dumfries and Galloway

A white lady haunts the castle, believed to be Marion of Dalpeddar, who may have been murdered by her husband. She disappeared in 1590, but in 1875 the skeleton of a blonde woman was found buried in the fabric of the castle.

Sandringham, nr Kings Lynn, Norfolk

Sandringham was bought by the future Edward VII in 1862 when he was Prince of Wales, and there have been numerous reports of footsteps in the servant's quarters, coupled with doors opening and lights being turned on. Most of the haunting seems to take place around Christmas. A ghost strips the bedclothes from freshly made beds, and heavy breathing is heard in an empty room.

Sandwood Bay, nr Cape Wrath, Highlands

Over 300 years ago, a Polish ship was wrecked here. A few witnesses visiting this remote spot have seen the apparition of a headless sailor. He is described as being bearded and wearing heavy sea boots, and tends to be seen on the beach.

Sankey, nr Warrington, Cheshire: Buttermilk Bridge

The terrifying manifestation of an old woman with a horrific face has been seen here on many occasions. She is described as wearing a black shawl and having a cackling laugh. It is thought that she was one of the women who sold buttermilk to the workmen who constructed the bridge.

Sarratt, nr Watford, Hertfordshire: Rose Hall

The grandparents of the ghost writer, Peter Underwood, once lived here. They claimed to have seen a headless phantom in the house.

Sawston Hall, nr Cambridge, Cambridgeshire

When Edward VI died in July 1553, the scheming Duke of Northumberland (father of Lady Jane Grey) sent a message to both Mary and Elizabeth demanding their immediate presence in London. Elizabeth claimed she had an illness, and suspected Northumberland's motives. Mary began the journey, but was warned it was a trap. One of her escorts, Andrew Huddleston, suggested that as they were not too far away from Sawston, where it was reasonably safe, they should stay there overnight. Mary spent the night of 7 July sleeping in the now-famous four-poster bed in the Tapestry Room. Robert Dudley, Lady Jane's husband, was en route to Sawston, but Mary escaped and Sawston Hall went up in flames. When Mary became queen, she built a new manor house for the Huddlestons in 1584. Mary's ghost has been seen in the house and grounds, carrying a prayer book. An unknown grey lady haunts the Tapestry Room and the sound of a spinet is heard in the Long Gallery. A watchman called Cuttriss stalks around the grounds.

Saxmundham, Suffolk

In a field just outside the market town, witnesses claim to have seen the manifestations of several ghosts dancing. The witnesses have not been able to get close enough to identify the period of clothing, but there appear to be at least eight or nine apparitions.

Scampton, nr Lincoln, Lincolnshire

The grave of Nigger, the dog that belonged to the famous Dambuster leader Guy Gibson, can be found at this RAF base. The black Labrador was killed on the day of the raid, but can still be seen at all times of the day and night in and around the base.

Scarborough, North Yorkshire: Scarborough Castle

Piers Gaveston, Edward II's favourite, haunts the castle. He was captured here before being taken to Warwick for execution. His ghost appears to be headless, which is consistent with his beheading, and he is often seen in the ruin on the cliff top. The manifestation is particularly unpleasant, as aside from being headless it also appears to be very aggressive. It will try to tempt people onto the wrecked battlements and at the crucial moment the apparition will charge

the unsuspecting victim, hoping to make them fall or leap to their deaths to avoid him.

Scarborough, North Yorkshire: The Three Mariners

Built in the 1300s, the former pub is no longer a public house but is vacant. The pub stands behind more recent buildings on the seafront and is apparently riddled with secret passages and concealed cupboards that were once used to hide smuggled contraband and criminals. There are many legends attached to the inn. The American John Paul Jones apparently hid here after being shipwrecked, and a ship's figurehead used to stand above the inn's entrance, which was known locally as Elvira. It is said that Elvira left her position on the wall of the pub and would knock at fishermen's doors to warn them of storms. The haunted room in the pub is believed to house the spirit of a headless woman. One witness saw the apparition in the early morning and refused to set sail as a result. He warned his colleague, who unfortunately disregarded him and was killed the same day during a storm at sea. Another witness has reported being aware of an unseen hand tugging at her bedclothes in the middle of the night.

Schiehallion, nr Aberfeldy, Tayside

Another black dog, of an altogether more malign nature than most other canine apparitions, is said to haunt this peak in the Highlands. It may be encountered in the gulleys surrounding the mountain. There are also tales of water spirits living in the lochs nearby.

Scole, nr Diss, Norfolk: The Scole Inn

Dating from around 1655, this magnificent coaching inn is haunted by a white lady. She was the lover of a highwayman that used the inn as a secret base, but she was discovered and murdered by her husband. Her apparition can be seen in one of the rooms on the first floor and on the main staircase.

Scone Palace, nr Perth, Tayside

Despite the fact that the floors here are wooden, many witnesses have distinctly heard the sound of footsteps on stone flooring. The manifestation responsible for the footsteps is unknown, but he is generally referred to as the 'Boring Walker'.

Scotch Corner, nr Richmond, Yorkshire: Great North Road

Tom Hoggett, the highwayman, came to his end one stormy night when, pursued by officers of the law, he fell into a pond and drowned. The ghost of Tom Hoggett still patrols the Great North Road between Boroughbridge and Scotch Corner. He is a fast-moving figure in an ankle-length coat, carrying a bulls-eye lantern.

Scotney Castle, nr Lamberhurst, Kent

In 1259, Walter de Scotney, steward to the Earl of Gloucester, poisoned him and other nobles during a feast. Some of the guests died, but the Earl survived. Scotney was tried and hanged in Winchester. In 1720, the then owner, smuggler Arthur Darrell, was outlawed and died abroad in the same year. At his funeral, a tall figure in a black cloak stood among the mourners. Suddenly it exclaimed, 'That's not me', and disappeared. In 1924, the coffin was opened and found to be full of stones. The castle also houses the ghost of a customs officer, who was killed by one of Darrell's men and thrown into the moat. The apparition is seen emerging from the moat to hammer on the door of the castle.

Scrap Faggott Green, Great Leighs, Essex

Pilgrims used the village inn en route to Canterbury, but the hauntings only began in the 1940s. In the 16th or 17th century, a local woman was executed for witchcraft and was buried, with a stake through the heart, at Scrap Faggott Green. The US Army removed a boulder which had been placed over the grave in order to improve road access to a nearby base. Immediately afterwards, the parish church clock started chiming backwards, the bells rang by themselves, hens stopped laying, milk cows dried up and geese disappeared. After a while, the haunting seemed to settle on the pub, which experienced great poltergeist activity over a period of time, during which clothes were strewn around rooms and footsteps were heard walking along the upstairs corridors, door handles rattled and curtains were pulled off their rails. A black shape was seen in one of the bedrooms and a figure was encountered standing by an old fireplace. If the haunting is not related to the spirit of the witch, then it is possible that it is associated with the murder of a small child, perpetrated in front of her screaming mother. This was said to have happened many years ago.

Scrooby, Nottinghamshire

John Spencer murdered the toll-keeper and his wife at this village near Bawtry in 1779. The Great North Road used to pass by the village and he killed them for the money that they had collected. As a lesson to others, Spencer was hanged and gibbeted on the spot, but you may still be able to see the phantoms of the two victims and Spencer re-enacting the murder.

Scunthorpe, Lincolnshire: Scunthorpe General Hospital

The manifestation of a nurse, said to come from the Old Frodingham Hospital, makes regular visits to the new hospital. She is described as wearing long clothes, partially covered by a long apron. Whenever she is seen, there is an almost overpowering smell of violets in the air. She is associated with good fortune, as when she visits desperately ill young children, they always recover.

Seafield Bay, nr Cattawade, Suffolk

The screams of witches can be heard in the night at this place. This harks back to the time when Matthew Hopkins, the Witchfinder General, tortured suspected witches. It is said that the loudest and the most agonised cries come from the spirit of Elizabeth Clarke.

Seahouses, Northumberland: Beadnell House

The ghost of a naval officer haunts this Victorian mansion on the Northumbrian coast. He has been seen in and around the house in full uniform.

Seahouses, Northumberland: Longstone House Hotel

A child that has not only been seen but also makes a lot of knocking noises haunts room 6. Although the identity of the ghost is not known, it is believed that the apparition has haunted the building for many years.

Sea Palling, Norfolk: The Hall Inn

The building is believed to date back to the 16th century, and has, among others, the apparition of a grey lady. She has been seen sitting on the window ledge of the television room – the room suddenly drops in temperature when she makes an appearance. A blue shadow, a column of grey smoke and the smell of tobacco also haunt the pub.

Seaton Delavel Hall, nr Blyth, Northumberland

A grey lady haunts the hall, and is described as being slim and pensive. She can be seen standing looking out of a window in the west wing. It is believed that she awaits her lover, who never returned.

Sedgemoor, nr Bridgwater, Somerset

Where the River Carey becomes King's Sedgemoor Drain, a ghostly band of soldiers can be seen. They appear weary and ragged, and the distant sounds of battle and faint calls accompany them. On 3 July Monmouth's ghost can be seen fleeing from the battlefield. Strangely, the battle actually took place on 6 July. The sweetheart of a local man, killed by soldiers after being forced to race a horse, drowned herself on Sedgemoor Levels. Her spirit is seen accompanied by the sound of her lover's running feet and laboured breathing, as well as the thunder of galloping hooves. Whether this is the famed rider in flowing white is unknown, as this horseman is seen on a large, heavy horse, but not heard.

Seend, nr Devizes, Wiltshire

A phantom funeral procession has been seen in these parts on several occasions. It is not, however, known why this manifestation is so persistent.

Selborne, nr Alton, Hampshire

Gilbert White, the naturalist, once lived here, and his ghost has been seen in the garden of the cottage he loved. The priory here has phantom monks and a spectral dog. The latter died over a century ago and it is said that it was a companion of a racehorse trained at Selborne. Popular belief has it that the dog is still looking for its old friend.

Selside, nr Settle, North Yorkshire: No.1 Salt Lake Cottages

One of the houses in this row of railway cottages is haunted by the spirit of a platelayer who was killed on the track many years ago. The manifestation tends to make its presence felt in the front bedroom, either as a drop in the temperature or, more chillingly, as an apparition getting into bed alongside the occupants.

Selside Hall, nr Kendal, Cumbria

The old yew tree in the grounds of the hall was once used to hang sheep thieves, and it is thought that the spirits of one or more of these are behind the hauntings at the place. Prior to the hall being connected to an electric supply, a ghost would run around the hall putting out all of the candles and lamps as quickly as they were lit.

Semley, nr Shaftesbury, Wiltshire: Pyt House

Molly the housemaid was hanged for scalding her illegitimate daughter, Betty, to death. At the time, she was in the service of the Bennett Stanford family, and one of the male members of the family was said to be the father of the child. Betty's bones were kept on the grounds and on the three occasions that steps have been taken to bury them elsewhere, terrible calamities have befallen the household. A wing of the house caught fire, the male heir died and then a daughter died.

Send, nr Guildford, Surrey: Boughton Hall

The spirit of an elderly man who is seen smoking a pipe while he walks upstairs haunts the hall. Witnesses also report that there is the strong smell of tobacco in the air. It is believed that the man was a former owner of the house.

Sennen Cove, nr Penzance, Cornwall

The victim of a shipwreck haunts a rock off the shore, and is known as the Irish lady. Witnesses have seen a woman hanging from the rock, waving to catch the attention of on-lookers. The woman had managed to get to the rock after the ship she had been on sank offshore, and she held on for several hours while vain attempts were made to save her. Eventually, she slipped below the waves and now haunts this spot.

Sevenoaks, Kent

A 17th-century coaching inn here was once the home of the singer Vince Hill. His bedroom had horse-box doors with metal latches. Throughout the Hills' two-year occupation of the building, they heard thudding noises coming up the stairs and attempting to open the door. Every time they investigated they discovered nothing at all, nor any explanation locally for the haunting. After these activities occurred on three or four occasions when his wife Anne was alone in the house, they decided to sell.

Shaftesbury, Dorset: Gold Hill

Up the steep cobbles of Gold Hill, the ghosts of two men with packhorses carry the body of Edward the Martyr, who was murdered at Corfe Castle in 979. Edward was murdered by his stepmother and was buried at Shaftesbury Abbey at the top of the hill.

Shaftesbury, Dorset: The Grosvenor

This 18th-century inn is haunted by a grey lady, said to be seen in and around the pub. It may be the apparition of a woman who died in one of the bedrooms many years ago. Witnesses also report the strange phenomenon of beer going missing from the cellar, despite the fact that it is locked.

Shaftesbury, Dorset: Shaftesbury Abbey

The unusual sight of a phantom monk walking on his knees has been seen among the ruins of the abbey. He appears along the outer wall and vanishes at a particular spot in the wall. The assumption is that the spirit is unaware of the fact that the ground level has been raised. Legend has it that the ghost wears a brown habit and is actually a priest who conceals a key to the abbey's treasures. Apparently he died of a heart attack before he could reveal to the last abbess where he had concealed the hoard.

Shap Fell, nr Penrith, Cumbria

A spectral black dog haunts the A6 over Shap Fell, and is said to appear prior to an accident occurring on this dangerous stretch of road. Others believe that it is the appearance of the hound that actually causes the accident in the first place. Certainly the sight of a large black dog leaping across the road and jumping over a wall to fall 300ft would test the mettle of the best driver.

Shardlow, Derbyshire: The Lady in Grey Restaurant

The apparition of a grey lady gives this 18th-century building that once belonged to the Soresby family its present name. The ghost is said to be that of Jeanette Soresby, who moves from one of the bedrooms across the landing and into another bedroom. Witnesses describe her as being aged about 20 and dressed in Victorian clothes. Other witnesses have reported feeling something brush past them in the garden.

Shebbear, nr Holsworthy, Devon

The Devil's Stone in the churchyard is ritually turned on 5 November each year after the bells have been rung to scare away the Devil. If it is not turned, then the Devil will wreak havoc on the village. Two sad spirits haunt the village pub: that of an old man with a grey beard and a young girl. The man was murdered at the inn and the little girl witnessed the killing.

Sheffield, South Yorkshire: The Carbrook Hall Hotel, Attercliffe Road

This hotel is opposite the Meadowhall retail park and originates from the end of the 16th century. A former landlady, Linda Butler, is said to have seen the ghost of a Roundhead soldier near the doorway. She also reported seeing a little old woman in a mob cap. Other witnesses have reported seeing a former customer known as Fred, as well as a monk and an Edwardian lady. The staff and regular customers have also witnessed a black shadow that walks past the taproom window. Landlords have claimed that on the way upstairs they have felt something or someone brush past them, although they could see no one.

Sheffield, South Yorkshire: The Old Queen's Head, Pond Street

This building is the oldest surviving domestic building in the city. Dating back to the 15th century, the building was first mentioned in an inventory of the 6th Earl of Shrewsbury's property made in 1582. The pub has the reputation of being one of the most haunted places in the city. One particular ghost has been seen near the old stone fireplace and is believed to be an old man with jugs of beer in his hands. The snug has been the focus of many strange happenings in the past. The door to the room, which is bolted at night, is often found open in the morning. The cellar in the pub, where workmen uncovered a well, has been the site of unexplained footsteps and lights that come on and go off by themselves.

Sheffield, South Yorkshire: Sheffield Royal Infirmary

A grey nurse haunts the surgical block of the hospital, tending dying patients. She is dressed in a very old-fashioned uniform and the temperature drops considerably for a short period of time. On several occasions, the apparition has been seen to offer glasses of water to patients, usually a sign that they will soon die. On one occasion, when a patient refused to take the water, the patient made a full recovery.

Sheffield, South Yorkshire: Turret House

Once part of the hunting lodge of the Earl of Shrewsbury, this place was one of the many used to imprison Mary Queen of Scots. She appears as a grey lady.

Sheldon, nr Bakewell, Derbyshire: Magpie Mine

Suitably haunted and cursed, this abandoned mine houses the apparition of an old miner who was said to have died in an accident underground. He appears to be able to walk or stand on water.

Shelsey Walsh, nr Worcester, Worcestershire: Court House

Lady Lightfoot was imprisoned and then murdered here. She appears riding in a phantom coach. The coach pulls up to the house, circles around it and then passes through the building. Her apparition, screaming in terror, accompanies the whole scene.

Shepton Mallet, Somerset

A white lady, who was beheaded here in 1680, haunts the 300-year-old former army prison. Banging noises, heavy breathing, oppressive feelings and icy chills have all been reported. Prison officers have claimed to feel icy chills and resistance when trying to lock doors. The wartime gallows site boasts the figure of a man in a World War Two uniform. The library is built on the site of death row and numerous ghostly sightings have been reported here.

Sherborne Castles, Sherborne, Dorset

Sherborne boasts not one, but two, castles, predictably named the Old and New Castles. Sir Walter Raleigh was given the manor of Sherborne in 1592, but having failed to make the Old Castle comfortable, he started to build the New Castle. Raleigh's ghost has been seen on regular occasions since his execution in 1618. The Old Castle has a further claim to fame. All its owners have, apparently, become cursed following an oath made by Osmond, one of William the Conqueror's followers, who stated that if the castle was no longer in church hands, then all those who owned it would suffer misfortune. Lady Chatterton, writing in 1878, described a confused scene that she could only characterise as a number of men fighting. From this time on the room from which she viewed the scene has been described as the Haunted Room. Apparently the room below the Haunted Room is renowned for being the place to listen to the sound of bodies being thrown from the window of the room above.

Sherrif Hutton, North Yorkshire

The apparition of Nance, an 18th-century farmer's daughter, is said to haunt these parts. She was to marry a coachman, Tom Driffield, but instead she married and had a child with a highwayman. She fled when she realised that he was already married, but died of exposure despite Tom's help. She promised to protect Tom and his descendants from beyond the grave. Once she helped Tom steer his coach through thick fog and on another occasion saved his son from highwaymen. Nance now helps lorry drivers in bad weather conditions, travelling ahead of the truck so that the driver can see that the way ahead is clear.

Sherrington Manor, nr Selmeston, East Sussex

The house is haunted by a strange figure in

brown. Although it has been seen on a number of occasions, there is no indication of the identity of the apparition. It is popularly thought to be a monk.

Shipton Court, nr Burford, Oxfordshire

Somewhere in this building is a sealed room that contains the exorcised spirit of a ghost. The nature of the haunting that provoked the exorcism is not known, nor is the location of the secret room.

Shocklach, nr Whitchurch, Cheshire

The churchyard contains the graves of many of the Brereton family. Legend has it that the ghosts of the entire family return to the churchyard once a year for a get-together.

Shotley Bridge, Spring Lane, nr Consett, Co. Durham

Jack Arthur was a 22-year-old paper-mill worker at the local mill. He lodged with Jack Rutherford, the postman. In November 1895, a lively argument was heard between the two about Jack's drinking and gambling habits. By the following morning, Jack had completely disappeared. The ghost of Jack has been seen many times, dressed in Victorian working clothes.

Shrewsbury, Shropshire: The Albright Hotel and Restaurant, Ellesmere Road

There has been a building here since before the writing of the Domesday Book and it was used during the English Civil War as a garrison. It is haunted by a dark cloaked figure, often seen standing at the foot of a bed. There are also reports of knocking noises, which in some cases are extremely loud.

Shrewsbury, Shropshire: The Dun Cow

The ghost of a Dutchman, hanged for the murder of a servant, haunts the pub. At the time he was staying in Shrewsbury with Prince Rupert. The odd apparition of a monk in a brown robe that is said to glitter has also been seen. The manifestation has a tendency to throw things at people.

Shrewsbury, Shropshire: The Nag's Head

In one of the attic rooms there is a painting of an old prophet on the back of a cupboard door. The hauntings in this pub seem to be related to this, as it is said that those who see the picture will go mad. As a result a coachman hanged himself, a woman threw herself out of the window and was crushed by a bus and an army officer shot himself. They all haunt the building.

Shrewsbury, Shropshire: Prince Rupert Hotel

Formerly known as Jones's mansion, the building was used by Prince Rupert as his headquarters during the English Civil War. However, the haunting relates to a bridegroom who hanged himself after his best man took his bride from him. His spirit has been seen in room 7 and the passageway leading to it.

Shrewsbury, Shropshire: St Julian's Church

During the 1800s, a man died in the Lion Hotel. The body was buried in the churchyard after a short service. As the gravediggers were completing their work they could hear screams. The following day the screams continued until the coffin was dug up. Prising open the casket, they discovered that the man had been buried alive and there were scratch marks on the inside of the lid and his fingers were worn to the bone. The ghost of the unfortunate man justifiably haunts the graveyard.

Shrewsbury, Shropshire: Shrewsbury Castle

An ogre that was once said to menace the town haunts this 14th-century building, now a museum. It is seen dragging away a young girl called Fanny, who was its ninth victim. The ogre is known as Bloundie Jack, and he killed eight of his wives in addition to Fanny. He kept the fingertips and toes of his victims in a drawer. He was eventually hung, drawn and quartered and his head was impaled on a pole.

Shrewsbury, Shropshire: Shrewsbury Railway Station

In 1887 the roof over platform 3 fell in, killing a Shrewsbury councillor. He was crushed to death in the train carriage. On many occasions, a strange, shadowy figure has been seen sitting or standing near to the entrance.

Shuckburgh Hall, nr Southam, Warwickshire

Lieutenant Sharp of the Staffordshire Militia asked Sir Stewkley Shuckburgh for the hand of his daughter in marriage. Whether the old man disapproved of soldiering or Sharp himself is not known, but not only did he say no, but he also forbade Sharp to see his daughter again. Sharp went for one last walk in the gardens with Shuckburgh's daughter, shot her and then shot himself. The pair of them haunt the hall.

Shute, nr Axminster, Devon

Many years ago, a coachman was murdered by his mistress at Shute Pillars. Consequently, the coachman haunts the village, but he is without his coach and horses.

Shute Shelve Hill, nr Axbridge, Somerset

At the Hanging Field, there are three ghosts. Two are said to be male and the other female. This unholy trinity were executed for the murder of the woman's husband.

Silent Pond, nr Dorking, Surrey

The spirit of a murdered Saxon maiden haunts the pond. She has been seen by a variety of different witness over nearly 1,000 years.

Silton, nr Gillingham, Dorset

A robed priest, who moves toward the altar and then heads for the vestry, where he disappears, haunts the church. Unconfirmed reports seem to suggest that he was a parish priest here in the 19th century.

Simonside, nr Rothbury, Northumberland

A terrifying manifestation haunts this part of the Cheviot Hills. Many years ago a hunchbacked dwarf had a habit of preying on travellers in the area. He would kill them and then cook them over a fire before eating them. His ghostly form still stalks the landscape.

Sissinghurst Castle, nr Cranbrook, Kent

During the reign of Queen Mary, Sir John Baker, or Bloody Baker, as he was known, lived here. He built the castle, but he also had the unpleasant habit of torturing and murdering Protestants. The castle is haunted by one of the victims of this purge, a priest.

Sizergh Castle, nr Kendal, Cumbria

The Strickland family lived here for over 700 years, and during one of the many wars against the Scots, the then lady of the castle was locked up in the main tower by her husband. His instructions were that she was not to be released until he returned home. Whether he died or simply decided never to come back is unknown, but the woman

GHOSTS OF GREAT BRITAIN

eventually went mad and then died. She now haunts the castle, along with Catherine Parr, who haunts the Queen's Room. She was Henry VIII's sixth wife, and stayed at the castle on a number of occasions.

Skene, nr Aberdeen, Grampian

In 1724 the infamous warlock, Alexander Skene, died here. Legend has it that he would drive his coach to the village graveyard and dig up the bodies of un-baptised children. He would feed the bodies to his familiars, a hawk, a magpie, a jackdaw and a crow. His manifestation is seen driving across the loch in his phantom coach on New Year's Eve.

Sker House, nr Porthcawl, Mid Glamorgan

The tortured spirit of a girl who was chained up the in the house by her wicked father, haunts the building in the form of the sound of chains being dragged across the floor. It is also said that the nearby Sker Rocks are haunted by a phantom shipwreck that predicts a real disaster at sea.

Skibo Castle, nr Clashmore, Highlands

On one occasion many years ago, Skibo Castle was left in the sole charge of a manservant, who persuaded his former sweetheart to visit him at the castle. When the girl failed to return home that evening an intensive search was made, including the castle in spite of the protests of the manservant. She was never found and shortly afterwards the servant left the district. Soon afterwards people living in the castle were startled by screams that were heard coming from the castle corridors and by the sight of a young woman who always appeared to be in a state of terror. Many years later some repairs were being made to the castle, during which a young woman's

bones were found in the very spot where the apparition usually disappeared. The remains were buried elsewhere and the apparitions ceased.

Skinburness, nr Wigton, Cumbria

Screams are heard from just out to sea on stormy nights. They are said to originate from a ferry that sunk here many years ago. Eloping lovers used the ferry as a quick way to get across the Solway Firth to Gretna Green.

Skipsea Castle, nr Bridlington, East Yorkshire

The ghost of Lady de Bevere haunts the mound that marks the site of the castle. She was married to Drogo de Bevere and was the niece of William the Conqueror. Drogo was a vicious and unpleasant man, who eventually murdered Lady de Bevere. Her ghost has been seen both during the day and at night.

Sledmere, nr Driffield, East Yorkshire: Sledmere House

The monument to the World War One dead pays tribute to those who made the ultimate sacrifice. However, their restless spirits are seen marching through the grounds of Sledmere House. It is believed that these apparitions replay their last walk through the village before they were transported to France, where they were killed.

Slough, Buckinghamshire: Upton Court

The ghost of a woman wearing a bloodstained nightdress haunts Upton Court. It is not known who the woman was or why she haunts the place, but the apparitions have been reported for many years.

Smarden, Kent: The Chequer's Inn

In the early 19th century a soldier was killed

here. His apparition has been seen on a number of occasions, clearly identifiable in his uniform of the period.

Smethwick, West Midlands: Black Patch Park

Queen Henty was a gypsy who lived in the Romany camp based in the park in the early 20th century. The apparition is described as being an old woman with a long, black dress and a red cape. She is also described as having very long, black hair. Witnesses have seen her on a pathway a little way from a narrow bridge.

Smethwick, West Midlands: Warley Abbey grounds

A grey lady, appearing as a tall woman in a grey coat, is believed to be the apparition of a murdered heiress to the estate. Warley Abbey, built in the 18th century, was demolished in the mid-20th century. The apparition appears where the original front door stood, walks along a pathway and then vanishes.

Smithills Hall, nr Bolton, Greater Manchester

Sir Roger Barton, the Catholic owner of Smithills Hall in 1555, interrogated the Protestant martyr George Marsh here. During the questioning, Marsh cursed the building, leaving the impression of his foot when he stamped on the stone floor near to the chapel. Marsh haunts the hall and the coach house is said to have the spirit of a grey lady in residence.

Snape Castle, nr Ripon, North Yorkshire

Catherine Parr haunts the home that she shared with her second husband, Lord Latimer, whom she married after the death of

Henry VIII. Latimer died in 1542, but it is Parr's ghost that is seen, in the form of a young girl with blonde hair, in a blue dress.

Snodhill, nr Hereford, Herefordshire

Built in around 1660, this was the former home of the Prosser family. All of the manifestations that haunt the buiding seem to be related to the family in some way. A ghostly funeral cortège, footsteps and rustling silk have been experienced. The cortège is supposed to warn of an imminent death in the family.

Snowdon, nr Llanberis, Gwynedd

Bordering on mythology are the manifestations of Bwbach Llwyd and Brenin Llwyd. The first is a brown goblin that is often mistaken for a shepherd. If followed, it will lead you into danger. The latter is said to live at the top of a mountain and will eat anyone who becomes lost there.

Soham, nr Ely, Cambridgeshire

Joseph Hempsall fell into the bogs that used to blight this area before the Fens were drained. His ghost appeared to some of his friends and led them to his body. The spirit apparently told them that he wished to be buried in Wicken, but he was interred in Soham instead. As a result, until his remains are taken to Wicken, his spirit haunts the area between the two villages.

Solway Firth, Dumfries and Galloway

Two ghost ships appear here that may have originally been the invention of smugglers. The *Betsy Jane* was wrecked on Gilstone Rock on Christmas Day and the *Rotterdam* was lost with all hands. Its appearance is said to foretell a sea tragedy.

Southampton, Hampshire: Bitterne Manor

Near the Northam Bridge, across the River Itchen close to the manor, the apparitions of Roman soldiers are to be seen.

Southampton, Hampshire: The Dolphin, High Street

At 2am, you may be fortunate enough to see the floating manifestation of Molly, a former cleaner. She is apt to pass through several rooms in the early hours, presumably following her usual cleaning route. Witnesses report that she appears to be friendly. The hotel was extensively modernised in 1751, which may account for the fact that Molly does not know where the doors are now.

Southampton, Hampshire: Southampton General Hospital

Two ghostly nuns haunt this former workhouse. In the early 19th century, an inexperienced nun gave the wrong medicine to a patient who died in agony as a result. Shortly afterwards she committed suicide by taking the same overdose. The ghostly figures are said to be that of the nun and her patient, who often appear at the bottom of patients' beds, dressed in habits.

South Cadbury, nr Wincanton, Somerset

There is an Iron Age fort on the hill here, said to be the burial place of King Arthur. He appears with his knights as they rise from their graves on Midsummer's Eve, galloping down the hill and into the distance. They have been seen and heard by witnesses.

Southend-on-Sea, Essex: Cluniac Priory

The ruins of the priory in Prittlewell Park are said to be haunted by ghostly monks, which perform age-old rituals as they did when they were alive.

Souther Fell, nr Keswick, Cumbria

A phantom army has appeared here since the middle of the 18th century. It usually makes an appearance on Midsummer's Eve at around 8pm. In 1745 a group of nearly 30 people witnessed it, which included horsemen and carts. When they investigated the route in the morning, they found no trace of the army's passing.

Southerndown, nr Bridgend, Mid Glamorgan

The Earl of Dunraven was a notorious shipwrecker. He would light beacons inland in order to confuse the ships. Unfortunately, one of the passing vessels that was wrecked had his son on board and he was drowned. A blue lady haunted Dunraven's castle, which has now been demolished, and the ghost of the Earl can be seen on the beach.

Southfleet, Kent

A very well-documented ghost of a nun, or perhaps a nurse, haunts the rectory. The female apparition is short, dumpy and wears a brown dress. In the past a friary stood here, where it is said three nuns were seduced by monks and then bricked up in the walls to prevent a scandal.

Southport, Merseyside: Palace Hotel

In 1969, strange voices were heard coming from empty rooms and the second floor corridor, and the lift began moving up and down. This was all the stranger as the electricity had been cut off and the building was about to be demolished. The only possible explanation related to the time when the building was used to care for victims of sea disasters. Some died there, and there is a tale of a man who had committed suicide on the second floor.

South Tidworth, Wiltshire

A drummer was committed to Gloucester jail in 1661. His drum was sent to Magistrate Mompesson's home at Tedworth. Not only did the drum sound itself, but numerous poltergeist occurrences befell the household. The demon drummer was then committed as a witch and transported. The ghost returned and the drumming continued.

Southwick Hall, nr Oundle, Northamptonshire

This 14th-century manor house is haunted by a grey or blue lady described as being tall and slim. Her dress has a pointed collar. She tends to be seen in the chapel beside the altar and then moves through the Priest's Room to a staircase, where she then vanishes. In the Oak Room there is said to be the spirit of a child.

Southwold, Suffolk: Gun Hill

In the 1880s the guns here were fired in salute of a local dignitary. Unfortunately, one of the guns exploded, decapitating an artilleryman. His ghost has been seen standing by the second canon on the right, fully recognisable in his period uniform.

Southwold, Suffolk: Old Vicarage

The ghost of a woman who, besides being seen, has also produced some very mysterious noises, haunts the old vicarage. On one occasion, sounds of someone falling down the stairs were heard and several people ran to see if they could offer assistance, only to find that the stairway was empty and there was no visible cause for the noises. The sound of the clanking of chains was heard on several occasions coming from a disused attic, and the creaking of a chair was also heard, followed by the sounds of a deep sigh. On many occasions, people sleeping in an old four-poster bed in the spare room reported that they had been woken up to find the figure of a woman standing by their bed.

South Zeal, Devon: Oxenham Arms

The inn is a 14th-century manor house built on the site of a 12th-century monastery. It is therefore surprising that ghostly monks have not been seen. The resident manifestation takes the form of footsteps in one of the corridors and the sound of something being dragged across the floor. It may be that the haunting has some connection with the fact that one of the rooms has a granite monolith as the main feature.

Sparkford, Somerset: South and North Barrow

King Arthur and his mounted knights, accompanied by foot soldiers, have been seen on the ancient causeway between South and North Barrow on Midsummer's Eve. King Arthur haunts the nearby Arthur's Hunting Causeway on Christmas Eve. It is said that their horses have silver horseshoes, and one has been found quite recently. Cadbury Castle is said to be the site of King Arthur's Camelot, so it is not surprising that King Arthur has been seen in this area. Other witnesses have reported that the armed knights carry flame-tipped lances.

Speke Hall, nr Liverpool, Merseyside

A white lady haunts the Tapestry Room and disappears through a wall that may once have been an entrance to a secret passage. The house was used to hide priests and is said to have a number of concealed passages and priest's holes.

Spedlin's Tower, nr Lockerbie, Dumfries and Galloway

The tower dates from around 1480, and the head of the Jardine family arrested and imprisoned a local miller called Porteous there. He locked him in the dungeon and rode off to Edinburgh. Unfortunately he had the key to the cell in his pocket and the man starved to death. From then on the man's spirit haunted the tower, despite the fact that an exorcism was performed. The ghost was said to have escaped and followed the Jardine family to Cumbria. It is presumed that the hungry and restless spirit still plagues the Jardines to this day.

Spetchley, nr Worcester, Worcestershire: The Red House

A female apparition that is said to be harmless and helpful haunts the stairs. It is not known who she is and nobody has been able to describe the clothes she wears, so it is impossible to date her.

Spinney Abbey, nr Wicken, Cambridgeshire

Approximately a mile from Wicken Fen stands the former farmhouse called Spinney Abbey. The name was derived from an old priory that once stood on the site. Phantom monks, who are heard singing, haunt the building, and one has been seen walking along a pathway in the grounds. Mysterious lights and a female figure have also been reported. Spinney Abbey was built by Mary de Bassingbourne and Beatrix Malebise for Augustin friars in 1217. In 1406, the then abbot of Spinney was murdered by one of his monks, and Oliver Cromwell's son, Henry, farmed here immediately after the Restoration. He is said to have been murdered with a pitchfork by one of Charles II's men, who were travelling through the area on their way from Newmarket. It is also reported that the pigs and horses that are kept in the grounds often get boisterous and make a lot of unexplained noises. The ghost who walks along the path in the early hours of the morning is believed to be the monk who murdered the abbot in 1406. He wears a brown habit and the hood fully covers his face so that no features are visible.

Spofforth Castle, nr Harrogate, North Yorkshire

A bluish-white figure plunges from the top of the 13th-century tower. Witnesses state that only the top half of the body is visible and that it disappears when it hits the ground below.

Spondon, nr Derby, Derbyshire: St Werburgh's Church

Amazingly, a blue lady was photographed near the vestry door in the 1970s. She is also said to haunt the former vicarage.

Springfield, nr Chelmsford, Essex

Springfield Place, near the church, is said to be haunted by a phantom that resembles a malformed dwarf. It was extensively reported after World War Two and was described by one witness as a 'funny man'.

Springhill, Co. Londonderry, Northern Ireland

Built in the 17th century, the house is haunted by a black lady who has often been seen standing at the top of the stairs. She was seen to approach a room, throw her hands up in horror and then vanish. The apparition has also been seen near the back door, where it almost collided with a member of staff. The ghost is believed to be that of the wife of Colonel Conyngham, who served in the Crimean War.

Spurstow, nr Nantwich, Cheshire: Dead Man's Lane

A rather unpleasant local squire was overheard planning to murder one of his tenants and abduct the man's daughter. In the execution of this plan he was ambushed and decapitated by the tenant. The squire's ghostly funeral procession is seen passing down the road.

Stainton, nr Penrith, Cumbria

Following the dissolution of the monasteries, the local baron pulled down the monastery and built himself a new house with the masonry. While doing so he disturbed many of the monks' graves in the cemetery. Soon after he rode to the site but his horse reared up and threw him. The baron's neck was broken and his phantom can be seen riding on Baron's Hill, overlooking the town.

Staithes, nr Whitby, North Yorkshire: Boulby Cliff

In 1807, Hannah Grundy, a fisherman's wife, was decapitated by a rock fall while she was walking along the beach. She is usually seen in April, the month of her death, as a transparent figure walking on the beach, picking up stones and casting them into the sea.

Stamford, Lincolnshire: The Garden House Hotel

An apparition that has the ability to peer in from the outside haunts the top floor of the building, which formerly housed the servant's quarters. Room 18 seems to be the most affected area. When guests are staying there curtains are pulled open and the faint sound of a man breathing heavily can be heard.

Stanbridge, nr Dunstable, Bedfordshire

A ghostly hitch hiker has been seen on a number of occasions, waiting for a lift on Station Road. It was particularly well documented in 1979.

Stanbury, nr Haworth, West Yorkshire: The Old Silent Inn

Although Bonnie Prince Charlie hid here in 1745, a former landlady haunts the pub. She was a great cat-lover and used to attract stray animals by ringing the bell beside her back door so that she could feed them. Her ghost has been seen on many occasions on this spot, despite the fact that the back door has been bricked up.

Stanton Harcourt Manor, nr Oxford, Oxfordshire

Lady Alice Harcourt was murdered in Pope's Tower while the rest of the family were celebrating mass. It is said that her spirit was exorcised many years ago. Despite this, two ghosts remain in the pond and will reappear if it ever dries up. The first is that of a phantom coach and horses and the second is the apparition of a woman who drowned herself.

Stanton St Bernard, nr Devizes, Wiltshire

The apparition of a woman whose corpse was defiled by a greedy sexton appears in the doorway of the dining room of the manor house on the anniversary of her funeral. Chillingly, the sexton attempted to steal the woman's rings from her corpse as she was lying in the coffin. Unable to remove the rings from the woman's swollen fingers, he chopped them off with a knife.

Staple, Somerset

The 'Woman of the Mist' appears in the hills around here and is usually described as an old woman carrying a bundle of sticks. She has been seen in these parts on regular occasions.

Steeple Morden, Cambridgeshire: Moco Farm

The ruins of Moco Farm are haunted by the ghost of Elizabeth Pateman, who was murdered by her master in 1750 because he thought that she was about to implicate him in the murder of a visiting peddler, whom he had killed and thrown down a well. Elizabeth, a 19-year-old servant girl, was overheard by her master telling her lover that she had a secret to reveal. Absolutely convinced that she was referring to the murder of the peddler, the master killed her to be sure of her silence. Elizabeth's ghost is now regularly heard, crying out in pain and terror as she did when she was done to death with a knife and coulter (a blade from a plough).

Stiffkey, nr Fakenham, Norfolk

In the 18th century a woman who was gathering cockles was drowned in the marshes. Witnesses report hearing screaming on foggy nights near an area called Blacknock.

Stiperstones, nr Shrewsbury, Shropshire

On 22 December each year all the ghosts that haunt Shropshire are said to meet here. It is said that if you see them then you will die. One surviving witness has suggested that they are talking together as if having a debate.

Stirling, Central Scotland: Stirling Castle

Stirling Castle was built in the 15th century to replace a wooden fort. It was a favoured place of Mary Queen of Scots. Not only was she crowned in the chapel in 1543, but she lived there for some considerable time. She is often connected with sightings of the green lady. In later years sightings of the green lady have been related to potential disasters in the castle. The castle also boasts a pink lady, supposedly dating back to times when jousts took place near Lady's Rock. The apparition of a young girl has been seen walking between the castle and the church nearby.

Stirling, Central Scotland: Stirling Youth Hostel

A monk, or perhaps a priest, has been seen on a number of occasions leaning over beds in one of the rooms. He is dressed in robes and is said to be an old man with a big nose.

Stock, nr Chelmsford, Essex: The Bear Inn

The ghost of Charlie 'Spider' Marshall haunts the pub. He was an ostler at the pub at the end of the 19th century and earned his nickname by walking sideways like a spider-crab. Spider would often perform his other trick, scrambling up the chimney of the tap-room fireplace and emerging from the chimney in the bar parlour. Occasionally, however, he would stay up the chimney for some time to un-nerve the customers. The only way to bring him down was to light a fire in one of the fireplaces to smoke him down. There was a small loft at the junction of the two chimneys where Spider would sit listening to his friends entreating him to come down. One Christmas Eve, however, Spider would not come down, even when fires were lit to smoke him out. It was assumed that he had died of suffocation at the junction of both chimneys, but at no time did anyone make any attempt to remove his body and it is presumed that his remains are still inside the chimney. His ghost is often seen, although it is reported that he is smaller in stature than he was in life. He has been seen wearing his white breeches. The pub is also haunted by the sound of footsteps in the middle of the night and there is often a suffocating presence felt in the private quarters.

Stockport, Greater Manchester: Dukinfield Chapel

This is said to be the centre of considerable poltergeist activity. On one occasion in 1646, a phantom drummer appeared and disrupted the service so much that the congregation had to abandon the chapel.

Stockton on the Forest, nr York, North Yorkshire

Close to the site of the Battle of Stamford Bridge, a ghostly army is said to re-enact the bloody conflict between the Anglo-Saxons and the Danes. It was here that Harold fought his last successful defence of the English crown before heading south to Hastings where he met defeat at the hands of William the Conqueror.

Stogumber, nr Bridgwater, Somerset: Heddon Oak

The mutilated bodies of some of Monmouth's men were left hanging at Hedden's Oak. Although the hanging tree was cut down in 1979, many witnesses have reported the sound of groans, clanking chains, creaking leather, hoof beats and strangling noises. Others have felt as if they are being choked when in the area. As if this was not enough, Woden, mounted on his white horse and leading the Wild Hunt, was seen in the vicinity as recently as the 1960s. Apparently the Wild Hunt sped through the village, although nobody dared to look. Sight of the Wild Hunt brings death and disaster.

Stoke-by-Nayland, Suffolk: Thorington Hall

Thorington Hall, a gabled farmhouse built in the late 16th century, is haunted by the ghost of a girl wearing a brown dress tied at the waist with a piece of cord. She has been seen walking along an upstairs corridor and the sound of her footsteps has also been heard in that corridor and in other parts of the house.

Stoke Dry, nr Uppingham, Rutland: St Andrews Church

The ghost of a woman accused of being a witch is said to haunt the church. The rector at the time locked the unfortunate woman in a room above the porch and left her to starve to death.

Stondon Massey, nr Brentwood, Essex

In the 18th century the graveyard and church were haunted by Richard Jordan. After his death his spirit was so restless that the corpse had to be dug up and wrapped with chains before reburial.

Stonehenge, Wiltshire

Surprisingly, there are no accounts of hauntings here until the 20th century. In 1912 a Royal Flying Corps aircraft crashed, killing the two pilots. It landed in a wood where there is now a memorial to the dead airmen. The phantom aircraft continues to crash on regular occasions, and has been seen by a number of people more intent on looking at Stonehenge.

Stoneleigh, nr Kenilworth, Warwickshire

During the reign of Queen Victoria a cyclist was killed in an accident while heading down the hill toward the River Sowe. Several witnesses claim to have seen his apparition making this last journey.

Stonor Park, Buckinghamshire

Voices emanate from empty rooms, and nun's footsteps are heard walking across the floor and down the stairs, where a cupboard door is opened. On other occasions people have felt someone touch their face in bed at night. Dogs are wary of the back garden; they often sense something and back away from it, growling.

Stourmouth, nr Ramsgate, Kent: The Rising Sun, The Street

This public house is said to be over 400 years

old and has been used for a wide range of purposes including a ferry house and a bakery. Whether the ghost of an old gentleman relates to one of the former incarnations of the building is unknown, but several regulars as well as the landlord have seen the apparition on a number of occasions.

Stover, Devon

The bridge that crosses the River Bovey is said to be haunted by 'something waving its arms and running alongside', according to a witness in 1961. Staff from a nearby private house would never go near the bridge at night. This may well be the Jew's Bridge, where a poor Jewish peddler was murdered.

Stow Bardolph, nr Downham Market, Norfolk: The Hare Arms

For unknown reasons a former landlord by the name of Capon went mad and killed himself after he had eaten a pie made by his wife. Unfortunately we do not know what was in the pie, but the man's spirit can still be seen in the pub.

Stowford, Devon: Hayne Manor

The ghost of a pageboy murdered by a butler haunts this place near Launceston. A man with a head under his arm has also been seen and his appearance is said to foretell the death of the owner of the house. It is also said that the grounds boast a black dog of unknown origin.

Stow-on-the-Wold, Gloucestershire: Chappen Street

Odd poltergeist activity has taken place in this semi-detached house. On a series of occasions, the family living there were continually subjected to rapping sounds. Water was also seen to be pouring out of the walls. They stated that they had seen a child's hand that had suddenly changed into a man's hand. On one occasion, they heard a voice claiming to be one of the builders of the house, who had died on 15 February 1943.

Stow-on-the-Wold, Gloucestershire: King's Arms Hotel

The hotel dates from the 15th century, and King Charles I was said to have stayed here. However, it is not the monarch that haunts the hotel, but an old lady and a young boy. The former is described as wearing black, with her grey hair in a bun and a pendant around her neck. The boy is around 7 years old and both have been seen in the lounge area.

Stradey, nr Llanelli, Dyfed: Old Stradey House

The apparition of Lady Mansel is said to haunt the building, accompanied by the sound of organ music.

Straffan, Co. Kildare, Republic of Ireland

The area is haunted by the ghost of a railway guard, who has been seen walking at night along a stretch of the local railway line carrying a lamp. The apparition is thought to be the guard of an express train that broke down on 5 October 1853. A luggage train was following some distance behind and it ploughed into the express train, unfortunately killing 16 people and injuring another 30. During the enquiry it came to light that the guardsman had forgotten to attach a lantern to the rear of the train and that the train was travelling in excess of the restricted 20mph. It is thought that the spectral guard patrols the line at night, carrying his lamp to make up for his former negligence and to ensure that there is not a repetition.

Strata Florida Abbey, nr Aberystwyth, Dyfed

On Christmas Eve the manifestation of a ghostly monk can be seen trying to rebuild the wrecked altar of this Cistercian abbey. He works by flickering candle light.

Stratford-upon-Avon, Warwickshire: Ettington Park Hall Country Club

The apparition of a ghost known as Lady Emma has been seen walking down the terrace beside the arched entrance, wearing a long gown. She is a very old white lady, and when she reaches the wall she disappears through it. Sometimes ghostly footsteps will be heard and on one occasion a guest felt something soft being drawn over their face.

Stratton, nr Bude, Cornwall: Binhamy Castle

Only the moat remains of the castle, but Sir Ralph de Blanc-Minster, who died while on crusade in 1270, haunts the area. He shares this haunting place with the apparition of a white hare.

Stretton, Rutland: Stocken Hall

Three ghosts haunt this hall, which now serves as an open prison. The first is that of a black lady, thought to be the manifestation of a girl who was strangled in the attic. She is seen walking along a corridor with her head lowered. An opaque phantom of a small white dog has been seen on the stairs. The apparition of a man murdered at the hall in the early part of the 19th century, after having been accused of stealing sheep, has been seen hanging from the bough of an oak tree.

Stubley Old Hall, nr Rochdale, Lancashire

There are several ghosts here, including a Parliamentarian soldier that is seen leaning against a fireplace and the apparition of a small girl who has been seen skipping in the fields. Of these we know very little, but much has been recorded of two other manifestations. An apparition of a Cavalier, thought to be the spirit of Ralph de Stobbeley, has been seen in a part of the building that used to house his apartment. He is described as wearing a blue velvet jacket and black trousers. He tends to appear near a striking stained-glass window, and is accompanied by an odd 'churchy' smell. Fatima, a young woman and an accomplished harpist, was said to be engaged to marry Ralph de Stobbeley. Before they could marry, he left for the Crusades, and she died before he returned. Her ghost is seen leaving a candle in the window to guide her lover home. Fatima's ghost is not averse to tomfoolery, and she has been active in the local pub too, where she trips newly-wed brides, ruffles their hair and tugs at their jewellery and veils, perhaps in recognition of the fact that they have accomplished something that she was unable to do. There is a portrait of Fatima in the hall. Some say that her spirit is a malicious one. Ralph was unfaithful to her in life. When he eventually married, he died on his wedding night after hearing ghostly harp music emanating from the woods. Perhaps this was Fatima's revenge?

Studham, nr Dunstable, Bedfordshire

Disappearing into a yellow-blue mist, the apparition of a short, blue man with a beard and tall hat has been seen on the common. He is thought to be of foreign origin, as witnesses did not recognise the language he was speaking.

Studland, Dorset

Many years ago a naval deserter robbed and murdered a man who was crossing the heath land with his donkey. On 22 December the donkey reappears as a white donkey, looking for its master.

Sudbury, Suffolk: St Gregory's Church

In the vestry of St Gregory's Church is the preserved head of Simon of Sudbury, Archbishop of Canterbury, who was beheaded by the supporters of Wat Tyler (leader of the Peasant's Revolt) in June 1381. Today the head is so shrivelled that it looks more like a skull. The body is buried at Canterbury. Mysterious footsteps have been heard in the church and it is thought that Simon causes them.

Sudeley Castle, nr Winchcombe, Gloucestershire

Dating from the 12th century, the castle is haunted by a former housekeeper called Janet. She has been seen wearing a mob cap, a white blouse and a long, faded pink and white cotton skirt. She has appeared in the main bedroom and the Rupert Room. Janet lived in a cottage in Rushley Lane and did not let death get in the way of her devotion to the castle.

Sunderland, Tyne and Wear: The Cauld Lad

A castle once stood on the site of the pub, and the haunting probably relates to a murder that occurred in the 17th century. The pub is named after a murdered child that has been seen naked, running around the building. Another witness claims to have seen the apparition of a figure in a grey suit. It only appeared for a second or two and then vanished.

Sunderlandwick Hall, nr Driffield, East Yorkshire

Many years ago, the son of an owner of the hall killed an African servant while abroad. Somehow linked to this murder is the sound of wet feet slapping on the stone floor in one of the corridors.

Sunninghill, nr Windsor, Berkshire: Berystede Hotel

Eliza Kleininger was killed in a fire that nearly gutted the house in 1886. She worked for the Standish family and still haunts the hotel. It is said that she roams the house searching for her lost possessions.

Sutton, Co. Dublin, Republic of Ireland

In November 1696, the packet-ship *William* left Holyhead bound for Ringsend, Dublin, carrying 80 passengers. The ship was battered on the rocks by a strong gale, with the loss of all lives except for the captain and galley-boy. The captain, who later gave evidence at a public inquiry, said that lights had been seen in the area around the rocks and, thinking that it was safe to guide his ship toward them, he had done so and smashed into the rocks. This would suggest that wreckers were to blame for the disaster, for at that time they were very active in the area, luring ships onto the jagged rocks to seize any cargo and valuables that they could lay their hands on. The phantom packet-ship has been seen on many occasions since that time and ghostly lanterns have also been seen, still enticing ships to their doom on the rocks.

Sutton Cheney, nr Hinckley, Leicestershire

In 1485 King Richard III met his end at the Battle of Bosworth Field. The battle site is not haunted by Richard, but by two simple soldiers who appear as a headless foot soldier and a phantom horseman.

Sutton Coldfield, West Midlands: The Gate Inn

This former 18th-century tollhouse is said to be haunted by an apparition that resembles a Cavalier. He is described as wearing a red cloak and appears as a hazy figure for a few seconds in one of the bedrooms. He has also been seen walking into the pub and on each occasion a sudden drop in temperature accompanies him.

Sutton Coldfield, West Midlands: The New Hall

A white lady haunts the Red Landing. She is believed to be the wife of Henry Sacheverell, who died in the 17th century. She is said to haunt the house as a result of the fact that he left the hall to the elder of his two illegitimate sons. A ghostly coach is seen galloping along the drive, and just outside the gates a woman in dark clothing with a dog has been seen by a number of witnesses.

Sutton Place, nr Guildford, Surrey

Despite having been owned by two American millionaires, William Randolph Hearst and Paul Getty, the house is haunted by a white lady.

Swanbourne, nr Winslow, Buckinghamshire

The village of Swanbourne is haunted by the ghost of a green lady, thought to be the ghost of Elizabeth Adams, whose husband Thomas was murdered by thieves in October 1627, leaving her with four children to support. Elizabeth is said to have died of a broken heart shortly afterwards.

Swansea, West Glamorgan: The Grand Theatre

The ghost of Dame Adelina Patti, who opened the theatre in 1897, may be the white lady that haunts the building, leaving a smell of violets in her wake. Alternatively, the apparition may be that of an actress called Jenny who was drowned when the *Titanic* sank in 1912 after hitting an iceberg.

Swinscoe, Staffordshire

Three Jacobites were buried at Swinscoe, near Ashbourne, when they were ambushed during Bonnie Prince Charlie's retreat from Derby in 1745. Their graves are said to be haunted by a black dog that is locally known as Padfoot.

Swinton, nr Doncaster, South Yorkshire

The amusing sight of the apparition of a woman called Mary riding a large, black pig has been seen near the river here. While her husband was busy drinking himself into a stupor, she slaughtered his favourite pig. The drunken man chased Mary down to the river where she drowned.

Swinton, Greater Manchester: Wardley Hall

A clause in the lease of this property stipulates that the skull housed here cannot be removed. It rests in a niche in the wall of the staircase. If it is removed then disaster will strike the building. Two stories may give some insight into the nature of the hauntings and the purpose of the skull. During the reign of Charles II, Roger Downes owned the house. In 1676, he was in London carousing with cronies when he attacked a fiddler for refusing to play for him. The nightwatchmen arrived to deal with the disturbance and Lord Rochester drew his sword and offered them a fight. Downes kicked the sword out of his friend's hand, which probably saved the man's life, but was struck over the head by one of the other watchmen himself. He died from the assault and was returned to

Lancashire and buried in Wigan Church. In 1779, his coffin was opened and the top of his skull was missing. It is presumed that this was on account of the post mortem. The skull may, alternatively, belong to Edward Barlow. He was the son of Sir Alexander Barlow, of nearby Barlow Hall. Edward was a Catholic and at the age of 54 was hung, drawn and quartered on 10 September 1641. He was known as Father Ambrose and was captured by 400 baying Protestants while celebrating mass at Morely Hall on 25 April 1641. The Minister of Leigh led them. After his execution, his head was placed on a pole in the tower of the Old Church at Manchester. Later, the head was taken to Wardley Hall. It is believed that the Roger Downs was created to fool people about the actual identity of the skull. On one occasion during the 19th century, the skull was thrown into the moat. The result was inevitable and the haunting so intense that the moat was quickly drained and the skull was returned to its niche.

Syderstone, Norfolk: Syderstone Hall

Amy Robsart, wife of Robert Dudley, who died at Cumnor Hall in Berkshire, and whose death was thought to have been caused by her husband and Elizabeth I, lived at Syderstone Hall before her fateful marriage. Her ghost was seen at the Old Hall shortly after her death and continued to appear there until the hall was demolished. After the hall was finally pulled down, the ghost moved to the nearby rectory. The building now houses Amy's apparition and other poltergeist activity. There are also tales of a phantom highwayman seen galloping toward the village green.

Sykes Lumb Farm, nr Preston, Lancashire

When the Wars of the Roses broke out, Old Sykes and his wife buried their wealth in earthenware jars deep beneath the roots of an old apple tree in the orchard. Unfortunately, they died soon afterwards and their relatives could never find their fortune. The ghost of Dame Sykes was seen walking along the road which crossed the Lumb, and sometimes she was seen standing in the old barn. A local farmer finally plucked up the courage to follow her and she silently guided him to the old apple tree and pointed downwards. When the last jar had finally been lifted out, the apparition vanished, but some claim to have seen her in the vicinity to this day.

T

Talkin to Tyttenhanger House

Talkin, nr Brampton, Cumbria: The Blacksmith's Arms

This pub is haunted by the spirit of Maggie Stobbart, who kept it at the beginning of the 20th century. Presumably she enjoyed her work so much that she has found it hard to leave the place.

Talland, nr Looe, Cornwall

Richard Dodge was the parish vicar 1713–1747. He was also a ghost hunter and exorcist. Perhaps the more unsavoury aspect of his life was his smuggling activities. During his career he was said to battle with the Devil at night, and no god-fearing folk would dare to peek out of their windows. He used Bridle Lane as a route to move his contraband, claiming that it was a centre for evil manifestations to discourage people from passing that way at night.

Tallentire, nr Cockermouth, Cumbria: Tallentire Hall

A young woman was murdered here many years ago. Her headless phantom can be seen walking around the hall and at the window of the room where she was murdered. A vivid red fungus was said to have grown just after her death.

Talley, nr Llandeilo, Dyfed: Talley House

A secret passage is said to link the Old Manor House with the nearby ruined abbey. It is probable that the manifestation of a cloaked man, perhaps a monk or priest, has religious origins.

Tamar River, Cornwall and Devon border

The banks of the river are haunted by a pack of hounds led by the renegade priest Dando. He and his pack are only seen on Sunday mornings.

Tamworth, Staffordshire: Tamworth Castle

This Norman castle replaced the Saxon fort once owned by Alfred the Great's daughter. It is believed that she may be the white lady that is said to haunt the Tower Room and the staircase leading to it. One investigator actually managed to record the strange moans and whisperings. The apparition appears in a white dress with grey shoes and is said to be rather indistinct. Some claim that she has also been seen in the nearby meadow.

Tantaloo, nr Ramsey, Isle of Man

A grey lady, thought to be of Victorian origin, has been seen at the site of an old mill. She is described as wearing a grey cloak and waves a strange hat at hikers. The apparition disappears after just a few seconds.

Tantonbie, nr Stanley, Durham: The Oak Tree Inn

This much added-to public house has several manifestations, including a phantom drinker in the bar, strange noises on the upper floor and a spirit that appears to enjoy locking customers in the men's lavatory.

Taunton, Somerset: Castle Hotel

This building was once part of the castle itself and is often haunted by the ghost of a female violinist. She has been seen in the room known as the 'Fiddlers Room'. Not only has strange and haunting violin music been heard, but guests have also complained of feeling movement around their beds and a hand smoothing the bedclothes.

Taunton, Somerset: County Museum

Heavy dragging sounds and the tramping of boots have been heard in the building. These may well be related to the assizes presided over by Judge Jeffreys, as Monmouth's rebel soldiers were dragged into the Great Hall to meet their fate. One of the curators has seen a pair of ghostly hands and another a flaxen haired young woman in a 17th-century dress. There is also the ghost of a Cavalier, who has been seen on a stairway landing. He is a fully formed apparition with long boots and a pistol and sword in his hands.

Taunton, Somerset: The Crescent

Mrs Maria Anne Fitzherbert, the wife of George IV, is said to have been seen in this area. She appears as an elderly woman, dressed in a black silk dress with black mittens on her hands. She has all the appearance of a 'real' person, although she never responds if spoken to and often disappears if cornered.

Taunton, Somerset: The Tudor Tavern

The infamous Judge Jeffreys haunts the room named after him in this inn. He has been seen on several occasions, complete with his wig.

He apparently stayed at the tavern directly after the fall of Monmouth, when he held his assizes.

Tavistock, Devon: The Bedford

This 15th-century inn was built on the site of a Benedictine abbey, but all that remains of the older structure is a porch and gateway. The apparition of a young girl has been seen walking through the bedrooms of the hotel and is also reported to have visited the restaurant area. It is not known whether the ghost relates to the earlier period of the site or has a shorter history.

Tavistock, Devon: Betsy Grimbal's Tower

This was once the gatehouse of an abbey that stood on the site. It is haunted by Betsy Grimbal, who is said to have been murdered by a soldier on the spiral staircase in the tower. Her ghost can be seen staring out of one of the windows and is usually the warning of an impending disaster.

Tavistock, Devon: Kilworthy House

Judge Glanville's daughter haunts this 16th-century house, which was rebuilt in around 1800. She was in love with a sailor, but her father wanted her to marry a goldsmith. The girl, her servant and her lover were tried for the goldsmith's murder. The judge was her father and he sentenced them to death. The ghost of the daughter has been seen dressed in a cloak and hood. A door to the courtyard will bang violently even on the calmest of evenings. Several witnesses have also heard the rustling of silk.

Teesside Airport, nr Darlington, Co. Durham

Halifax and Lancaster bombers operated from here during World War Two. The ghost of either pilot Mynarski or pilot McMullen haunts the Teesside Airport Hotel, formerly the Canadian Officer's Mess. The former won a posthumous VC, and the latter steered his stricken bomber into countryside to avoid crashing into Darlington. Interestingly, they were both members of Squadron 428, the Ghost Squadron.

Temple Newsam, nr Leeds, West Yorkshire

Temple Newsam is said by many to rival Hampton Court in beauty. Not surprisingly, the complex of buildings is home to a number of ghosts and apparitions. The ghost of a young boy who emerges from a cupboard has been seen on a number of occasions, and a Templar knight stalks the Darnley Room. Lord Halifax saw a blue lady at Temple Newsam in 1908. On the upper floor the indistinct sounds of music and dancing from a phantom ball can be heard. Ghostly screams emanate from the south wing.

Tenby, Dyfed: St Mary's Church

A ghostly priest, believed to be a former parish vicar, haunts one of the corners of the church. Locals believe that the apparition may date from the Reformation period, as the robes he wears resemble those worn then.

Testwood House, nr Totton, Hampshire

The drive is said to be haunted by a man in a heavy, double-breasted overcoat. A phantom face can be seen at the window of the house. There is also the ghost of a woman in the attic. Apparently a manservant murdered the cook and dragged her body down the drive. There is also an unconfirmed story of a ghostly coach with four horses.

Tetcott, nr Holsworthy, Devon

Although the Queen Anne mansion was

pulled down, the original manor house and building still remain. It is haunted by the last of the Arscotts (1718–1788), who was a great huntsman and associated with the Wish Pack (or Wild Hunt).

Tewin, Hertfordshire

The ghost of Lady Catherine haunts Tewin Water. The phantom of Lady Sabine can be seen at Tewin House. In her lifetime, Lady Anne Grimstone denied the Resurrection and doubted the very existence of God. Her argument continued onto her deathbed in November 1716, when she said, 'if there is any truth in the Word of God, may seven trees grow on my grave'. Lady Grimstone's grave is in the eastern part of Tewin Graveyard. A multi-trunked sycamore and several ash trees have forced open the stonework of the tomb and have almost completely engulfed the original railings.

Tewkesbury, Gloucestershire: The Berkeley Arms

This building, constructed in 1430, has been haunted by the sound of mysterious footsteps for a number of years. The sound emanates from one of the upstairs corridors. In the 1970s renovation work revealed a small, cobwebbed room containing two history books of England dated 1820. The discovery did not affect the haunting. However, witnesses report that strange tapping sounds can now be heard above the bathroom. Perhaps another room still needs to be revealed?

Tewkesbury, Gloucestershire: Deerhurst Priory

The ghost of an old woman, dressed in clothes dating from World War One, including a long, green coat with a large collar, a cloche hat, black shoes and open-backed gloves, has been seen in and around the priory. She stares at witnesses, has an ill effect on dogs and has a very disturbed look about her. Several witnesses have described her as being hostile and aggressive. There does not seem to be any indication of who this woman was or what her intentions are now.

Tewkesbury, Gloucestershire: Tudor House Hotel

The strange figure of a woman dressed in a long, white gown has been witnessed on a number of occasions. She appears inside the haunted bedroom, but disappears as she reaches the door. The ghost of a black Labrador can also be seen on the main staircase landing. Little is known about the history of the house to connect either of these manifestations to it, but the building dates from around 1540 and was, at one time, the Court of Justice. Before it became a hotel, the Revd Samuel Jones based his academy in the building.

Thame, Oxfordshire: The Birdcage Inn

The unhappy spirit of a leper who was locked in one of the rooms before being stoned to death haunts one of the bedrooms. Witnesses have reported feeling extremely cold in this room and they have been kept awake by continuous knocking noises.

Thames Ditton, nr Kingston-upon-Thames, Surrey: The Home of Compassion

A ghost that was photographed in 1962 has haunted the building for many years. It may well be a Benedictine nun, as they used to run this home as a place for the elderly. The ghost is generally seen near the chapel and wears grey robes.

Thetford, Norfolk: The Bell Hotel

Former landlady Betty Radcliffe was murdered by her ostler lover in room 10. Betty is rarely seen but does leave fingerprints inside the glass protecting a 17th-century mural.

Thetford, Norfolk: Warren Lodge

Built in the 12th century, this building was originally constructed as a place to breed rabbits. Later it became a refuge for lepers. It is one of these unfortunate individuals that is still said to haunt the site. He is described as having a hideous face.

Theydon Bois, nr Epping, Essex

Deep within Epping Forest is the Iron Age hill fort of Ambersbury Banks. Queen Boadicea and her daughters are said to haunt this ancient site.

Thickthorn Down, Dorset

The ghost of the first Lord Shaftesbury is seen driving a coach with a coachman who carries his head under his arm.

Thirlmere, nr Keswick, Cumbria

Deep beneath the waters of the lake lies Armboth House, which was said to be the meeting place of all the ghosts of the Lake District on Hallowe'en. Climbers attempting Castle Rock have described an ill feeling in the area. It is believed that the ghosts have chosen this as their new meeting place.

Thirlwall, nr Haltwhistle, Northumberland

The ghost of a young boy is said to have haunted the common here for over 400 years. It is said that he was an orphan, made homeless by his uncle. There is also a phantom dwarf that stands guard over a treasure at the bottom of a well.

Thornton Abbey, nr Grimsby, Lincolnshire

Not only does the spirit of the wicked abbot, Thomas de Gretham, whose skeleton was found in a bricked up room sitting at a table, haunt this area, but the very fabric of the building also seems to be cursed. Stones from the abbey were used to build Ferriby Sluice and a new house built by Sir Vincent Skinner, both of which collapsed.

Thorpe-le-Soken, nr Clacton, Essex: The Bell Hotel

The apparition of Kitty Canham, an 18th-century bigamist, is said to haunt room 6 of this hotel. Not only has a shadowy, female figure been seen, but a heavy wardrobe has also been moved. Kitty is buried in the churchyard next door.

Thorpe Market, nr North Walsham, Norfolk: The Elderton Lodge Hotel

Built in 1780 as a hunting lodge for the Earls of Suffield, this was a favoured meeting place of Edward Prince of Wales and Lillie Langtry. The apparition of a chambermaid who hanged herself from the staircase in the servant's quarters haunts it. Several guests have reported seeing her standing at the foot of their beds and tugging their bed covers.

Threave Castle, nr Castle Douglas, Dumfries and Galloway

Archibald the Grim, 3rd Earl of Douglas and Lord of Galloway, built the castle in 1370. In 1455 King James II besieged and stormed the castle. It may be these events that have spawned rumours of ghostly voices and music in and around the castle. An American film crew attempted to record the sights and sounds of the castle. They discovered nothing in particular, apart from the fact that several crew members felt decidedly uneasy during the attempt.

Thurlton, nr Great Yarmouth, Norfolk

In August 1809, Joseph Bexfield drowned when he fell into a dyke. He was a wherry man and should have known the area well, but he is said to have been led astray by flickering lights. Joseph's ghost can still be seen wandering around the marshes.

Thurnham Hall, nr Lancaster, Lancashire

A green lady, thought to be Elizabeth Dalton, haunts this old hall. She lived there in the 19th century and shares the site with a ghostly Cavalier.

Thurstaston, nr Birkenhead, Merseyside

The ghost of an old woman who murdered a child haunts the hall. The nearby common boasts the sounds of screams and groans, and it is believed that the spirits of smugglers who were killed by customs officers haunt the area.

Tideswell, nr Bakewell, Derbyshire: The George Hotel

A spirit rises from the grave and heads for Wheston Hall. She is described as wearing a nightgown and having fair hair. She murdered her husband and buried him in the orchard. A Victorian barmaid called Old Sarah, who is said to be eternally searching for her husband, haunts the hotel itself.

Tidmarsh, nr Reading, Berkshire

The ghost of a young boy rises from the waters of the River Pang near the rectory. He drowned there and can be seen on full moon nights in June.

Tidworth, Wiltshire: Tedworth House

In March 1662, the local magistrate John Mompesson visited nearby Ludgarshal to investigate a former army drummer who was attempting to obtain money with forged documents. William Drury admitted his fraud and his drum was confiscated. He was ordered to be held in custody until a report was received from his former commanding officer. Drury promptly escaped. Several weeks later, the bailiff sent the drum to Mompesson at Tedworth House. He was away in London, but while he was away, his wife heard strange knocking sounds outside the front door. When Mompesson returned, he too heard the noises and went out to investigate, armed with a pair of pistols. He found nothing and returned to bed, but the knockings continued and this time seemed to emanate from the roof of the house. Drumming was then heard for five nights in a row, followed by three nights silence. Suddenly, the noises moved into the house, beginning in the room where the drum had been. Mompesson had already had the drum destroyed by this point. While Mrs Mompesson was pregnant and for some time after, there was no drumming, but soon the noises restarted. The children were getting fretful and the only place that the Mompessons could think of putting the children at night was the loft. Disturbances began there too, and soon chairs and shoes were seen to fly through the air and everything possible was thrown at a visiting vicar. The Mompessons moved the children out of the house, except for their eldest daughter. Whenever she fell asleep, the poltergeist activity and noises started. After the children came home, the hauntings took another form; this time something tugged at their hair and bedclothes. Ultimately, a series of grotesque apparitions were seen throughout the house at night, culminating in Mr Mompesson taking a shot at one of them, a grotesque form with red blazing eyes. Meanwhile in 1663, William Drury was committed to trial for theft. He boasted to another inmate that he had the power to plague a man in Wiltshire after having his drum taken from him. He was tried and found not guilty of witchcraft. Drury did not escape justice, as he was later transported on a charge of stealing a pig. As soon as he left England, after two years of disturbances, the manifestations and noises abruptly ceased at Tedworth House.

Tilty, nr Saffron Walden, Essex: Tilty Abbey

A Cistercian abbey was built at Tilty in 1153. As a result of its sacking by King John in 1215, a headless monk remains to haunt the site. Apparently the monks fought King John's soldiers and one was decapitated. During World War Two an excavation revealed a headless skeleton.

Tintagel, Cornwall

King Arthur may have been born at Tintagel, and Camelford could be Camelot. The King of Cornwall is said to have sent his wife Igerne here to protect her from the advances of Uther Pendragon, King of Britain. Merlin enabled Uther to impersonate Gorlois to seduce Igerne. Arthur was the product of the union, and his spirit is said to haunt Tintagel.

Tintern Abbey, nr Chepstow, Gwent

Founded in 1131, this Cistercian abbey was extensively enlarged during the 13th and 14th century. It is haunted by the ghost of a monk who has been seen praying near one of the arches on the west side of the abbey. If he is approached he will vanish.

Tisbury, Wiltshire: Wardour Castle

Built in 1768 on the site of the castle defended by Lady Blanche Arundel against the Parliamentarians, Wardour Castle may be haunted by Blanche herself. A ghostly figure has been seen walking across the lawns just before dusk, dressed in the costume of her period.

Toddington, Bedfordshire: The Bell

The ghost of a young girl, said to have been imprisoned in one of the bedrooms, may explain the intense poltergeist activity that occurs here from time to time. Glasses have been broken and strange noises heard in the middle of the night.

Todmorden, nr Halifax, West Yorkshire

The Gabriel Hounds, Yorkshire's Wild Hunt, are said to race down Cliviger Gorge and vanish just to the east of the town.

Tonbridge, Kent: The Cardinal's Error

The inn is said to be haunted by a woman in a large hat. It is strongly believed that she may have been a former landlady or perhaps a regular customer.

Torquay, Devon: The Old Spanish Barn

The building was originally used as a monk's storehouse, and in 1588 it was used as a temporary prison for the crew of the *Nuestra Senora del Rosario*. This vessel had been captured by the navy and towed into Torquay. Conditions were not ideal for the 400-strong crew of the ship. The building was overrun with rats, which brought sickness and disease. The Spanish sailors were soon dropping like flies. One of the 'sailors' was in fact a Spanish girl, who had been smuggled on to the ship in order to be with her lover, Don Pedro de Valdez. She was one of the first to die and was discovered to be a woman by the priest giving her the last rites. Her apparition has been seen in the park by the waterfront. She walks dejectedly toward the entrance to the barn, with her face downcast.

Torquay, Devon: The Palace Hotel

Formerly the home of Dr Henry Philpotts, the Bishop of Exeter, who built the villa next to the hotel before the two buildings were joined together, the hotel is haunted by Philpotts in full ecclesiastical uniform.

Torquay, Devon: St John's Church

Both the church and the former choir school Montpellier House (also the vicarage) claim the apparition of Henry Ditton Newman, who died in 1885. Within the church the organ played by itself at his funeral and this has happened on several other occasions, particularly after the organ was replaced in 1956. It is also said that a man who committed suicide in 1953 haunts the church itself.

Torquay, Devon: Torre Abbey

A phantom coach containing the apparition of Lady Cary haunts the avenue that leads from the abbey. Witnesses report that she is wearing a very fine dress and that the apparition is absolutely silent.

Torrington, Devon

A ghostly black dog is said to haunt the area, although its apparition has not been seen very recently. The town itself is said to be haunted by ghostly soldiers, presumably related to the Battle of Torrington in 1646. Several witnesses have heard loud noises that they describe as being like a group of motorcyclists roaring by. Witnesses have also heard strange male and female voices shouting.

Totton, nr Southampton, Hampshire: Testwood House

The drive is said to be haunted by a man in a heavy, double-breasted overcoat. A phantom face can be seen peering out of the windows of the house. There is also the ghost of a woman in the attic. Apparently a manservant murdered the cook and dragged her body down the drive. There is also an unconfirmed story of a ghostly coach with four horses.

Traquair House, nr Peebles, Borders

The ghost of an old lady, thought to be Lady Louisa Stuart, the sister of the last Earl of Traquair, haunts the grounds. A phantom highlander, said to be Bonnie Prince Charlie, who stayed at the house just before the Battle of Culloden, guards the gates. As he left he said that the gates should never be opened again until a Stuart sat on the throne of England. Consequently they have never been opened to this day.

Trearddur Bay, nr Holyhead, Gwynedd

The apparition of a woman in a long, old-fashioned dress has been seen near the caravan site and cricket pitch. Local residents claim that she is the ghost of a woman who died just before World War Two. She is said to appear at the edge of the field nearest the sea and then disappear over the edge, as if she has fallen.

Trelawnyn, nr Rhyl, Clwyd: Gop Hill

Standing at over 40ft high, this tumulus is said to be the burial site of a Roman centurion. Whether this is the case or not, a tall figure sat on a white horse has been seen leading a cohort of legionaries in the area.

Trent, nr Sherborne, Dorset

This may be the place where King Arthur had his sword thrown prior to his death. However, the haunting relates to a terrible coach accident dating from the 17th or 18th century. Witnesses have reported hearing screams and galloping hooves. All of the coach's passengers were drowned in Trent Barrow.

Treryn Dinas, nr Porth Curno, Cornwall

Witches haunt this place. Whether they were executed here or whether they have decided to stay in a spot that they made their home is unknown.

Trottiscliffe, nr Maidstone, Kent: The Pilgrims' Way

A ghostly giant dog is said to haunt the village and the surrounding area, particularly the part that is associated with the Pilgrims' Way.

Tunbridge Wells, Kent: Broomhill Road

The strange figure of a man that appears at a bend in the road which used to be the site of an old hunting lodge has scared many motorists in this area. The buildings had lain derelict for many years and nobody seemed to be willing to buy them on account of the haunting. The apparition is believed to wear a grey suit.

Tunstead, nr Chapel-en-le-Frith, Derbyshire: Tunstead Farm

Returning home from campaigning with Henry IV in France, the wounded Ned Dixon discovered that his cousin had assumed that he had died. Ned's wife and cousin then murdered him and buried him in the garden. From then on they seemed to be plagued with ill luck, until a witch told them to bring Ned's skull into the house. Unfortunately 20th-century investigations discovered that the skull thought to be that of Ned was in fact a woman's, but it is still believed to be a good omen to the house. It is also believed

that Dickey, as he has become known, still haunts the area.

Turton Tower, nr Bolton, Lancashire

A black lady has been seen on many occasions on the spiral staircase here. There is also a degree of poltergeist activity, which is blamed on the Timberbottom skulls kept in the tower.

Tutbury, nr Burton-on-Trent, Staffordshire: Ye Olde Dog and Partridge Inn

A rich and varied history no doubt provides plenty of reasons for the hauntings here. At one stage this 15th-century building was a manor house and then a coaching inn. A young girl of about 10 years old haunts it. She is known as Gracie, and is said to have been hanged in room 33. Many people have seen the girl or heard her skipping and singing. She is also responsible for some poltergeist activity, as well as noises that are heard in the middle of the night.

Twerton, nr Bath, Somerset

Six people in a council house saw an old man 'with a horrible, wrinkled skin' in 1975, on three successive nights. The figure was described as being big and black, with no definite face. Investigations have not revealed anything about the sighting that could shed light on the manifestation.

Twycross, nr Ashby-de-la-Zouch, Leicestershire

In 1800 John Massey murdered his wife and daughter and was subsequently executed and gibbeted for his crimes. The gibbet post still stands on the spot where Massey hung for 20 years. The apparition of Massey in the gibbet can be seen, along with the ghosts of his young daughter and his wife, who both drip with water.

Tydd St Giles, nr Wisbech, Cambridgeshire: Hannath Hall

A grisly story lies behind the haunting of the hall that dates back some 150 years. When Joseph Hannath's wife died he was so distraught that he could not bear to bury her corpse for 6 weeks. The spirit that is still active in the house may be hers or that of a maidservant, who committed suicide as a direct result of Joseph's actions. Some believe there is also the ghost of a young, fair-haired boy who was murdered here.

Tynemouth, nr Newcastle, Tyne and Wear

Viking chieftain Olaf was wounded when his men attempted to loot the priory. He was nursed back to health by the monks, converted to Christianity and became a monk and then a prior. Later the Vikings raided again and his brother was killed in the attempt. Olaf died of grief, praying in the chapel. His apparition is seen looking out to sea on fine days when the wind is coming from the east. There is also a story of a ghostly border collie that used to watch its master cross the Tyne in a boat every day. The faithful hound would wait for its master to return, until one day the man did not come back. The collie waited on the spot until it died. Its ghost can be seen near the Collingwood statue and its body is preserved in the Turk's Head Inn.

Tyttenhanger House, nr Colney Heath, Hertfordshire

Sir Henry Blount's ghost is seen here. He was a royalist and well-seasoned traveller who lived in the house between 1602 and 1682.

U and V
Uplyme to Vernham Dean

Uplyme, Devon: The Black Dog

Legend has it that a phantom black dog became friendly with a local farmer and lived with him rather like a pet. For some reason the farmer chased the dog away and it disappeared through a ceiling, leaving behind it a pile of gold coins. It was this money that was used to establish the pub. The phantom dog is still said to haunt the area but does not appear to be particularly dangerous to humans.

Uplyme, Devon: The Old Rectory

The mother of 19th-century occupants haunts the rectory. The apparition was seen in 1873 by Revd Brooke de Malpas, who saw the old lady sat in an armchair. He deliberately sat down on the apparition and it promptly disappeared.

Upminster, Essex: Upminster Golf Club

A young white lady haunts the first floor hallway of the club house. The building is thought to have been the site of an 11th or 12th-century monastery. It is believed that she dates back to the 17th century and was kidnapped from Havering. She was hidden in the house and then murdered and her body hidden in a room now overlooking the car park.

Uppark, nr Petersfield, West Sussex

Sir Harry Fetherstonehaugh is closely associated with Lady Emma Hamilton and was a close friend of the Prince Regent. He died in 1846 at the age of 92, but not before he married a dairymaid at the age of 70. His ghost is often seen in the Red Room.

Upton Court, nr Marlow, Buckinghamshire

On Friday nights you may be unlucky enough to see the ghost of a woman wearing a bloodstained nightdress. She is popularly believed to be a woman who was either murdered near here or was a murderess herself.

Usk, Gwent: The Cross Keys Hotel

There are two theories attached to the hauntings in room 3 of this hotel. The most plausible is that the apparition is that of a serving girl who committed suicide in the room. Alternatively the manifestation may be that of a monk who was killed during the reign of Elizabeth I.

Utkinton Hall, nr Chester, Cheshire

At some time during the Tudor period a priest managed to transfer the spirit of a ghost that had been haunting the house into the body of a blackbird. It is said that the great profusion of blackbirds around the house is a direct result of this action.

Uttoxeter, Staffordshire: Gladstone Pottery Museum

The figure of an old man with grey hair and side whiskers, wearing a short brown coat, has been seen in the building on a number of occasions by members of staff. It is believed that he is the ghost of a man who originally worked in the Victorian Pot Bank.

Valley, nr Holyhead, Gwynedd

The Romans fought the Welsh here in AD 60, and as a result Roman soldiers have been seen marching around the edge of the airfield that now occupies the site.

Velly Farm, nr Hartland, Devon

The ghost of a Cavalier walks through the rooms at the back of the house and is popularly believed to be a deserter or refugee from one of the defeats of the royalists toward the end of the English Civil War.

Ventnor, Isle of Wight: The Royal Hotel

A green lady haunts the top two floors of the hotel. She has rarely been seen, but witnesses have reported a considerable drop in temperature between the first and second floors. It is not known why the apparition haunts the building.

Verdley Castle, nr Midhurst, West Sussex

It is said that the unhappy spirit of the last wild bear in England haunts the remains of this old castle. The bear was, apparently, killed near here.

Vernditch Close, nr Bower Chalke, Wiltshire

A house stood here in which a man was murdered. His ghost returns to the scene of the crime and re-enacts his last moments. It is said that you can hear the three chops of the axe that it took to behead him.

Vernham Dean, nr Andover, Hampshire

In 1665 the plague struck this small village, which is now haunted by the apparition of the vicar at the time. He fled in order to save his own skin. On a number of occasions a bent, shadowy figure has been seen walking up Conholt Hill, along the route taken by many of the villagers who tried to escape death.

W

Wadebridge to Wynch Cross

Wadebridge, Cornwall

On 8 February 1840 Edmund Norway, captain of the merchantman *Orient*, proceeding from Manila to Cadiz, wrote: *'About 7.30pm, the Island of St Helena NNW distant about 7 miles; shortened sail and rounded to with the ship's head to the eastward. At 8, set the watch and went below; wrote a letter to my brother, Nevell Norway. About 20 minutes, or a quarter before ten o'clock, went to bed, fell asleep and dreamt I saw two men attacking my brother and murder him. One caught the horse by the bridle and snapped a pistol twice, but I heard no report. They then struck him a blow and he fell off his horse. They struck him several blows and dragged him by the shoulders across the ground and left him. In my dream there was a house on the left hand side of the road. At four o'clock I was called and went on deck to take charge of the ship. I told the second officer, Mr Henry Wren, that I had a dreadful dream – namely that my brother was murdered on the road from St Columb to Wadebridge but I felt sure that it could not be there as the house would be on the right hand side of the road; so that it must have been somewhere else'.* When Edmund docked, two men had already been arrested for the murder of his brother. William and James Lightfoot were convicted and hanged at Bodmin on 13 April 1840. They had encountered Nevell on the road to Wadebridge and much of the story tallies with what Edmund had seen in the 'dream'. After robbing the body they had dragged it into a stream on the left-hand side of the road, where it was eventually found. The house had been on the right of the road the last time that he had seen it, but the road had been moved and the house was now on the left.

Wadebridge, Cornwall: Molesworth Arms Hotel

Tracing its history back to the 16th century, this public house is said to be the point at which a phantom coach begins its journey each year. At midnight, on New Year's Eve, the spectral coach drives through the courtyard, pulled by four horses and driven by a headless coachman.

Wadesmill, Hertfordshire: The Feathers Inn (formerly the Prince's Arms)

Originally built in 1615, this public house changed its name in 1670. The building had a successful career as a coaching inn, but was the scene of an unfortunate accident in the 18th century, which has led to the present haunting. A young, fair-haired girl's ghost has been seen both inside and outside the public house. She was killed when a London-bound coach ran her over.

Wadsley, nr Sheffield, South Yorkshire

A white lady can be seen on the common between 9 and 11pm each evening. Although we do not know who she is, she does appear to be somewhat upset and waves her arms in the air.

Walberswick, Suffolk: Blytheswood (Westwood) Lodge

The ghost of a woman seen wearing a white silk dress haunts Blytheswood Lodge, sometimes called Westwood Lodge. One of the many people to have seen her is an old gamekeeper, who after seeing her several times in quick succession, refused to go anywhere near the house after dark. In 1972, three policemen stayed one night at the house in the hope of seeing her. She is known to have been there that night, as she was said to have sprung a booby-trap set for her, but she was not seen. The waiting officers felt a drop in temperature at about the same time as the trap was sprung.

Walberswick, Suffolk: Walberswick Parish Church

George Orwell saw the ghost of a man here during the 1930s. The apparition was also witnessed in the 1980s and has been seen since then, wandering around the ruined chancel.

Walford's Gibbet, nr Castle of Comfort Inn, Nether Stowey Somerset

The 18th-century charcoal burner and murderer John Walford haunts the path. It is also said that there is a smell of putrid, rotting flesh. At Dead Woman's Ditch, the ghost of Walford's wife Jenny has also been seen. Jenny was pregnant by John when he married her in June 1789. Their marriage lasted just 17 days before he murdered her. John had loved Ann Rice, and she was the only one who wept when he was hanged and strung up in a cage for a year and a day.

Wallingford, Berkshire: The George Inn (Hotel)

Originally the George Hotel was the dower house of Wallingford Castle, and was used at that time for the families of deceased guardians of the castle. During the Civil War the Parliamentarians besieged the castle. After a siege lasting four months the garrison commander agreed to surrender the castle to Cromwell's troops and the castle was destroyed. The George was one of the few buildings to survive the Great Fire of Wallingford in 1675. The hotel is famous for its Teardrop Room, so-called because of the teardrop pattern that has been drawn on one wall. The teardrops are pear-shaped, crudely drawn and have been painted on the plaster of the wall. The room is haunted. Samuel Pearse, a 17th-century landlord, killed his daughter's lover Sergeant John Hobson in 1626. The daughter went insane shortly afterwards and was locked in what was to become the Teardrop Room. It is said that the teardrop designs were made from a mixture of her tears and soot. In 1968, a guest woke up in the early hours of the morning to find the girl standing by her bed. There were tears streaming down the apparition's face, it turned and disappeared into the wall. Another room in the hotel has the sad apparitions of two children that have been seen standing by a washbasin. In the cellar, there is considerable poltergeist activity in the form of tapping on the beer barrels.

Wallington Hall, nr Cambo, Northumberland

Although this site once housed a mediaeval castle and Tudor mansion, the present building dates from around 1688. It has several ghosts, including that of the sounds of a bird flapping against the windowpanes. The bedrooms are haunted by the sound of an invisible phantom, whose heavy breathing has been heard quite recently by people spending the night at the hall. The ghost is thought to be either that of Sir John Fenwick, or someone connected with him. He was executed in 1697 for his part in the assassination attempt on William III. William took Sir John's horse, White Sorrell, for himself, but the animal stumbled on a molehill and the monarch subsequently died from the injuries he sustained in the fall.

Wallington House, nr Newcastle, Tyne and Wear

Ghostly birds are said to peck at the windows of this old house and other witnesses claim to hear spirits banging and crashing around in the middle of the night.

Walmley, nr Sutton Coldfield, West Midlands

The unfortunate village idiot of Erdington found himself being interrogated by the Duke of Cumberland's men in 1745 while they were in hot pursuit of Bonnie Prince Charlie's army. Feeling that he was hiding something from them, they shot him and cut his head off and threw it into an oak tree at New Shipston Farm. The skull remained untouched until 1827 when the tree was cut down. The ghostly skull is said to float around the area looking for its body.

Walsall, West Midlands: The White Hart Inn, Caldmore Green

A young girl's mummified arm and hand are two of the more grisly exhibits to be seen at Walsall's Central Library. The mummified remains, thought to have once been a hospital exhibit, were probably at some time injected with a preserving agent. The arm was found, along with an English Civil war period sword, in the White Hart. Pacing feet and sobbing have been heard in the attic area of the building and a female apparition has been seen on the upper floor, accompanied by the traditional sensation of coldness. The building was originally a Tudor manor house and two murders are known to have been committed here. Some Parliamentarian soldiers killed a man called Menzies in the building during the Civil War and during the 18th century an argument between two men ended in the death of one of them. In 1900, a servant girl took her own life in the attic. Back in the late 1950s, a landlady saw a white shape at the bottom of her bed and in 1955 the landlord investigated noises coming from the attic. When he reached the room, the sobbing ceased, the floor was covered in dust and there were no footprints to be seen, but in the middle of the room was a table and on it was the clear handprint of a child.

Walworth Castle, nr Darlington, Durham

Built in 1189, this castle houses the ghost of a grey lady, said to be the apparition of a pregnant maidservant who was bricked up in a spiral staircase. The staircase resounds to the echoes of footsteps. The ghost of a young stable boy often pulls the bedclothes from guests' beds. He was murdered here many years ago.

Wandlebury, Cambridgeshire: The Gog Magog Hills

Phantom dogs haunt the hills and the hill fort, along with the apparition of a ghostly knight.

Wanlip, nr Leicester, Leicestershire

Rassalas Morjan was a rescued slave who died in 1839 and was buried in the churchyard. Several witnesses claim to have seen the apparition of a small black boy near the church.

Wansford, Cambridgeshire: The Nene Valley Railway

A stationmaster and his pet were both killed in the Warwell Tunnel several years ago. The cat, Snowy, had wandered into the tunnel and his deaf master failed to hear a train coming up behind him. They were both killed but only Snowy haunts the area.

Warblington, nr Havant, Hampshire

Margaret Pole, the Countess of Salisbury, was executed at the Tower of London but appears as a headless ghost near the castle and the churchyard.

Warblington, nr Havant, Hampshire: The Old Rectory

In 1695, at the site of the Old Parsonage, a whistling ghost began its haunting. It is believed that the apparition was none other than a former parson who had fathered a number of illegitimate children with one of his servants and then murdered them all.

Waresley, Hants: Vicarage Farm

The ghost of a small boy, John Minney, haunts the 15th-century Vicarage Farm. He died there of meningitis in 1921, aged only four. The ghost, which has been seen as recently as the mid-1960s, has made frequent visits to the place of his death. It was seen in 1961 by an Australian visitor, who was sleeping in the room in which John died 40 years before. The visitor awoke in the middle of the night to find the extremely thin boy kneeling by the bed, crying for his mother. It is said that the sight of the apparition had a profound affect on the witness.

Warkworth Castle, nr Alnwick, Northumberland

The ghost of Margaret Neville, wife of the 1st Earl of Northumberland, haunts the path from the castle to the hermitage. This is perhaps another example of an apparition that finds it difficult to leave a place that played a significant part in the life of the person.

Warleggan, Cornwall: The Old Rectory

The ghost of the Revd Frederick Densham, who died in 1953, has been seen walking through the rectory and wandering in the garden. By all accounts he was a rather eccentric man, and held the post as vicar from 1931. From the beginning, he did not endear himself to his parishioners, especially when he had the church and rectory painted in garish colours, which the Bishop of Truro had him remove at a cost of £25 to Densham. As time went on, fewer people came to listen to his sermons and he eventually resorted to filling the pews with cardboard cutout

people so that he could preach to a full church. By 1933, following a string of complaints from the parishioners, the Bishop of Truro ordered an enquiry to find out why the church was so empty. He had received five complaints. Densham had closed the Sunday School, ran services at times to suit himself, had erected a barbed wire fence around the rectory gardens and had threatened to sell the church organ, which had been bought as a memorial to the villagers that had fallen in World War One. Perhaps the most damning charge was that he had misappropriated church property for his own use. Paradoxically, the Bishop sided with Densham and this resulted in the whole of the Church Council resigning and no one turning up to any of his services. Densham was undeterred and simply filled the rest of the pews with his trusty cardboard figures. In 1953, after conducting a service to his cardboard congregation, Densham was found at the bottom of the stairs of the pulpit, lying in a crumpled heap. There was a horrific expression on his face.

Warlingham, nr Croydon, Surrey

Following a bungled highway robbery, all of the passengers on a coach passing Slines Green Pond drowned after the horses bolted into the water. The spirits of the unfortunate victims of this accident now haunts the area. It does seem that the highwaymen lived to tell the tale as he does not haunt this area.

Warminster, Wiltshire: St John's Road

A strange, cowled figure has been seen at No.14, sometimes in the hall or the stairs. It is believed that a monastery once stood in this area and that the apparition dates from the pre-Reformation period.

Warslow, nr Leek, Staffordshire

A headless rider, mounted on a white horse, is believed to be the ghost of a knight. The warrior had been killed and decapitated in a battle with the Scots and his horse had brought the remaining part of his body home. You are most likely to encounter this apparition on the moorland between Warslow and Onecote.

Warwick, Warwickshire: Warwick Castle

The ghost of Sir Fulke Greville, an Elizabethan chancellor who was murdered by his manservant, haunts the Bogey Room. Witnesses also speak of sudden drops in temperature when he appears.

Washer's Pit, nr Fontmell Magna, Dorset

Before the road was cut through this area, a barrow housed strange, gibbering ghosts called Gabbygammies. The turf around the barrow was said to have always been scoured. When the barrow was destroyed to make way for the road, the creatures shifted their home to the pond at Ashmore.

Washford, nr Watchet, Somerset

The railway here was closed in 1917, but the haunting relates to a fatal accident on the line in 1857. Two trains collided on the line running along the valley to Roadwater. Since then trains have been heard despite the fact that the track has been removed.

Washington, nr Newcastle upon Tyne, Tyne and Wear: The Old Hall

A grey lady, thought to be a member of the Washington family of which George Washington was a member, is said to haunt an upstairs corridor of the old hall. The 17th-century building houses a number of family portraits and it is widely believed that the apparition bears a strong resemblance to them.

Waterfoot, nr Rawtenstall, Lancashire: Railway Inn

For some years the Railway Inn has been haunted by the ghost of a woman, known affectionately by the locals as Jane, who is described as being a tall lady, dressed in grey, who walks through guests' bedrooms and has even been seen passing through a partitioning wall. Jane is prone to removing guest's bed sheets while they are asleep. There are no clues to who Jane may be or why she has chosen to haunt the inn. A bricked up room was discovered at the inn, but it is not known whether this has any particular significance.

Waterford, Co. Waterford, Republic of Ireland

Eli Hayson was awakened by the sound of footsteps on Christmas Eve in the 1850s. He could hear them on the waterfront near to his house. He got up to investigate and saw a figure running toward his front door. More figures followed, apparently chasing the first. As he stared out, he realised that the first figure was Jack, his twin brother. Eli was confused, as he had thought that his brother was in Cork on the boat *Thomas Emery*. The chasing figures were dressed in sailor's clothes, but had stag's head masks. Suddenly, the scene went dark as a large cloud obscured the moon and when the light returned all of the figures had gone. Three days later Eli's father received a letter from the captain of the *Thomas Emery* telling him that his son had fallen overboard and drowned while he had been sleepwalking. At the inquest in Cork, despite the fact that the family stated that Jack had never walked in his sleep, the verdict was 'Found Drowned'. The Hayson's were convinced that Eli's vision meant that Jack had died as a result of foul play, but enquiries led them nowhere. Twenty years passed and Eli found himself sitting in the lounge of a hotel in Cork. The landlord told him that an old man called Matthew Webster was on his deathbed and wanted to see him before he died. Eli went to see him that night and learned that Matthew Webster's son Tom, who had died two months before, had been on duty the quay at Cork many Christmas Eves ago. Around midnight he heard footsteps and saw three men in sailor's clothes with animal masks walking down the quay toward the schooner *Thomas Emery*. He followed them and saw them chase a man, who jumped into the water to escape. Tom tried to save the man, but the other three sailors grabbed him and were about to kill him. Something changed their minds and he was forced to swear that he would tell no one of what he had seen. Tom never discovered who the men were, but he had told his father that the date was 24 December, the same night that Eli had seen the figure of his twin brother trying to get into his cottage at Waterford.

Waterlooville, nr Portsmouth, Hampshire

The figure of a young girl, believed to be a hitch hiker who was killed on the road many years ago, haunts Hulbert Road. On many occasions motorists have swerved to avoid her figure in the road.

Watford, Hertfordshire: Cassiobury Park

Lord Capel was executed on 9 March 1649 for supporting the king against the Parliamentarians. His ghost is said to appear on the anniversary of his death each year. It is not clear whether he appears headless or as a complete apparition. The Earls of Essex once owned this part of Hertfordshire.

Watford, Hertfordshire: The Palace Theatre

Built in the early 20th century, this building is haunted by mysterious footsteps, strange sounds and drops in temperature. The haunting seems to centre on the stage and one of the dressing rooms. It is strongly believed that it is the ghost of a former stagehand.

Watherstone, nr Stow, Lothian

A phantom lorry has been seen travelling along the A7 from Stow to Edinburgh and local inhabitants have noticed the speedy but silent approach of this rather old-fashioned looking vehicle. It is driven by what has been described as an evil-looking man, and travels along an old sheep track on the approach to Watherstone Hill before joining the main road. Several accidents have been caused by motorists swerving to avoid the apparition.

Watton, nr Beverley, East Yorkshire

Elfrida was a nun made pregnant by a monk, who then denounced her and had her executed. She now haunts the ruins of the abbey with other headless ghosts. Two of these may be the spirits of a woman and a child who were murdered by Roundheads in the aftermath of the Battle of Marston Moor.

Waverley Abbey, nr Farnham, Surrey

Still searching for his entrails, the disfigured apparition of a monk is said to haunt the grounds of the abbey. For some reason he was hung, drawn and quartered on the site. It is believed that he must have perpetrated a crime and that the authorities considered it important to make an example of him.

Wayland Wood, nr Watton, Norfolk

The two ghostly children that haunt Wayland Wood are thought to be the original children of the story of the *Babes in the Wood*. At the spot where the two children were left to perish by their uncle's servants, two ghostly figures have been seen wandering hand-in-hand through the trees, looking for the path that would lead them home. Unexplained wailing noises have been heard in the dead of night at this spot.

Weare Giffard, nr Bideford, Devon

The spirit of Sir Walter Gifford walks from the gatehouse to the church in search of his wife. He died in 1243. The hall is also haunted by a rude ghost that shouts 'Get you gone!' if he sees you.

Wedmore, nr Glastonbury, Somerset: The George Inn

A woman in Edwardian-style clothing with a high-necked blouse and long, black hair streaked with grey has been seen as a reflection in the bathroom mirror. Another witness stated that she appears to be wearing a long, black skirt and that the spirit simply walked straight through her door. After a few seconds, wherever it appears, the apparition fades away.

Wellingborough, Northamptonshire: The Lyric Theatre

The ghost of a man called Daniel haunts the former Lyric Theatre in Midland Road. He died on the site before the cinema was built in 1935. Others believe that the haunting relates to the fact that it was built on the graveyard of a Congregational chapel, or that the haunting is related to the ghost of a bankrupt manager who hanged himself in the cinema. Whatever the explanation, the apparition appears as a white shape that flits across the balcony and makes strange, tapping noises.

Wellington, Somerset

A phantom hitch hiker haunts the road between Wellington and Taunton. The apparition tends to appear on wet nights and flashes a torch and often throws itself in front of oncoming trucks.

Wellow, North Somerset

In the garden of a cottage is St Julien's Well. The ghost of a white lady haunts it. She is thought to have been murdered, and her body concealed in the well.

Wells, Somerset: King Charles's Parlour

Dating back to the mediaeval period, this pub houses the apparition of a ghostly figure that appears on the Jacobean stairway. Some witnesses have reported hearing the sound of a harpsichord, an unseen presence brushing past them and the sound of heavy footsteps on the landing.

Welshpool, Powys: Powys Castle

Three ghosts haunt this castle, including a man in a gold lace suit and hat who is said to have been murdered there after finding a hidden box full of secret documents. A white lady has also been seen walking around the grounds and a phantom horseman rides up to the castle and disappears.

Welton, Lincolnshire: The Black Bull

Strange noises have been heard in the pub, including footsteps walking up the 18 stairs to the restaurant and doors opening and closing. Nothing has ever been seen in this old coach house, despite a number of detailed investigations.

Wembdon, nr Bridgwater, Somerset

On the hill the ghost of a woman in an opaque shawl with glaring eyes can be seen. She is thought to either be a witch or a woman who died in a blizzard.

Wendover, Buckinghamshire: Ellesborough Parish Church

A tall, mediaeval-looking apparition has been seen by a number of witnesses gliding into the church and vanishing near one of the memorial tablets. The organist and several other regular visitors to the church have all experienced the manifestation. The ghost is oblivious to the fact that anyone is around and repeats its short journey from the door to its vanishing point.

Weobley, nr Hereford, Herefordshire

The preaching cross in the churchyard is said to have strange ghostly properties. In addition to this, if you walk around the cross at midnight seven times, reciting the Lord's Prayer backwards, the Devil will emerge.

Weobley, nr Hereford, Herefordshire: Dunwood Farm

Old Gregg haunts Dunwood Farm after having been poisoned by one of his family. He apparently did not realise that he was eating stewed toad for his supper.

West Auckland, nr Bishop Auckland, Co. Durham

Galloping at speed over the countryside toward Hampsterly is a ghostly rider mounted on a grey horse. Witnesses have said that his face is covered in blood and that he looks terror-stricken.

West Bay, nr Bridport, Dorset: The Bridport Arms

This 17th-century thatched building has received recent interest as one of the sets for the television series *Harbour Lights*. Some members of the cast and crew experienced an altogether less explicable aspect of the building. While filming was taking place the crew were dumbfounded to see a stain in the shape of a human head appear on the ceiling. Numerous other witnesses have felt a strange presence in the building, which manifests itself by rattling beer glasses, interfering with the plumbing and making the sound of footsteps ascending the staircase. Despite enquiries there does not seem to be an obvious reason for the hauntings.

West Bromwich, West Midlands: Manor House Restaurant

The Manor House has two ghosts, both from the days when it was the Old Hall. Footsteps have been heard coming from upstairs and members of the restaurant staff have reported seeing a little old lady, thought to be an 80-year-old grandmother who burned to death after falling into the fire. Several members of staff have also reported seeing a man with a black beard looking out of one of the windows.

West Clandon, nr Guildford, Surrey

The ghost of Elizabeth Knight, dressed in cream satin, haunts the house built for Lord Onslow. She unfortunately died before the house was completed.

Westgate, nr Stanhope, Co. Durham: Park House Pasture

During the 18th century a merchant intent on collecting debts from customers in Weardale disappeared near Park House Pasture. Nearly a generation later his skeleton was found and it is thought that he was murdered by some of his debtors. Several witnesses have seen a phantom horseman riding around the fields, complete with blood streaming from his body. The apparition vanishes near where the skeleton was discovered.

West Harptree, Somerset: Richmont Castle

A ghost in a long cloak and black hat haunts the ruins of Richmont Castle. The apparition has also been seen at the wishing well. At

Devil's Batch a dark knight has also made himself apparent. There is also a tale of the ghost of a lady who walks the balcony outside the castle.

West Hendred, nr Wantage, Oxfordshire

The ghost of a man killed in a road accident haunts the village of West Hendred. The figure, wearing a cap and an overcoat, has been seen by several unfortunate motorists, dashing in front of their cars. On all occasions, however, there was no bump and when the shaken motorists investigated, there was no sign of the man.

West Kennett, nr Marlborough, Wiltshire

On Midsummer's Day a ghostly priest, believed to be a Druid, enters the Neolithic tomb contained in a long barrow. He appears at sunrise with his strange companion, a white dog with red ears.

Westleton, Suffolk

Westleton Walks are said to be haunted by strange, formless apparitions, thought to be in some way related to smuggling activities that occurred here on a grand scale in the past. Alternatively the smugglers could simply have made the story up in order to scare people away.

West Lulworth, Dorset: The Castle Inn, Main Street

The apparition of an old woman haunts this 16th-century public house. It is said that she is particularly active in the garden where she died. The pub has been extended to include the crucial spot and therefore she has been seen in the building. She seems to have the habit of turning off electrical appliances.

West Malling, nr Maidstone, Kent

This site operated as an airfield during World War Two, and a spitfire pilot made an emergency landing and skidded his aircraft across the grass until it hit a brick wall. At that point, a brick smashed through the windscreen of the aircraft and killed him. A ghostly flying brick that is said to hurl itself at passing cars now haunts the airfield.

Weston-on-the-Green, nr Oxford, Oxfordshire: Weston Manor Hotel

A nun called Maud paid frequent visits to her monk lover until she was caught and burned at the stake. She is often seen in the hotel's best bedroom and is popularly called Mad Maud.

Weston Rhyn, nr Oswestry, Shropshire: Tyn-y-Rhos Hall

Miss Phillips was tortured and executed by the Roundheads after they found a priest hidden in the hall. She makes her appearance as a white lady.

West Peckham, Kent

Diamond Cottage, the home of Jack Diamond, the notorious highwayman, was burned down after being struck by lightning one Friday 13. Since then, every Friday 13 ghostly figures have been seen near the remains of the old cottage, and on occasions the sounds of a girl screaming have filled the air. Jack Diamond has been said to have been seen walking from the cottage, 'a little old man, with no legs, walking like a mist'.

West Raynham Airfield, nr Fakenham, Norfolk

During the 1960s, a Canberra bomber was attempting to land at the airfield in appalling weather conditions. The cloud cover was low and the aircraft was nearly out of fuel. Suddenly a World War Two vintage Mosquito fighter-bomber appeared just below the Canberra and waggled its wings to indicate that the other aircraft should follow it. Believing it to be one of the few serviceable Mosquitoes based at Duxford, the pilot obeyed and emerged from the cloud cover just over the airfield. When the pilot called to thank the Mosquito pilot, he discovered that no such aircraft had been out of its hanger that night and that the markings on the aircraft he had seen belonged to a Mosquito squadron that had operated from West Raynham during the war. The specific aircraft had crash-landed in appalling weather and all of the crew had died.

West Stoke, nr Chichester, West Sussex

In 894 the Saxons brought marauding Vikings to battle here. The yew trees in Kingley Vale are said to mark their resting places. Strange shapes and figures have been seen flitting in and out of the trees.

West Witton, nr Leyburn, North Yorkshire: Ivy Dene

This 300-year-old building is haunted by a strange figure, often seen sitting in a window seat smoking a clay pipe. Not only does the apparition carelessly flout the no-smoking policy in the hotel, but he also seems to leave the room extremely smoky and smelly. The figure has also been seen at the top of the stairs.

West Wratting, Cambridgeshire

A ghostly white lady is said to haunt the area from Spanney's Gate to West Wratting House. A scarier story associated with this area and nearby Balsham tells of a terrifying hound, or Shuck Monkey, which has the face of an ape.

West Wycombe, Buckinghamshire: The George and Dragon

Built in 1720 on the site of an inn thought to have been here since the 14th century, the pub sign depicts the slaying of the dragon by St George. Several ghosts haunt the inn, but perhaps the best known is the apparition called Sukie. Sukie was a serving wench, young and attractive with long blonde hair, said to be a terrible flirt and have a real passion for men. By the age of 16 she already had quite a reputation and the other servants of the inn called her 'Your Ladyship'. Sukie did not intend to spend her life as a serving girl. Three local men were attempting to court her, but her aspirations were higher than being the wife of a farm hand. When a handsome stranger arrived to stay at the inn, Sukie fixed on him and was determined to marry him. From his bearing, clothes and obvious richness, Sukie thought that he might be a highwayman and this only served to heighten her interest. The three would-be suitors now had a common purpose in scaring the man away from the woman they all wanted and put their own rivalry aside. In their drunkenness, they hatched a plot to deal with the situation. They had another hotel servant tell Sukie that the man wanted to meet her in the chalk caves at midnight. She was to wear a white gown. She arrived that night and waited for the man, but the three men arrived instead and teased her. She threw stones at them and managed to fall and fracture her head. The three men brought her back to the inn, but she died the following morning. She was buried in the white dress and only a few days later the hauntings began. She has often been seen gliding down the corridor in the early hours of the morning, complete with the white dress. The room in which she slept still has a cold atmosphere. The other major apparition at the pub is that of an 18th-century traveller who was robbed and murdered in the inn.

Witnesses have heard his footsteps in the upper floors of the building.

West Wycombe, Buckinghamshire: West Wycombe Park

Built by Sir Francis Dashwood, a libertine politician and free-thinker and founder of the notorious Hellfire Club, this mansion is haunted by a smiling monk. It was seen by a number of witnesses, including Noel Coward, and is said to disappear as quickly as it appears. The Music Room is said to be haunted by a charming female ghost.

Wexford, Tullamore, Co. Wexford, Republic of Ireland

During the 1880s, Lord Dufferin, later the British Ambassador in Paris, was on holiday at Tullamore. One night, at around 2am, he awoke to see a hunchbacked figure staggering about on the lawn under the weight of a coffin. Dufferin went downstairs to find out what the man was up to. He saw the apparition's repulsive face when it turned to look at him, then it disappeared before his eyes. His host knew nothing of the ghost, but Dufferin was not to regret what he had seen. Several years later, Dufferin, now the Ambassador in Paris, was attending a function at the Grand Hotel. As he was about to enter the lift, along with his secretary and the hotel manager, he saw the same apparition, which this time appeared as the lift operator. Dufferin would not get in the lift and watched as it ascended to the fifth floor. At this point, the cables snapped and the lift plummeted to the bottom of the shaft. All the passengers inside were killed. Despite investigations, the identity of the phantom lift operator was never discovered.

Wharton Hall, nr Kirby Stephen, Cumbria

The evil Lord Wharton, whose hobbies included terrorising his neighbours and tenants, had a heart attack while riding and was left blinded. Since the stroke occurred on Ash Fell, his ghost is doomed to try to find its way home unaided.

Whiston, Delph Lane, nr Liverpool, Merseyside

Many years ago a seaman fell into a quarry here after trying to take a short cut home after visiting his girlfriend. It is said that his apparition retraces his last steps.

Whitby, North Yorkshire

A rather mysterious ghost called Hob, said to have a grudge against travellers, haunts the area around Whitby. He has been seen appearing in front of cars, forcing them to skid, and mysteriously car tyres have been let down, another act attributed to Hob. However, his favourite pastime is to turn signposts round, causing confusion to passing motorists not familiar with the roads around this Yorkshire seaside town.

Whitby, North Yorkshire: St Mary's Church

A phantom coach is said to drive along Green Lane toward the churchyard. The ghostly passengers leave the coach and walk to the grave of a seaman. His spirit then rises and joins them and they return to the coach, which then goes down Church Steps to plunge into the sea.

Whitby, North Yorkshire: West Cliff

A mysterious cloud-like apparition can be seen moving down the cliff-top toward the beach. It is said that this manifestation only occurs on clear days.

Whitby, North Yorkshire: Whitby Abbey

St Hilda founded the abbey in the 7th century, but it was burned by the Vikings and later rebuilt by the Normans. St Hilda herself has been seen looking out through one of the abbey's windows. The ghost of Constance de Beverley also haunts the abbey; she was bricked up alive in the dungeons for having fallen in love with a knight called Marmion and broken her vows. The story was used in a novel by Sir Walter Scott. She is seen on the stairways of the dungeon, begging and pleading to be released. On the nearby cliff top, a horse-driven hearse, with a headless coachman, can be seen plunging over the edge.

Whitchurch, Shropshire: Blaney's Lane

A massacre occurred here following the Battle of Evesham in 1264. A number of soldiers from Prince Edward's army were ambushed here and slaughtered and their bodies were thrown into the river. The ghostly apparitions still make their sad progress to the place of their deaths.

Whitley, nr Godalming, Surrey: King Edward VI School

Many years ago one of the pupils was killed after a prank on the stairwell. As a result, staff and pupils have seen the pale figure of a young boy lying on the stairs. It usually appears at around 4.30pm for a few seconds before fading away.

Whittington, nr Kinver, Staffordshire: Whittington Common

In 1812 William Howe murdered a local farmer. He was hanged and gibbeted on the site of the crime. Unsurprisingly his ghost haunts Gibbet Lane. He shares this place with the ghost of a young girl, whose body was found in 1906 with a rusty dagger sticking out of her ribs.

Whittington, nr Kinver, Staffordshire: Whittington Inn

Dick Whittington, three times Lord Mayor of London, haunts the pub. He owned land near here. He is also seen riding in a phantom coach outside the inn. It is claimed that Lady Jane Grey also haunts the building, together with a more violent apparition that pins people down in their beds.

Wichenford, nr Worcester, Worcestershire: Wichenford Court

Lady Washbourne was said to have murdered a French prisoner in 1405 after he had spurned her advances. First she poisoned him, and then she stabbed him in the back. Her apparition is seen holding a goblet in one hand and a bloody knife in the other.

Wickford, Essex

The roundabout is the haunting place of a girl hitch hiker. Apparently she is the spirit of a motorcycle accident victim who hitched a ride and then died in a crash. It is said that Anne Boleyn's coach also clatters along a neighbourhood road in the dead of night.

Wickham, nr Newbury, Berkshire: The Five Bells Inn

Thought to be around 400 years old, part of the building is thatched. It is in this older area of the building that a white lady has been seen. She seems to favour one of the bedrooms and is described as being quite young. A sudden drop in temperature accompanies the manifestation.

Widecombe in the Moor, Devon: Jay's Grave

A grave by the roadside marks the burial site of a young girl called Mary Jay. She hanged herself in a barn that stood on the site during the 19th century. Mary had come from a workhouse and committed suicide after the only person in her life that had given her attention, her lover, abandoned her when she fell pregnant. Ever since her body was buried, fresh flowers have miraculously appeared on the grave. Witnesses have also seen the hunched figure of an old man with a dark blanket covering his head and upper body standing beside the grave. It is believed that this is the apparition of her lover, attempting to atone for deserting Mary and causing her suicide. An interesting note here is that the witnesses have claimed that the blanket stops about a foot from the ground and that the apparition does not have any legs.

Widecombe in the Moor, Devon: The Old Inn

Old Harry has haunted this pub for many years and is often seen wandering around the building. He is thought to have been a regular at the establishment. There are also ghostly sobs, perhaps those of a child. They may be the cries of Mary Jay, who is buried by the roadside.

Wigglesworth, nr Settle, North Yorkshire

A woman who drowned while scooping water out of the nearby stream has become a considerable hazard on the road west of the village. A number of motorists have nearly come to grief avoiding her as she steps out in front of cars in the middle of the night.

Wigton, Cumbria

Several ghosts are said to haunt the Wigton area, including a phantom in Church Street and a headless apparition in New Street.

Wilbury House, nr Cholderton, Wiltshire

The spectral form of a friendly Retriever dog will follow visitors up the drive to the house. It is believed that this is the apparition of a former pet.

Wilden, nr Bedford, Bedfordshire: Wilden Manor Farm

The farm itself is said to be haunted, and the road from Wilden to Ravensden is said to be haunted by the ghost of a woman. She is a witch-like figure with an evil expression and wears black, trailing clothes.

Wilderhope, nr Much Wenlock, Shropshire

The horse of Major Smallman, a supporter of the royalists, haunts the area close to the Plough Inn. Smallman escaped imprisonment in the manor house and made the horse jump into a 100ft drop in order to escape his pursuers. He managed to grab hold of the branch of an overhanging tree.

Willingdon, nr Eastbourne, East Sussex

A woman dressed as an Edwardian motorist haunts the main road. At dusk she waves at drivers to avoid the car in which she and two men were killed, although the car is not visible to witnesses. Another version of the story suggests that the woman was a female golfer who died in a car crash in the 1920s.

Willington, Bedfordshire: Willington Manor

Willington Manor was certainly in existence at the time of Henry VIII, but after two major fires the house is now mainly Georgian in appearance. Two of its most famous occupants were Sir John Gostwick, Master of Hounds to King Henry in the 16th century, and Sir Joseph Godber, former Secretary of State for Foreign Affairs. There are no recorded sightings of a ghost at Willington

Manor, but there have been numerous reported incidents of heavy footsteps and the tinkling of a bell. Dogs have been particularly upset, especially in the early hours of the morning. There is no story to account for the hauntings, but during the course of some reconstruction work in the early part of the 20th century, the skeleton of a man was found bricked up in a wall.

Willington, Northumberland

In the 1830s, a mill house occupied by Mr Unthank and Mr James Proctor, the mill's partners, stood amid the handful of cottages and the vicarage next to the flourmill. The mill had been built in 1800. When the partners bought the mill, they had already heard rumours that the house was haunted. At the time, as they were to hear themselves, it was restricted to the sound of someone operating a mangle. This was odd, as there was no mangle in the building. Mr Unthank lived there relatively peacefully for the first three years, and it was then Mr Proctor's turn to live in the house with his family. Proctor was a Quaker and very sceptical about the presumed haunting. The family brought with them Mary Young, their loyal and trusted servant, and she experienced much of the haunting in the next few years. In January 1835, the sounds of footsteps were heard on the unused third floor. It was thought that the ghost had to be that of man as the footsteps were very heavy. Whenever the family heard the noises, they all ran up the stairs to try to catch the intruder, but always found the rooms empty. They even covered the floor in flour to try to see the footprints, but again, nothing was visible. The haunting spread to the rest of the house, doors opened and closed, footsteps were heard coming down the stairs and bolts were drawn. Outside they could hear someone walking on the gravel, then beds were shaken and something hammered on the floorboards. Later the apparition started whistling and was heard to be dropping heavy sacks on the floor. On several occasions, the family heard a box being dragged across the room. It was not until Whit Monday 1835 that the household first saw an apparition. It was Mary Young who experienced it. She heard footsteps heading toward the kitchen where she was working. She saw a woman in a lavender dress walking upstairs and then disappearing into a room on the first floor. A few days later Isobella, Mary's sister, saw a white towel moving around on its own, and again the heavy footsteps were heard. The feeling of an icy-cold hand touching her face awakened Mrs Proctor. Her two sisters felt their four-poster bed being lifted up with them in it when they came to stay. They also saw a grey lady walk out of a wall at the back of the bed and lean over them. Soon afterwards Mary Young's boyfriend, Thomas Davidson, encountered a ghostly white cat. On 23 June 1840 Mr Proctor, an elderly servant, Mr Edward Drury, Mr Thomas Hudson and a dog lay in wait for the apparitions. At first they heard the footsteps, then a woman coughing, and then the grey lady appeared and moved toward Drury, who promptly fainted. Shortly after this, a bald cleric was seen floating about three feet above the floor on the second floor. In 1853, the clairvoyant wife of a local pitman was able to solve the haunting mystery. She told the story of a priest who had refused to allow a woman to confess to the crime that she had committed several years before and as a result, she killed herself.

Wimbourne, Dorset: Wimbourne Minster

The Revd Percy Newall haunts King's House, West Borough. He lived there during the late 19th century. He tends to appear at 6am with a bible tucked under his arm, and makes his way to the upper floor. The ghost then produces a key, opens a sealed door and disappears inside.

Winchcombe, Gloucestershire: Cheltenham Road

The ruins of the abbey, which includes the shrine of the martyr King Kenelm, resound to the sound of music and chanting monks at midnight. A tall, dark figure is seen on the road near the railway station, in a hollow by the cemetery, walking about a metre from the ground. A ghostly monk has been seen at Pyke Bank. More recently, a cyclist's bicycle was bewitched at Margaret's Hollow by an unseen force, making him dismount. When the machine was checked there was nothing mechanically wrong with it.

Winchelsea, East Sussex: The Queen's Hotel

Either the ghost of a tenant farmer who once lived there haunts this former farm, or it is the apparition of a landlord who died at the end of the 19th century. His coffin was laid out in the bar prior to burial. The ghost of a black man in a red uniform has also been seen in the churchyard. In addition to this, the ghosts of the Weston brothers, who were local highwaymen, have been seen in the area. They were hanged at Tyburn in 1783.

Winchester, Hampshire: Castle Hall

The cells below Castle Hall are the haunting place of a man in a frock coat and a tricorn hat. He has been seen by several witnesses disappearing through one of the walls.

Winchester, Hamsphire: The Eclipse Inn

Dame Alice Lisle, who was executed at Winchester on 22 September 1685, haunts the pub. She was born in 1614 and married John Lisle, who was later to be made Lord Lisle by Oliver Cromwell. John Lisle helped to draw up the sentence for Charles I and also administered the oath when Cromwell became Protector of England. Lord Lisle fled the country after the Restoration and lived in Switzerland with Alice. In August 1664, the royalist Thomas MacDonnell assassinated him and Lady Alice returned to Moyles Court. On 20 July 1685 John Hicks wrote to her. He was a non-conformist minister and in deep trouble for his preaching. She agreed to hide him, and he arrived a few days later with another man. What Alice did not know was that Monmouth was after them, as they had fought at Sedgemoor on 6 July. A local informer brought Colonel Penruddock, with a troop of cavalry, to the house. He had a score to settle with the Lisles as his father, John Penruddock, had been sentenced to death by Alice's husband. She was tried at Winchester on 27 August 1685, before Judge Jeffreys himself. She was sentenced to be burnt at the stake, but after King James II interceded, she was simply beheaded, at the age of 71, on 22 September 1685. She was subsequently found not guilty in 1689. She was held as a prisoner on the top floor of the Eclipse before her death and still haunts the room where she listened to the scaffold being built for her below. She is described as being a grey lady who causes the temperature of the room to drop. She occasionally puts her ghostly hand on the shoulder of a guest or a member of staff. She also haunts Moyles Court, her home, near Ringwood.

Winchester, Hampshire: Quarry Road

Despite two attempts at an exorcism, a house in Quarry Road still has three ghosts. One is a nun, the second a lady in white and the third a tall man in black, with brass buttons. The latter stands and smiles. Spectral hands have drawn curtains and the smell of perfume mingles with the stench of death.

Winchester, Hampshire: Winchester Cathedral

In 1957 an amazing photograph was taken of some 13 phantoms standing in front of the altar. A limping monk haunts the Close and it is believed that he was one of these 13 figures.

Windslade, Hampshire: Spring Wood

Near Hackwood House, in Spring Wood, lies a spot called Polly Peachum's garden, which is said to be haunted by a grey lady. It is not known who she is.

Windsor, Berkshire: Theatre Royal

A girl called Charlotte was killed in the gallery when the theatre burned down in 1908. It is interesting to note that she now haunts the new building.

Windsor, Berkshire: Windsor Castle

Elizabeth I haunts the library and has also been seen on the castle walls. The Canon's House is said to be the haunting place of Charles I. George III has been seen in the room in which he was kept during the last years of his life. He was insane during this period. Outside, Herne the Hunter appears in the Park. Herne was Warden of the Forest to Henry VIII, who can be seen in the Deanery. Herne committed suicide rather than be tried for witchcraft. He is the master of the Wild Hunt and appears clothed in the skin of a stag with antlers on his head. He appears regularly with his pack in the Long Walk. There is also the ghost of a sentry to be seen in Long Walk; he committed suicide there.

Wingham, nr Canterbury, Kent: The Red Lion

The ghost of a man who committed suicide in the 19th century haunts the pub. Witnesses have described him as being quite normal-looking, until he suddenly vanishes.

Winnats Pass, nr Castleton, Derbyshire

In 1758 three lead miners murdered Henry and Clara, who were eloping to get married. Their ghosts can be heard begging for mercy amid the rain and wind in the pass. The miners were not very lucky after their robbery and murder; one hanged himself, one went mad and the third was crushed to death in a rock fall.

Wisbech, Cambridgeshire: The Bowling Green Tap

A ghost called Charlie who resembles a Quaker haunts this pub, and often causes violent or mischievous poltergeist activity.

Wistman's Wood, Dartmoor, Devon

A ghostly funeral cortège of monks dressed in white robes has been seen in this area. There are also tales of phantom hounds and a figure riding a skeleton horse.

Witheridge Hill, nr Ipsden, Oxfordshire

Along the track through the woods here is a stone wall. A ghostly woman, believed to be a witch, sits there brooding.

Withycombe, nr Minehead, Somerset

Outside the south door of the church is the tombstone of Madam Joan Carn of Sandowne Manor. She was a famous 16th-century witch, who murdered three husbands. She was drowned in the Witch's Pool at Sandhill Farm. When she was buried, mourners returned from putting her coffin into the ground to find her apparition back at her home, frying eggs and bacon in the kitchen. Her spirit has been exorcised from the farm, but her ghost is said to be returning to Withycombe Church, where her coffin is buried, at the rate of one cock stride per year.

Wittering, Cambridgeshire: RAF Wittering

A ghostly bomber that made an emergency landing here during World War Two is said to swoop down toward the airfield. It hit the control tower, causing many fatalities. As a result a ghostly airman has been seen walking away from the area of the control tower.

Wittersham, Kent

Dozens of witnesses have seen the figure of a little old woman wearing a dark cloak walk across the road from the entrance to Sweatman's Cottage toward Poplar Farmhouse. She appears to vanish before she reaches the gate. Popular local opinion links her to the murder of a man in a nearby house nearly 200 years ago. Witnesses describe her as being a perfectly formed figure who only becomes odd-looking when she reaches the gate.

Woburn, Bedfordshire: Woburn Abbey

Woburn Abbey was built on the site of a Cistercian abbey by Francis Russell, 3rd Earl of Bedford, in 1626. The present buildings date from around 1744, but the original abbey was closed during the Dissolution in 1538. The abbot at the time was to rue his condemnation of Henry VIII and his proposed divorce of Catherine of Aragon and subsequent marriage to Anne Boleyn. The abbot and two other clerics were left hanging from the branch of an oak tree near the south front of the house. The ground below the oak is still bare. In 1953, the 12th

Duke of Bedford was found shot dead on his estate in Devon, and his son, the 13th Duke, inherited Woburn at the age of 36. Death duties swallowed up £4.5 million and the house required a maintenance budget of over £150,000 a year. It was at this point that Woburn became one of the first stately homes to open its doors to the general public. Soon after the new Duke took up residence, hauntings became obvious. At first it began with doors opening and closing by themselves. The ghost is said to be the apparition of a black servant of the 3rd Duke of Bedford. Burglars broke in and nearly strangled him to death and then locked him in the Masquerade Room. Once they had finished searching around for loot, they threw him out of the window and drowned him in one of the lakes. The summer house in the park is haunted by the wife of the 11th Duke of Bedford, known as the Flying Duchess. She moved into Woburn in 1891, but was not allowed to be involved in the running of the house or the upbringing of her son. She qualified as a nurse and built her own small hospital at Woburn. In 1934, she flew herself to South Africa, but three years later she died when her Gypsy Moth crashed on the east coast of Africa. Other ghosts at Woburn include a monk seen in the crypt and the Sculpture Gallery, and the figure of a tall gentleman wearing a top hat.

Wold Newton, nr Grimsby, Lincolnshire

A strange, flickering light and the sound of ancient harvesters at work can be seen and heard in a barn at harvest time.

Wolfeton House, nr Dorchester, Dorset

Built in 1505, the house is haunted by three ghosts. The first is a descendent of Sir Thomas Trenchard, who built the property. The second is a suicide victim, the wife of another descendent, who cut her own throat and now roams about what was the Great Chamber, as a headless lady in black. The third is a phantom priest that can be seen in the gatehouse.

Wolverton, Godstow Nunnery, nr Oxford, Oxfordshire

In 1177 Rosamund Clifford, Henry II's mistress, died here. She may have been poisoned by Eleanor of Aquitaine. The hauntings seem to have their root in the 16th century, when grave robbers desecrated her tomb. She now appears as a grey lady and can be seen, accompanied by ghostly singing, near the old nunnery on 1 May.

Wombourne, Staffordshire: Holbeche House

The remaining conspirators implicated in the Gunpowder Plot of 1605 were tracked down to this place near Wolverhampton. Witnesses speak of phantom riders, the sound of horses and other noises that commemorate their capture and death.

Wonson, nr Gidleigh, Dartmoor, Devon

At the manor four Cavaliers are sometimes seen playing cards. One of the former owners of the property gambled the house away. Also, unseen hands tuck people into bed and smooth down the pillows.

Woodchester Park, nr Stroud, Gloucestershire

This unfinished Victorian mansion has several strange apparitions, including two American soldiers who were based at the secret laboratory there during World War Two, a gamekeeper who was torn to pieces by his dogs, a headless horseman, a ragged dwarf and a Roman centurion.

Woodcroft Castle, Helpston, nr Peterborough, Cambridgeshire

Built in the 13th century, this castle was besieged by Colonel Woodhead's Roundheads in 1648. After his brother was killed Woodhead led the attack himself, storming Michael Hudson's defences. Hudson tried to hide by clinging to the battlements but was spotted and had his hands chopped off. He was retrieved from the moat and had his tongue pulled out. Hudson shares this site with two Roundheads, one of whom died when a canon blew up and the other who exhibited Hudson's tongue around the country but died in poverty.

Woodham Ferrers, nr Chelmsford, Essex: Edwin's Hall

Edwin's Hall was the home of Edwin Sandys, Archbishop of York in 1619. There are said to be three ghosts that haunt the place. The first is a Cavalier, the second is a girl who drowned in the lake and the third is a more sinister 'thing' that stalks the orchard.

Woodhorn, nr Morpeth, Northumberland: St Mary's Church

Shortly before Tom Chalkley's parents received the telegram telling them that their son had been killed in World War One, they saw his ghost, complete with the wounds that had killed him. In the lane outside the church a skeleton, dressed in miner's clothing, rides a bicycle.

Woodstock, Oxfordshire: The Bear Hotel

Room 16 at the Bear Hotel seems to be the centre of a very strange poltergeist phenomenon. Things are moved, lights are switched on, drawers are opened and footsteps are heard. It is believed that this is the work of a man who fell or was pushed from the roof in the 17th century.

Woodstock, Oxfordshire: Blenheim Palace

Blenheim Palace boasts but one ghost, that of a Roundhead soldier. He has been seen sitting next to the fire in one of the bedrooms.

Woodstock, Oxfordshire: Woodstock Palace

This building stood by the lake and was haunted by a dangerous poltergeist given the name the Devil of Woodstock. At one stage the building was used as a garrison during the English Civil War and the soldiers and the royal commissioners were forced to leave it as a result of his activities.

Wookey Hole, nr Wells, Somerset

Although the caves have witch connections, the ghost of an old woman who smells of mould reputedly haunts a nearby Victorian cottage. She is seen with clutching hands and a desperate facial expression. An attempted exorcism in 1912 failed to rid the cottage of its inhabitant.

Wool, nr Wareham, Dorset: Woolbridge Manor

It is said that only members of the Turberville family can see the phantom coach that appears on Christmas Eve. It is said to leave the manor and head across the heath toward their other old home at Berer Regis.

Woolpit, nr Bury St Edmonds, Suffolk

A phantom wolf or dog is said to come out of a hole in the ground near the village. This haunting seems particularly plausible, as the village has derived its name from the word 'wolfpit'.

Wootton Wawen, Wootton Hall, nr Alcester, Warwickshire

The grey lady that haunts this house is said to be Mrs Fitzherbert, who lived here. She was first the mistress and then the wife of the Prince Regent. Her haunting is accompanied by the smell of perfume.

Worbarrow Bay, nr Weymouth, Dorset

Around 300 years ago a smuggler was trapped here by custom's officers and stoned to death. As the moon is waning he can be heard thrashing about in the water, trying to avoid the missiles.

Wormit, nr Dundee, Tayside: The Tay Bridge

On 28 December 1829 the Tay Bridge disaster caused the deaths of many passengers on board the train that plunged into the water when the bridge collapsed. A ghostly train now crosses a phantom bridge. Many witnesses have seen the train heading toward the site of the old bridge and then abruptly disappearing.

Wormsley Grange, nr Weobley, Herefordshire

At midnight, the phantoms of a woman in silk and a man in black stalk the building. Legend has it that you can only see these apparitions if you were born between 11 pm and 1 am.

Worcester, Worcestershire: Worcester Cathedral

The precincts of Worcester Cathedral, especially College Green, are haunted by the ghost of a bear, seen standing on its hind legs. The ghost, which has been seen many times, once appeared to a sentry posted in College Green during the Civil War. He fired a musket shot at it but to no effect. The terrified Roundhead sentry deserted his post.

Worstead, nr Norwich, Norfolk

A white lady appears at midnight on Christmas Eve in the church. Many years ago a campanologist attempted to kiss her, but abruptly went into a fit and died.

Worthing, West Sussex: The Connaught Theatre

A grey lady dressed in a Victorian costume has been seen in the building, and witnesses have also heard a piano being faintly played.

Wotton-under-Edge, Gloucestershire: The Ancient Ram Inn

This 800-year-old former pub is owned by John Humphries, who over a three-year period experienced more than 80 supernatural phenomena. The centre of activity seems to be the Bishop's Room, which is said to be home to five ghosts. A photograph taken in 1999 shows a blurry figure on the stairway. It is believed that the pub was constructed on a pagan burial site. Witnesses claim to have been pushed against walls, knocked over, had their beds shaken at night and felt something like an animal clawing at their bed.

Wotton-under-Edge, Gloucestershire: Newark Park

Built in around 1570, primarily as a hunting lodge, Newark Park was enlarged toward the end of the 18th century. Witnesses have heard disembodied voices, rustling silk and resounding footsteps. Strange lights and a sudden drop in temperature often accompany these.

Woughton on the Green, Buckinghamshire

The ghost of Dick Turpin can be seen in these parts. The village blacksmith, according to local legend, was made to put Black Bess's hooves on back to front in order to confuse anyone who sought to follow Turpin.

Wrotham, Kent

A figure in a grey suit trimmed with silver, wearing a cocked hat, appears to strangers. They only ever see him three times. He also laughs menacingly at them. The house in which he is seen suffers from sudden drops in temperature and doors are flung open if they are closed before 10pm. At this particular location, a man murdered his brother and then threw him out of the window.

Wycoller Hall, nr Colne, Lancashire

Guytrash Lightfoot is a phantom dog believed to be a harbinger of death. The Cunliffe family lived in the hall until 1819. One of them murdered his wife and is doomed to replay the killing on its anniversary each year. Another Cunliffe married a West Indian woman but threw her overboard on the way home. She appears as a black lady, so clearly had the ability to follow her murderer back to Wycoller Hall. A further Cunliffe appears as a phantom horseman whose horse breathes fire from its nostrils. He tried to get the horse to take him up the staircase, but both were killed.

Wyke, nr Bradford, West Yorkshire: High Fernley Hall

Quite how he did it we will never know, but a brother whose woman left him for his sibling cut his own head off. Before he carried out the grisly deed he warned that he would haunt the house, which he has done since 1742. Nearby Hellfire Corner is also visited by a headless horseman, which could be the slighted brother.

Wynch Cross, East Sussex: The Roebuck Hotel

This hotel is said to be haunted by an unseen spirit who seems to cause particular problems in the middle of the night.

Y
Yarmouth to Youlgreave

Yarmouth, Isle of Wight

The Old Mill is said to be haunted by a malicious spirit that seems intent on strangling anyone who approaches the building. Other witnesses have heard rattling chains and have supported the assertion that some spirit intends violence.

Yattendon, nr Newbury, Berkshire

A black or grey lady is said to haunt the Old Rectory here. She is said to be quite friendly and actually helps find lost items.

Yatton Keynell, Wiltshire: The Old Rectory

The Old Rectory is said to be haunted by an unseen spirit. It does not appear to be malicious or malignant in any way.

Yeolmbridge, Cornwall

The Wild Hunt haunts this spot. It was seen by a man crossing the bridge who was told by the Master that if he ever got in the way of the hounds again he would be struck dead. For years he avoided the bridge but one day he took a lift from the driver of a carriage. He never arrived home. His body was found on the bridge the next morning.

York, North Yorkshire: The Angler's Arms

Three unseen ghosts haunt this pub in Goodramgate. One is said to be old and very evil, but the second is a friendly young girl, perhaps related to the strong smell of lavender. The third is a malignant spirit in the cellar.

York, North Yorkshire: The Cock and Bottle

The ghost of an ugly man with a big nose, believed to be George Villiers, the 2nd Duke of Buckingham, is said to haunt this pub in Skeldergate. He seems particularly bothered by customers wearing crucifixes and is prone to pull them off their necks.

York, North Yorkshire: Holy Trinity Church

During the dissolution of the monasteries, the abbess of the convent was killed by one of the soldiers that had come to close the building. She usually makes her appearance on Trinity Sunday, gliding across the church in her nun's habit. Thomas Percy, who led an uprising during the reign of Elizabeth I, haunts the churchyard. He was captured and beheaded at York and the churchyard is said to be the resting place of his head.

York, North Yorkshire: Marmaduke's Restaurant

Based in Goodramgate, the building is haunted by Marmaduke himself, who hanged himself in 1715. He was crippled and lived on the top floor of the building.

York, North Yorkshire: St William's College

Two brothers robbed and murdered a clergyman during the Tudor period. After the deed the elder brother told his sibling to hide from the authorities. He promptly explained that the younger brother had committed the murder. The younger one was found, tried and executed. The elder brother, clearly full of remorse, has haunted the building ever since. He is rarely seen but his footsteps are often heard.

York, North Yorkshire: Theatre Royal

This 18th-century theatre is said to be haunted

by a grey lady, believed to be a nun, who wears a hood or a cowl. After a few seconds the phantom fades and disappears. An attempt to exorcise the ghost was made many years ago but does not appear to have been successful. The theatre is also said to be haunted by the inexplicable sound of organ music and the apparition of an actor killed during a stage fight.

York, North Yorkshire: Treasurer's House

The apparitions of Roman soldiers are seen in and marching through this building. They have been seen on a regular basis for at least the past 60 years. Excavations in the cellar revealed that there was a Roman road beneath the floor, which explained why witnesses had seen the apparitions appear from the knees up. There was some dispute about the description of the soldiers until it was revealed by later research that the figures seen were not legionaries, but auxiliary troops of the later Roman period.

York, North Yorkshire: York Minster

The choir stalls are said to be haunted by a man sitting in Dene's pew, thought to be Dene Gale who died in 1702 and was buried in the Minster. One witness encountered the apparition of a stonemason who asked her whether she liked the carvings on the West Door. He approached and said 'I carved that. Do you like it?' When the woman turned to look at the man again, he had disappeared.

York, North Yorkshire: York Museum

An enormous temperature drop accompanies the sighting of an apparition believed to be an old man searching for books in the library. It is said that every fourth Sunday at 8.40pm a particular book drops from the shelf onto the floor.

Youlgreave, nr Bakewell, Derbyshire: Youlgreave Hall

Many witnesses claim to have seen the manifestations of a Roundhead and a Cavalier fighting one another on a particular night in November. On the road to Middleton you may encounter a phantom coach with four horses accompanied by a pack of dogs.

Z

Zeals House to Zennor

Zeals House, nr Mere, Wiltshire

The ghost of a grey lady comes down the stairs, leaves the house and walks into the woods beyond the lake. She was the daughter of the master of the house, who eloped with a servant and was never seen again. At the end of the 19th century a female skeleton was dug up in the woods and a stone now marks the resting place.

Zennor, nr St Ives, Cornwall

A man dressed in 19th-century working man's clothes is said to cycle up the lane toward Foage Farm. His face is covered in blood. He is believed to have been the victim of a mining accident. The Tinner's Arms is sometimes blighted by severe poltergeist activity that usually precedes an electrical storm.

Websites

http://freespace.virgin.net/martin.lightburn/ghost.html
This Spectred Isle – A Gazetteer of British Ghosts
A fairly useful site in terms of its coverage of mainland UK, some very short entries and occasional personal comment. The site is under construction, but worth looking at.

http://www.fortunecity.com/roswell/minnetonka/572/links2.html
Useful link page, mainly American orientated but some useful general ghost links and UK material.

http://www.geocities.com/Area51/Hollow/8719/contents.html
Haunted inns of Great Britain and other links. Some useful material, but aimed at the American market. Includes sites that offer overnight accommodation.

http://www.hants.gov.uk/discover/house.html
Typical county site that offers good links and information about historic houses (some haunted) in the Hampshire area.

http://mindquest.net/paranormal/whiterabbit/whiterabbit1.html
Haunted Hotels, ghost walks and more… Offers a limited selection of hotels and B&Bs that are haunted.

http://www.hauntedvalley.com/a-z.htm
Ghosts, Haunted Places and Paranormal Encounters in the Longdendale Area. An in-depth site offering information on hauntings restricted to this area.

http://www.derbycity.com/ghosts/ghosts.html
Derby is said to be the most haunted city in the UK. Extensive information on the majority of hauntings in and around the city.

http://members.tripod.com/zurichmansion/index2.html
Haunted mansions around the world. Good links to interesting information, and some audio narration.

http://www.castleofspirits.com/peterunderwood.html
The master ghost-hunter's home page. An opportunity to see the man, his extensive bibliography and his views on ghosts.

http://www.joinme.demon.co.uk/storymenu.htm
Ghost Pages UK. Potentially a good site, but still has many blank pages at the moment. Some good material in finished sections.

http://www.ghostcity19.freeserve.co.uk/
Tom Slemen's homepage. Some good links and out-takes from his existing and forthcoming books.

http://www.uktouristinfo.com/myst/ghosts.htm
Mysterious Britain – British Ghosts and Haunted Houses. Current links tend to take you to general council sites.

http://www.virtual-shropshire.co.uk/ghosts/index.htm
Ascott-Davies promotional page, with several ghost stories from the Shropshire area.

http://www.wewomen.co.uk/search/Mystical_and_Occult/
Interesting site with good links to a variety of paranormal information.

http://www.geocities.com/Area51/Dreamworld/7611/
Another good jump site in the making, with useful paranormal links and some information on general York based hauntings.

http://www.mystical-www.co.uk/
Much of Andrew Green's work appears on this site. It contains some good coverage of UK hauntings under the title of Ghosts of Today.

http://www.borleyrectory.com/
This incredible site covers just about every aspect of the Borley hauntings in minute detail.

Ghost Tours

Bath
http://www.ghostwalksofbath.co.uk/
Extensive tour run since 1974.

Bedford
http://www.bedford.gov.uk/bedford/tic/guided%20walks.htm
Bedford Ghost walk and Halloween tours.

Cambridge
http://www.ghostclub.org.uk/camghost.htm
Leaving King's College three times a week.

Canterbury
info@concorde.ltd.uk
Canterbury tour of pubs and the cathedral.

Chatham
http://www.fortamherst.org.uk/
Ghost walks through half a mile of underground tunnels.

Chester
Mo Parker on 01244 402445
Chester ghost tour.

Colchester
Derek on 01206 582924
Colchester ghost walk.

Derby
http://www.selvatico.co.uk/derbyuncovered/DHC-ghost.htm
Derby ghost tours, including pubs or a ghost tour by bus.

Dorset
http://www.dorset-info.co.uk/dorset_tours/
Link site for tours in Dorset.

Dublin
Tel 00 353 1 661 8646
The Zozimus Experience (Walking Tour) of Dublin
Tel 00 353 1 703 3151
Dublin Ghost Bus Tour

Edinburgh
http://www.mercat-tours.co.uk/
Edinburgh ghost walks.

London
http://www.london-ghost-walk.co.uk/
Leaving Bank underground station every evening.

http://www.scoot.co.uk/ghostwalk/
London ghost walk leaving Blackfriars almost daily.

Norwich
http://www.norwich-ghost-walks.co.uk/main.htm
Ghostly Norwich walking tour.

Nottingham
http://www.ghost-walks.co.uk/
Nottingham and Lincoln orientated ghost tours.

Rye
Jean Hulme on 01797 223432
Haunted Rye walk.

Winchester
Tel: 07990 876217
Ghost tour of historic Winchester.

Whitby
mrpunch@globalnet.co.uk
Whitby ghost walk.

Ghost Club
http://www.ghostclub.org.uk/ghosttours.htm
Good link site to the Ghost Club and numerous tours, including some abroad.

Bibliography

Banks, Ivan *The Enigma of Borley Rectory* Foulsham, 1996.

Braddock, Joseph *Haunted Houses of Great Britain* Dorset Press, 1991.

Bradford, Anne and Barrie Roberts *Midland Ghosts & Hauntings* Quercus, 1994.

Brooks, John *Britain's Haunted Heritage* Jarrold, 1990.

    Cornish Ghosts & Legends Jarrold, 1981.

    Ghosts and Legends of Wales Jarrold, 1987.

    Ghosts and Legends of the Lake District Jarrold, 1988.

    Ghosts and Witches of the Cotswolds Jarrold, 1986.

    Ghosts of London Jarrold, 1982.

    The Good Ghost Guide Jarrold, 1994.

    Railway Ghosts Jarrold, 1985.

Bunn, I. and M. Burgess *Haunted Lowestoft* BSIG, 1975.

Byrne, Patrick *The Second Book of Ghost Stories* Mercier, 1974.

Chard, Judy *Haunted Happenings in Devon* Obelisk, 1994.

Clarke, David *Ghosts & Legends of the Peak District* Jarrold, 1991.

Clarke, Stephen *Ghosts and Legends of the Monmouth District* Monmouth Beacon, 1965.

Daniel, Clarence *Ghosts of Derbyshire* Dalesman, 1977.

Eyre, Kathleen *Lancashire Ghosts* Dalesman, 1976.

Forman, Joan *Haunted East Anglia* Jarrold, 1984.

    The Haunted South Jarrold, 1989.

Green, Andrew *Ghost Hunting, a Practical Guide* Garnstone, 1973

    Ghosts in the South East David & Charles, 1976.

    Ghosts of Tunbridge Wells John Hilton, 1978.

    Haunted Houses Shire, 1975.

    Haunted Inns & Taverns Shire, 1995.

    Mysteries of London Napier, 1973.

    Mysteries of Surrey Napier, 1972.

    Mysteries of Sussex Napier, 1972.

Haining, Peter *Ghosts* Sidgwick & Jackson, 1974.

    The Ghost's Companion Gollancz, 1975.

Hallam, Jack *Ghosts of the North* David & Charles, 1976.

    Ghost's Who's Who David & Charles, 1977.

    Haunted Inns of England Wolfe, 1972.

Hartley, Mark and Julie Wareing *The Bridgnorth Ghost Book* Artscape, 1989.

Hayes, Patrick *Ghost Stories of Erdington* Brewin, 1996.

Hillsdon, Sonya *Jersey Witches, Ghosts & Legends* Jarrold, 1984.

Hippisley-Coxe, Antony *Haunted Britain* Pan, 1973.

Holzer, Hans *Ghosts* Chancellor, 1998.

Hymas, Maureen *Dorset Folklore* Wessex, 1981.
    West Country Inns with a Tale Wessex, 1986.
MacNaghten, Angus *Windsor Ghosts* Luff, 1976.
    More Berkshire Hauntings Luff, 1977.
McCarthy, Christine *Some Ghostly Tales of Shropshire* Shropshire Books, 1988.
Marsden, Simon *The Haunted Realm* Webb & Bower, 1987.
Mills West, H. *Ghosts of East Anglia* Countryside, 1991.
Moss, Peter *Ghosts Over Britain* Sphere, 1979.
O'Donnell, Elliott *Scottish Ghost Stories* Jarrold, 1975.
Osborne-Thomason, Natalie *The Ghost-Hunting Casebook* Blandford, 1999.
Poole, Keith *Ghosts of the West Country* Jarrold.
Price, Harry *Poltergeist* Studio Editions, 1994.
Roberts, Andy *Ghosts and Legends of Yorkshire* Jarrold, 1992.
Robertson, James *Scottish Ghost Stories* Warner, 1996.
Sampson, Charles *Ghosts of the Broads* Jarrold, 1973.
Scott, Michael *Irish Ghosts and Hauntings* Warner, 1994.
Scott-Davies, A *The Ironbridge District Ghost Book* Artscape, 1988.
    The Shrewsbury Ghost Book Artscape.
Slemen, Thomas *Haunted Liverpool* Pharoah, 1996.
Spencer, John and Anne *The Encyclopaedia of Ghosts and Spirits* Headline, 1992.
    The Ghost Handbook Boxtree, 1998.
Townsend, Marchioness and Maude Ffoulkes *True Ghost Stories* Senate, 1994.
Underwood, Peter *Ghosts and Phantoms of the West* Bossiney Books, 1993.
    Ghosts of Cornwall Bossiney Books, 1983.
    Ghosts of Devon Bossiney Books, 1982.
    Ghosts of Dorset Bossiney Books, 1988.
    Ghosts of Kent Meresborough Books, 1985.
    Ghosts of North Devon Bossiney Books, 1999.
    Ghosts of Somerset Bossiney Books, 1985.
    The A-Z of British Ghosts Souvenir, 1971.
    This Haunted Isle Harrap, 1984.
    West Country Hauntings Bossiney, 1986
Westwood, Jennifer *Albion* Granada, 1975.
Williams, Michael *Cornish Mysteries* Bossiney Books, 1980.
Williams, Michael *Paranormal in the West Country* Bossiney Books, 1986.